Contents at a Glance

Continued on next page

Contents at a Glance

Continued from previous page

Creating
Web Pages

Preston Gralla
Matt Brown

Sams Publishing, 800 East 96th Street, Indianapolis, Indiana 46240 USA

Creating Web Pages All In One

International Standard Book Number: 0-672-32690-6

Library of Congress Catalog Card Number: 2004091352

Printed in the United States of America

First Printing: May 2005

08   07   06   05   4   3   2   1

Trademarks

All terms mentioned in this book that are known to be trademarks or service marks have been appropriately capitalized. Sams Publishing cannot attest to the accuracy of this information. Use of a term in this book should not be regarded as affecting the validity of any trademark or service mark.

Warning and Disclaimer

Every effort has been made to make this book as complete and as accurate as possible, but no warranty or fitness is implied. The information provided is on an "as is" basis.

Bulk Sales

Sams Publishing offers excellent discounts on this book when ordered in quantity for bulk purchases or special sales. For more information, please contact

   U.S. Corporate and Government Sales

   -800-382-3419

     ales@pearsontechgroup.com

      tside of the U.S., please contact

       al Sales

        pearsoned.com

Acquisitions Editor
Linda Harrison

Development Editor
Jonathan A. Steever

Managing Editor
Charlotte Clapp

Project Editor
George E. Nedeff

Copy Editor
Jessica McCarty

Indexer
Chris Barrick

Proofreader
Leslie Joseph

Technical Editor
John Traenkenschuh

Publishing Coordinator
Vanessa Evans

Series Designer
Gary Adair

About the Authors

Preston Gralla is the author of more than 30 books, including *How the Internet Works*, *How Wireless Works*, *Windows XP in a Snap*, and *eBay in a Snap*. He has written about technology for dozens of newspapers and magazines, including *USA Today*, the *Los Angeles Times*, *PC Magazine*, *Computerworld*, the *Dallas Morning News* (where he was a technology columnist), and many others. He was a founding editor of both *PC Week* and *PC Computing*, and an executive editor at CNet/ZDNet. As a well-known technology expert, he has made numerous appearances on television and radio, including CNN, MSNBC, *ABC World News Now*, the *CBS Early Show*, and many others. He has won numerous awards for his editing and writing, including Best Feature in a Computer Publication from the Computer Press Association.

Matt Brown is a San Francisco Bay-area consultant who has worked on creating Web pages for a number of years. He has edited more than 20 Dreamweaver and Photoshop books over the years, contributing most recently to *Macromedia Dreamweaver MX 2004 Demystified* (Macromedia Press).

Dedication

Thanks—as always—to my wife, Lydia, and my children, Gabe and Mia, for help, support, tea, and comfort. And thanks to Linda Harrison of Sams Publishing for trusting me with this project. Also, many thanks to Jon Steever, George Nedeff, Jessica McCarty, Chris Barrick, and John Traenkenschuh.

—Preston Gralla

We Want to Hear from You!

As the reader of this book, *you* are our most important critic and commentator. We value your opinion and want to know what we're doing right, what we could do better, what areas you'd like to see us publish in, and any other words of wisdom you're willing to pass our way.

You can e-mail or write me directly to let me know what you did or didn't like about this book—as well as what we can do to make our books stronger.

Please note that I cannot help you with technical problems related to the topic of this book, and that due to the high volume of mail I receive, I might not be able to reply to every message.

When you write, please be sure to include this book's title and author as well as your name and phone or e-mail address. I will carefully review your comments and share them with the authors and editors who worked on the book.

E-mail: webdev@samspublishing.com

Mail: Mark Taber
          Associate Publisher
          Sams Publishing
          800 East 96th Street
          Indianapolis, IN 46240 USA

Reader Services

For more information about this book or another Sams Publishing title, visit our website at www.samspublishing.com. Type the ISBN (excluding hyphens) or the title of a book in the Search field to find the page you're looking for.

PART I

Getting Started Building Web Pages

IN THIS CHAPTER

✔ Start Here

You've already taken the first step in building a website—you've got this book in your hands. Now it's time for step two: Learn how websites work, learn about HTML, take a close look inside web pages, and find out all the steps you'll take when you build a site. In this chapter, you'll lay all the groundwork for building a great website.

How Websites Work

Before you learn how to build a website of your own, you'll first need to understand how one works. And to understand that, we'll first take a look at how the Internet itself works.

Let's take first things first: The Web (formally called the World Wide Web) is not the same thing as the Internet. The terms are often used interchangeably, but in fact, they're different. The Web is only one part of the Internet. There are many other parts as well—and in fact, the Web was developed many years later than many other parts of the Internet.

The Internet is a vast network of computers connected to one another, communicating and offering information in many different ways. One way is the Web. But there are other ways as well, including email, discussion areas called Usenet newsgroups, and the FTP (File Transfer Protocol). We'll cover FTP more (later in this chapter) because you'll be using it when you build a website.

Computers on the Internet connect with each other using what are called protocols—essentially standards, conventions, and rules that govern how they communicate with one another. Different parts of the Internet use different sets of protocols. The Web's protocol is the **Hypertext Transfer Protocol**, known as **HTTP** for short. Acute observers will recognize that acronym because it always precedes any website's address. Putting those letters in front of the address alerts computers that they should communicate using HTTP.

▶ KEY TERM

Hypertext Transfer Protocol (HTTP)—The communications language, or protocol, used by the World Wide Web.

Whenever you visit a website, your web browser contacts a computer on the Internet called a **web server**. When it makes that contact, it asks the server to send information to it, and the server happily complies. The server sends to your browser the web page and any files associated with that page, and your web browser displays it on your computer.

▶ KEY TERM

Web server—A computer on the Internet that contains web pages, and that delivers those web pages to computers that contact it.

By the way, you'll often come across the terms *website* and *web page*. The terms are often used interchangeably, but they're not quite the same thing. A web page is one individual location, whereas a website is made up of multiple web pages.

How Web Servers Work

Web servers are at the heart of the Web, and when you build web pages, you're going to spend time with servers. So you should get to know one before you visit. Web servers can be any kind of computer. They can be Windows-based PCs, Macintoshes, or computers that run the Unix operating system, or a popular variant of Unix called Linux. These servers run software called web server software—the software that speaks HTTP.

Every server on the Web has its own unique number, called an **IP address**, such as 130.94.155.164. There's no way for human beings to remember every single number of every single website, so the server also has a domain associated with it, such as **gralla.com**. When you type in the address of the website, special servers on the Internet called **DNS servers** translate that address into an IP address, and your web browser goes to the right location.

▶ KEY TERM

IP address—A unique number, such as 63.240.93.138, that identifies a computer on the Internet. In order for a computer to be connected to the Internet, it must have an IP address.

▶ KEY TERM

DNS (Domain Naming Service) server—An Internet server that translates web addresses such as **www.samspublishing.com** to 63.240.93.138. When you type in a web address, the request is first sent to a DNS server, which translates the address into an IP address. Your computer then uses the IP address to contact the website you want to visit.

You won't be running a web server yourself. Instead, a company called a hosting service or an Internet service provider (ISP) runs the servers.

For someone to visit a website you build, you'll have to put onto the server the files that make up the site. There are two primary ways to do this:

- You can create the files first on your own computer, and then upload the files to the server—that is, send it from your PC to the server. You'll usually upload the files using FTP by running special FTP software on your computer. You'll learn how to do this in Part III, "Build Your Own Website Using Netscape Composer."

- You can use built-in design tools so that you'll create the site right on the server itself, rather than first building it on your computer. You'll learn how to do this in Part II, "Building Your Own Website on GeoCities," Part V, "Make Money Building Auctions on eBay," and Part VI, "Build a Blog."

Understanding Web Page Addresses

When you visit a web page, you type in a web address, also known as a *URL (uniform resource locator)*. That URL contains precise instructions on where that page is located on a specific web server. The URL can be simple—just the name of a site, such as **http://www.samspublishing.com**. Or it can be much more complicated, and point to a specific location on that site, such as **http://www.samspublishing.com/title/0672326906**.

▶ KEY TERM

URL (uniform resource locator)—An Internet address that uniquely identifies a location on the Internet, such as **http://www.google.com**.

There's method behind the seeming madness of the confusion of slashes, characters, and dots that make up a URL. As you'll see as you use this book, you'll need to understand that method in order to build your website. This image shows you a URL with all the parts labeled.

The parts of a URL.

- **Protocol**—This determines what kind of Internet protocol should be used. For the Web, it's HTTP.

- **Domain name**—This directs the browser to the proper web server on the Internet. Behind the scenes, DNS is translating that domain into IP numbers. Note the first three letters in front of the domain, www.

- **Pathname**—This identifies the directory on the server where the page is located.

- **Filename**—This is the file itself that the browser is looking for. The file has to end in a .htm or .html extension for the browser to recognize it as a web page.

So, when someone types this URL into a browser, it uses the HTTP protocol to connect to the **samspublishing.com** server, and gets the allin1.htm web page in the /books directory. Note that this URL is an imaginary one, so it won't work—we use it here only as a fictional example.

What Is HTML?

Many websites are filled with graphics, colors, sophisticated layouts, interactivity, and even music and videos. So you might think that to build a page or a site requires superhuman feats of programming. In fact, it's easy to build web pages and sites. That's because no programming is required. Pages are built using the *Hypertext Markup Language (HTML)*. Throughout this book, you'll build web pages in a variety of ways, such as by filling in forms on a website, or by using a program such as Netscape Composer. But when you build those pages, behind the scenes the website or program is taking your instructions and creating HTML pages, which are then posted on the server. You can also create HTML pages without use of an HTML tool by simply typing in HTML code into a text file.

▶ KEY TERM

Hypertext Markup Language (HTML)—The language of the Web. A language used to build pages that contain instructions on how to display web pages.

When your browser visits a web server and requests to see a page, the server sends back to it an HTML page, which the browser then displays. This page is, in fact, nothing more than a text document—in other words, it's a document made up of letters, numbers, and a few special characters. Codes known as HTML *tags* on this page tell the browser how to display information.

▶ KEY TERM

Tags—HTML tags are instructions that tell browsers how to display information. Tags are surrounded by brackets, like this: **<B>**. Generally, there is a beginning tag, like **<B>**, which tells the browser to display text as bold, and an ending tag, like **</B>**, which tells the browser to stop displaying the text as bold. The actual tag itself is merely a code to give instructions to the browser and isn't displayed itself.

For example, tags tell the browser how large to make text, what fonts to use, how to place the text, and similar information. And the tags also tell the browser how to display graphics and multimedia on the page. These graphics and multimedia are contained in separate files. The HTML document tells the browser where to find these files, and how they should be used on the page. Tags are enclosed in brackets, like this: **<P>**.

HTML can get quite complicated, but no matter how complicated it gets, the page itself is a plain-text page built using HTML tags.

▶ TIP

On the Web, the world is an open book, literally. It's easy to take a look at the HTML code that builds any page you visit. If you're using Internet Explorer, click the View menu and choose Source. The actual code for the HTML page will open in a new window, in either Notepad or WordPad. If you're using Netscape Navigator, click on the View menu and choose Page Source. The code for the page will open in a separate window.

A Look at a Simple Web Page

The basics of HTML are rather simple. To show you how simple, let's take a look at a very basic web page. We'll look at the code that builds the page itself, and then at how the page looks in a browser.

Here's the HTML code for the page:

```
<HTML>
<HEAD>
<TITLE> The Pick of the Best </TITLE>
```

```
</HEAD>
<BODY>
<H1> Welcome to Preston's Picks</H1>
<P>
If you're looking to find out about the best books, movies and CDs,
you've come to the right place. Welcome to Preston's Picks,
your guide to everything good in the world.
</P>
</BODY>
</HTML>
```

And here's how the page looks in a browser:

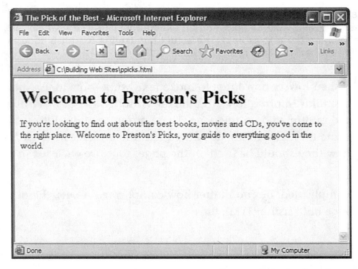

Here's how a web built by the nearby HTML code looks in a browser.

You'll notice that this page is as basic as it gets. There are no graphics and no links. We're not going to go into the details of HTML right now, but take a look at the code and then examine how the page looks in a browser to get a feel for it.

The page is just made up of text. We can add a graphic and a link to it by adding a few simple HTML commands. Keep in mind that the graphic itself is a separate file from the HTML page. The HTML page tells the browser where to find the graphic to display, but the graphic itself is a separate file from the HTML page.

Shown here is the graphic we're going to add. Its filename is **criticup.gif**. I'm also adding some HTML code that will include a link. I've highlighted the new HTML code that I've added. Don't worry if you don't understand the code yet. In fact, throughout this book, you'll build web pages without having to use HTML, although a working knowledge of HTML is a good idea so that you can tweak your pages. You'll learn the basics of HTML in Chapter 2, "The Basics of HTML." We just wanted you to get a sense of what HTML looks like here.

```
<HTML>
<HEAD>
<TITLE> The Pick of the Best </TITLE>
</HEAD>
<BODY>
<H1> Welcome to Preston's Picks</H1>
<P>
If you're looking to find out about the best books,
movies and CDs, you've come to the right place. Welcome to
Preston's Picks, your guide to everything good in the world.
</P>
<IMG SRC="criticup.gif"><A HREF="http://www.fsbassociates.com/
fsg/corrections.htm">The Corrections</A> is a
scathing and hilarious look at life in contemporary America.
</BODY>
</HTML>
```

Here's the graphic that will appear on our new web page.

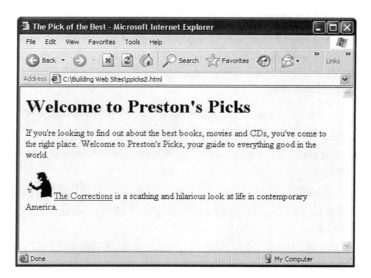

And here's the new web page, complete with graphic and link.

The Anatomy of a Web Page

The web pages we just showed you are pretty simple. The pages you're going to build will be far more complex. But all web pages, no matter how simple or how complex, are built largely the same way, and made up of the same components. In this section, we'll take a look at those common components—the anatomy of a web page. We're going to look at both the HTML code that builds the page, as well as what the page looks like in the browser. We'll take the page we've just built and use that as a starting point, but add a few extras to the page as well.

How the Page Appears in a Browser

We'll start off with the anatomy of a web page, as it appears in a browser.

▶ **NOTE**

Not all browsers display the same HTML page exactly the same. Internet Explorer might display a page slightly differently than Netscape Navigator or another browser. So when building a web page, it's a good idea to view it in both Internet Explorer and Netscape Navigator. But because the vast majority of people use Internet Explorer, you should in general design your pages for that browser.

As you can see here, we've added a few new elements to the page that we've already built. The callouts on the figure detail different parts of the page. Note that this is a very basic web page, with only the very simplest elements.

Here are more details about basic elements of the page:

- **Title**—This is what appears in the browser's title bar. Don't confuse this with the main heading on a web page (in this instance, "Welcome to Preston's Picks"). On a web page, the title is only what appears in the title bar, and is not a heading on the page itself.

- **Headings**—These divide up the web page. You can have up to six levels of headings on a web page. The two largest are shown here.

- **Text**—You can format text on a web page in many different ways, such as using boldface, italic, different fonts, and different colors.

- **Background**—You can change the background of your web page in several ways. The simplest is to pick a particular color. You can use graphics as backgrounds, as well.

- **Links**—These are the heart of the Web. Links can be not just to other web pages, but can perform other functions, as well. For example, this page includes a link that, when clicked, launches the browser's email program and addresses an email.

- **Horizontal line**—A simple way of dividing a web page is by adding a horizontal line, also known as a horizontal rule.

- **Graphics**—Graphics are great for web pages, but you have to be careful to keep them as small as possible so that it doesn't take a long time to load the page. Commonly, web graphics are in .JPG or .GIF formats. Web pages also can have multimedia content, such as video or music.

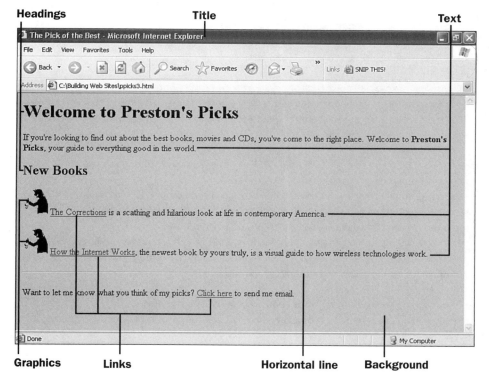

A closer look: Here are the basic parts of any web page.

How the Page Appears as HTML Code

Now that you see the basic components of a web page, it's time to take a look behind the scenes and examine the HTML code that produced it. Don't worry if you don't understand most of what you see—we're just going to look at the basic components of an HTML page.

Here's the code that produced that page, along with details about the basic components of the HTML file:

```
<HTML>
<HEAD>
<META NAME="description" CONTENT="Preston Gralla
picks the best of books, movies and CDs">
<META NAME="AUTHOR" CONTENT="Preston Gralla">
<TITLE> The Pick of the Best </TITLE>
</HEAD>

<BODY>
<BODY BGCOLOR="CCCCCC">
<! -- Remember to include new editions of my books -- >
<H1> Welcome to Preston's Picks</H1>
<P>
If you're looking to find out about the best books,
movies and CDs, you've come to the right place. Welcome to
<B>Preston's Picks</B>, your guide to everything good in the world.
</P>
<H2>New Books</H2>
<P><IMG SRC="criticup.gif"><A HREF="http://www.fsbassociates.com/
fsg/corrections.htm">The Corrections</A> is a
scathing and hilarious look at life in contemporary America.</P>
<P><IMG SRC="criticup.gif"><A HREF="http://www.amazon.com/
exec/obidos/tg/detail/-/0789729733/qid=1096580232/sr=8-1/
ref=sr_8_xs_ap_i1_xgl14/103-7003297-3323050?v=glance&s=books&n=507846">
How the Internet Works</A>, the newest book by yours truly, is a visual
guide to how wireless technologies work.</P>
<HR>
<P>Want to let me know what you think of my picks?
<A HREF="mailto:preston@gralla.com">Click here</A> to send me email.

</BODY>
</HTML>
```

- **Header**—This portion of the HTML document includes information that describes the web page, such as its title. A great deal of information can go in the header, not just the basic information you see here. For example, it can include JavaScript code—a technique for adding interactivity to web pages—as well as linking the page to style sheets, which can give many pages on a single website the same basic style elements, such as colors and fonts.

- **Meta tags**—These are tags in the header that aren't displayed, but instead are used as a way to let search sites and indexing sites know about what kind of content is on the web page. The tags typically contain keywords and descriptions.

- **Body**—This portion of an HTML document contains the actual content itself, including text, graphics, and multimedia, as well as information about the background, colors, text, and similar information.

- **Background**—You can specify that the background of a page be a specific color. As you'll see later on in the book, there are many different ways to do this, including typing in the name of a specific color, or using codes, like you see here. In this instance, the background color is gray. You also can specify that the background be a picture.

- **Comments**—A lot of time, when you're putting together an HTML page, you'll want to put in comments to yourself or anyone else who might look at the HTML code. You might want to put in a comment that reminds you why you coded a page a certain way, or possibly a reminder to yourself to update the comment. When comments are put on an HTML document, they'll be ignored by the browser and won't be displayed.

- **Headings**—These tell the browser how large to make text that you want to use as headings. HTML lets you use up to six levels of headings.

- **Links**—These are at the heart of the Web. With HTML, you can link from a web page other web pages or any kind of Internet resource, including multimedia and files.

- **Images**—HTML makes it easy to display graphics, or play music or video on web pages.

How You'll Build Websites

Okay, so you now have a good understanding of how websites work, what HTML is, and you have an inside view of the anatomy of a web page. But how does it all come together? How do you actually build a website?

First, a brief rundown of the relevant information you've learned already in this chapter:

- Web pages sit on a web server on the Internet. When someone visits a web page, he or she is asking a web server to send a web page. The person's web browser displays the web page.

- Web pages are built using HTML code. A web page is a plain-text document that instructs a browser how to display the document. It includes links, including links to graphics.

- You can build web pages using specialized software, such as FrontPage, or a simple text editor, such as Notepad.

With that in mind, let's take a look at how you'll actually build websites. Here are the basic steps you're going to take:

1. **Decide on what type of website you want and its content.** Often, this is easier said than done. Will this be a personal web page, telling the world about you, your family, friends, and hobbies? Will it be for your small business, or for a group such as a parents' organization? Before you do anything else, be clear about the information you want to present, and the tone you want your site to have, whether it be chatty, informal, informative, or authoritative.

2. **Organize the content and draw up a site map.** After you know the kind of site you want, decide the kind of content you want to put on it. Then draw up a site map. Will it be one page? Two? Three? Building a site is like building a house: Without a firm foundation, it'll fall apart. You'll learn more about organizing your content and drawing a site map in Chapter 3, "Planning Out Your Web Site."

3. **Find a home for your website.** You'll have to decide where your website is going to live. If you build it on a site such as GeoCities that includes web-building tools, your site will live on that site. But if you use a tool such as Netscape Composer in which you create web pages on your computer and then upload them to a web server, you'll need to put your site on a web server somewhere. Your ISP might provide free web space, so that might be a place to start. But there are also many sites on the Internet that provide server space as well. These sites are called web-hosting services. For more information about how to choose a hosting service, see **12 About Choosing a Hosting Service**.

4. **Assemble the graphics you'll need.** Any self-respecting website includes pictures. You can find pictures for free on the Web, you can buy them on CDs, you can create your own with graphics programs, or you can capture them with a scanner or digital camera.

5. **Build your web pages.** Either use tools built into the site itself, or use a tool such as Netscape Composer.

6. **Upload everything to your web server.** If you build your pages using a tool such as Netscape Composer, you'll upload your files to the hosting service. If you build a site using tools on the website, such as on GeoCities, as soon as you build the page they're available—you won't need to upload the pages, although if you're using graphics you create, you'll have to upload those.

7. **Get the word out and draw in visitors.** What happens if a tree falls in the forest and no one hears it? Probably the same thing that happens if you build a website and no one visits it. Publicize your site to friends, family, and the entire Web.

That pretty much covers all the steps you'll take. So let's get started. Turn to the next chapter, "The Basics of HTML."

2

The Basics of HTML

IN THIS CHAPTER:

Throughout this book, you'll learn to build web pages primarily through visual, easy-to-use tools such as Netscape Composer, and online sites such as GeoCities and eBay.

The great thing about those tools and services is their simplicity. To build a web page, you don't need to know a thing about coding or using HTML (Hypertext Markup Language), the underlying language of the Web.

But there may well be times when you want to customize your web pages more than those sites or tools allow. Perhaps you'll want to change an image size, jazz up some text, or change the layout in the way those tools don't let you. In that case, you'll turn to HTML.

In this chapter, you'll learn the basics of HTML, beginning with learning what a tag is, all the way through building an entire page using HTML.

1 **About HTML**	
✔ **BEFORE YOU BEGIN**	→ **SEE ALSO**
Just jump right in.	**2** Use HTML Tags

1

Hypertext Markup Language (HTML) is the basic language of the Web. Web pages are built using HTML. When you send your browser to a web page, you're actually visiting a page that contains HTML codes. Those codes tell your browser how to display the page, and your browser then shows you a page, based on what the codes tell it to display and how to act.

▶ KEY TERM

Hypertext Markup Language (HTML)—A language that uses a set of codes that tells web browsers how to display pages when they visit a site.

There is an official standard for HTML—a set of rules that define exactly how the language is used and works. The standard is set by a nonprofit organization called the World Wide Web Consortium, or W3C for short.

▶ WEB RESOURCE
http://www.w3.org/TR/html401/

This site contains the entire official HTML specification for free on the Web. The specification details how every HTML tag and feature works, in exquisite and occasionally mind-numbing detail. As this book went to press, the current standard was version 4.01.

In the ideal world, every site would follow the W3C HTML standard, and every browser would display web pages in precisely the same way. Because we don't live in an ideal world, many sites use nonstandard tags that are designed to work with a specific browser such as Microsoft Internet Explorer or Netscape Navigator. For example, the web-authoring program, Microsoft FrontPage, creates many tags that can only be properly viewed in Internet Explorer. And Internet Explorer and Netscape Navigator at times display the exact same web page differently, even though that page may use W3C-standard HTML tags.

The lesson here is that whenever possible, use standard HTML when building your website.

One more lesson in all this is that when building your web page, you should view it in both Internet Explorer and Netscape Navigator. That way, you'll pretty much know how all your visitors will see your site, not just a portion of them. You might also want to test the site using the Opera and Firefox browsers as well.

Although at first HTML may seem difficult to understand, in fact, it's not very difficult to master. After just a few minutes, you'll be able to build your first web page. So let's get started by teaching you the basics: how HTML tags work.

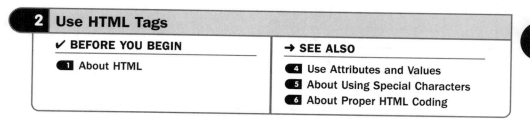

2 Use HTML Tags

✔ BEFORE YOU BEGIN	→ SEE ALSO
❶ About HTML	❹ Use Attributes and Values
	❺ About Using Special Characters
	❻ About Proper HTML Coding

2

Just as the English language follows rules of grammar, HTML follows certain rules as well. These rules are not nearly as complicated as grammatical rules, but if you want a browser to understand the web page you're building, you'll have to follow them.

At the heart of these rules—and the core of HTML—are tags. HTML tags tell a browser how to display the elements of a page. The tags themselves aren't displayed, though; those remain invisible to people visiting a site.

In this task, you'll learn how to use HTML tags—specifically, how to make text on a web page boldfaced. Although making text boldfaced is simple, the rules for creating tags are the same for making text boldfaced as they are for more complicated HTML commands.

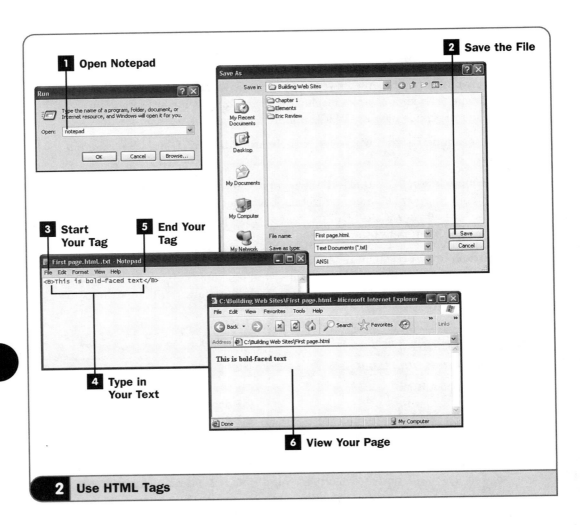

1 Open Notepad

HTML pages are text files that contain commands that tell browsers how to display pages. So Notepad is a good tool for learning basic HTML, because you can easily create text files with HTML commands in it. To run Notepad, click the **Start** button, choose **Run**, type **Notepad**, and press Enter.

2 Save the File

In this exercise (and the rest of this chapter), you're going to view the results of what you do in Internet Explorer or another browser. Before you can do that, you need to save your file. Save it and give it an extension of **.htm** or **.html**. When you give a file that extension name, a browser such as Internet

Explorer recognizes that it's a web page. If you don't give it that extension, you won't be able to view it in a browser, when it's on your own hard disk, or when it's on the Web. Be aware that when you save a file in Notepad, it often insists on a file name ending in **.txt**. Make sure that when you have your page in Notepad, you select All Files from the dropdown file type list, and choose a filename that ends in **.htm** or **.html**.

3 Start Your Tag

Tags are put between a < (called a left-angle bracket) and a > (called a right-angle bracket.) There are no spaces between the brackets and the tag. Tags come before the text they affect. So to issue the HTML command that will tell a browser to display boldfaced text, type this before the text: **<B>**. This is called an *opening tag*. It doesn't matter if the content of your tag is upper-case or lowercase. So to make text bold, you can type either **<B>** or **<b>**. As a general rule, though, it's a good idea to use lowercase, because if you get to advanced web work using something called XHTML, you'll have to use lower-case letters.

▶ **KEY TERM**

Opening tag—A tag that tells a browser how to display text or an element on a web page.

4 Type in Your Text

The text that the tag affects comes after the tag itself. So type in the text that you want to appear bold—for example, **This is boldfaced text**.

5 End Your Tag

Your HTML should now look like this: **<B>This is boldfaced text**. Now you need to end the tag, to tell the browser to stop displaying what follows as boldface. So after the text, type in **</B>**. This second tag is called the *closing tag*. Closing tags always use the forward slash symbol /. You can think of a set of tags as a container that performs an action on what's inside the container.

▶ **KEY TERM**

Closing tag—A tag that tells a browser to stop displaying text in a certain way, or to stop displaying an element on a web page.

6 View Your Page

To see the results of what you've done, open Internet Explorer or another browser, and choose **Open** from the **File** menu. Click **Browse** and browse to the folder where you've saved your **.html** or **.htm** file. Double-click the file. The file will be displayed—and the text in it will be bold.

---

3 About Empty Tags and Nesting

✔ BEFORE YOU BEGIN	→ SEE ALSO
2 Use HTML Tags	**6** About Proper HTML Coding

3

HTML tags sound pretty simple, don't they? Well, it's time to get a little bit confusing. As it turns out, not all tags require closing tags. Some require that you only use opening tags—for example, the paragraph tag <P>. When you want to start a new paragraph, you put the <P> tag in front of it. But when you want to end a paragraph, you don't need to put a closing tag at the end. So how does your browser know when to separate the paragraphs? It's simple. Put a <P> tag at the beginning of every paragraph. You can, however, put a </P> tag at the end of each paragraph if you'd like. However, that </P> tag is optional.

How do you know which tags don't absolutely require ending tags? There's no rhyme or reason to it—you'll have to memorize which require ending tags and which don't. Go to **http://www.w3.org/TR/html401/** to find out which require ending tags and which don't—it's the official HTML site.

Now it's time to get even more confusing. Some tags *never* use a closing tag, and are commonly called *empty tags*. Although the <P> tag can use a closing tag, these empty tags won't work with closing tags. Some common empty tags are <HR>, which draws a horizontal rule across a page, and <IMG>, which places a graphic onto a page. Table 2.1 lists all the empty tags in HTML 4.01, which is the most recent standard. I won't go here into what each are used for. Head to **http://www.w3.org/TR/html401/** for more details.

▶ **KEY TERM**

Empty tag—An HTML tag that does not get a closing tag, and that will not accept a closing tag.

TABLE 2.1   The Complete List of Empty HTML Tags

<AREA>	<FRAME>	<LINK>
<BASE>	<HR>	<META>
<BASEFONT>	<IMG>	<PARAM>
 	<INPUT>	
<COL>	<ISINDEX>	

By the way, you might notice that <P> isn't considered an empty HTML tag. That's because you *can* use the closing tag </P> along with it, and the browser will understand the closing tag. Empty tags don't have any closing tags, and browsers will choke if you try to use closing tags with them.

How to Nest Tags

There will be times when you're going to need to insert one set of tags inside another set of tags. You might need to do this, for example, when you want a set of words to be boldfaced, and you also want some of those words to be italicized. Or, for example, you might have a set of words that are boldfaced, and you want some of them to be hyperlinks—in other words, they can be clicked upon and will send the browser to another location.

Doing this is called *nesting*. There's a rule you should follow when nesting tags: First, close the tag that you've most recently opened, and then close the other tag. If you don't, you might confuse the browser and you might not display what you expect to.

▶ KEY TERM

Nesting—To place one set of HTML tags inside another. For example, when you want to make text boldfaced and italic, you would nest the tag for italic **<I>** inside the tag for boldfaced **<B>**.

Let's take an example. Let's say you want to have text displayed like this in a browser:

Bold *Italic*

The proper way to nest the tags is like this:

<B>Bold <I>Italic</I></B>

Notice that the **<I>Italic</I>** is nested within the **<B>** and **</B>** pair of tags. That's because you're making the first text bold, and then you're adding italic.

In the same way, let's say you want to display this text in a browser:

Bold Italic

3

There are two proper ways to nest this:

<B><I>Bold Italic</I></B>

or

<I><B>Bold Italic</B></I>

The point here is that when you nest tags, the innermost tag should be closed before you close the outermost tag. So in the first instance, you're using the closing tag </I> before the closing tag </B>, because the <I> and </I> pair of tags are inside the <B> and </B> tags. In the second instance, you're using the closing tag </B> before the closing tag </I>, because the <B> and </B> pair of tags are inside the <I> and </I> tags.

It's important to always follow this way of nesting because there will be times that you nest tags within tags within tags—you can go as many levels deep as you want. If you don't follow rules for nesting, you'll lose track of which is being nested inside which, your web page will look a mess, and it will be difficult for you to figure out what went wrong.

4

▶ **NOTE**

Most tags aren't single letter tags like **<B>** and instead are made up of several contiguous letters—for example, **<HEAD>**. When using tags made up of several contiguous letters, don't put a space between any of the letters. So **<H EAD>** won't be understood by a browser, although **<HEAD>** will.

4 Use Attributes and Values

✔ **BEFORE YOU BEGIN**	→ **SEE ALSO**
2 Use HTML Tags	**5** About Using Special Characters
	6 About Proper HTML Coding

To give you more control over how your pages look and work, you can use what are called *attributes* and *values* along with tags. An attribute modifies the tag and gives you options about how the tag should function. So, for example, a **FACE** attribute lets you specify what font should be used on a web page. A value is paired with an attribute, and lets you further customize the attribute—for example, to specify the size of a font that you're choosing.

▶ **KEY TERMS**

Attribute—A modification of an HTML tag that lets you choose options over how that tag should be used—for example, by choosing a font to display on a web page.

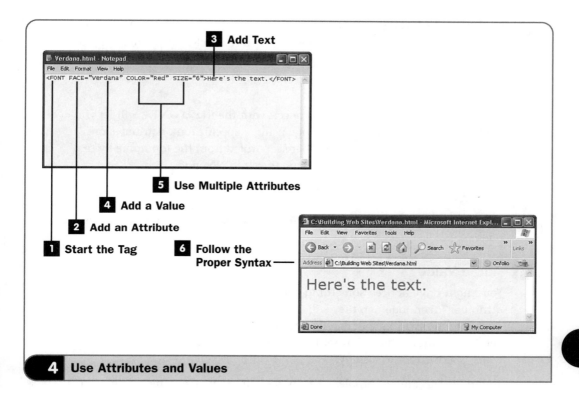

3 Add Text

5 Use Multiple Attributes

4 Add a Value

2 Add an Attribute

1 Start the Tag

6 Follow the Proper Syntax

4 Use Attributes and Values

4

▶ KEY TERM

Value—A piece of information paired with an attribute that lets you customize how the attribute is used.

In this task, you'll learn how to use attributes and values—specifically, how to use them to change the font on a web page. As in the previous tasks, we'll be doing it in Notepad.

1 Start the Tag

You can't use an attribute by itself; it has to work in concert with a tag. So before using the attribute, start the tag. In our instance, we're going to specify how text should be displayed on a web page using the **<FONT>** tag. The **<FONT>** tag gives you control over how text is displayed on a page. By itself, however, the tag doesn't do anything—if you use the tag pair **<FONT>** and **</FONT>** around text, the browser in normal circumstances won't do anything special to the text. The tag needs an attribute in order to work.

Start the tag as you normally would any tag, by typing **<FONT**. Don't put in the closing bracket **>** yet, though, because before we close it, we're going to add an attribute.

2 Add an Attribute

The attribute **FACE**, when used in concert with the tag **<FONT>**, will let you tell browsers to display text on a page using a specific font. Attributes are placed inside the opening tag, and are separated from the tag name by a space, like this: **<FONT FACE>**. So type that into Notepad.

3 Add Text

Follow the tag and attribute by text. This is the actual content of your web page.

4 Add a Value

You might have noticed something odd about our **<FONT FACE>** tag and attribute. Taken together, they still don't tell the browser what font to display. There are many fonts that can be displayed on a browser, and the browser as yet doesn't know which browser font to display, because we haven't yet told it which specific font to display.

To handle this kind of problem, attributes can use values, which define exactly how the attribute should be used. In our example, we want our text to be displayed using the Verdana font. In that case, we'd use the value of Verdana. To add a value, you use the = sign, followed by a pair of quotation marks, and inside the quotation marks you place the value, and then close it all off with an ending bracket, like this: **="Verdana">**.

So here's how the tag and attribute would look, along with the closing tag. It's making the text **"Here's the text"** appear in the Verdana font.

<FONT FACE="Verdana">Here's the text.</FONT>

▶ NOTE

Although many tags use attributes—in fact, often *require* them—not all tags can use attributes. For example, the comment tag **<!--- --->** can't use attributes. When you use the comment tag, all the text after the tag will not be displayed in a browser. It's often used by HTML coders to remind themselves why they coded a page in a certain way.

5 Use Multiple Attributes

There will be times when you will want to use more than one attribute per tag. For example, when placing an image on a page, you'll want to detail the location where it can be found on the Web, and you might also want to use attributes for where it should be placed on the page and how large it should be. And in our example, displaying text, you might want to not only use a particular font, but you might also want to say how large that font should be, and also what color to make the text.

In those cases, you'll use more than one attribute per tag, and each attribute may have an associated value. It doesn't matter what order you put the attributes in. But you have to follow the same syntax for multiple attributes that you do for a single attribute. So first comes the tag, then a space, then the attribute and its value if there is one, then a space and the next attribute and value if there is one, and so on.

Turning back to our example, let's say we want to have text displayed in the Verdana font, be colored red, and be large-sized. You'd add each of those attributes inside the opening tag, one after another. Here's what the entire tag, along with its attribute and multiple values, would look like:

<FONT FACE="Verdana" COLOR="Red" SIZE="6">Here's the text.</FONT>

▶ **NOTE**

An HTML tag, along with one or more attributes and their associated values, can be quite long. When you create an HTML tag and use attributes and values along with it, the entire result is called a string.

6 **Follow the Proper Syntax**

Make sure you follow the proper syntax. If you look at the tag, attribute, and value, you'll get a sense of the proper way to string them all together. To drive it home, here is the basic syntax for using tags, values, and attributes:

- An attribute is separated from its tag by a space.

- A value is connected to its attribute by an equal = sign.

- Values are surrounded by quotation "" marks.

- Attributes and values go *only* in the opening tag. They are never used in the closing tag. So, for example, when you close the <FONT> tag, it's always with </FONT> and never includes attributes such as **FACE**, or values such as "**Verdana**".

▶ **TIP**

As you've learned, tags aren't case sensitive—they can be either upper- or lowercase. However, some values *are* case sensitive—for example, filenames or URLs. So as a rule, get into the habit of typing in values using the proper case—even better yet, get in the habit of using lowercase.

4

5 | About Using Special Characters

✔ BEFORE YOU BEGIN	→ SEE ALSO
2 Use HTML Tags	**6** About Proper HTML Coding

There are certain characters and symbols that you can type into your word processor, but that won't display on a web page. For example, if you put the symbol for copyright © into the text on a web page, it won't display properly. The same holds true for many other symbols and characters, such as letters in a foreign language such as ç.

In order for those special characters and symbols to be displayed on a web page, you'll need to use special code. You denote the special code by prefacing it with a & symbol. Then following the & symbol, you use a name code or a numeric code that will tell the web browser exactly which symbol to display. For a name code, you just type in a name, but for a numeric code, you have to put a # after the & and before the number. Then directly after that name code or numeric code, you place a semicolon ; with no space between it and the code.

For example, to display the © symbol on a web page, you would use the coding

©

or

©

Each will work, so whichever you want to use is up to you.

▶ NOTE

There have been several versions of HTML—the version is now up to 4.01—and along the way the powers-that-be at the W3C introduce new tags and attributes into the language, and try to expunge some tags and attributes that it believes are no longer useful. A tag or attribute that the W3C discourages from being used is called *deprecated*. These tags and attributes will still work in browsers, but the W3C prefers that coders instead use new tags or techniques. Many deprecated tags, however, remain in widespread use. For example, the nearly ubiquitous **FONT** tag is a deprecated tag. The W3C prefers that coders use what are called style sheets to determine fonts, rather than using the **FONT** tag.

Note that not every special character has a name code as well as a numeric code, although all have numeric codes.

One other reason you'll want to use these special characters to display text is that browsers interpret certain symbol instructions or tags, and so won't display them. For example, let's say you want to display the text <P> on a web page. If you type in **The tag <P> starts a new paragraph.** your browser will display the following image, which is not at all what you want it to do.

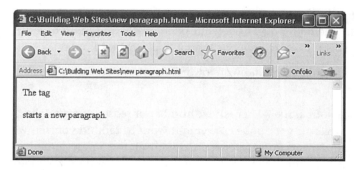

*Here's what your browser will display if you type **The tag <P> starts a new paragraph.***

Instead, you should type in **The tag <P> starts a new paragraph.**, which will display the following:

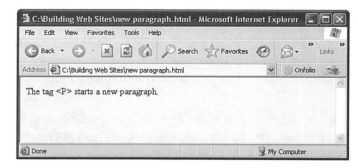

*When you type **The tag <P> starts a new paragraph.**, this is what the browser displays.*

For a list of special characters and symbols, and the codes you need to use for them, go to **http://www.w3.org/TR/html401/sgml/entities.html**.

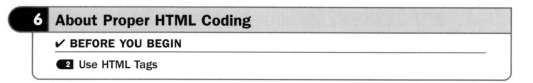

6 About Proper HTML Coding

✔ **BEFORE YOU BEGIN**

2 Use HTML Tags

When you start coding pages, you'll notice that they can get very messy looking very quickly. So messy looking, in fact, that unless you pay attention to keeping everything neat, clean, and proper, you'll soon lose your way. This is especially a problem if you come back to edit a page later. If you coded the original page willy-nilly, it will be very difficult for you to recode it.

Because of that, it's a good idea to pay attention to your coding style—the way that you place HTML code on a page. Code your page neatly and in an organized fashion and you'll save yourself tremendous amounts of time and angst.

Follow this advice, and you'll go a long way toward creating clean code that's easy to follow and edit:

- **Use comments on your page**—There are a number of reasons you might want to use comments on your page. You might want to remind yourself why you coded something a certain way, or remind yourself to change content. And you might also use comments to describe a certain section of the page—for example, a complex table—so that it's easy to locate when you need to edit your page. To put a comment in a page, start it with <!-- and end it with --> like this: <!-- **This is a comment** -->.

- **Indent your code to make it easier to follow**—Some coders find that if they indent certain portions of their code, it can be much easier to follow and edit. This is particularly true when editing tables (see Chapters 6, "Using the Advanced Editor for Building Web Pages," and 9, "Organize Text with Tables and Rules"), which can sometimes make anyone go cross-eyed. Inserting indentations won't affect how your page looks, but it will make it easier to edit.

- **Color code your tags**—Another way to make it easier to edit your code is to color code your tags. This way, you can more easily pick out relevant information. Many HTML editors let you do color coding of tags.

- **Be consistent in your use of upper- and lowercase**—Tags can be either uppercase or lowercase. Choose which you prefer, but don't mix the two—it'll be harder to follow your code.

7 Set Up a Web Page's Basic HTML Structure

✔ BEFORE YOU BEGIN	→ SEE ALSO
2 Use HTML Tags	**6** About Proper HTML Coding

You now have a fresh, empty document in front of you. The first thing you'll need to do in order to create a web page is to set up the page's basic structure.

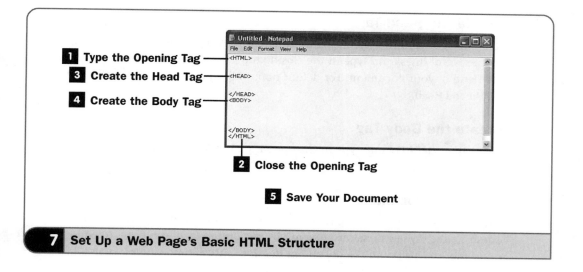

1 Type the Opening Tag

3 Create the Head Tag

4 Create the Body Tag

2 Close the Opening Tag

5 Save Your Document

7 Set Up a Web Page's Basic HTML Structure

There are two basic parts of an HTML page: the head and the body.

- **The head** includes information about the document itself, such as the title. (The title is what appears in the title bar of the browser—it doesn't appear in the body of the page.) It also is where you can include information about your web page so that search engines such as Google can find it and index it. And the head might also include scripts that will automatically be run by visitors, such as JavaScript. The only thing in the head that will be displayed is the title. Everything else will not appear on a page.

- **The body** is what contains the actual information that will be displayed by the browser. What you put there is up to you—the sky's the limit.

With that in mind, let's set up the page's basic structure.

1 Type the Opening Tag

Open Notepad, and at the top of the document, type in the opening HTML tag <**HTML**>. This tells any browser visiting your page that the document is an HTML document.

2 Close the Opening Tag

After you create the opening tag, press Enter a number of times, and at the bottom of the document type in the closing HTML tag </**HTML**>. This closes the <**HTML**> tag.

3 Create the Head Tag

Scroll back toward the top of the document, and type in the <HEAD> tag. Go down several lines, and type in the closing tag </HEAD>. You've now defined the Head of your document. For details about filling in the Head, see **8 Add a Title and Head**.

4 Create the Body Tag

Below the </HEAD> tag, type in the opening <BODY> tag, go down several lines, and type in the closing tag </BODY>.

5 Save Your Document

Save your page, making sure to give it an extension of **.htm** or **.html**. If it doesn't have those extensions, it won't be recognized as a web page. Keep in mind that at this point, the document doesn't contain any content—you'll be filling it in throughout the rest of this chapter.

▶ NOTE

8

The standards-setting body W3C, keeper of the official HTML flame, recommends that every web page include a special **!DOCTYPE** tag that alerts a browser to what version of HTML was used when coding the page. A typical such tag would be at the top of an HTML document like this:

<!DOCTYPE HTML PUBLIC "//W3C//DTD HTML 4.01 Transitional//EN">

The truth is, there's no real need to put that in because it appears to have no effect on browsers. In fact, some of the most popular sites on the Internet, such as **Yahoo!** and the tech site **CNet** don't use that tag. If you use an HTML editing program, it may well put the tag in for you. There's no need to take it out. But if you're creating your page using a text editor or some other tool that doesn't put the tag in automatically, there's no real need to spend your time to put it in.

8 Add a Title and Head

✔ BEFORE YOU BEGIN	→ SEE ALSO
2 Use HTML Tags	**6** About Proper HTML Coding
7 Set Up a Web Page's Basic HTML Structure	

Now that you have a basic structure filled in, it's time to start building out your page. Let's start with the head.

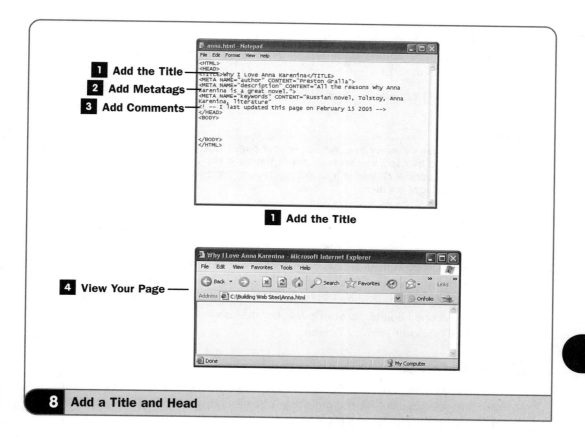

1 Add the Title

2 Add Metatags

3 Add Comments

1 Add the Title

4 View Your Page —

8

8 Add a Title and Head

For a simple HTML page, there are only a few things you need to add:

- **Metatags**, which will contain information about the document, such as keywords that describe it. With keywords, the page will be more accurately indexed by search sites such as Google, and so your page will more easily be found by people.

- **The title**, which will appear in the title bar of the browser.

- **Comments** that you might want to appear in the head.

The only one of these three things that you have to add is the title, by the way. So if you don't want to add comments or metatags, you can ignore that.

1 Add the Title

Nothing could be simpler than adding a title. Just enclose it between **<TITLE>** and **</TITLE>** tags, like this:

<TITLE>Why I Love Anna Karenina</TITLE>

▶ NOTE

It's a bad idea to use colons or backslashes in your page's title. Some operating systems don't allow them to be used, and so you'll cause trouble if you try to use them. And if you need to use a special character in a title, such as a foreign letter, you'll have to use number or name codes for them.

Because titles are only displayed in the title bar of the browser, you may well be tempted to simply type in the first thing that comes to mind for a title, such as **Welcome to my First Web Page**. Resist that, at all costs. The title is much more important than you realize. When a search engine indexes your site, the first thing it looks at is the title. So a good descriptive title will make it more likely that your page will be found by people using search engines. And if someone bookmarks your page, the title is what appears in that person's Bookmarks or Favorites menu.

8

2 Add Metatags

Now that you have a title, it's time to add metatags. There are many different uses for metatags, but for the website you're designing, the most important is to provide information about your site to search engines. The more information you provide to them, the more likely your site can be found on them, and the more visitors will come your way. And because you're building a site that you'd like the world to see, more visitors is better than fewer.

Keep in mind that you're not *required* to add metatags. Whether you want to is thoroughly up to you.

Metatags don't use closing tags, and can use many different attributes and values. In fact, anyone can make up their own attributes for them. No matter what metatags you use, they won't affect the way the page is displayed, because information in them is hidden.

The attribute you need to know about is the **NAME** attribute, because that's the one that describes the content of your site. Let's say that you want search engines to know that you're the creator of the website. Here's how you'd use the metatag and the **NAME** and **CONTENT** attributes (assuming that your name is Preston Gralla, that is):

<META NAME="author" CONTENT="Preston Gralla">

In it, we're defining the author of the document as Preston Gralla.

Search engines commonly look for several different metatags. Here are the other important ones, and how they're used.

Description

This enables you to add a description of your website that offers more information than the title. It's particularly useful if you have a web page without a great deal of text. Some search engines will take your description and display it on the search results pages. Here's how you use it:

<META NAME="description" CONTENT="All the reasons why Anna Karenina is a great novel.">

Keywords

This lets you add descriptive keywords that are useful in helping index your page and determining what category of page it is. And it will help people find your page if they happen to type in one of the keywords you've entered. You separate the keywords by commas. Here's how you use it:

<META NAME="keywords" CONTENT="Russian novel, Tolstoy, Anna Karenina, literature"

8

3 Add Comments

Adding a comment is as simple as it gets. Simply enclose your comments inside the comment tag. Note that the comment tag doesn't take a closing tag. Here's how to do it:

<! -- I last updated this page on February 15 2005 -- >

4 View Your Page

If you haven't already saved the page, save it now. View it in your browser. If you've done your coding correctly, the browser will actually be blank at this point, except for the title bar. So why view it now? To make sure that you haven't made a coding error. You'll notice a coding error if anything displays in the browser. You also want to proofread the title as well.

9 Add and Format Text

✔ BEFORE YOU BEGIN	→ SEE ALSO
2 Use HTML Tags **7** Set Up a Web Page's Basic HTML Structure	**6** About Proper HTML Coding

In the last task, **8 Add a Title and Head**, we finished coding the head, but the head doesn't have a great deal of information that's going to be displayed—in fact, the only thing displayed from the head is the title, and it will be displayed in the title bar of the browser. So it's time to get to work filling your page with content.

The content will go in the body of your page—in other words, between the <BODY> and </BODY> tags.

1 Create Headings

The first thing you should do is organize your page into headings—the major points that you want to make, or the main information you want to present. You can organize the page into major headings, and then several levels of minor headings beneath each major heading. HTML allows for six levels of headings in all. Start with the major headings, and if those need to be subdivided, put minor headings beneath them. You can then further subdivide minor headings, and so on.

To create a heading, use the heading tag, which requires an opening and closing tag, like this:

<H1>Anna Karenina Was Tolstoy's Greatest Novel</H1>

To change the size of the heading, change the number next to the **H**. The number **1** is the largest-sized heading, and the number **6** is the smallest heading. Make sure that when you close the tag, you include the number of the heading as well—in other words, use the tag **</H1>**, not **</H>** when closing an **<H1>** heading. Here are the sizes of six headings:

- H1—24 point
- H2—18 point
- H3—14 point
- H4—12 point
- H5—10 point
- H6—8 point (9 point on the Macintosh)

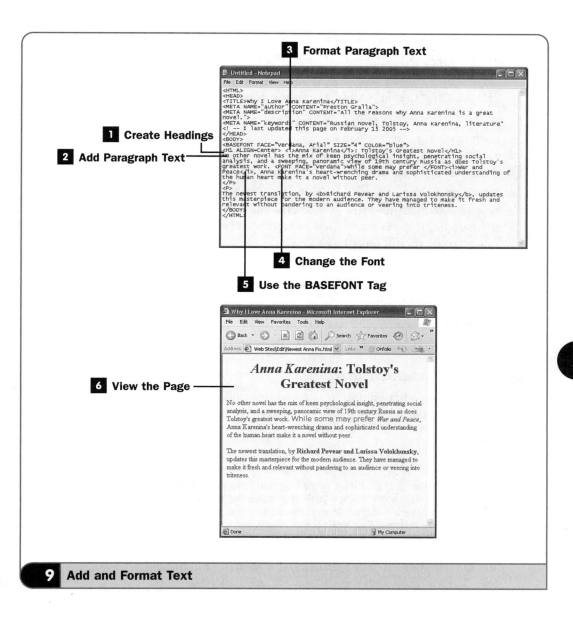

3 Format Paragraph Text

1 Create Headings

2 Add Paragraph Text

4 Change the Font

5 Use the BASEFONT Tag

6 View the Page

9 Add and Format Text

▶ **TIP**

It's best to keep your web pages short. People tend not to spend a great deal of time on any single web page; they get antsy and click away. Long pages also take a long time to load. So keep individual pages simple and to the point. Try not to have more than three major headings on a single page. If you have more than that, look at the content you're presenting, and try to break it up into more than one page.

You also have control over how the heading sits on the page—aligned left, aligned right, or centered. To do that, use the **ALIGN** attribute. Here's how to center the heading:

<H1 ALIGN="Center">Anna Karenina: Tolstoy's Greatest Novel</H1>

To align the heading to the left, type **Left** as the value, and to align it to the right, type **Right** as the value.

2 Add Paragraph Text

Now it's time to put some text on the page. Inline, underneath the heading, type in text. Note after you use the **<H>** and **</H>** tags, you don't need to use the paragraph tag to start a new paragraph. The **<H>** tag pair includes a line return, as do several other tags.

When you're done with your first paragraph, end it with the **</P>** tag. HTML doesn't absolutely require that you do this, oddly enough, but it's a good idea to get used to doing it.

To start a new paragraph, type in **<P>**. Type in the text. Keep adding as many paragraphs as you want that way.

3 Format Paragraph Text

We now have a reasonable enough–looking page. But the text in the paragraph could use some help, by changing colors and fonts, and using boldface and italic.

▶ NOTE

There's a text-handling tag that lives in infamy, and may well be the most reviled tag ever invented—the highly annoying **BLINK** tag. Surround text with **<BLINK>** and **</BLINK>** and your text will blink in maddening fashion. Don't ever use it; you'll only chase people away. Internet Explorer doesn't recognize the tag anyway; it will only make text blink when viewed with Netscape Navigator.

You add emphasis to text by making it boldfaced or italicizing it. To italicize text, surround text with the **<I>** and **</I>** tags, like this:

<I>War and Peace</I>

To make text bold, surround it with the **<B>** and **</B>** tags, like this:

<B>Richard Pevear and Larissa Volokhonsky</B>

You can also nest the **<B>** and **<I>** tags, to make text bold italic, like this:

<B><I>Anna Karenina</I></B>

If you're nesting the tags, make sure that you close off the innermost one before closing the outermost one. In other words, close the most recent tag you've created before closing off earlier tags. (For more details, see **3** **About Empty Tags and Nesting**.)

You can use the italic tag with headings, not just for text. So if you want to italicize words in a heading, it will look like this:

<H1 ALIGN=Center><I>Anna Karenina</I>: Tolstoy's Greatest Novel</H1>

Don't bother to try to use the **<B>** tag with a heading, though. By default, heading tags are boldfaced already.

4 Change the Font

There will be times when you want to change the font on your page, and to do that, you use the font tag **<FONT>** and **</FONT>**. It lets you change the font of the text, but goes beyond that: With it, you can also change the size of the text and the color of the font, among other things.

To change the font, use the attribute **FACE** along with the **<FONT>** tag, like this. (For more details about using attributes and values, see **4** **Use Attributes and Values**.)

<FONT FACE="Verdana">While some may prefer</FONT>

That will change the text to the Verdana font.

There's a problem using the font tag to specify a particular font, though. The browser will only display the text in that font if the PC doing the browsing has that specific font installed. If the font isn't installed, the font won't be changed—it will stay as the Times New Roman font that a browser normally displays.

To get around the problem, you can use several fonts as values, separated by spaces and commas. The browser will try to use the first font, but if it isn't installed, it will instead use the second font, and so on. If none of the fonts are on the system, the browser will use Times New Roman. Here's how to specify several fonts:

<FONT FACE="Verdana, Arial">While some may prefer</FONT>

You can also change the font size, using the **SIZE** attribute, and a number between 1 and 7, like this:

<FONT SIZE="4">While some may prefer</FONT>

9

The default size for a font is **3**, so if you use a number below 3, you'll be making the text smaller, and if you use a number above 3, you'll be making the text larger.

To change the color of text, you use the **COLOR** attribute. There are two types of values you can use along with this attribute in order to specify a color. You can type in the names of any of 16 common colors, such as red, blue, and so on. Or else you can specify the color using *hexadecimal* code. This gives you greater control over the precise color, but is a bit harder to do. For our purposes, for this chapter, we'll go with typing in a color name. Here's how you do it:

<FONT COLOR="blue">While some may prefer</FONT>

All of these attributes can be used at once to specify the font, size, and color, like this:

<FONT FACE="Verdana, Arial" SIZE="4" COLOR="blue">While some may prefer</FONT>

The resulting text will be in the Verdana font, will be blue, and will be larger than normal text.

▶ KEY TERM

Hexadecimal—A numbering system that uses 16 unique symbols, the numbers 0 through 9, and the letters A through F. These symbols are used individually, or combined. So, for example, the number 15 is represented in the decimal system by F.

5 Use the BASEFONT Tag

If you want to change all the text on your web page to a specific font, you can use the **BASEFONT** tag. It's an empty tag, which means that it doesn't use a closing tag.

The **BASEFONT** tag uses the same attributes and values as does the **FONT** tag. So putting the following tag at the beginning of the body of your document will force all text to be in the Verdana font, blue, and larger than normal.

<BASEFONT FACE="Verdana, Arial" SIZE="12" COLOR="blue">

6 View the Page

If you haven't already saved the page, save it now. View it in your browser. Look for any errors, such as the font being the wrong type or size.

---

10   About Creating Hyperlinks

✔ BEFORE YOU BEGIN	→ SEE ALSO
2 Use HTML Tags **7** Set Up a Web Page's Basic HTML Structure	**11** About Adding Graphics

The heart of the World Wide Web is its capability to link to other web pages, resources, and information. So now we're going to cover how to put links on your page.

You use the anchor tag <A> and </A> to link from your website to another **URL**. The **URL** you link to can be anything on the Internet—a web page, a video, or a file, for example. When you link to a web page, that page will appear in your browser. When you link to something other than a web page, what happens will be determined by what exactly you're linking to, and how your computer has been set up. For example, if you link to a music file, the file might either download to your computer, or start playing on your computer.

▶ KEY TERM

URL (uniform resource locator)—An address on the Internet, such as **http://www. samspublishing.net**.

10

Let's say that on your page, you want to put a link on the word *Tolstoy's* that, when clicked upon, will send the browser to the **www.ltolstoy.com** site, a site devoted to Leo Tolstoy and all his works. Here's how to create the link using the anchor tag:

<A HREF="http://www.ltolstoy.com">Tolstoy's</A>

In this instance, the text **Tolstoy's** will show up as a link on your web page, and when clicked on, will send a browser to the site **http://www.ltolstoy.com**. As you can see, the anchor tag uses the HREF attribute to specify a URL to which you link. The URL has to be surrounded by quotation marks.

Note that you have to use the full URL to the page to which you're linking, including the **http://**.

When you put a link on your page, it shows up as the familiar underlined text you see on the Web. The text that is underlined and linked from—in our instance, the word *Tolstoy's*—is often called a label.

When you link, you can link not just to the home page of a site, but to any individual page on the site. So, in our example, if we want to link the word **Tolstoy** to a page on the **www.ltolstoy.com** site that contains his biography, our link will look like this:

<A HREF="http://www.ltolstoy.com/about/biography.html">Tolstoy's</A>

► **TIP**

When coding your page, try to keep labels as short as possible. Making entire sentences show up as links makes the page very hard to read. If possible, keep the labels to several words or fewer. Using a brief description of the destination page as the link text is much more useful to visitors than simply using the nondescriptive **Click Here**.

---

11 About Adding Graphics

✔ BEFORE YOU BEGIN	→ SEE ALSO
2 Use HTML Tags	**10** About Creating Hyperlinks
7 Set Up a Web Page's Basic HTML Structure	**79** About Image Information
	99 About Image Information

11

The Web would be a pretty dull place if it was made up only of text. So you'll often want to add graphics to your pages.

To add a graphic, you use the image tag, **<IMG>** and **</IMG>**, along with the source (**SRC**) attribute. Here's how to use it:

<IMG SRC="http://www.ltolstoy.com/picture.jpg"</IMG>

Note that when you point to a graphic, you need to include its location—where it can be found on the Web—not just its name.

If, though, you are going to put your graphic in the same location on the same web server as the web page that points to it, you don't need to include the location (although if you do, it won't hurt).

So, to reiterate, to place a graphic on a page, you use the image tag in this format: **<IMG SCR="*filename*">** where "*filename*" includes both the location and name of the file itself.

When you place a graphic on a page, there might be a great deal of white space to the right of it. That's because when you place a graphic, the graphic is placed on the left side of the page, and no text will appear to the right of the graphic. Instead, any text will appear underneath the graphic, as you can see in the following figure.

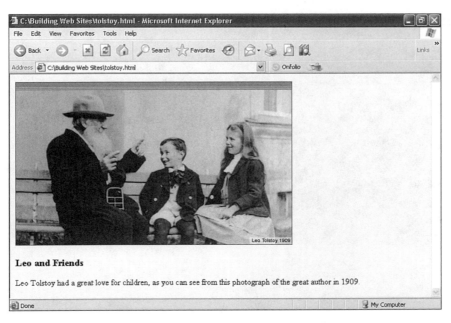

Too much white space to the right of a graphic can seem awkward.

There's an easy way to fix that. You can use the **ALIGN** attribute to wrap text around an image. The image can be aligned to the right or to the left, and the text will wrap around it in both cases. Here's how to align the graphic to the left. When you do this, text will automatically wrap around it to the right:

<IMG SRC="http://www.ltolstoy.com/picture.jpg" ALIGN="left"</IMG>

The following figure shows how the page looks by aligning the image to the left and wrapping text around it.

11

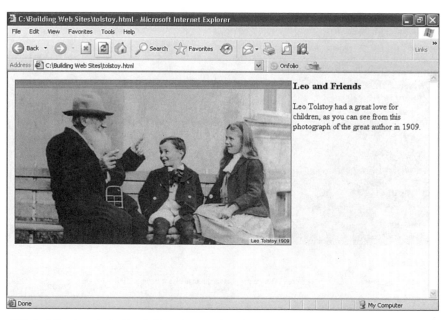

Aligning the image to the left and wrapping the text around it.

If you use **ALIGN="right"**, it will look like the following figure.

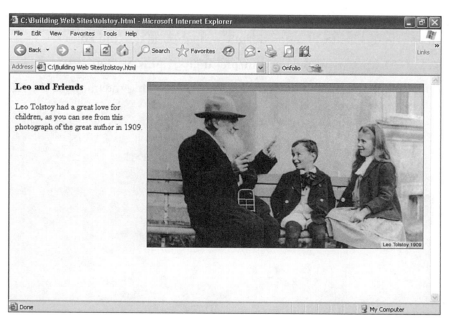

Aligning the image to the right and wrapping the text around it.

▶ **TIP**

When creating graphics for the web, use the **.gif**, **.jpg**, or **.png** file formats, because those are the only ones that all browsers will recognize. Also, if you're going to use a graphic to create an image map, there's some help on the Web. Go to **http://www.htmlgoodies.com/tutorials/image_maps/index.php** and **http://www.ihip.com/** for help.

---

12 About Choosing a Hosting Service

✔ BEFORE YOU BEGIN	→ SEE ALSO
1 About HTML	**20** Explore GeoCities

Before you can start building your website, you need to find a home for it. A web-*hosting service* will house your web pages, and offer you help and tools in building and maintaining it. A good one will also offer extras such as graphics you can use, and even website-designing software. There are many hosting services you can use, ranging from ones provided by your Internet service provider (ISP) to free hosting services to those that charge you a monthly fee.

12

▶ **KEY TERM**

Hosting service—A service that will let you post your pages to it, and keep all your pages on its server, so that people can visit it.

When people visit your website, they're actually visiting a web server—a computer on the Internet that delivers web pages. You get your web page site to a web server by uploading it from your computer, where you created it, to the server, where other people can visit it. When a web server houses a website, it's called hosting a site. A server frequently has more than a single website on it, and so it can host many sites at a single time.

A web-hosting service is a company that houses websites. There are many different kinds of services, offering many different levels of service. Before you can build a website, you need to find a service to host your site. Although there is a wide variety of different services, there are generally three hosting services from which you'll choose:

- **Your own ISP**—Almost every ISP, including America Online, includes web hosting as part of its basic service. Often, this hosting is bare bones, and offers little beyond the most basic features, but sometimes ISPs have more substantial offerings as well.

- **A free web-hosting service such as Yahoo! GeoCities**—These services frequently offer many kinds of extra features, such as web-based site-building tools and extra storage. In return, you might have to agree to put advertising on your website. For more information about building pages on **Yahoo! GeoCities**, see ㉚ **Explore GeoCities**.

- **A for-pay hosting service, such as Verio.com**—These kinds of services give you a lot of storage space for your website, make sure that visitors can get high-speed access to your site, offer solid technical support, and might have many different extras, such as prebuilt "shopping carts" for people who want to build sites that let visitors buy items.

Which service you choose will depend on your needs, and your pocketbook. In general, though, unless you're building a site for a business, there's usually no need to spend money for a hosting service.

Things to Consider When Choosing a Hosting Service

Here are the basic things you'll look for in a hosting service:

- **How reliable is it?** In other words, can people reach your site or is it frequently down? And when people reach it, will the web pages be delivered with reasonable speed? There's only one way to check this out: Visit sites that the service hosts and see if they're alive or dead, and if they're delivered in a timely way.

- **How much storage space do you get?** You'll need space to store your website. The HTML pages themselves don't take up a lot of space because they're only text files, which tend to be small. But graphics and multimedia files such as music files can take up a great deal of space, so find out how much storage space you'll need. Sometimes, at an ISP for example, you might only get about 10MB of storage space. That small amount of storage space often doesn't go far, so try to opt for more. More is always better.

▶ NOTE

When checking to see how much storage space you'll get on a hosting service, ask whether that amount of space has to accommodate email messages stored on the email server. Some hosting services give you an email box, and the storage space you get for your website might be less than you think because it will have to accommodate your email messages as well. Note that you'll only have to pay for email that is actually on the mail server. After your email software connects to the mail server, it downloads it, and the email won't take up any server storage space. Still, check before deciding on a hosting service.

- **How much bandwidth do you get?** When people come to your site, they download web pages and other information from the server to their computers. The amount of information downloaded this way is referred to as *bandwidth*. Most hosting services allow you a certain amount of bandwidth, and then start charging after that. Often, you'll get several gigabytes per month, which is more than enough for most personal sites. But if you are building a site for a non-profit group or a business, you might need more than that, so find out how much you'll be charged for bandwidth above a certain amount.

- **What kind of technical support is offered?** When building and publishing a website, you can run into countless complications. So you'll want good technical support from your web-hosting service, if at all possible. How to find out if technical support is good? Before you sign up, call the technical support number and see how long you're put on hold, or else send an email and see how long it takes before you get a response. If you're on hold a long time or it takes a long time to get a response, you'll know the technical support leaves much to be desired.

- **How easy is it to publish your site?** Ask the hosting service how you'll publish your website. At most hosting services, it should be straightforward and easy, but you should check before you sign up.

▶ **TIP**

To publish a website, you upload it from your computer to your web-hosting service. In order to upload, you'll usually be given a password and username, as well as the location of the directory to which you're going to upload. Keep all that information in a safe place, because without it, you won't be able to publish your site.

13

- **What kind of extras are offered?** Some sites offer shopping cart software, others offer features to specifically work with certain page-creation software such as Microsoft FrontPage, and still others might give you several email inboxes. Check out the extras before you order.

13	**About Posting Your Page**
✔ **BEFORE YOU BEGIN**	→ **SEE ALSO**
12 About Choosing a Hosting Service	**20** Explore GeoCities

A web page sitting on your computer is no good to anyone. You can do all the hard work of coding you want, but if you can't post your site to the Web, no one will visit. If a tree falls in the forest and no one hears it, did it truly fall?

We don't know the answer to that philosophical question, but we do know that if you don't post your website, it's as if it didn't exist.

In order for your site to be live, it has to be uploaded to a web server—that is, all the files that make up your site, including the HTML files, graphics, and any other files, have to be sent from your computer to the computer on the hosting service that will have your files.

How you actually post your page will vary from site to site, and so there's no way to provide the exact details of how you post a web page here. Make sure that you write down all the information sent to you from your hosting service, including file directories and locations, passwords, and usernames.

But no matter how you post your page, there are a series of steps you should take before posting.

Check Your HTML Markup

First, you should check whether there are errors in your HTML markup. No matter how careful you are, no matter how experienced, and no matter how many times you check your markup, you've probably made an error or two. Don't worry, you're not alone—even the professionals make mistakes. And it's not as if HTML is a particularly logical language.

If you're using an HTML editing program, it may well have a feature that will automatically check your HTML for you. It will go through your HTML and check it for errors, bad syntax, and similar problems, and then recommend changes, or make the changes for you. These are incredibly helpful tools, so if you're using an HTML editing program, use that feature.

If it doesn't have that feature, you should preview all your pages and then go over them with a fine-toothed comb for errors.

Check Your Links

It's not just your markup that can be a problem. It's also very easy to make errors when linking to files or graphics. So you should check your links as well, to make sure that they're not broken. You've no doubt clicked on dead links when surfing the Web—remember how annoying that was? You don't want your visitors to be similarly frustrated. So check your links before posting.

Again, the better HTML editors include link-checking features. If you don't use an HTML editor, or yours doesn't have a link checker, click every link on every page, to make sure they work.

You can also download a free link-checking program that will check your pages for bad links. It's called Xenu's Link Sleuth, and is available for free at **http://home.snafu.de/tilman/xenulink.html**.

Other Final Checks

There are a few other final checks you should make before publishing your site. First, check it for spelling and typographical errors. Many HTML editors include a built-in spell checker, so use it before posting. But don't rely solely on it, because it won't be able to catch misuses (*its* for *it's*, for example). Check your punctuation as well, and give your pages a final read.

You should also view the final pages in both Internet Explorer and Netscape Navigator. (You may also want to check them on Opera and Firefox as well.) Pages coded properly for one browser might display incorrectly in another browser, so always preview your pages in both browsers. There are many versions of both browsers, but it's always best to preview your pages in the most recent versions.

For more details about publishing your site, see Chapter 12, "Publish Your Site."

13

3

Planning Out Your Website

IN THIS CHAPTER:

There's a sign that used to be hung at some commercial websites: "It's the content, stupid!" It was a shorthand way of reminding people that, at heart, the Web is a way to give people information or entertain them—in other words, give them content. All the graphics, videos, animations, and cool web techniques in the world aren't useful if there isn't solid content on the site, organized well.

That holds true whether you're building web pages for fun, friends and family, or for profit. So in this chapter you'll learn how to decide what content you want to present, and after you've decided that, you'll learn how to make a site map and build navigation so that your content will be presented as clearly as possible. And building a site map ahead of time is also the best way for you to organize your work, as well.

14   About Planning Your Site

✔ BEFORE YOU BEGIN	→ SEE ALSO
Just jump right in.	**15** About Focusing on What You Want to Present

The hardest work you'll do building a website comes well before you ever touch even the smallest bit of HTML code. It has nothing to do with the Internet, and nothing to do with computing. In fact, it has nothing to do with technology at all. It has to do with first deciding on why you want to build a website, and then determining what you want to present on it.

It sounds simple, but in fact it's very, very hard to do. You've probably come across dozens of websites that confuse you or that don't ever quite come to the point. The great odds are the problem wasn't with the designers or coders—the problem was that the people creating the site weren't quite clear on why they were creating it. The next time you come to a website that you don't think is particularly good, take a few minutes to examine it and see why. You'll probably find out it's because the site has a confused focus, and no clear point or message.

You don't want to fall into the same trap. So before you do a lick of work, stop. Then start thinking. Take enough time planning your site, and building it will be a breeze.

15 About Focusing on What You Want to Present

✔ BEFORE YOU BEGIN	→ SEE ALSO
14 About Planning Your Site	**16** Match Your Design and Content to Your Audience

Before working on your site, there are several steps to take. First, as outlined in **14** **About Planning Your Site**, decide why you want to build a website. Is it to share news with friends and family? Pontificate about world events? Try to sell auction items?

Based on that, you need to decide on what kind of website you want to build. There are three basic kinds of websites you might want to create:

- A **personal site**, where you might simply want to share your hobbies or personal musings with the world on a site or **blog**.

▶ KEY TERM

Blog—A website that is in diary-like format, in which there are a series of short, dated entries. Many blogs also allow for readers to post comments on the site.

- A **website for a non-profit group**, such as a youth soccer league, or school, in which you want to share information about the group.

- A **business site**, in which you publicize your business, or take orders over the Internet.

▶ TIP

As a first step in deciding on what you want to present, consider writing a mission statement. A mission statement is one or two sentences that describe succinctly the point of your site—in short, its mission. When drawing one up, make sure it's not too long. A too-long mission statement usually means that you can't decide on the primary reason you're building a website.

Keep in mind that you shouldn't try to mix and match these sites. In other words, don't try to create a website that is both a personal site and a business site. Your customers might not really appreciate having to read about your pet chinchilla, or your collection of vintage license plates.

Why Build a Personal Site?

Got a hobby you want to share with the world? Need to get something off your chest? Do you want your own personal soapbox?

15

Those are just some of the reasons why you might want to build a personal website or blog. Many people create them to keep in touch with friends and family, or just to announce to the world, "I'm here!" And they're great places to post pictures of yourself, your family, and your vacation. (For more information about blogs, turn to **180 About Blogging**.)

In fact, the only reason you might want to build a personal website is just for the fun of doing it.

No matter your reason, though, your personal website should be as much as possible a personal reflection of yourself. You can also make the design as informal as you want, and can disclose only the information about yourself that you want. In short, when it comes to building a personal website, the only real rules you need to make are your own. You can be as wild or staid as you want.

Why Build a Website for a Non-Profit Group?

Just about any non-profit group could make good use of a website. Whether it's an amateur theater group, a neighborhood association, a parent group, a youth soccer league, a charitable organization, or almost any other kind of non-profit group, there are good reasons to build a website for it.

15

One of the main reasons for building this kind of website is to get the word out about the group—for example, to do fund-raising, get people to join, or get people to take some kind of action. Calendars, information about upcoming events, basic information about the group, and contacts are just some of the other kinds of basic information you'll put on this site. This type of site will have to be more formal-looking than a personal site.

▶ TIP

In addition to doing good, building a website for a non-profit has another benefit as well—it can help you in your career. When you build one, you'll get real-world, practical experience that will make your resumé stand out from others.

One more thing to keep in mind when building this site: Often, it will require the input of many people, and many people may have to sign off on it before it's posted. So if you're building this sort of site, leave plenty of time for others to review it.

Why Build a For-Profit Site?

If you have a small business, the benefits of building a website are fairly obvious. It's a great way to get new customers, to keep in touch with existing customers, and to keep in touch with suppliers. And you can also use your website to take orders, as well.

This kind of website should be the most formal looking of the three major types of sites. And considering that the site is intended to make money, you should think about spending more for a hosting service than you will for a personal website or non-profit website. It'll be worth your while to pay extra for a site that has substantial backup. And in any event, if you want to take orders over the Web, you might have to pay extra for a hosting service that offers this feature.

▶ **TIP**

Sometimes it's a good idea to mix business and pleasure. If you have a personal website, consider posting your resumé there and updating it regularly, even if you aren't looking for work. It's free, it's easy to do, and you never know what kind of work it might bring your way.

---

16 **Match Your Design and Content to Your Audience**

✔ BEFORE YOU BEGIN	→ SEE ALSO
14 About Planning Your Site	**17** Organize Your Site's Content
15 About Focusing on What You Want to Present	

16

So now you've taken the first step—you've decided what kind of website you want to build. Now comes an even harder part. You have to figure out who your target audience is, what kind of content to put on the site, and then match the design of the site to the information you want to present and your target audience. In this task, you'll learn how to do all that.

1 **Define Your Audience**

Knowing the kind of site you want to build isn't enough—you also have to define what kind of audience you're after. And the best way to define your audience is to ask yourself questions about who they are. Be as specific as possible. Here are some basic questions to ask. Don't stop here, though. Add questions of your own.

- If you're designing a site for a for-profit business, will the audience be existing customers, new customers, or potential investors?

- If you're designing a site for a for-profit business, will visitors expect to be able to do business with you right on the Web, or will they use the Web to get information, and then contact you in some other way?

- If it's a personal site, are you only interested in designing it for people you already know, or for strangers as well?

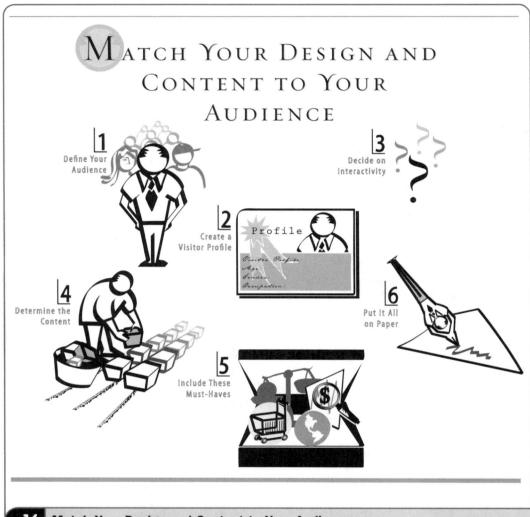

MATCH YOUR DESIGN AND CONTENT TO YOUR AUDIENCE

1 Define Your Audience

2 Create a Visitor Profile

Profile

Visitor Profile
Age
Gender
Occupation

3 Decide on Interactivity

4 Determine the Content

5 Include These Must-Haves

6 Put It All on Paper

16   Match Your Design and Content to Your Audience

- If it's for a personal site, will your visitors be primarily family members, or other people as well?

- If it's a site for a non-profit group, are you designing the site for members of the group so that they can communicate with one another, or are you designing it to do outreach in the community? Or do you want to combine the two purposes in some way?

- Do you expect more men or more women to visit, or an equal number of both?

- What is the average age of your expected visitor?

- How technically savvy are they?

- How frequently do you expect them to visit?

2 Create a Visitor Profile

After you answer these questions, you've got a good start on understanding your intended audience. Based on your answers, write a short profile of who your primary visitors will be. Be as specific as possible. Keep in mind that the content and design of your site should be aimed primarily at them, so you want to define them as comprehensively as you possibly can. You might also want to create a profile of your secondary visitors or even tertiary visitors. You can design part of the site for them as well. But don't let that distract you from the main point of this exercise—deciding who is your target audience.

3 Decide on Interactivity

No matter who your audience, make sure to ask yourself one basic question about them: Will they want interactivity of some sort with the site, with you, or with your business or group? For example, if they want to be able to get answers to questions, or to contact you directly, make sure to include a link that they can click on to send you email. And if you're creating a blog, decide whether you want to let visitors post comments. (See **193** **Limit Who Can Comment on Your Blog**.)

4 Determine the Content

You now should have a profile of your target audience. Now it's time to figure out what kind of content they want.

Start off in brainstorming mode. Don't expect to be able to figure this out in a logical manner. Get a piece of paper and a pen, and start off by writing down a comprehensive list of everything you think your target audience would want from your website. Keep referring back to your audience description, and focus on your primary audience first. Don't worry about trying to organize the information at this point—just keep writing down ideas. And don't think yet about how you might present the information; that comes later.

Just in case you need some help to get you started with figuring out what kind of content you should have, here's a very short list of things to consider, for each kind of the three main types of websites you might want to create.

16

Personal Website

- Hobbies and interests

- Education

- Resumé

- Public diary

- Personal ramblings

- Photos

Website for Non-Profit Group

- Name and purpose of the group

- Calendar

- Notices of upcoming events

- How to donate money

- Articles or publicity about the group

- Contact information

- News

For-Profit Website

- Name and purpose of the business

- Contact information

- Product list or list of services

- Online buying, or information on how to buy offline

- Shipping and warranty information

- Directions on how to get to the company

- Feedback form or email contact information

5 Include These Must-Haves

No matter the kind of website you're building, there are three piece of information that should be on it. You should include contact information—and if it's a personal site, you'll probably only want to include an email address rather than a phone number so that you don't get crank calls. You should also include an "About" statement, which describes the purpose of the site or group. And you should also have a FAQ area. FAQ stands for Frequently Asked Questions, and it's a list of common questions that people might ask. You'll be amazed at how much a simple FAQ page can help your visitors.

6 Put It All on Paper

Make sure that you put everything down on paper—don't assume you'll remember it all. Don't worry about organizing all your material at this point. Just get it down on paper. In the next task, you'll find out how to organize it into a coherent whole.

---

17 Organize Your Site's Content

✔ BEFORE YOU BEGIN	→ SEE ALSO
15 About Focusing on What You Want to Present	**14** About Planning Your Site
16 Match Your Design and Content to Your Audience	

17

Now that you've gone to so much effort to list all the content you might want on your site, it's time to get it all organized. At this point, you should have a large, sprawling list of ideas. If you've done your homework, there's far more information than you'll ever be able to publish. In fact, if there's not more information than you can possibly use, you've probably done something wrong.

So how to put that mass of information into a more coherent whole? Follow these steps, and you'll start to get it all into shape.

1 Group Related Ideas

Study your ideas for a while, and you'll notice that they fall into related topics. For example, on a personal web page, you could group together all your hobbies and personal interests, or you could group your resumé with information about your current job. On a non-profit website, you could combine email and phone contact information with driving directions on how to get to the group's headquarters.

Also, put related interactivity together. You might want visitors to your site to be able to chat with one another, be able to sign a guestbook, or take interactive polls of some kind. If so, put them all in one area.

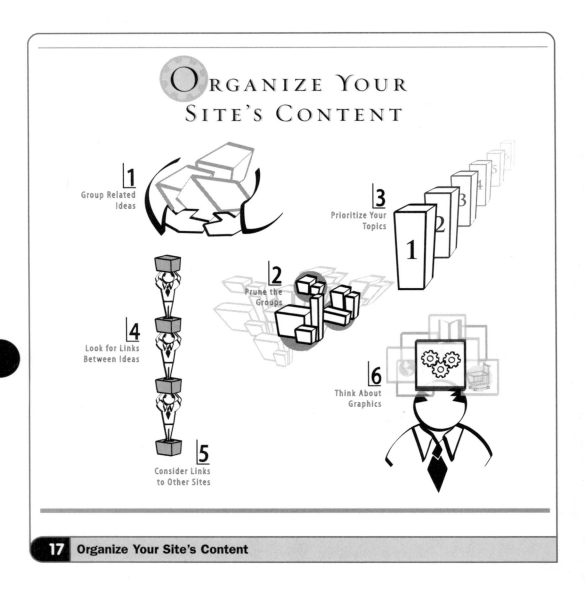

Organize Your Site's Content

1 Group Related Ideas

3 Prioritize Your Topics

2 Prune the Groups

4 Look for Links Between Ideas

6 Think About Graphics

5 Consider Links to Other Sites

17

17   Organize Your Site's Content

▶ NOTE

A web page can have as little or as much information as you want on it. If you include a great deal of writing on it, the page simply scrolls...and scrolls...and scrolls. But how much information is too much? Keep your information as bite-sized as possible on the Web, otherwise you'll lose people's attention. A good rule of thumb is that you shouldn't have more than about 350 words per page. There are exceptions, of course—for example, if your page is made up of short diary entries in a "blog"-like fashion, a page can be longer because people can pick and choose among those snippets. But in general, when it comes to the Web, less is more. Also, keep in mind that too many graphics on a page will make the page load very slowly, so you want to keep them under control as well.

2 Prune the Groups

Too many groups spoil the site. These groups that you've just created will become the main sections of your website. You should limit them to no more than between five to seven. If you have any more than five to seven of them, people will soon get lost—and in fact, when people come to the site, they might see how sprawling the site is and not even bother to stay.

So either cut out the groups that are peripheral, or else combine several groups into one. Under each group, list all the information that you want to have in that group.

3 Prioritize Your Topics

You should now have five to seven topics, with several (or many) ideas under each of those topics. But not all ideas are created equal—some are more important than others. So prioritize. Put a 1, 2, or 3 next to each of your ideas, according to its importance, with a 1 being the most important. (You shouldn't number your topics, but rather the ideas under each topic.) When it comes time to design your site, you'll probably want to start only with the number 1s on your list. If you want to grow it from there, you can move to the number 2s and number 3s.

4 Look for Links Between Ideas

The heart of the Web is the capability to link pages to one another. So look at your information and start thinking about which pages should be linked to which. You can't link every page to every other page, because that quickly becomes far too confusing. But you will notice ideas that should be linked to each other. For example, if you have a page that mentions each member of your family, and also have a page with photos, you'll want to link the names of your family members to their photos, and vice versa.

5 Consider Links to Other Sites

It's a good idea not only to link to pages on your own site, but also to other websites as well. Although you might think doing so will send people away from your site, that isn't the case. If people know they can find good links from your site to other useful or entertaining sites, they'll keep coming back to yours for more.

▶ TIP

People love clicking around the Web and are always looking for new sites to visit. So on your personal website, consider creating a favorite links page. Describe each and why you like the site. Rather than a single, long list, group the links into related subjects—for example, sports, cooking, travel, and so on.

6   Think About Graphics

When you start building your website, you'll find out that one of the most difficult problems is getting fresh sources of graphics. So it's never too early to start thinking about what kind of graphics you'll want to use—the more time you spend thinking about what they should be and how you can find them, the better.

---

18   Build a Site Map

✔ **BEFORE YOU BEGIN**	→ **SEE ALSO**
15 About Focusing on What You Want to Present	**14** About Planning Your Site
17 Organize Your Site's Content	

By now you know the content you want on your site. You should have five to seven main topics, and under each of those topics, several ideas, each with a number-1 priority. For now, we'll forget about the number-2 and number-3 priorities. You can add them later if you want.

How to get all that information from your outline to a living website? The best next step is to build a site map. A site map is a clear, visual representation of every page on your site, and will show how those pages fit into the site's organization. In essence, a site map is a flowchart that shows every page on the site and details how visitors will move through the site.

You can draw a site map freehand on a large sheet of paper, or else you can use some kind of graphics or drawing program. I greatly encourage you to draw it freehand. I've found that if you use a graphics or drawing program, you spend more time trying to understand how to use the program, fiddling with color, figuring out how to draw snazzy lines, and other time-wasters than you actually do getting any work done. A very rough hand-drawn sketch is fine at this point.

I also recommend getting a very large piece of paper—as large as you can find. Get large, oversized pads at an art store or office supply store.

For every page on your site, you'll draw a rectangle. When pages link to one another, draw lines from one to another. For each page, write down the main topic.

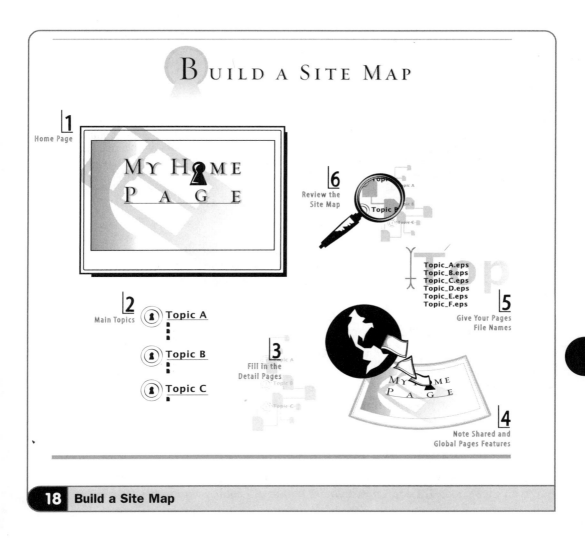

18 Build a Site Map

1 Start with the Home Page

At the top of the site map, draw a rectangle and label it **Home Page**. The home page is the front door to your site. It's the first view of your site that your visitors will have. The home page should tell at a glance the name of your site, its purpose, and lay out the directory and navigation of the various topics on the site. It frequently has more than just navigation and a directory of information on it, though—it often has some kind of content as well, depending upon what kind of site you're building. For example, if it's a site for a non-profit group, you might have information about an upcoming fund drive. If it's a personal site, you might have photos of a recent trip you took, or a holiday greeting. And if it's a commercial site, you should have information about the product or service you're selling, and a way for people to order it.

▶ **TIP**

For some incomprehensible reason, some web designers insist on putting a page in front of the home page. This pre–home page often is little more than a logo or animation of some kind, and you're supposed to click on the logo or the animation in order to enter the site. I can't think of a worse way to try and get people to your site. All this does is drive people away, because many people won't bother to click on the logo or animation. When people are browsing the Web, they often have very little time or patience, and it's your job to make things easy for them, not force them to click for no apparent purpose.

2 List the Main Topics

Beneath the home page, in a row, draw rectangles for all your main topics. Remember, there should be no more than five to seven of them—and fewer is fine. (For more information, see **17 Organize Your Site's Content**.) In each rectangle, write in the topic. Draw lines from each topic page to the home page.

3 Fill in the Detail Pages

You're ready to round out the map. It's time to put in the detail pages—the topics that you've put number 1s next to in your brainstorming outline. Draw a rectangle for each, label each rectangle, and put them in a third row, beneath the main topic row. Draw lines from each main topic to the detail pages that are associated with that topic.

4 Note Shared and Global Pages and Features

Most websites have pages and features that are linked to and from many other pages. For example, if you're building a commercial website, on every page on your site, you might have a link to your site's privacy policy. If you're building a site for a non-profit group, you might have a link on many pages or even on every page to a member sign-in form. And if you're building a personal website, you might have a link on every page to an **About Me** page.

If you try drawing lines from every page on your site to all of these global pages and features, your site map will soon be so filled with lines that it will look like nothing more than a bowl of spaghetti. So instead of drawing those lines, come up with symbols or letters for each of those pages or features. Then on each page that will link to them, draw the symbol. Draw rectangles for each of the shared and global features and pages, label them, and note their symbols.

▶ **TIP**

When mapping out a site, it's easy to overlook pages that you'll need to create—sometimes there are "hidden" pages that you need to create. For example, if you have a form that you ask people to fill in, there will need to be a page that appears after the person has filled in and submitted the form. So follow the flow of your site, and make sure that you've listed every single page that you might possibly need.

5 **Give Your Pages Filenames**

After you've gotten what you believe to be a final page map, you should give your pages filenames. Every page on your site will have to have its own filename, and it's a good idea to come up with filenames now, before you start coding. That way, you can come up with a comprehensive plan for naming files. There are a few things you need to keep in mind when naming files:

- **Filenames usually end in .htm or .html**—Most of the files you create will use **.htm** or **.html** as a file extension. If the site is hosted by a Windows server, the filenames generally end in **.htm**. Ask your web-hosting service whether your site is hosted by a Windows computer.

- **Keep filenames short**—Not only will this make it easy to remember them, but short filenames are easier for people to type into their browser. Also, avoid embedded spaces in filenames because they can be hard to reference in links.

- **Use logic in naming pages**—They should relate to the content of the page, and there should be a reason why you pick certain names. For example, don't use numbers to name pages unless there's a logical purpose to those numbers. In many cases, the home page's filename must be **index.htm** or **index.html**. If not, the server software administrator might have to configure the server for a different filename.

▶ **TIP**

A very useful way to fine-tune and finalize your site map is to put all the pages on a wall and organize them as they will be on the site. Each page should be on its own separate sheet of paper. Tape them to the wall and organize them the way you want them on the site. Seeing the site large like this is an excellent way to fine-tune its organization. It's easy to move pages around and reorganize them, and seeing them this size somehow makes the site more real as well. You might also want to use larger-sized sticky notes for this purpose.

6 **Review the Site Map**

You should now have a comprehensive site map. Before you begin coding and designing, feel free to re-jigger it, moving pages around, eliminating

18

some, and adding new ones. After you have a complete site map, you might want to consider making a neat copy using a graphics or drawing program, or better yet, a flowcharting program.

▶ **TIP**

After you've created your website, you'll at some point begin adding new pages and taking away old ones. When you do that, make sure to update your site map. If you don't, you'll soon lose track of the organization of your site, and it will be difficult to maintain it and grow it. Many larger websites have a page with a linked-up site map that users can use to navigate the site instead of the navigation found on the home page. Consider building one of these for your site.

19   **About Designing Your Site's Navigation**

✔ **BEFORE YOU BEGIN**

🔟 Organize Your Site's Content
🔞 Build a Site Map

19

There's one more thing to consider before you begin creating your site—how people will navigate through it. It's important to create a way for people to know at a glance what's available on your website, and to let them quickly jump to where they want to go.

You do all that through designing navigation for your site, the way that people will get around. You should have common navigation for all your pages. If you change the navigation, people will quickly become disoriented and lost, so keep the navigation consistent throughout.

Navigation consists of buttons or links that people can click on to get to the main areas of your site. Typically, the main areas of the site you'll want people to navigate to are the five to seven major topics you've created on your site map.

As a rule, navigation should go down the left side of each page, or else across the top (and sometimes the bottom) of each page. For navigation, you can use simple HTML links, or else buttons or even graphics. The following figure shows navigation along the top of a website—in this instance, the Sams Publishing site.

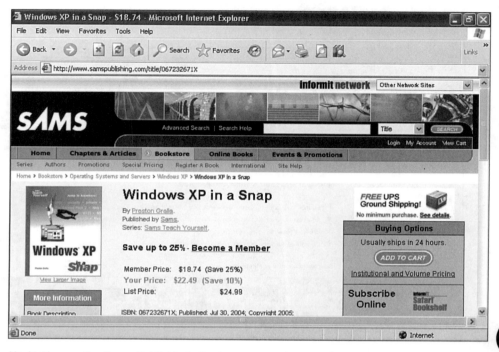

Navigation on the Sams Publishing site goes across the top of the page.

In addition to links to your five to seven major topics, you might also want to have navigational links on every page to global features or topics, as outlined earlier in this chapter. You might, for example, want to have links on every page to an **FAQ** or **Help** area, or an **About Me** area in addition to the topic areas. In that case, you should separate these special, global areas from your main content areas. If that's the case, you'll want to use left-side navigation combined with top or bottom navigation. Typically, if you organize your site's navigation this way, the main topic areas will go down the left side of the page, and the links to global features will go at the top or bottom of the page. The following figure shows this combination of top and side navigation, on the InformIT website.

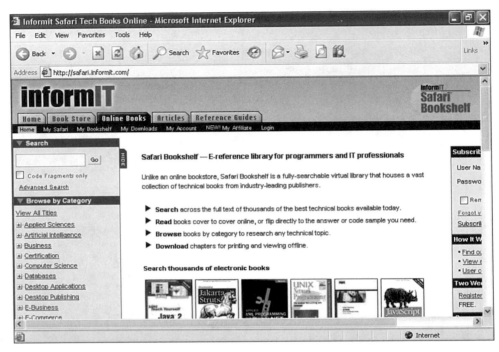

19

You can combine left-side navigation with top navigation, as shown here from the InformIT website. Many sites use the left-side navigation for main content areas, and the top navigation for links to common global pages or features.

When designing your navigation, however, keep in mind that, in general, simpler is better. Complex graphics serve only to confuse. And if you do use graphics instead of buttons, make sure to include text with them as well. Not everyone in the world will know that a picture of a cherry is meant as a link to a list of your favorite fruit.

▶ **TIP**

In addition to a site map, consider creating a style guide for your site—a document that covers the colors you'll use, the mood of your site, the tone of your writing, and details of word usage—for example, whether you'll use *email* or *e-mail*. You want to be as consistent as possible in everything you do, and having a written record of your style will make sure that you are.

Using "Bread Crumbs" on Your Site

Remember the story of Hansel and Gretel? As they were led by a witch deeper and deeper into the forest, Hansel scattered bread crumbs behind them so that they would be able to find their way back home.

The Web is often as confusing as a deep forest, and if you want to help your visitors find their way, you can use a Hansel-like technique called breadcrumbing. (For now, we'll forget that Hansel's bread crumb strategy didn't work because the forest's birds had eaten all the bread crumbs after he scattered them.)

Bread crumbs are, in essence, a trail of links put somewhere near the top of a page that lets you step back up through the hierarchy of a website, anywhere along the way.

Let's take an example. Say that you've created a page for your non-profit group, the **Cambridge Frisbee League**. There are several main areas on the site, including one titled **Schedule**, one titled **Rosters**, one titled **Rules**, and so on. Each of these areas has a number of pages beneath it. For example, the Schedule area has 12 pages, one with a schedule for each month of the year. If you were on that page, the breadcrumbing would look like the following figure. This enables you to see where you've been on the site, and quickly jump to a previous level. If you build a site with even more levels than this, breadcrumbing is even more useful.

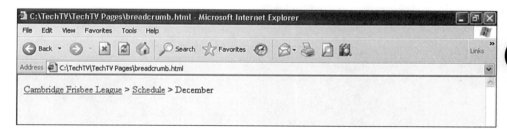

Using breadcrumbs is a good way to help people know where they've been and how to return there.

PART II

Building Your Own Website on GeoCities

IN THIS CHAPTER

4

Getting Started Building Web Pages on GeoCities

IN THIS CHAPTER:

Making a website on Yahoo!'s GeoCities is about the easiest way to get on the Web anyone could imagine. The basic service is free, but your site will show advertisements that GeoCities puts up on your site. If you don't want advertisements, you have options of upgrading to one of three services with fees from $5 to $11 or more per month, depending on the features you want to use.

GeoCities is one of many free hosting services from companies on the Web. GeoCities has a great range of features available for you to use to build free websites and has a very easy path to upgrade to one of several paid services that enable you to add features to your account, such as FTP access for uploading files, multiple email accounts, and domain hosting.

20 | Explore GeoCities

✔ **BEFORE YOU BEGIN**

Just jump right in.

20

Yahoo! GeoCities was one of the first large-scale, free web-hosting services on the Internet. All hosting companies at the most common level do the same thing: They host HTML documents that are served to viewers' browsers, where they are interpreted and displayed for viewers to read. In the beginning of the Web, everyone had to write his or her HTML by hand. HTML is a simple language that is easy to learn, but many beginners still found that the process of displaying the message could be overwhelming.

Because HTML was so easy to write, it was possible to create an application to write web pages and websites that would live on a server and be available for users who had no idea what HTML was all about. Today, there are many options from which to choose on GeoCities that range from free hosting and web page design to commercial-grade web hosting.

1 Go to http://www.geocities.com

You should see the GeoCities home page, where you can select from the various services GeoCities offers.

2 Click on GeoCities PLUS

This is the page in which you can order the GeoCities Plus plan, where you can get 25 megabytes (MB) of storage for your site and get no ads on your website. In the free service, you get 15MB, which is plenty for most people starting on the Web, but you also get advertisements you don't want to have in the long run. Click on the Back button before proceeding to step 3.

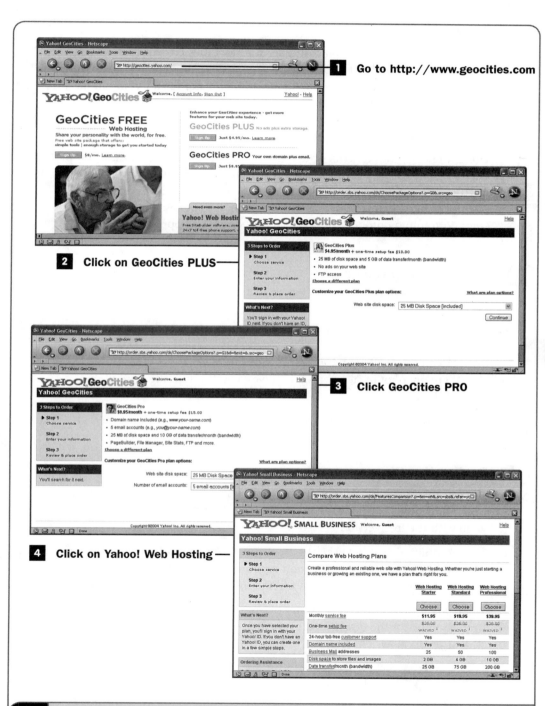

1 Go to http://www.geocities.com

2 Click on GeoCities PLUS

3 Click GeoCities PRO

4 Click on Yahoo! Web Hosting

20

20 Explore GeoCities

3 Click GeoCities PRO

This is the page in which you can order the GeoCities Pro package, which gives you the capability to point to a domain name at your site, an email account under your domain name, and 100MB of storage for your email. Click on the Back button before proceeding to step 4.

4 Click on Yahoo! Web Hosting

This is the page that describes the different professional plans for hosting that GeoCities offers. The packages here offer 2–10 gigabytes (GB) of storage, 25–100 different email addresses per domain, and advanced scripting with PHP and Perl, which is used to create dynamic web pages where users can enter data into a database or order products from a shopping cart.

---

21 Sign Up for Services

✔ **BEFORE YOU BEGIN**

Just jump right in.

21

In this task, you'll learn how to set up an account on GeoCities. This is a long task, but there are a lot of steps and you have to go through them all at one time, so buckle up, here we go.

Over time the steps might vary as GeoCities grows and changes, but you will need to go through the same steps, even if they are arranged differently.

1 Go to http://www.geocities.com

The welcome page for Yahoo! GeoCities shows several different options from which to choose, but these are all the paid options for service. We are going to go with the free version of GeoCities.

The main differences between the services are the amount of space you are allowed to use, the number of email accounts you are allowed to create, and whether you have your own domain name, such as **tacothechook.com**.

We're going to use the free version of GeoCities for this task. Click on the **Sign Up** button under the description of the free services. On the page that loads, click **Sign Up Now**.

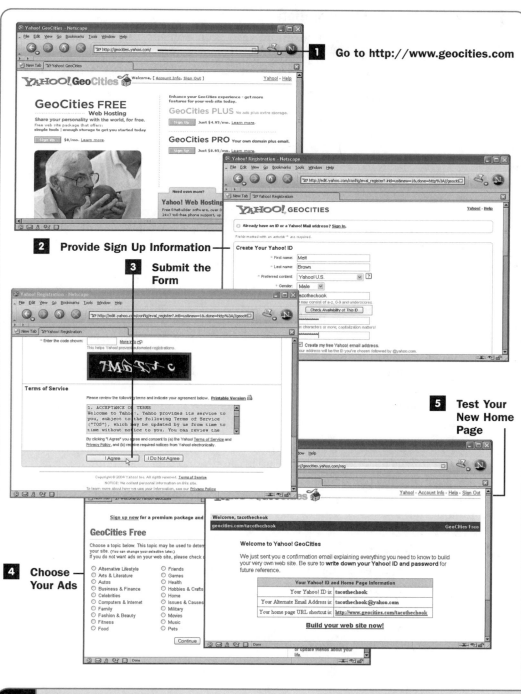

1 Go to http://www.geocities.com

2 Provide Sign Up Information

3 Submit the Form

5 Test Your New Home Page

4 Choose Your Ads

21

21 Sign Up for Services

2 Provide Sign Up Information

Fill in your name in the text boxes provided. Your name is used by GeoCities to personalize your service. When you go to your account, it calls you by the name you provide here, so enter something you want to see yourself referred to.

Choose your **ID**. Your ID is what your website is going to be called, as well as the name you are going to use to log in to the site and the name for your email account.

▶ TIP

Remember to write down your password. (Yes...I have learned that one the hard way—more than once.)

Select the check box to get your **Yahoo! mail** address. A Yahoo! email account is free, and you can use it to register for other services later. You might also want to use that address for people to contact you from your website. Sometimes it is useful not to use your main email address because it will help you to avoid receiving spam.

The information you supply in the next section of the form will help you recall your password if you ever forget it. Select a question and answer so that if you forget your password, you can provide some information for Yahoo! to send you your password. It also asks you for an alternative email account. If you have forgotten your password, you won't be able to get into your Yahoo! email account to get the password Yahoo! sends you, so it sends the password to the alternative email account.

At the bottom of the form is a box with a picture of some letters and maybe some numbers distorted and out of line. You need to copy the characters you see there into the box above the picture to guarantee you are a real person and not a computer program someone is using to make a website for questionable purposes.

3 Submit the Form

Click on the **I Agree** button. If you have made an error in the form or left a field empty that you need to fill out, a page will come up that tells what else you need to fill in.

Submit the form and write down the information that is returned and keep it in a safe place. Click on the **Continue to Yahoo! GeoCities** button.

4 Choose Your Ads

You are presented with a choice of what sort of advertisements you want to see on your page. You must have the ads in the free service, but you at least get to ask GeoCities to give you ads related to your site. Select one option and click on the **Continue** button.

5 Test Your New Home Page

You are presented with your Yahoo! ID, your alternate email address, and the URL or web address of your new page. Click on the link to your new page and go to your new home page!

22 Use Yahoo! PageWizards to Create a Page

✔ **BEFORE YOU BEGIN**

21 Sign Up for Services

22

Now that you have a Yahoo! GeoCities account, you can create your site. With Yahoo! GeoCities, you can create your website a few different ways. For the initial site, you are going to use the Yahoo! Quick Start PageWizard, which is very easy to use and gives you a good-looking home page using templates that are provided for you by GeoCities.

1 Go to Your New Page

This is where your changes are going to appear when you are finished creating your page. For now, all you will see is the starting point for you to build the site. On this page, you can access several tools to build your pages. You are going to use the **Yahoo! PageWizards** in this chapter. The **Yahoo! PageBuilder** will be covered in the next chapter.

▶ **NOTE**

Yahoo! PageWizard enables you to create pages through a web-based interface, where you fill in the blanks and use a template to create your page. Yahoo! PageBuilder enables you to work with the page in a much more hands-on way, with access to each item on the page and even access to the source HTML code.

The **File Manager** tools are for you to create blank pages and to move files around or rename them.

Click on **Yahoo! PageWizards**.

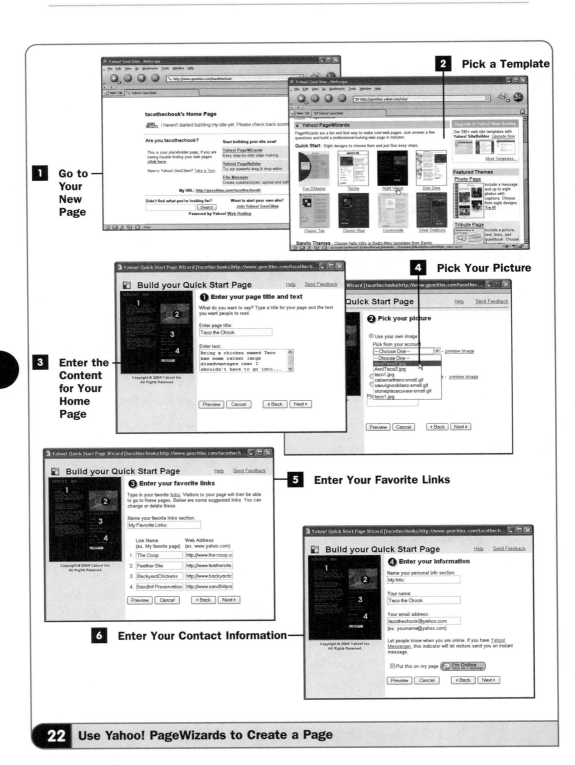

22 Use Yahoo! PageWizards to Create a Page

► **TIP**

For printing your pictures on your printer at home, you want to have images that are very large and detailed so the pictures come out looking sharp and not grainy. For the Web, you want small images that are cropped correctly to show only what you want to see on the page and that download fast. No one will want to spend time on a page if she has to wait a long time for the pictures to download.

▣2 Pick a Template

Find the Quick Start designs at the top of the page.

Below the Quick Start section are Sanrio themes if you need to create a Hello Kitty sort of page, and below the Sanrio themes are popular themes you can use for special occasions. You can explore these if you like. Each one has a wizard that will walk you through using them.

In the right column there are other templates, such as a Tribute Page (if you need to do that tribute to your favorite band of the '80s), or want to put up a quick photo album for your in-laws.

Click on the link for the wizard of your choice. (For this chapter I picked one of the Quick Start templates called **Night Vision**.)

Click on the **Begin** button.

The PageWizard lets you select another page style or you can keep the one you selected already. You can preview the page design you chose in your browser by clicking on the **Preview** button.

Click on the **Next** button.

▣3 Enter the Content for Your Home Page

Enter the title and the main text of the page. The title and initial text of the page are used by search engines to classify your page, so taking the time here to put in good, descriptive titles and then getting right to the point in the first paragraph of the page can make your page easier to find.

When you're done, click on the **Next** button.

▣4 Pick Your Picture

On this screen you can pick a picture you have already uploaded or choose to upload a new image for your page. Because you have just created your account, you probably haven't uploaded any images yet, so we are going to upload an image.

22

Make sure the **Use Your Own Image** button is selected and then click on the **Upload New Image** button. In the new window that opens, click on **Browse** and select an image to upload. Click on the **Upload** button.

You can also decide not to have a picture on the page by selecting the **Don't Use an Image** button or you can use the default image.

You can also add a caption to the photo in the text box at the bottom of the wizard.

When you're done, click on the **Next** button.

5 Enter Your Favorite Links

On the next screen, you can enter links for sites that visitors to your page might want to visit. In the **Link Name** column on the left, enter the text you want your visitors to see. In the **Web Address** column on the right, enter the web address for each link.

When you're done, click on the **Next** button.

6 Enter Your Contact Information

22

These are the final two steps of the Yahoo! Quick Start PageWizard where you can add a link for people to contact you through email or even through Yahoo! Messenger if you have it installed.

Click on the **Next** button when you add your information.

Name your page on the next screen of the wizard. This is the text that shows at the top of the browser window when visitors come to your site.

When you're done, click on the **Next** button. You have now completed your first web page on GeoCities.

▶ TIP

Be sure to write down the web address so you can find the page again and your friends will be able to find you on the Web. Later on, we are going to change the address to make it easier to find, but for now be sure to keep this address written down.

---

23 **Edit Your Page**

✔ BEFORE YOU BEGIN	→ SEE ALSO
20 Explore GeoCities	**24** Use the PageBuilder
21 Sign Up for Services	
22 Use Yahoo! PageWizards to Create a Page	

Using the PageWizard to edit an existing page is very similar to creating the first page. When you open the PageWizard using the same template as you used to create the page, you will be able to open the page and change the items rather than start a new page.

❶ Go to Your Home Page at Yahoo! GeoCities

Open your home page at the address you wrote down. From the home page, open the **PageWizard**.

❷ Edit Your Page

In the PageWizard, click on the template you used to create your new page.

After you have used the PageWizard, you have a choice of creating a new page or editing an existing file. Pick any of the files you have created with the template in the drop-down list and click the **Next** button.

❸ Change the Template

After you have edited the page, you can select a different template. The PageWizard knows where the content on your page is and how to change the template and move the existing content to the right place in the new template.

After you have selected a new template or if you don't need to select a new template, click on the **Next** button.

❹ Edit the Content of the Page

In the PageWizard, you can change any of the existing content on the page.

When you change or add content through the wizard, you'll want to keep a few things in mind. The changes you make will be added to the page right after the text that is currently in the text area. You can highlight text, though, and replace it entirely.

23

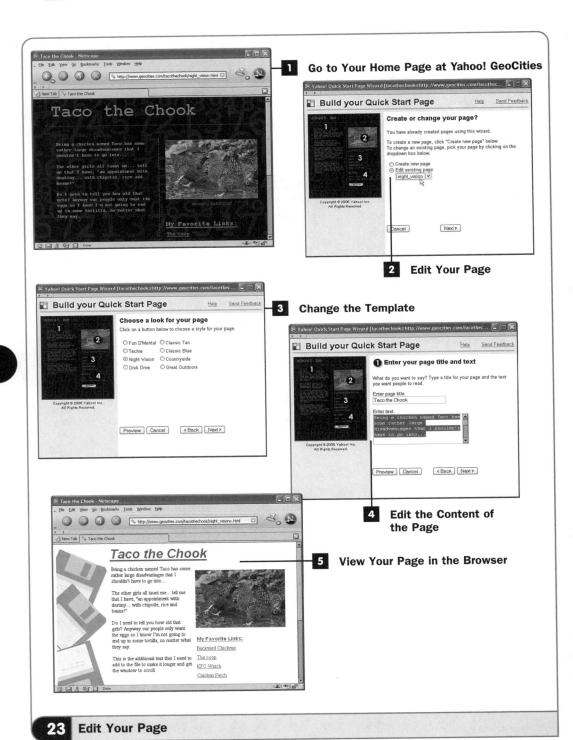

1 Go to Your Home Page at Yahoo! GeoCities

2 Edit Your Page

3 Change the Template

4 Edit the Content of the Page

5 View Your Page in the Browser

23

23 Edit Your Page

Using the PageWizard only lets you operate in the areas of the templates where there is existing text. If you want to add text to areas where there is not any text, you'll need to use the **PageBuilder** or the **Advanced Editor**.

When you get to the area to change the links, you can select one of the links you added, highlight the **Link Name**, and change it to whatever new link you want to feature.

▶ TIP

If you are familiar with web addresses, you might have seen addresses with **http://** in front of the address. In PageWizard, you don't have to add **http://**.

▶ TIP

If you go to the page to which you want to link, you can copy the link from the address bar in the browser and then paste that into the **Web Address** field in the Yahoo! Quick Start PageWizard. If you copy and paste an address, there is a better chance of getting the address right.

When you are done with the changes to the page, you can save the page to a new name if you want to keep the original page and the edited version, or you can save the edits over the page you started with.

23

5 View Your Page in the Browser

Go to your page in the browser and note that the changes you made to the page are saved and visible online.

5

Use the Yahoo! PageBuilder to Build Advanced Pages

IN THIS CHAPTER:

Creating a web page using the *wizards* is a pretty cool start to having presence on the Web, but you will outgrow that simple website very quickly. In this chapter, you will use the PageBuilder to add features to your site that will make visitors spend more time on your site and gain more information from it.

▶ KEY TERM

Wizards—Cool technology that walks you through a series of questions. These questions enable the program—the wizard—to do a lot of the work for you. These wizards build the page they think you want. For a page built to your exact needs, you must use the PageBuilder.

---

24 Use the PageBuilder

✔ BEFORE YOU BEGIN

22 Use Yahoo! PageWizards to Create a Page

24

The **PageBuilder** is a powerful tool that gives you a lot more flexibility than the **PageWizard**, but with that flexibility comes more choices and requires a little more work than **PageWizard**.

1 Go to Your Page at GeoCities

Go to your page at GeoCities that you made in Chapter 4, "Getting Started Building Web Pages on GeoCities."

When you open your home page at GeoCities, you should still see the placeholder page that says that you haven't started building your site yet. That isn't true, but we haven't set the pages you have built to automatically load when someone comes to your site.

In the last chapter, in the right column of the placeholder home page, you selected the **PageWizards**, which enabled you to pick a template and build your page through a four-step process.

We are going to use the **PageBuilder**, which will give you a lot more control for building your pages.

Click on the link for **PageBuilder**.

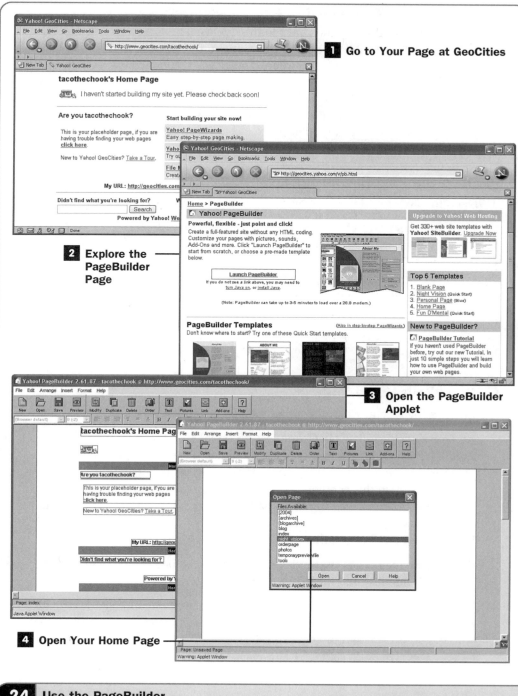

1 Go to Your Page at GeoCities

2 Explore the PageBuilder Page

3 Open the PageBuilder Applet

4 Open Your Home Page

24

24   Use the PageBuilder

2 Explore the PageBuilder Page

The right side of the page has links to the top five templates and links to tutorials for **PageBuilder**. There is also a link to the Message Boards, where you can ask other users your questions.

On the left of the page is the link to start the **PageBuilder** applet.

On the bottom left of the page is a list of the templates available for the **PageWizards**, which you used in the last chapter, and below that there are **Popular Themed Templates** for different special events and types of pages.

3 Open the PageBuilder Applet

Open the **PageBuilder** applet by clicking on the **Launch PageBuilder** link.

The **PageBuilder** applet will open in a new window.

▶ TIP

You need to have Java installed and turned on to use the **PageBuilder**. There are links to help you with Java just below the **Launch PageBuilder** link.

24

Also, PageBuilder is intended for use on PCs running Windows. Mac users will see a warning. Last, do not close the small pop-up window. It's not an ad for cheaper insurance or low mortgage rates. This window controls the PageBuilder load process.

4 Open Your Home Page

Click on the **Open** icon at the top of the applet window.

An **Open Page** window opens and lists all the files in your site. For now there should be several files. You should see the index file, which is the page that opens when someone types in your address and it is the page that opened when you started this chapter. If you have previewed any templates in earlier tasks, you might see the **temporarypreviewfile** that is generated to give you a preview as you work. There might be other pages available to you if you have created any in the earlier tasks.

Click on the file named **night vision** (the file you've been working on in the **Files Available** list) and then click the **Open** button.

You might see an alert that warns you that changes made in PageBuilder will make the page unusable in PageWizard. Continue on because you will not be working on these pages in PageWizard.

25 Add Text and Graphics to the Page

✔ BEFORE YOU BEGIN	→ SEE ALSO
22 Use Yahoo! PageWizards to Create a Page	**9** Add and Format Text **11** About Adding Graphics **43** Add Text and Links

What makes a website popular with web surfers? Your website will have viewers if it has interesting content and is pleasant to read. If you want many viewers, your website must be understandable.

Think about the best sites you know of—the places you want to go and spend time. They probably don't have bells and whistles, or beeping sounds when you roll over things. On the other hand, they probably don't contain a lone paragraph of content and not much else, either.

Add text and graphics to your site as often as you can. Add information and keep the images fresh to keep your visitors coming back.

■ Add Some Text to Your File

25

Place the cursor at the end of the text in the file. Let's add some interesting content. Type more text to fill out the text block.

In this view, your page is more like a word or text processor.

When you entered your text into the **PageWizard**, you wrote it in a **Text Editor** because you couldn't really see what you were typing in the text area of the wizard. Here in **PageBuilder**, you have the real layout of the page visible to you so when you type, you can see what you are entering in the context of the rest of the page.

■ Change the Font Attributes

Highlight the first paragraph in the main text block and set the font to the typeface and size of your choosing.

You can use tools that should be familiar to you from word processors in **PageBuilder** that were unavailable in the **PageWizard**.

You can set the font, font size, and alignment of the text in the box from side to side and top to bottom; bold, italic, and underline; and the color of the text or background.

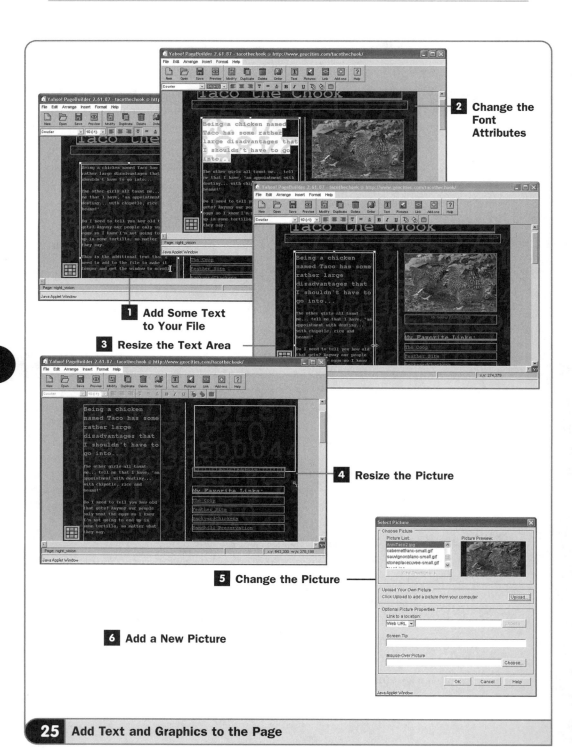

2 Change the Font Attributes

1 Add Some Text to Your File

3 Resize the Text Area

4 Resize the Picture

5 Change the Picture

6 Add a New Picture

25 Add Text and Graphics to the Page

3 Resize the Text Area

Resize and move the text area by clicking on the text area to bring up the resize handles.

One thing that might be new to you is that each piece of text and picture is in its own box. This is how the layout of the page is done, which is different than how a word processor does it. The little squares on each side and corner of the text box are called **resize handles**. Click on the **resize handle** on the upper-right corner and your cursor should change into a two-headed arrow. Now you can drag it in toward the center of the box, and the box and text get narrower and move down the page a little more. If you click in a little from the edge of the **resize handle**, your cursor will change into a four-headed arrow. Now when you drag, you will move the entire text box, not just the corner or the side to resize the text box.

4 Resize the Picture

Resize the picture by clicking on the picture on the right side of the page.

Your picture box works like the text box you just worked on. Click on the lower-right **resize handle** and drag the handle in toward the center of the image. Notice that as you move the handle, the picture disappears while you are dragging but the shape of the box never changes. It always stays the same shape as the original picture. Now click on one of the **resize handles** on the side of the picture box and move that. Notice that the box changes shape, getting wider or narrower or taller or shorter. This is different than the way the text box works.

If you try dragging the edge of the text box over another element, the edge of the box turns red to indicate you are overlapping two elements. If you try to preview or save the page with overlapping elements, you will get a warning that the page can't be saved, so use the indicator to avoid overlapping elements as you work.

Sometimes you want to make a picture smaller or larger without distorting it and sometimes you want to change the shape and stretch the picture one way or another. In Yahoo! **PageBuilder** you can do either, just by moving the different **resize handles**.

5 Change the Picture

Change a picture by double-clicking on the picture on the right side of the page.

25

You can change a picture by double-clicking on the image to bring up the Select Picture dialog box. In the dialog box, you can select a new image and, if you need to upload a new image, you can do so from the dialog box.

► **TIP**

When you upload images and files to your website, you might run into problems with your files because of their names. On your computer, you can name files anything you want, but on the Web, files have some rules about naming that you need to know about. You can't use spaces in your filenames; instead, use underscores or dashes. **My Dog.jpg** won't work on the Web, whereas **My_Dog.jpg** will work. You also need to avoid any punctuation or symbols in your filenames. Last, there is a difference in filenames when uppercase and lowercase letters are mixed. My_Dog.jpg is different from my_dog.jpg. Most smart content authors use all lowercase letters in their filenames.

Because you only have the one image you uploaded in Chapter 4 on your site, you need to upload a couple of pictures to work with. Click on the **Upload** button and browse to an image you want to put on your site. In the **Upload** dialog box, you can upload up to five images at one time.

25

In the **Picture List** in the upper left of the **Select Picture** dialog box, click on **[User Files]** to see the files that are available for you to select to replace the existing picture on the page. You should see the new files that you just uploaded, as well as the original file you uploaded in Chapter 4. Click on one of the new images and then click the **OK** button at the bottom of the **Select Picture** dialog box to insert the image into the picture box.

When you insert the new image, it replaces the original picture, but it puts the new image in at the full size of the new picture, which may be larger or smaller than the image that was there. If that occurs, you might see a red grid overlaid upon the image. This is a message to you that the image is overlapping other boxes, which is not allowed in **PageBuilder,** so you need to resize and move elements until the red grid doesn't show up. To resize the image, you can simply click on one of the corners of the image and resize it as you learned in the last step.

6 **Add a New Picture**

Add a picture by clicking on the **Pictures** icon in the **PageBuilder** applet window.

When you click on the **Pictures** icon in the **PageBuilder** applet, the **Select Picture** dialog box comes up and you can pick a new image just as you did to replace the image in the previous step.

CHAPTER 5: Use the Yahoo! PageBuilder to Build Advanced Pages

95

26 Create Links to Other Pages

✔ BEFORE YOU BEGIN	→ SEE ALSO
22 Use Yahoo! PageWizards to Create a Page	**10** About Creating Hyperlinks **21** Sign Up for Services **43** Add Text and Links

One of the great benefits of the Web is the ability to link to multiple other locations that have information your visitor might want to have after looking at your page. You can create the links to other resources yourself with **PageBuilder**.

Remember, though, that you want to keep people on your site as much as you can, so posting multiple links to other places might not be the best way to do that. When the Web was young, it was a bunch of pages with a paragraph of information each that had 10 links to other sites that had a paragraph each and 10 links on each of those pages. A common thing beginners to the Web do is make too many links and not say enough. Make your site have content. Keep people there reading. Be a resource, not a signpost to other resources.

1 Select Text to Become a Link

26

Click on the text area in the **PageBuilder** applet, highlight a word or short phrase in your text, and click on the Link icon.

▶ **TIP**

Links should never span multiple lines or have too much content. People need a short summary of what information is provided if a link is followed. Most content authors use more than a word and less than a sentence. Too much information only makes links confusing and makes the reader wonder just what is returned if the link is followed.

2 Create a Link

In the **Hot Link** dialog box, you can link to a new page by selecting the **Web URL** from the **Link to a Location** drop-down box. In the text area next to the drop-down box, enter the address of the page to which you want to link. For example, you might want to link to CNN so that people can get to the latest news from your site, so you would enter **www.cnn.com**.

You can also set the text to link to pictures and files, such as music or Zip files, that you want people to be able to download from your site. One of the more interesting options here is to create a link that sends email from your page.

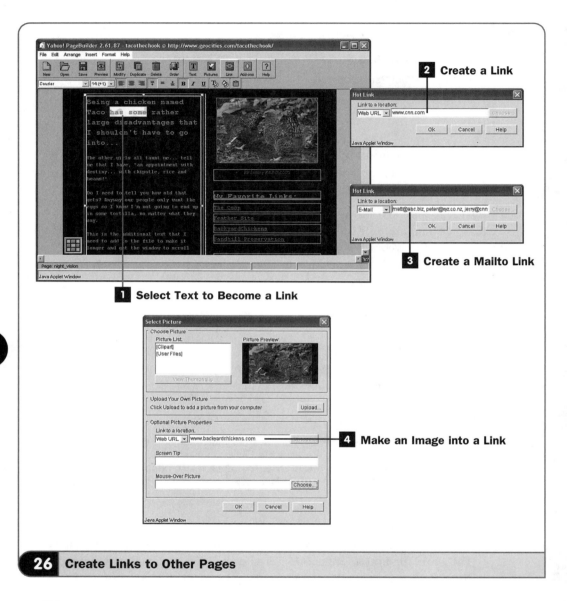

2 Create a Link

3 Create a Mailto Link

1 Select Text to Become a Link

4 Make an Image into a Link

26 Create Links to Other Pages

3 Create a Mailto Link

To create a link that opens a preaddressed email window from your website, select **E-mail** from the **Link to a Location** drop-down box. Instead of adding a URL in the text area, type in the email address for the person or people you want to send email to. If you want to email to more than one person at a time, separate each of the email addresses with a comma. This might be really useful if you are expressing a political position in which you want your visitors to act upon, for example. Say your piece on the page and then give them a link to write to the local council or even a senator or the president.

Click **OK** to set the link.

4 Make an Image into a Link

Double-click on an image. At the bottom of the **Select Picture** dialog box in the **Optional Picture Properties** section, you can link to a location and turn the picture into a link just like you can a piece of text. To make a picture a link, click on the **Link to a Location** drop-down box and select **Web URL**.

---

27 Add Special Features to Your Page

✔ **BEFORE YOU BEGIN**

20 Explore GeoCities
21 Sign Up for Services
22 Use Yahoo! PageWizards to Create a Page
24 Use the PageBuilder
25 Add Text and Graphics to the Page
26 Create Links to Other Pages

27

The **PageBuilder** applet has several special features you can add to your pages that you might want to use. It also enables you to create rollovers for images, which are especially effective for showing people they are rolling over an image that is active as a link.

▶ **TIP**

The term *rollover* isn't an accident that happens to small animals running in front of your car. A rollover is very similar to a ToolTip in a Windows application. In the same way a small pop-up informs you what a tool image does in a Windows application toolbar, a website rollover announces an image link to content elsewhere on the Web or on your website. These are nice touches to add to your website.

1 Add a Rollover to Your Page

Double-click on the image on the upper right of your page to open the **Select Picture** dialog box. At the bottom of the dialog box in the **Optional Picture Properties** portion, set the **Link to a Location** drop-down box to **Web URL**. The Screen Tip text will appear if your visitor holds his mouse over the picture without moving for a few seconds. You can set that if you like.

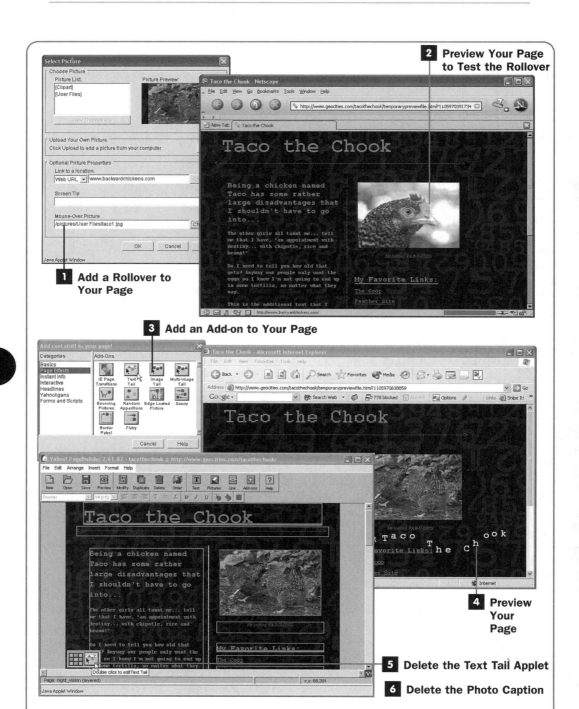

1 Add a Rollover to Your Page

2 Preview Your Page to Test the Rollover

3 Add an Add-on to Your Page

4 Preview Your Page

5 Delete the Text Tail Applet

6 Delete the Photo Caption

27

27   Add Special Features to Your Page

In the **Mouse-Over Picture** text box, choose another image. This will be the image that appears when your visitor moves her mouse over the image. The image you select will automatically be sized to the same size as the image that is there so that the rollover won't have images of two different sizes. Click **OK** to close the applet.

2 Preview Your Page to Test the Rollover

Preview the image by clicking on the Preview icon. When the page comes up, move your cursor over the image and see how the rollover works.

3 Add an Add-on to Your Page

Click on the **Add-ons** icon in the applet. In the **Add Cool Stuff to Your Page** dialog box, you have several categories of things that you can add to your page. You are going to add several in the next tasks. For now, click on the **Page Effects** option in the **Categories** list. In the **Add-ons** column on the right, click on the **Text Tail** Add-on.

In the **Text Tail Properties** dialog box, add a message that is appropriate for your site. Set the speed to medium and the size to medium. You can set any other settings any way you like.

4 Preview Your Page

Preview the image by clicking on the **Preview** icon. When the page comes up, move your cursor around the page and notice that the text you added follows your cursor around the page.

I know this one is a little flashy, but sometimes this works out really well on your page.

Some of the effects don't work on all browsers, so you might want to preview the page in several browsers to see how the effect will look for different viewers.

5 Delete the Text Tail Applet

Select the **Text Tail** icon on the lower-left corner of the **PageBuilder** applet and press the Delete key.

As you work, you might find that the components you add to your page need to be removed. You can't do that easily in the **PageWizard**, but in the **PageBuilder** you can take away items as easily as you can add them.

Items that are added to the page that can't be seen on the page, such as the **Text Tail** Add-on, are represented by icons on the bottom of the window. To remove them, simply select them and press the **Delete** key.

27

6 **Delete the Photo Caption**

For items such as images and text areas that have a visual representation on the page in the **PageBuilder** applet, simply select the item and press the **Delete** key.

---

28 **Use Page Stats**

✔ BEFORE YOU BEGIN	→ SEE ALSO
20 Explore GeoCities	**38** Use the Site Statistics
21 Sign Up for Services	
22 Use Yahoo! PageWizards to Create a Page	

As people visit your site, GeoCities counts and saves information about each visitor that can help you know general information about your visitors, such as what browser they are using and from what pages they visit. You are going to look at them in more depth in the next chapter.

Normally, these stats are only for you to see; however, you might decide you want to let your users see the stats for a particular page.

1 **Go to http://geocities.yahoo.com/stats**

The browser opens the **Site Statistics** page with all the pages listed that you have on your site.

2 **Allow Anyone to View Your Site Statistics**

In the upper-left side of the page, click on the **Options** link and, on the next page, click on the **Allow Anyone to View My Site Statistics** button; then click on **Save**.

You have to expressly allow GeoCities to display your site stats.

3 **Copy the Code for Your Stats Link**

In the **Adding a Public Page Stats Link** page, scroll down to the section labeled **Medium** and click on the **Select Code** button; then copy the code.

This is a little different than the other things you are adding to the page in this chapter. For the site stats, you need to pick which set of code you want to have—**Large**, **Medium**, or **Small**—and then copy the code and paste it in the page.

28

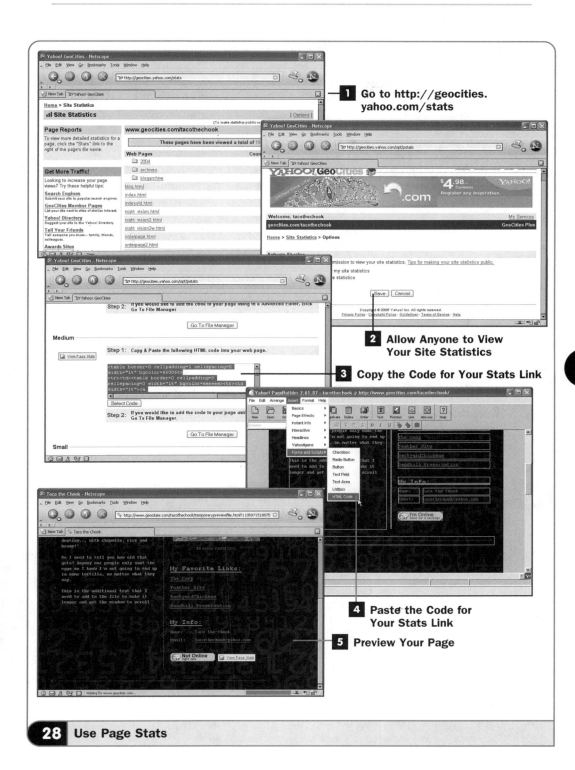

1 Go to http://geocities. yahoo.com/stats

2 Allow Anyone to View Your Site Statistics

3 Copy the Code for Your Stats Link

28

4 Paste the Code for Your Stats Link

5 Preview Your Page

28 Use Page Stats

The **Large** code block will be easy for people to see, but takes up a lot of space on your page. The **Medium** code block is easy to see, but doesn't take up much space. The **Small** code block only leaves a small icon on your page that people might overlook. You can decide which one you want to use for your page.

4 Paste the Code for Your Stats Link

Go to **PageBuilder** and, in your page, find a spot where you would like to insert the link to the page statistics. Click on the **Insert** menu and select **Forms and Scripts** and then **HTML Code**.

In the **Script Properties** dialog box, paste the text you copied into the **Script** area; you don't need to add a **Description**. Click **OK** to close the dialog box and paste the code onto the page.

5 Preview Your Page

Move the script box to where you want it on your page and then preview your page.

The site stats link you added only shows up when you preview the page. The representation you see in the **PageBuilder** is just a placeholder, so you can resize it and move it around to where you want it on the page.

The stats link you added will only show the stats for that page to your visitor. If you want to have more than one page show stats, you need to add a link to each page.

---

29 Add Hit Counters

✔ BEFORE YOU BEGIN	→ SEE ALSO
20 Explore GeoCities	**30** Add Stock Quotes
21 Sign Up for Services	**31** Add News Feeds and Weather Maps
22 Use Yahoo! PageWizards to Create a Page	**32** Add a Search Function

---

Having a web page means you want people to be able to see what you are writing and thinking. When they visit your page, you want to know how many people have been there. GeoCities makes it easy to add a hit counter to your page.

Hit counters have a mixed reputation in the industry. To some, hit counters are the "Billions and Billions Served" sign that makes a site look like fast food. For others, they are indispensable. If you want to have one, they are easy to add, but if you do, you might want to make it pretty inconspicuous.

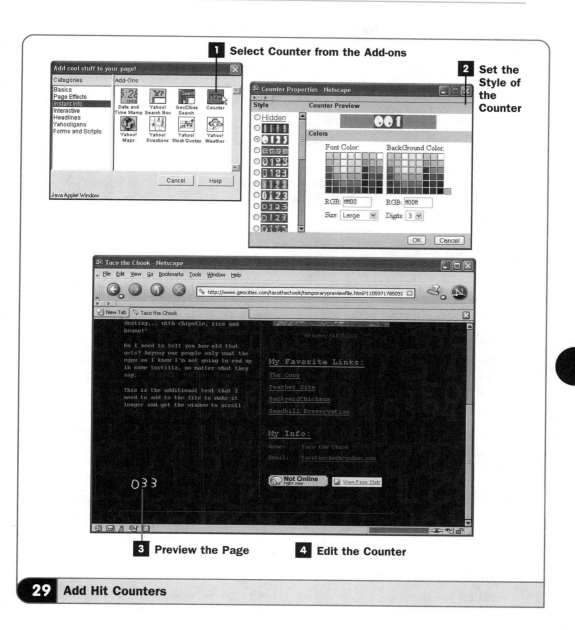

1 Select Counter from the Add-ons

2 Set the Style of the Counter

3 Preview the Page   **4** Edit the Counter

29 Add Hit Counters

▶ **TIP**

Hit counters track the number of downloaded files, not actual visitors. As you've learned in this book, web pages are a mix of HTML files and graphic files. The hit count varies a lot based on website design. The final hit counter issue? Pages with continuing low hit counts look more pathetic than useful.

1 Select Counter from the Add-ons

Click on the **Add-ons** icon. In the **Categories** list, select **Instant Info** and select **Counter** from the **Add-ons** in the right pane.

2 Set the Style of the Counter

In the **Counter Properties** dialog box, select a style and then set the colors for the font and the background color.

You can also change the size and the number of digits that show, so you can set the counter to six or seven places if you're ambitious and expect millions of visitors.

3 Preview the Page

When you click **OK**, a counter is placed in your page as an object that you can drag to the spot where you want to have it. Click on the Preview button on the toolbar to see how the counter looks on the live page.

4 Edit the Counter

Go back to the **Editing View** in **PageBuilder** and find the counter on your page. Double-click on the icon and, in the **Counter Properties**, change some of the properties and click **OK**.

30

▶ **TIP**

There are two schools of thought on counters as we mentioned previously—those who like them and those who think they look tacky. If you want a compromise between these two views, consider using colors for the counter that have low contrast with your background. That way, people who want to find it will, and those who don't won't see it at first glance.

---

30 Add Stock Quotes

✔ BEFORE YOU BEGIN	→ SEE ALSO
20 Explore GeoCities	**21** Sign Up for Services
	22 Use Yahoo! PageWizards to Create a Page
	29 Add Hit Counters
	31 Add News Feeds and Weather Maps
	32 Add a Search Function

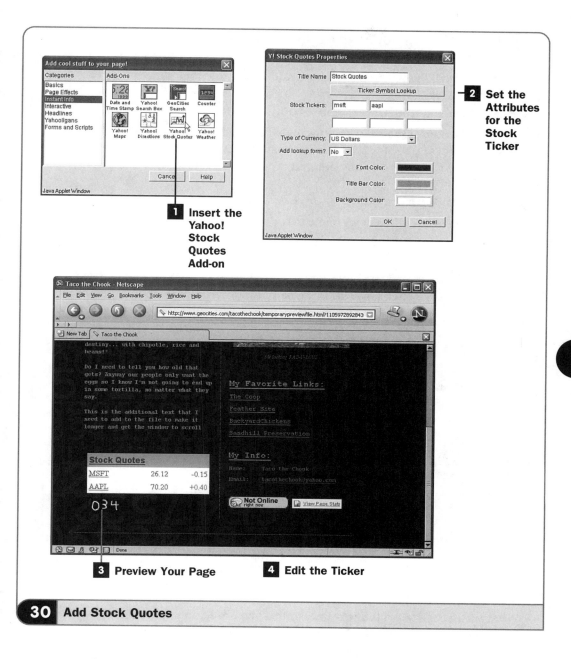

1 Insert the Yahoo! Stock Quotes Add-on

2 Set the Attributes for the Stock Ticker

3 Preview Your Page

4 Edit the Ticker

30 Add Stock Quotes

Another feature you can add to your site is a **Stock Quote** applet. This is a great way to provide your viewer with information about your investments or the stocks you think are hot.

1 Insert the Yahoo! Stock Quotes Add-on

Click on the **Add-ons** icon. In the **Categories** list, select **Instant Info** and then **Yahoo! Stock Quotes** from the **Add-ons** in the right pane.

2 Set the Attributes for the Stock Ticker

In the **Y! Stock Quotes Properties** dialog box, add a title for your stock quotes and set the **Stock Tickers** to the stocks you want to show on your page. If you don't know any offhand, Apple is **AAPL** and Microsoft is **MSFT**.

3 Preview Your Page

When you click **OK**, a stock quote ticker is placed in your page. Click on the **Preview** button on the toolbar to see how the counter looks on the live page.

Try clicking on the ticker symbol for each stock you added. On the **Yahoo! Finance** pages, you can get complete information on each stock, including historical price charts, news, technical analysis, SEC filings, and just about all you need to keep track of your stocks.

4 Edit the Ticker

Go back to the **Editing View** in **PageBuilder** and find the ticker on your page. Double-click on the icon and, in the **Y! Stock Quotes Properties**, change some of the properties and click **OK**.

---

31 Add News Feeds and Weather Maps

✔ BEFORE YOU BEGIN	→ SEE ALSO
20 Explore GeoCities	**21** Sign Up for Services
	22 Use Yahoo! PageWizards to Create a Page
	29 Add Hit Counters
	30 Add Stock Quotes
	32 Add a Search Function

What site isn't better with a weather map? If you are setting up a site that will cater to people from all over the country or the world, you can easily tell them what the weather is like on a daily basis without having to enter that information every day. You can also bring in news feeds from all over to help you produce content for your site.

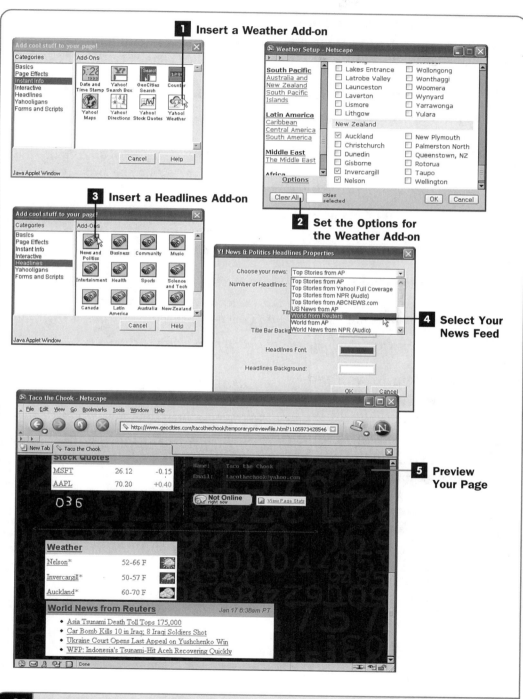

1 Insert a Weather Add-on

3 Insert a Headlines Add-on

2 Set the Options for the Weather Add-on

4 Select Your News Feed

5 Preview Your Page

31

31 Add News Feeds and Weather Maps

1 Insert a Weather Add-on

Click on the **Add-ons** icon. In the **Categories** list, select **Instant Info** and select **Yahoo! Weather** from the **Add-ons** in the right pane.

2 Set the Options for the Weather Add-on

In the **Weather Setup** dialog box, navigate to your location in the left column and pick your city on the right side of the dialog box.

There are weather reports from all over the world. You can get weather from New Zealand to Angola. You can choose to show more than one location, as well.

If you click on the **Options** button, you can set the color of the weather applet and the font color. You can also set the temperature to show as Fahrenheit or Celsius.

3 Insert a Headlines Add-on

Click on the **Add-ons** icon. In the **Categories** list, select **Headlines** and select **News and Politics** from the **Add-ons** in the right pane.

There are news feeds from all over the world from which to choose.

31

4 Select Your News Feed

In the **Y! News & Politics Headlines Properties** dialog box, select the news feed you want to use, pick the number of stories you want to show, and set the colors to match your background.

You will need to move the news applet and the weather applet to a part of your page that doesn't obscure your existing text. Just click on each applet and move it to where you want to have it on your page.

5 Preview Your Page

Preview your page to see your weather and news headlines.

32 Add a Search Function

✔ BEFORE YOU BEGIN	→ SEE ALSO
20 Explore GeoCities	**21** Sign Up for Services
	22 Use Yahoo! PageWizards to Create a Page
	29 Add Hit Counters
	30 Add Stock Quotes
	31 Add News Feeds and Weather Maps

Now that you have your page full of content, with applets and information simply oozing from the page, you need a way to let your visitors search the Web from your site. Fortunately, there is an easy to use applets in **PageBuilder** to do just that.

1 Add a Yahoo! Search Box to Your Page

Click on the **Add-ons** icon. In the **Categories** list, select **Instant Info** and select **Yahoo! Search Box** from the **Add-ons** in the right pane.

2 Move Your Search Box on Your Page

You will need to move the search applet to a part of your page that doesn't obscure your existing text.

3 Preview Your Page and Test Your Search Applet

Although there are no options you can set on the Search applet, you can go to the **Yahoo! Search** page and access all the features of **Yahoo!** directly from your page.

32

▶ TIP

This search applet will search the entire Internet, not just your website. Many people bookmark their favorite search engine, and you might not be adding a lot of value by including one on your website. Think carefully about all the features you'll add to your website. Websites that use too many of the effects and add-ons in this chapter can appear cluttered and tacky. Web design is a lot like good writing: Less is more.

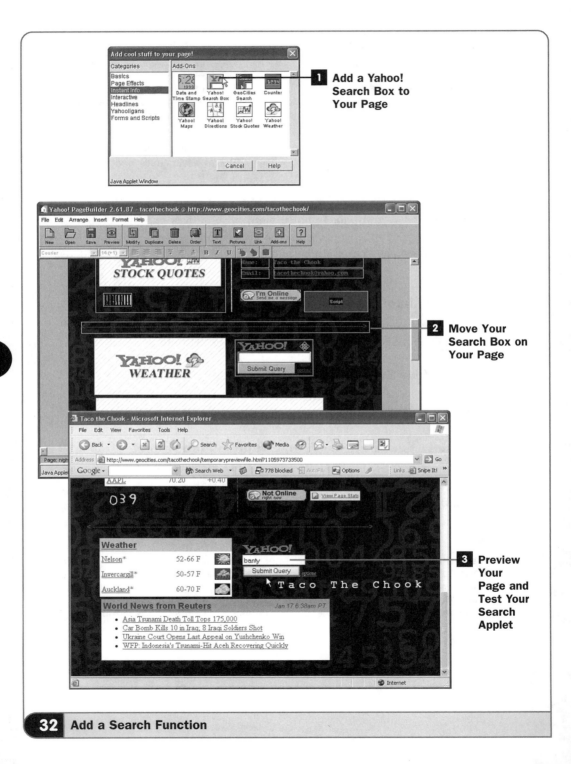

1 **Add a Yahoo! Search Box to Your Page**

2 **Move Your Search Box on Your Page**

3 **Preview Your Page and Test Your Search Applet**

32   Add a Search Function

6

Using the Advanced Editor for Building Web Pages

IN THIS CHAPTER:

The tools that GeoCities provides for you to build web pages aren't limited to visual editors such as PageWizard and PageBuilder. As you gain fluency building web pages and as you look into the wider range of things you can do with HTML, you have to find a tool that will allow you access to the HTML code that lies beneath every web page. GeoCities enables you to use its HTML Editor to access each page and even create pages from scratch.

HTML is not really that complicated if you learn it piece by piece as you saw in Chapters 1, "Start Here," and 2, "The Basics of HTML." In this section, you are going to create a file from scratch to get an idea of how the HTML Editor works. After you have a handle on how things work, you can dig a little deeper into HTML and try working on some more complicated files.

33 Use the HTML Editor

✔ BEFORE YOU BEGIN

6 About Proper HTML Coding

22 Use Yahoo! PageWizards to Create a Page

24 Use the PageBuilder

7 Set Up a Web Page's Basic HTML Structure

→ SEE ALSO

2 Use HTML Tags

Finding the PageWizard and PageBuilder tools is fairly easy to do from the home page of your site. Finding the HTML Editor takes a little more work because the HTML Editor is part of the File Manager. You are going to take a look at the File Manager later in the chapter, but in this task, you are going to access it to get to the HTML Editor.

1 Go to Your GeoCities Home Page

My address will be **www.geocities.com/tacothechook**. Your address will be whatever login name you chose when you established your account.

You should see the placeholder file that was created initially. Click on the File Manager link.

2 Open the File Manager

The File Manager entry page opens and asks what files it is supposed to show. Leave the defaults as they are and click on the Open File Manager link.

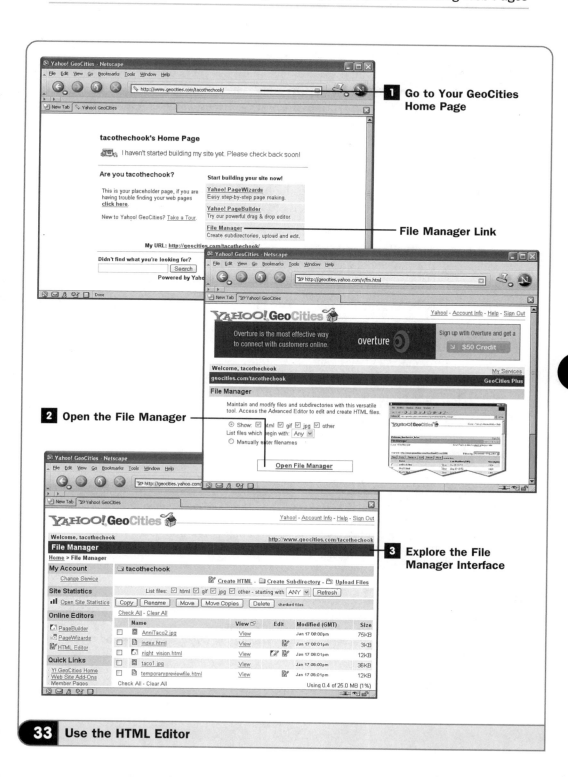

1 Go to Your GeoCities Home Page

File Manager Link

2 Open the File Manager

3 Explore the File Manager Interface

33

33 Use the HTML Editor

3 Explore the File Manager Interface

At the top of the page, you'll see a file list of all the files on your site. For now, you should have the **index.html** page, which is your placeholder that comes up when you type in your address at GeoCities. Some of you should have a file called night_vision.html, which is the page you created in PageWizard in Chapter 4, "Getting Started Building Web Pages on GeoCities," and modified in PageBuilder in Chapter 5, "Use the Yahoo! PageBuilder to Build Advanced Pages." You should also have a file called temporarypreviewfile.html, which is the file created to enable you to preview your file as you work. Finally, you should have the images that you uploaded.

If you have more files already, that's okay—it just means that you have added pages to the site already from the PageBuilder or PageWizard. Our goal is to explore and learn the interface, not require specific files.

Above the list of files are buttons that enable you to perform actions on the files. You are going to use them in a minute.

In the file list you will see the names of the files, a set of check boxes that let you select the files on which you are going to perform an action, the dates that the files were last modified, a link to view the files, a link to see stats of the HTML pages, and the sizes of the files.

At the bottom of the File Manager window there are stats that show how much disk space you have used and how much you have available.

33

▶ TIP

You might want to avoid editing pages you originally built in the PageBuilder or the PageWizard in the HTML Editor as you learn HTML. The pages developed in PageBuilder and PageWizard are reasonably complex and, if you have added any of the add-ons, there will be JavaScript in the file, which makes it harder to tell what is simple HTML and what isn't. After you have a few simpler files under your belt, you can give the more complicated files a shot.

▶ TIP

The green and blue PageBuilder or PageWizard icon in the Name list in the File Manager indicates that the file was built in PageBuilder or PageWizard. If you try and open one of these files to edit, you will get a warning that changes you make won't be saved if you reopen that file in the PageBuilder or PageWizard applet.

34 Create a Page

✔ BEFORE YOU BEGIN	→ SEE ALSO
6 About Proper HTML Coding	**2** Use HTML Tags
7 Set Up a Web Page's Basic HTML Structure	

Creating a page from scratch in the HTML Editor from the File Manager is easy, but requires you to know how to code from scratch (at least a little). For more information about **hand coding HTML**, see **6** **About Proper HTML Coding**.

1 Create a New Page

Click on the **Create HTML** link in the File Manager.

A new page comes up in the **HTML Editor** with the basic parts of the page added for you.

On the top of the interface is a space for a filename. Add that name now. After you have named the file, click on the Save and Continue button. The space to name the file disappears and the filename appears in its place.

2 Add a Title to Your Page

Highlight the word **Untitled** between the **<title>** and **</title>** tag and type "**Photo Album**". This is the title that will appear at the top of the window when the page is viewed.

This is the only thing you are going to add to the head of the document.

3 Add a Headline

Put your cursor on the line after **<body>** and type a good, engaging headline. I've named mine **<h1>Taco the Chook Presents – Photos</h1>**.

This sets a level-one heading—H1—in the document that tells the browser to display the type bold and large.

4 Add a New Paragraph

After the **H1** tag, create a new line and type **<p></p>**.

The paragraph or **<p>** tag is where all your text should go. You should have a beginning and end for the **<p>** tag, so add the **</p>** tag at the end. Add some text inside the tags to talk about the pictures you are going to include.

34

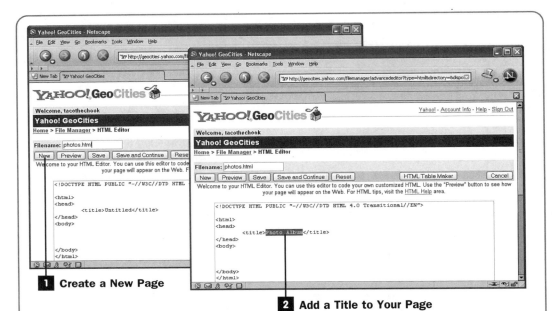

1 Create a New Page

2 Add a Title to Your Page

34

4 Add a New Paragraph

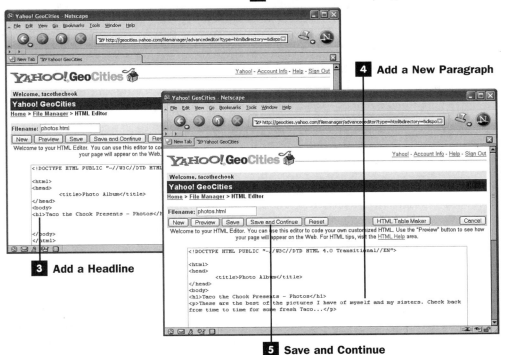

3 Add a Headline

5 Save and Continue

5 Save and Continue

Click the **Save and Continue** button at the top of the HTML Editor.

If you click on the **Save and Continue** button, it keeps the file open so you can continue editing. If you click on the **Save** button instead, your page is saved to the website, the **HTML Editor** is closed, and you are taken back to the **File Manager**.

▶ TIP

Congratulations on completing your first set of HTML codes, also called *tags*. Tags are placed between less-than (<) and greater-than (>) signs. Also, in many cases you must use an opening (****) and closing tag (****) to show the beginning and end of your tagged content. The closing tag begins with a slash (/). Not all tags follow these rules, but many do, like the Bold tag you've just learned in this tip.

---

35 Add a Table

✔ BEFORE YOU BEGIN	→ SEE ALSO
6 About Proper HTML Coding	**2** Use HTML Tags
7 Set Up a Web Page's Basic HTML Structure	**34** Create a Page

35

HTML pages were originally designed to work like a word processor: If you had a big chunk of text, it would flow down the page as if you had typed it on a type-writer. That would have been okay if computer screens were tall and narrow, but they aren't. So web design evolved and now tables are used to make the page work more like a newspaper. Tables were intended originally to display tabular information such as a spreadsheet, but web designers quickly learned to use tables to hold pictures and words so that they could display content in a better way for viewers to read.

1 Launch the Table Maker

Click on the **Launch Table Maker** button.

The Yahoo! GeoCities—HTML Table Maker dialog box helps you create code for tables and then enables you to preview the table. When you're done, it enables you to copy the HTML for the table into your page in the **HTML Editor**.

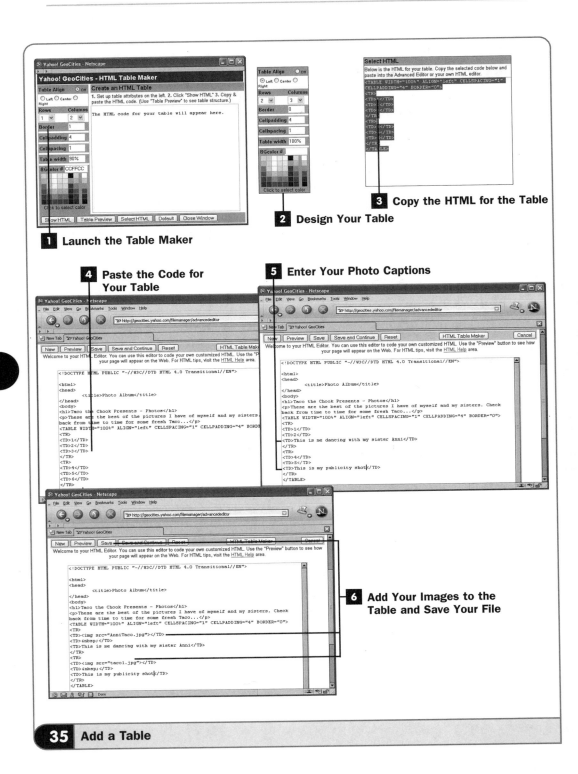

1 Launch the Table Maker

2 Design Your Table

3 Copy the HTML for the Table

4 Paste the Code for Your Table

5 Enter Your Photo Captions

6 Add Your Images to the Table and Save Your File

35

35 Add a Table

2 Design Your Table

You are going to use this table to display photos and captions. To demonstrate abilities, I will place photos in a column on the left, and captions will be on the right with a space between the columns. Of course, you can arrange them in any way you like.

In the Table Align section, I will set the alignment to Left. This will ensure that my text and pictures are all on the left side of their table cells. You should try options to get an arrangement you like.

Last, I will set the table to have two rows and three columns. I will set the border to 0 and leave the Cellpadding and Cellspacing at the defaults. Experiment with your own content. There are many options you can use with your content.

Tables are measured in either percentage of the browser window or pixels. Tables measured in percentages are not always the best choice because the table will resize as the window is resized. If you want your table to always be the same size, try setting the width to 700 pixels. In this case, set the table width to 100%. This means that the table is going to take up 100% of the available browser window.

35

The BGcolor is the background color of the table. If you leave this box blank, the table will simply sit on your page and not look any different than the existing background. If you set a background color, the table is going to stand out from the background. In this case, I have deleted the value from the BGcolor text area.

3 Copy the HTML for the Table

Click on the **Show HTML** button, copy the HTML by clicking on the **Select HTML** button, and then press Ctrl+C to copy the code. Close the window.

When you show the HTML, this writes the code needed for the table to be written to the window. To get it into your page, copy it from this window and then paste it into your page in the **HTML Editor**.

4 Paste the Code for Your Table

Place your cursor in the **HTML Editor** below the end of the <p> tag and paste the table.

Now that you have the table in the **HTML Editor** on the page, you can add content to the table.

5 Enter Your Photo Captions

Photo captions help explain your illustrations and why they are used. Readers like them, and in this task, we will create a few. I will designate where the captions go, but it is up to you to add the captions and experiment with the formatting.

Between the <td> tags where there is a 3, enter a photo caption for your first photo. Between the <td> tags where there is a 6, enter a photo caption for your second photo. HTML requires this information be placed in between certain tags. In this case, we are adding the information to the **Table Data** tags, or **td** for short.

▶ TIP

Be sure to place the caption information between the tags or the information may not be seen, or worse, it can corrupt the formatting and displaying of the table overall!

This will add the photo captions in the right column. There are three <td> tags in a row and they will be the individual cells of the table row. The third cell is the rightmost cell of the first row. The sixth cell is the rightmost cell of the second row.

35

6 Add your Images to the Table and Save Your File

As I work on the tacothechook website, I've prepared a few graphics. In this task, I will add them to the HTML content I've prepared.

Between the <td> tags where there is a **1**, I type **<img src="AnniTaco.jpg">**. Between the <td> tags where there is a **4**, I type **<img src="taco1.jpg">**. (You need to use the names of two of your own files you uploaded in Chapter 3, "Planning Out Your Website.") Be sure to type your own filenames exactly as shown.

▶ TIP

The **<img>** tag tells the browser to go get the picture that you listed in the **src=""** attribute. I am calling the pictures that I uploaded, but you will need to list the names of the files you uploaded in Chapter 3. For more information about **uploading files**, see **36** Preview and Use the Easy Upload.

Between the <td> tags where there is a **2** and a **5**, type **%nbsp;** and then click the **Save** button.

► KEY TERM

Non-breaking space ( )—A non-breaking space is a blank space in HTML that you want to have in some places. You might want to use them for dramatic effect. You might want to use them as part of your page formatting scheme. By default, HTML gets rid of more than one space in a row, so if you want to add more spaces, type in ** **.

---

36 | Preview and Use the Easy Upload

✔ BEFORE YOU BEGIN	→ SEE ALSO
6 About Proper HTML Coding	**37** Use the File Manager
7 Set Up a Web Page's Basic HTML Structure	

The pages you build and the edits you make to existing pages with the HTML Editor are saved directly to your website. The files don't reside on your local machine. However, if you want to add photos to your site or create a page locally, you will need to upload them to your site. With the free version of GeoCities, you can do that right in the **File Manager**.

You've done a lot of work on the page so far. You have been saving the files either by pressing the **Save and Continue** button, which keeps the **HTML Editor** open, or the **Save** button, which closes the file and returns you to the **File Manager**. It is important to keep your work saved as you go.

36

With some of the work done, you need to start interacting with the page as it is going to appear to your viewer. To do that, you should be previewing your file as often as needed.

1 Preview Your Page from the File Manager

Now it's time to see the results of our work! Find your new file (mine is **photos1.html**) in the **File Manager** and click on the **Preview** link to view your page.

The page comes up in a browser window. This page is a lot simpler than the ones you might create in PageBuilder and PageWizard (which are covered in other chapters of this book), but you did it with simple HTML code.

Notice that the images might not be the same size. This means that the largest picture sets the size of the cell and the width of the column in which it sits. The text, though, is all lined up in the right column. If you want to fix this, open the page in PageBuilder, select the image, resize it, and then look at the code to see how the HTML has changed.

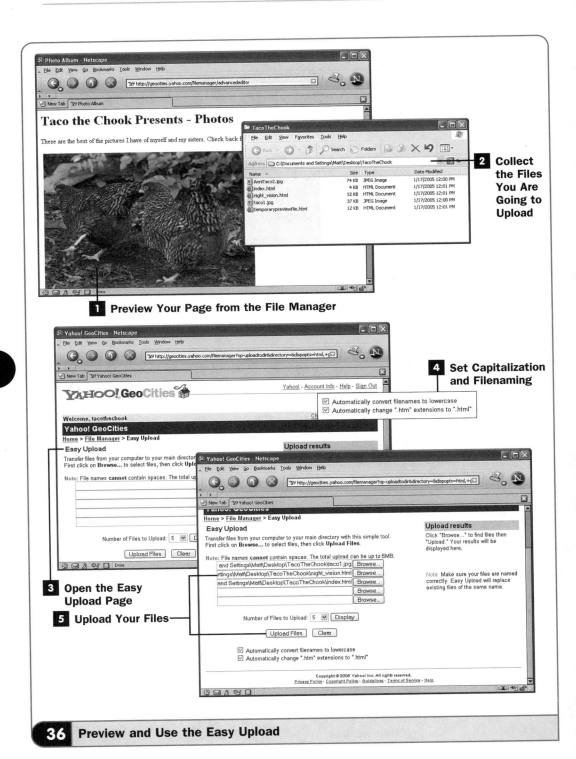

1 Preview Your Page from the File Manager

2 Collect the Files You Are Going to Upload

4 Set Capitalization and Filenaming

3 Open the Easy Upload Page

5 Upload Your Files

36   Preview and Use the Easy Upload

2 Collect the Files You Are Going to Upload

Get the files you want to upload on your machine.

The free service at **GeoCities** enables you to upload files, but you will have to select each file one by one. Keep them in one place to make it easy to find the files.

3 Open the Easy Upload Page

Go back to the **File Manager**. Click on the **Upload Files** button at the top of the **File Manager**.

The **Easy Upload** page appears. On the left side of the page is a **Text** area and **Browse** button for each file you want to upload. Below this is a button that enables you to show more than five upload boxes at one time on the page. Below this are buttons to upload the files or clear the form so you can start again.

4 Set Capitalization and Filenaming

Below the **Upload Files** button are two check boxes that are very important. The two things that cause the most problems in building a web page are the names of files not matching the way the files are capitalized in the links, and the use of **.htm** versus **.html**. Spelling and capitalization are critical when you are linking to files, so these choices might help you out a lot. I try to name all my files in lowercase with the **.html** extension so that if I do have a problem with a link not working on my page, I can easily look at the files on the server and see whether any are capitalized. If they are, I have found my problem and don't need to look any further.

Remember, though, that if you change the filenames to lowercase and you have referred to them with uppercase names, the files are not going to link correctly. If you work in all lowercase, you should use all lowercase for file-naming all the time.

▶ **TIP**

.htm or .html? Both file extensions are fine for the Web. Traditionally, though, web pages are named with the .html extension, and some viewers prefer to see their web pages named that way.

5 Upload Your Files

Click on the **Browse** button, select the files you want to add to your site, and click the **Upload Files** button.

36

The files you selected are uploaded to your site. If you upgrade to one of the paid services at **GeoCities**, you can upload whole folders of files rather than having to pick them one by one.

---

37   Use the File Manager

✔ BEFORE YOU BEGIN

22 Use Yahoo! PageWizards to Create a Page

13 About Posting Your Page

Now that you know how to create pages in the **PageWizard** and the **PageBuilder** and how to create and modify pages in the **HTML Editor** in **GeoCities**, you need to know how to handle your files in the **File Manager**.

1   Select the index.html File

In the **File Manager**, click in the check box to select the file called **index.html** and click on the **Rename** button.

Some filenames have special properties on the Web. One of those is index.html (or index.htm on some servers). These index filenames are the page that opens when someone types in your web address without typing a specific filename. In this case, when you type in your address to your site on GeoCities—for example, **www.geocities.com/tacothechook**, the actual page that opens is the **index** page.

Right now, the **index.html** page that you have on your site is the default page that everyone who creates an account on GeoCities has. This page has the links on it to the tools you have been using in this section. You should save this page, but you really want the page we discuss in Chapter 4 and modify in Chapter 5 to be the index page. If you haven't done these, don't worry; you can complete this step later.

2   Rename the index.html File

Click on the **Rename** button. In the **New Name** box, enter a good filename that is different from index.htm. (I use **tools.html**) and click on the Rename Files button.

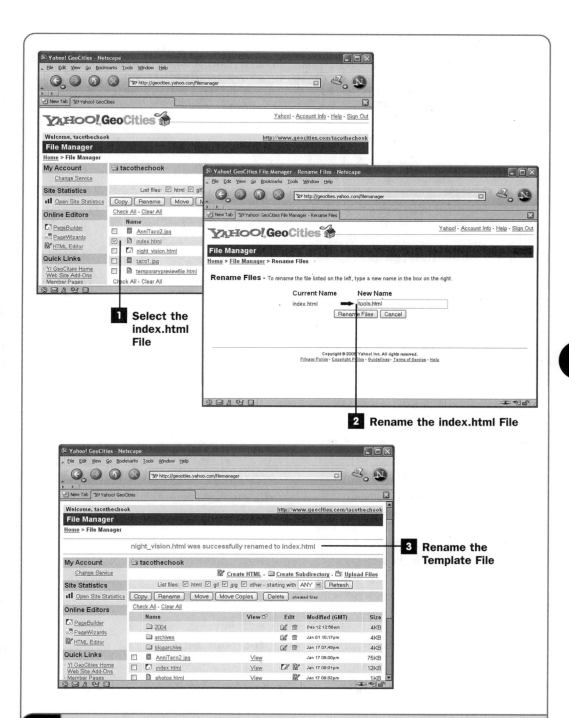

1 Select the index.html File

2 Rename the index.html File

3 Rename the Template File

37

37 Use the File Manager

▶ **TIP**

What *is* a good filename? A good filename is one that works on many types of computers. Try to use a consistent case for your filenames; most experts use lowercase letters. Also, avoid using special characters in the filename. Avoid punctuation marks (other than the period), slashes, and spaces. Your computer might have its own special restrictions for filenames, so check the online help. A filename standard that works on most platforms is 8.3, or eight initial letters, one period, and then a three-character extension like jpg that indicates the type of file.

A warning comes up telling you that you don't have an **index.html** or **index.htm** page any longer, which is true because you just renamed your **index.html** page to **tools.html**. If you were to type in your address for your index page at **GeoCities** right now, the page wouldn't open.

3 Rename the Template File

By now, you might have completed earlier chapters and will have a template file available for renaming. If not, you can always revisit this task. In the File Manager, click in the check box to select the file used with technologies like PageBuilder or PageWizard, the topics of Chapters 4 and 5. Mine is called night_vision.html. Click on the **Rename** button and change the name to index.html.

Now you have an index page again and it will come up when you go to your site instead of the placeholder that used to appear.

38

38	**Use the Site Statistics**	
✔ **BEFORE YOU BEGIN**	→ **SEE ALSO**	
13 About Posting Your Page	**28** Use Page Stats	

After you have your web page in place, **GeoCities** lets you see how people are accessing each page. You can see how many people are accessing your page, how many have each different screen resolution, how many use each browser, and what days bring in the most visitors. The **Stats** page in **GeoCities** even tells you the pages from which visitors come to your page.

1 Click on the Site Statistics Link for Your Site

The Site Statistics window comes up.

Click on the **Stats** link for your **index.html** page in the **Site Statistics** page.

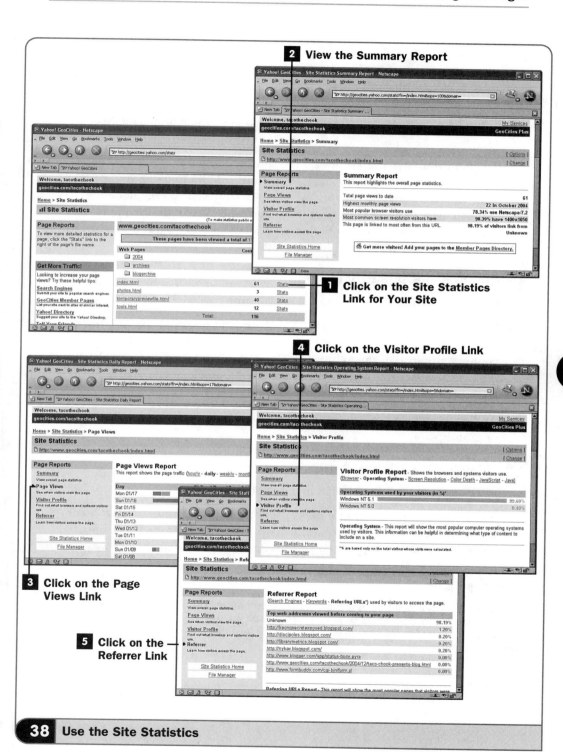

2 View the Summary Report

1 Click on the Site Statistics Link for Your Site

4 Click on the Visitor Profile Link

3 Click on the Page Views Link

5 Click on the Referrer Link

38

38 Use the Site Statistics

2 View the Summary Report

The **Summary Report** shows you the total views of the page to date. It shows the highest monthly views, what the most popular browser is, what the most common screen resolution is, and what page is linking to your page most. Using these statistics can help you make your page more usable for your viewers.

If you know that your users always use **Internet Explorer**, you might decide to use the **Internet Explorer Page Transitions Add-on** to make your pages blend into each other when you link pages in your site. You might decide that you want to make your page fit well on an 800×600 pixel monitor. If most of your visitors have higher screen resolutions, you might want to make your page design larger or with wider text areas.

3 Click on the Page Views Link

Click on the **Page Views** link in the left column.

The **Page View Report** shows you the hits on your pages by day. You can see whether there are a lot of people coming on a particular day and schedule your updates to your site to coincide with high viewer days. You can also use the **stats** to determine whether there has been a problem with your site that you haven't noticed (if people suddenly stop coming to your site).

At the top of the report, you can select to view the report by **hour, day, week,** or **month.**

4 Click on the Visitor Profile Link

Click on the **Visitor Profile** link in the left column.

By default, the **Visitor Profile Report** shows you the operating system breakdown for your visitors. You can also view the report by **screen resolution,** *color depth,* **browser type,** and whether **JavaScript** is enabled.

▶ KEY TERM

Color depth—Color depth is how many colors a computer is set to display. Older computers only display 256 colors or fewer—called 8-bit color. If your visitors come to your site and only can view 256 colors but your images use more, they will see images that are grainy or dithered.

5 Click on the Referrer Link

Click on the **Referrer** link in the left column.

By default, the **Referrer Report** shows what web pages people were on just before they went to your page. You can set it to see what search engine people use most often to find your site and see what keywords they use in the search engines to find you.

38

PART III

Build Your Own Website Using Netscape Composer

IN THIS CHAPTER

7

Getting Started with Netscape Composer

In This Chapter:

There are a number of great tools on the Web for creating web pages. In Part I, "Getting Started Building Web Pages," you learned about the basics of HTML and how pages worked. In Part II, "Build Your Own Website on GeoCities," you learned about building a website through a web service on GeoCities. In this part, you are going to work with a more advanced tool that will enable you to create pages locally on your machine that you can then upload to the Web.

Netscape Composer is one of the first web development applications that was available to users early in the history of the Web. It comes with the Netscape browser, so you might even have it already on your machine.

---

39   Download Netscape

✔ **BEFORE YOU BEGIN**	→ **SEE ALSO**
Just jump right in.	**21** Sign Up for Services

39

Before you begin this task, you can check to see whether you have Netscape installed. Many computers come with Netscape even if it isn't the primary browser. To see whether you have Netscape installed, check in your Programs on the Start menu and look for a Netscape folder. If you have Netscape installed, you don't have to do the steps in this task.

■ Go to http://www.netscape.com

The **Netscape** site is pretty interesting. Netscape is a *web portal* for the Web, as well as a company that makes a browser and a web development tool, so there is a lot of information on the page. Scroll down the page until you see Tools in the left column near the bottom of the page.

▶ KEY TERM

Web portal—A website you set as your home page from which you begin browsing every time you log on to the Internet. On a web portal, you usually find news and opinions, advertising, useful applications such as a search engine, and so on. By getting you to set the web portal as your home page, the site can sell more advertising, which pays for the features you find on the page. The advantage of making a web portal your home page is that you can get many of the things you need to have on the Web at once instead of going to multiple sites. The downside of web portals is that you often get too much information to digest at one time.

■ Click on the Browser Central Link

The **Browser Central** page is a great resource. Not only can you get the **Netscape** application, but you also can access all sorts of useful services and plug-ins for the browser.

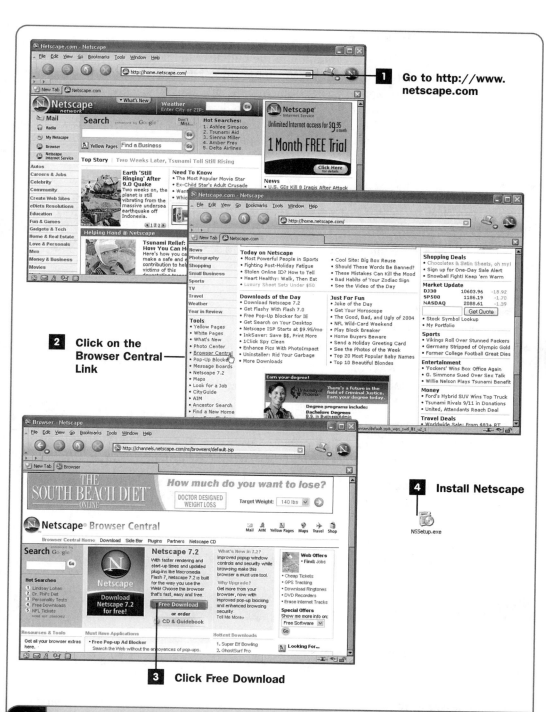

1 Go to http://www.netscape.com

2 Click on the Browser Central Link

4 Install Netscape

3 Click Free Download

39

39 Download Netscape

3 Click Free Download

Click on the **Free Download** button in the middle of the page to go to the **Netscape Download** page. Here you can download the latest version of Netscape. You also have a choice of buying the program on CD if you want to have a copy around that you don't need to download. This option is fairly handy if you want to install on multiple machines or like to have backups of your software, or for those with limited bandwidth.

▶ TIP

The **Must Have Applications** section on the Browser Central page is a great resource for browsing. Netscape has identified several things that really bother people while browsing, and has created links to multiple solutions for each annoyance, including Spyware being installed without your knowing it, getting spam and viruses, and having to sit through pop-up ads. Go through these links and try out some of the solutions when you have time.

4 Install Netscape

Double click on the **NSSetup.exe** file you just downloaded.

When the installer starts, click on the **Next** button, accept the license agreement, and click **Next** on the **Setup Type** screen to do a Recommended install of the application.

You can select extra components if you like as you go through the install process. At the end of the process, the installer downloads various components of the browser and installs them one by one. At the end of the install process, the new Netscape browser opens and the welcome page displays.

For this chapter, you need Composer, which is a part of the basic Netscape Navigator install, so you don't need to worry about which components are installed at this time.

Now that you have Netscape installed, you should find the **Netscape Navigator** application in the Programs section of your **Setup** menu.

40

---

40   About Netscape Composer

✔ **BEFORE YOU BEGIN**

   6 About Proper HTML Coding

Now that you have Netscape installed, you can access Composer and get an idea of what you can do with it.

Composer is designed to look and work as much like a word processor as possible, so it shouldn't be too difficult to get around.

At the top of the window is a row of icons to perform file actions, such as opening, closing, printing, and saving files. Next to the file actions are wizards to add links, images, and tables to the page, and to spell check the document.

Below the file actions are buttons to apply formatting to the text and images, such as alignment, color, and type size.

At the bottom of the window below the main work area are tabs that move from one view to another of the page. The normal mode is where you are going to do most of your work, the HTML Tags mode shows your page with the structure of the tags that make up HTML, the **<HTML> Source view** shows the code on the page, and the Preview mode shows how the page is going to look in the browser.

To help you get used to the different features, add some text to the page. You need to have a little content for some of the features to show up.

When you click on the **HTML Tag view**, the view changes to show your text wrapped in yellow HTML tag markers. On this page, because you haven't added any format to the text, all you see is the Body tag. You can view the page later and see more detail here. You also can work in this view to add content and the tags will change to match what you have done.

40

If you add anything that requires a new tag, you can double click on the tag marker and you can change the attributes of the tag in the Advanced Property Editor.

When you click on the **<HTML> Source view**, it shows you the actual HTML coding of the page. In this case, Composer is going to add some code that you might not recognize called the DocType and the **<meta content>** tag. These tags are important for code to be valid, but for now you don't need to worry about that.

You should see the **<html>**, **<head>**, **<title>**, and **<body>** tags that you are familiar with.

► TIP

There are many, many tags in HTML and you are probably going to only deal with a few of them. I would like to list all the tags that you can safely ignore, but I think it is easier to say that you should not edit a tag that you haven't seen before unless you consult an HTML tag reference.

41 Set Page Properties

✔ BEFORE YOU BEGIN	→ SEE ALSO
6 About Proper HTML Coding	**8** Add a Title and Head

Most things you want to do to a web page—such as editing text and adding pictures—involve working on the page, sort of like painting on a canvas. But what if you want to change the color of the canvas or replace it with velvet so that you can do Elvis or the dogs playing poker? On a web page, there is a split between the content on the page and the attributes of the page itself. With Composer, setting the page attributes is easily done.

1 Enter Page Title and Properties

Select **Page Title and Properties** from the **Format** menu. The **Page Properties** dialog box opens and gives you areas to enter text for the **Title**, **Author**, and **Description** of the page.

The **Title** field contains the text that appears at the top of the browser window when the page is viewed. A good title that describes what the page is about can help your viewers find your pages in search engines. If you just put your name or company name in the title for every page, you are not giving viewers or search engines much information about your site. Keeping your titles accurate and unique for each page in your site makes it easier to find information on your site.

The **Author** field is for you to enter your name or contact information so that people can find you. It is rarely used, but it does come up in search engines.

The **Description** field enables you to add a summary of the content of the page; this synopsis is used by some search engines to display a brief description of the page in the search results. A good page description can help your viewers find your page just like a good title can do.

2 Choose Format, Page Colors and Background

Select **Page Colors and Background** from the **Format** menu. The **Page Colors and Background** dialog box appears. By default, Composer gives your page no background image and leaves the colors of the text and links to the default of the browser.

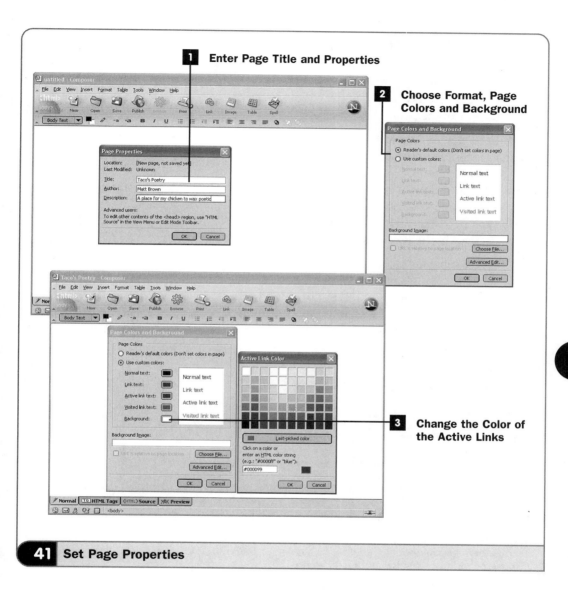

1 Enter Page Title and Properties

2 Choose Format, Page Colors and Background

3 Change the Color of the Active Links

41 Set Page Properties

▶ **TIP**

There are advantages in leaving the link colors at the browser's default because they are high contrast and easy to read. Also, they have significance to the viewer of the page; most people know that a piece of blue text with an underline indicates a link. When the link is purple, most viewers understand the link has been visited.

3 Change the Color of the Active Links

Now you can edit the colors for each type of text on the page. Editing the text colors in the page properties adds code to the page only once—not to every block of text to which you want to apply the color change—which reduces the size of the page and decreases the time it takes to download the page.

In the Page Colors and Background dialog box, click on the Use Custom Colors radio button and then click the button next to the Active Link text option. (Alternatively, click the color button for whatever type of text you want to change, such as **Normal Text** or **Visited Link** text.) The **Active Link Color** dialog box opens, with a table of the colors from which you can select. When you click one of the colors, it shows you the name of the color in *hexadecimal* in the text area at the bottom of the dialog box.

If you know the color you want to use, you can type its hexadecimal code directly in the text box and click **OK** to set your color choice. Otherwise, click the color in the table and click OK to return to the **Page Colors and Background** dialog box. Notice that the dialog box has been updated to show the color you selected as the color for the type of text you were editing.

42 ▶ KEY TERM

Hexadecimal—Hex is a system of numbering with a base of 16 rather than the base 10 with which we are familiar. Without going into too much detail on why computers like base 16 numbers, some explanation is necessary. A hex number looks like "#3366FF". The pound sign indicates to HTML that the following six numbers and letters are to be used as a single set of three two-digit numbers. The first set of two digits is the value for red, the second set is the value for green, and the third set is for blue. Together they tell the computer to display one color made up from red, green, and blue.

In hex, when you run out of the digits 0–9, instead of going on to 10, you go to a, and then b, c, d, e, and f. Thus, counting in hex is as follows: 0, 1, 2, 3, 4, 5, 6, 7, 8, 9, A, B, C, D, E, F. B equals 11 and E equals 14.

The sets of digits go from 00 to FF with 00 equaling zero and FF equaling 256. With 256 colors possible for red, green, and blue each, there are 256^3 colors possible. For those of you who aren't math heads, that is 16,777,216 possible colors.

42 Set the Page Colors and Background

✔ **BEFORE YOU BEGIN**

6 About Proper HTML Coding

In the Page Colors and Background dialog box (after you have the text and link colors set), you can use the same dialog box to set the background image and background color of the page.

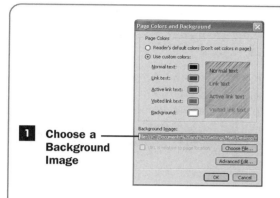

1 Choose a Background Image

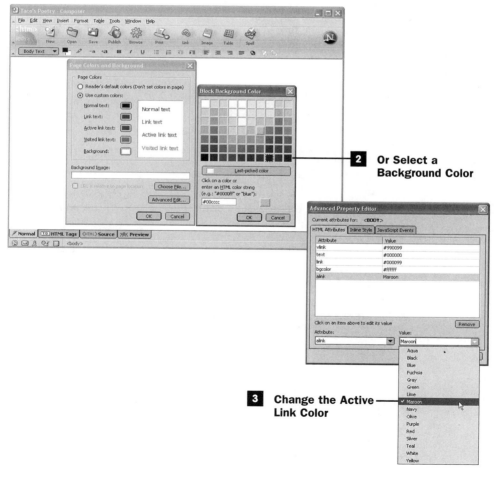

2 Or Select a Background Color

42

3 Change the Active Link Color

42 Set the Page Colors and Background

▊ Choose a Background Image

If it's not already open, choose **Format, Page Colors and Background** to display the **Page Colors and Background** dialog box.

If you want a background image for your page, you can browse to one and add it to your page. In the **Page Colors and Background** dialog box, click the **Choose File** button. Using the familiar Windows navigation system, browse to the image file you want to use as the background for your web page. The file must be either a JPG or GIF if it is to work in most browsers.

▶ TIP

In general, background images make your page hard to read. The more contrast that exists in the image, the harder the page is to read, regardless of the colors you choose for the text and links. For the best pages, use a very plain background image with very low contrast and select colors for the text that contrast enough with the background to stand out.

▊ Or Select a Background Color

Click the color button next to the **Background** option in the **Use Custom Colors** section of the **Page Colors and Background** dialog box. From the color table that appears, select a background color for the page.

If the color you select for your active links is too close to the color you select for the page background (if both are shades of blue, for example), the viewer might have trouble seeing the text against the background of the page. Choose your page background color with care.

For this example, in the color table, click the color swatch in the top row, second from the right. The color name at the bottom of the dialog box changes to **#ccccff**. This hexadecimal code specifies a color with quite a bit of red (the first two **cc** values), quite a bit of green (the second two **cc** values), and a lot of blue (the third group of values, **ff**). When the values are the same for each color (red, green, and blue), the result is a shade of gray. In this example, you have selected a light gray with a tinge of blue.

▊ Change the Active Link Color

Click the **Advanced Edit** button on the **Page Colors and Background** dialog box. The **Advanced Property Editor** dialog box comes up. You might not need to open this dialog box to set attributes until you become more proficient with JavaScript and other advanced techniques.

42

Right now you should see all the attribute–value pairs assigned to the **<body>** tag of the page. If you want to add another attribute to the **<body>** tag, click the **Attribute** drop-down list and select the attribute. Then click the **Value** drop-down list and choose from the available values for that attribute.

For example, click on the **alink** attribute (the active link text attribute) in the table at the top of the dialog box and then click the **Value** drop-down list. A list of colors comes up. Choose the color you want to use for all the active links on the page. The **Advanced Property Editor** is a different way to access colors; these named colors work in other places in Composer where you can enter color information.

▶ **TIP**

Because of the way the color information is written into the file, and the way the file is displayed in Composer, you might not see the correct color for the Active link until you preview the file. For the ease of use, you should set colors with either the regular **Page Colors and Background** dialog box or the **Advanced Property Editor** and not both on the same tag.

| **43** | **Add Text and Links** |

43

✔ BEFORE YOU BEGIN	→ SEE ALSO
6 About Proper HTML Coding	**1** About HTML
9 Add and Format Text	**2** Use HTML Tags
10 About Creating Hyperlinks	**26** Create Links to Other Pages

Having set the background color for your page and knowing where you can edit and change the page attributes (such as the title and description), you are ready to add text to the page. At this point, the Composer program works more or less like a word processor.

Now that you have your page filled in with some content and know how to format and edit it, you need to know how to create a link on your page.

1 **Type Some Text on the Page**

Click in the **main work area** of the **Composer** window and type some text. As you type, press the **Enter** key at the end of each line to begin a new line. Composer will wrap text like a word processor, but if you press the Return key, you are not creating a new paragraph in Composer—you are adding a line break.

You should get a few lines of text to work with. The lines of text should not have any vertical space between them.

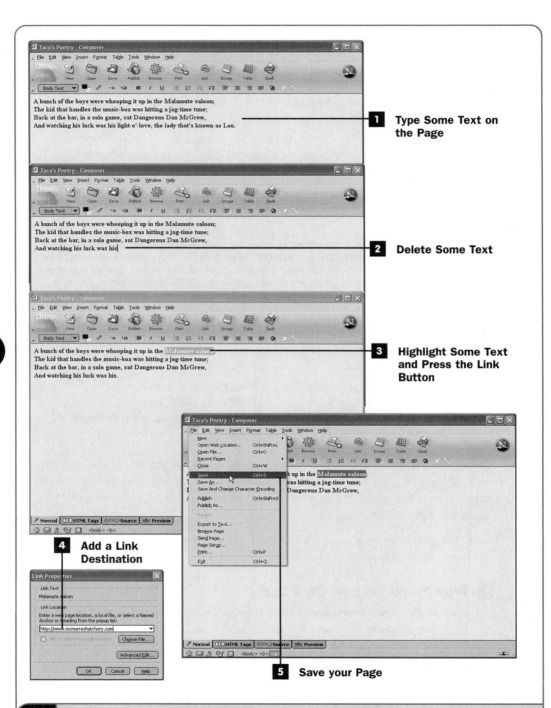

1 Type Some Text on the Page

2 Delete Some Text

43

3 Highlight Some Text and Press the Link Button

4 Add a Link Destination

5 Save your Page

43 Add Text and Links

2 Delete Some Text

Select some of the text you just entered and then press the **Backspace** key or the **Delete** key. Composer works just like a word processor or text editor and deletes the text. If you select across different paragraphs and delete, Composer is going to take care of the beginning and end paragraph tags that it created for you when you entered the text.

3 Highlight Some Text and Press the Link Button

The **Link Properties** dialog box comes up and you can either select a file on your machine from the **Choose File** dialog box or you can type in an address in the text area.

If you select a local file to which to link, you have to be sure to upload the file to the same location as the file on which you are working.

4 Add a Link Destination

In the **Link Location** text area, type in **http://www.mcmurrayhatchery.com**, click OK, and then save the file.

Be sure to add the **http://** part to the address. If you don't, the address won't work.

43

5 Save Your Page

When Composer saves your page, it saves only the page markup and not whatever graphics you might have added to the page. Your best practice is to keep your pages and their elements in one folder. When you keep your images in the same folder as your page, it makes the paths to your images shorter and easier to debug. When you have more and more graphics and pages, you might want to change that organization, but for now everything in the same folder is a good idea.

8

Work with Text

IN THIS CHAPTER:

You have started working with Netscape Composer and have built a simple page with text, so you should have a general sense of where things are in the program. Now you are going to dig into the formatting options and apply some of what you know about HTML.

44 Add Structure to Your Text

✔ BEFORE YOU BEGIN

6 About Proper HTML Coding
2 Use HTML Tags

→ SEE ALSO

9 Add and Format Text
25 Add Text and Graphics to the Page
43 Add Text and Links

As you learned in Chapter 2, "The Basics of HTML," HTML is a language of nested tags and everything that shows up on the page has to be in a containing tag. When you type text, by default it goes into the **<body>** tag, which is the highest-level container for content on your page. This isn't considered good for a well-designed page because the structure of the page is important to the browser. Generally, paragraphs should be enclosed in **<p>** tags, which give the text the correct structure and which create a vertical break between paragraphs.

Other tags are important to indicate the heading level for a block of text. If you are working on a longer document, you will have heading levels that help you organize. You might have three levels of information in your page. In HTML, you would use an **<h1>** for the top-level heading, then an **<h2>**, and then for the smallest subsections, you would use an **<h3>**.

Keeping these heading levels provides a structure or tree of your information.

■ 1 Open Your Sample File

Open the file you created in Chapter 7, "Getting Started with Netscape Composer." If you haven't completed that step, you can create a new file to use and add some text to work with.

■ 2 Format Your Text As a Paragraph

The text is converted from **<body>** text, which is unstructured, into **<p>** text, which has line breaks between each paragraph.

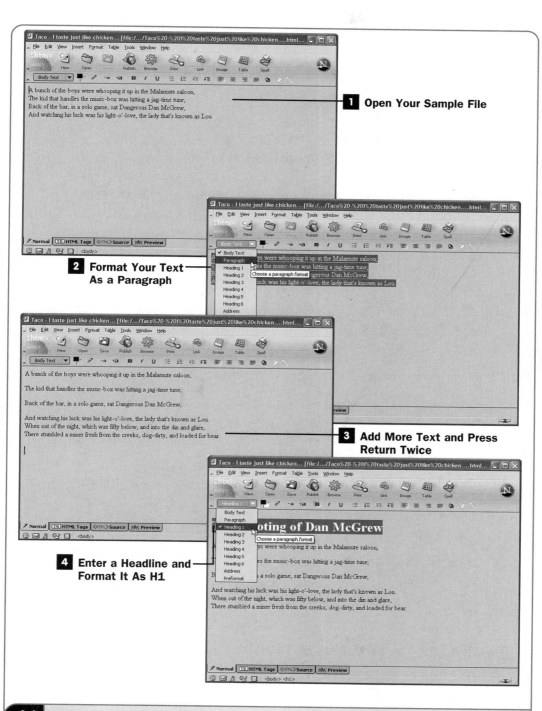

1 Open Your Sample File

2 Format Your Text As a Paragraph

3 Add More Text and Press Return Twice

4 Enter a Headline and Format It As H1

44

44 Add Structure to Your Text

3 Add More Text and Press Return Twice

When you press the **Return** key while typing in **Composer**, it adds a break or **
** tag to your text, which forces the next text to the next line. This is not the same as a paragraph tag, which represents a new logical unit or paragraph. When you press the **Return** key twice in a row, it ends the paragraph and starts a new paragraph.

4 Enter a Headline and Format It As H1

Put your cursor in front of the first line of text and enter a headline. Keep your cursor on the line and, from the format drop-down list on the **Format Toolbar**, select **H1**.

Giving a heading on a page an **<h1>** heading lets the browser know that everything from that **<h1>** to the next **<h1>** tag is related.

---

45 Add Color to Your Text

✔ BEFORE YOU BEGIN	→ SEE ALSO
4 Use Attributes and Values	25 Add Text and Graphics to the Page

45

In **HTML**, you can color your text as you would in a word processor to make a section of text stand out or follow a style guide. In **HTML**, you can also change the background for a line or paragraph like you would use a highlighter on paper.

1 Highlight the First Line of Text

Highlight text to tell **Composer** what you want to apply the color to, much like in a word processor.

2 Click on the Text Color Icon

The **Text Color** dialog box appears. Select a color that is going to stand out from the background and click OK. The text will change to the color you selected.

3 Highlight the First Line of Your Text Again

This time you are going to set the background for the part of the text you have selected. This will not affect the color of the text itself, but will set the background color.

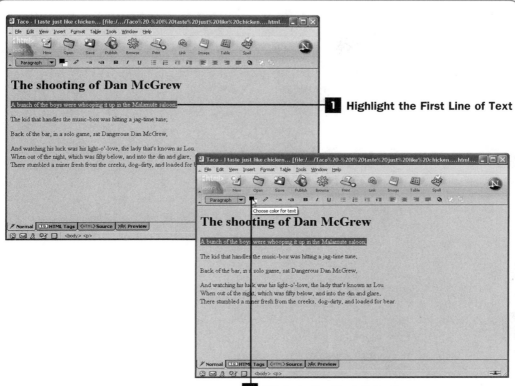

1 Highlight the First Line of Text

2 Click on the Text Color Icon

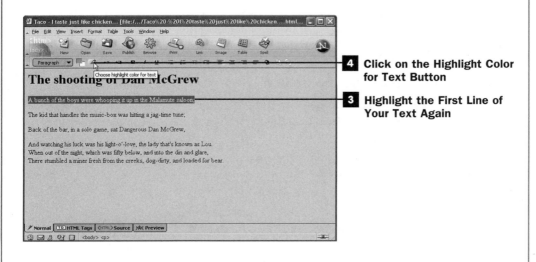

4 Click on the Highlight Color for Text Button

3 Highlight the First Line of Your Text Again

45

45 Add Color to Your Text

4 Click on the Highlight Color for Text Button

The **Highlight Color** dialog box appears. Select a color that is going to stand out from the background and click **OK**.

The text block, which runs from the beginning of the heading to the edge of the browser, is now the color you chose. Using highlights can be a great way to separate sections of a document.

---

46 Change Text Sizes and Styles

✔ BEFORE YOU BEGIN	→ SEE ALSO
4 Use Attributes and Values	9 Add and Format Text
	25 Add Text and Graphics to the Page
	43 Add Text and Links

46

When you set your headline to **<h1>**, the type increased in size. Each heading has its own display style that is associated with it. An **<h1>** tag has a size and weight of type that is determined by the browser. You can change that text or any text to display differently by selecting the text and applying the formatting options from the **Format** toolbar.

1 Highlight a Few Words of Your Text

You are going to explore different text changes you can bring to your web page. In my example, I create a highlight for your first line of text by making the text larger than the surrounding text and bold. You should highlight some text by selecting it.

2 Click on Either the Increase or Decrease Size Icon

Each time you click on the **Increase Size** icon, the selected text gets larger and is wrapped in the **<BIG>** tag. If you click on the **Decrease Size** icon, the selected text gets smaller.

3 Click on the Bold Icon

The **Bold** icon wraps the selected text in the **<STRONG>** tag.

4 Select Some Text and Set a Different Font

You can actually try a few of the formatting options here on the selection. The **Foreground Color, Decrease and Increase Size, Highlight Text Color, Bold, Italic,** and **Underline** buttons only affect the text you have highlighted.

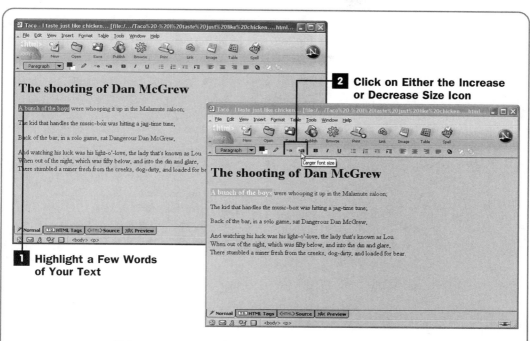

2 Click on Either the Increase or Decrease Size Icon

1 Highlight a Few Words of Your Text

3 Click on the Bold Icon

4 Select Some Text and Set a Different Font

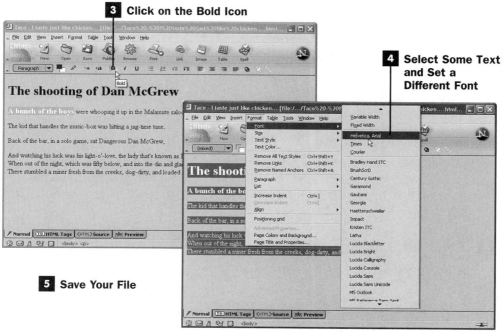

5 Save Your File

46

46   Change Text Sizes and Styles

5 **Save Your File**

You can keep using the same file to try other formatting options so you can see what different formatting options do in relation with each other.

---

47 **Edit Text**

✔ BEFORE YOU BEGIN	→ SEE ALSO
4 Use Attributes and Values	**9** Add and Format Text
6 About Proper HTML Coding	**25** Add Text and Graphics to the Page
	43 Add Text and Links
	44 Add Structure to Your Text
	45 Add Color to Your Text
	46 Change Text Sizes and Styles

47

Editing text is much the same as a word processor.

1 **Select a Word in the Headline and Type**

The text in the headline changes to what you typed.

2 **Select Some Text and Press the Delete Key**

The text is deleted, but the paragraphs are not merged and the format of each of the remaining pieces of text is not changed. If you were to do the same thing in a normal word processor, you would be left with one paragraph and one style.

3 **Select Undo from the Edit Menu**

You can undo multiple times. Each time you select **Undo**, the last action you performed is undone, and then the action previous to that, and so on. All the typing you do at one time is considered one action, so it will be undone as one action.

4 **Save Your File**

Save your file so you can use it in the next task.

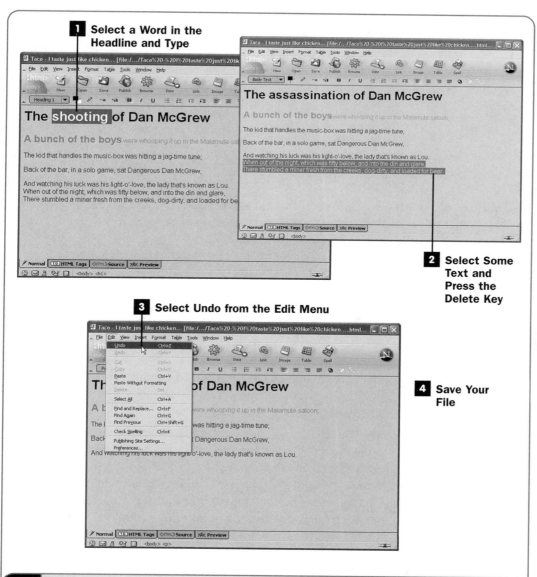

1 Select a Word in the Headline and Type

2 Select Some Text and Press the Delete Key

3 Select Undo from the Edit Menu

4 Save Your File

47

47 Edit Text

48   Use the HTML Views

✔ BEFORE YOU BEGIN	→ SEE ALSO
4 Use Attributes and Values **6** About Proper HTML Coding	**8** Add a Title and Head **9** Add and Format Text **25** Add Text and Graphics to the Page **43** Add Text and Links **44** Add Structure to Your Text **45** Add Color to Your Text

There are two HTML views in **Composer**: the **HTML Tags** view and the **<HTML> Source** view. You are going to use them both as you develop your pages. The **HTML Tags** view is going to help you understand how the tags interact with one another. It also gives you the ability to easily select the tags and apply properties to them. The **<HTML> Source** view is where you can access the actual code of the page and enter or change raw code.

1   Click on the HTML Tags View

Your page shows as it did in the **Normal** view but with markers in place for each of the tags on the page. At the top is the marker for the **<body>** tag, and at the beginning of each line of text is the marker for that paragraph.

2   Click on the Marker for the <big> Tag

There is a marker for the **<big>** tag on the second line where the text is bold. When you click on the tag marker, the contents of the tag are highlighted. While the tag is highlighted, you can drag it to any other location in the page. When you do that, you get everything between the beginning and end of the tag, which can be a problem sometimes in the **Normal** mode. You may drag more than you intend. Try to drag content in smaller chunks to avoid this problem.

3   Double-Click on the Marker for the <big> Tag

The **Advanced Property Editor** that you saw in Chapter 7 comes up so you can edit the attributes for the tag. You can also access the **Inline Style** for the tag and the **JavaScript Events** where you can add *cascading style sheet* information and hand-code **JavaScript**.

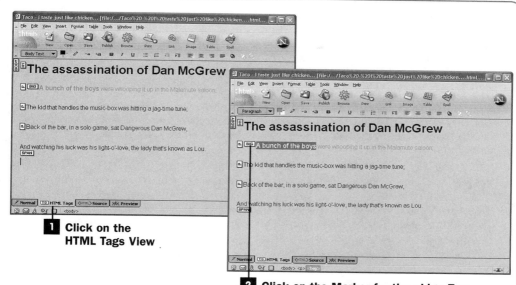

1 Click on the
HTML Tags View

2 Click on the Marker for the <big> Tag

3 Double-Click on the Marker
for the <big> Tag

48

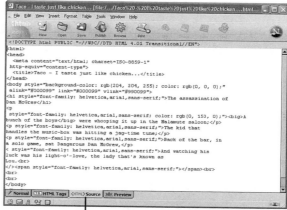

4 Click on the HTML Source
View Tab

48   Use the HTML Views

▶ KEY TERM

***Cascading style sheets*—Cascading style sheets (CSS) is a language related to HTML that the browser can read to impart visual styles to HTML pages. In web development, you might hear that best practice is to separate content from visual presentation. This allows your page to be very flexible in how it appears. Consider all the new devices that can surf the Web—and view your web page! You can have the same information displayed with a web browser on a computer, on a cellular telephone, on a kiosk, on an Internet-equipped television, or on who knows what! The only thing that would have to change is the style sheet, which tells the device how to show the same information differently (suited to each medium). There are a number of books that go into CSS in depth, but it is beyond the scope of this book.**

4 Click on the HTML Source View Tab

Now you can see the source code for your page with all the tags you have added in the chapter. If you want to edit the page by hand, you can do so in this view.

---

49 Add Lists

✔ BEFORE YOU BEGIN	→ SEE ALSO
6 About Proper HTML Coding	43 Add Text and Links

Presenting your data on the Web requires more planning sometimes than when you are writing for print media. On the Web, you have a limited amount of time to capture your viewers' attention, so you need to present your information in blocks that the viewer can digest easily. (This is like how newspapers try to get as much "above the fold" as they can so you don't need to unfold the paper to get the gist of what's going on.) One way to do that in **HTML** is to use bulleted or numbered lists with the main points of your information so the viewer can quickly decide whether the information is of interest.

1 Add a Heading

Put your cursor at the beginning of the text you have on your page and type a heading. In my case, it is going to be **Dangerous Dan McGrew Murdered in Bar-Room Mystery**.

This is going to be the first thing the viewer sees, so I want to have a catchy headline.

Set your headline as an **<H1>** from the **Paragraph Format** drop-down menu.

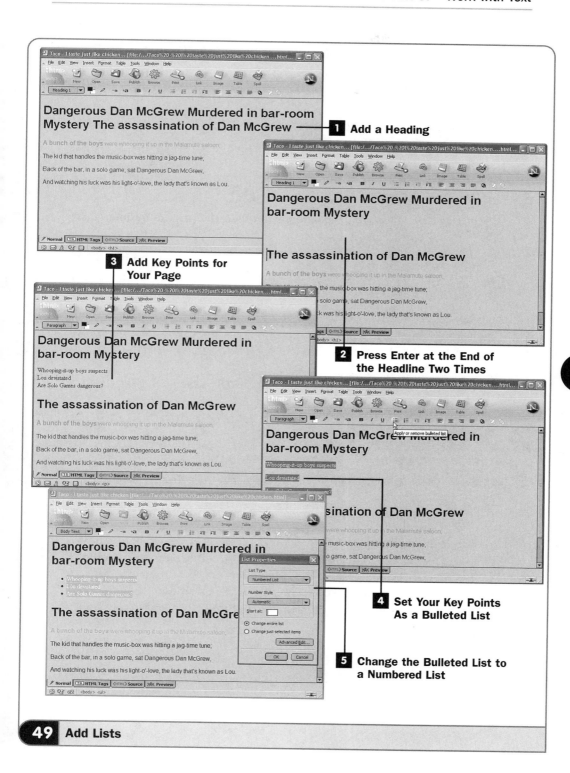

1 Add a Heading

3 Add Key Points for Your Page

2 Press Enter at the End of the Headline Two Times

4 Set Your Key Points As a Bulleted List

5 Change the Bulleted List to a Numbered List

2 Press Enter at the End of the Headline Two Times

This is going to give you the space to add your bullet points so that your reader will be able to scan to get an idea of the content of the entire page.

3 Add Key Points for Your Page

Enter a few key points about your page here and press **return** after each sentence.

4 Set Your Key Points As a Bulleted List

Highlight the sentences you just entered and then click on the **Bulleted List** icon from the **Format** Toolbar.

Your text should now be formatted as a bulleted list. Each line begins with a bullet. You can control what style bullet the list has by right clicking on a piece of the text and selecting **List Properties** from the context menu.

From the **List Properties** dialog box, you can also change the list from a bulleted list to a numbered list, which is useful if you are listing steps in a procedure or lesson like this one.

5 Change the Bulleted List to a Numbered List

50

---

50 **Add Special Characters**

✔ BEFORE YOU BEGIN	→ SEE ALSO
6 About Proper HTML Coding	**5** About Using Special Characters
	43 Add Text and Links

Special characters such as ç, ©, ®, and ¨ don't appear on your keyboard, but you might need them to add accents to letters or to show a trademark or copyright, for example. To add these characters in **HTML** (and others), you have to use a *character entity* and add it in the code. When you use **Composer**, though, there is an easy way to add special characters and accents to your page without touching the underlying **HTML** code.

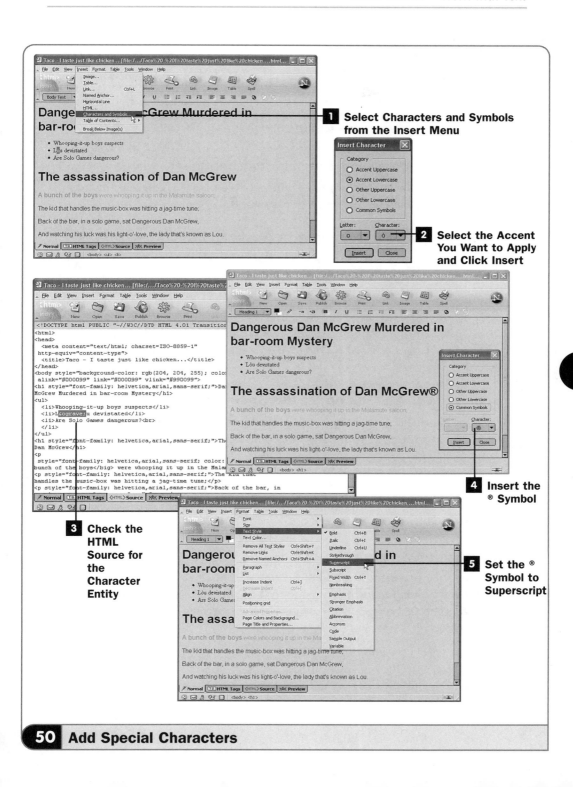

1 Select Characters and Symbols from the Insert Menu

2 Select the Accent You Want to Apply and Click Insert

3 Check the HTML Source for the Character Entity

4 Insert the ® Symbol

5 Set the ® Symbol to Superscript

50 Add Special Characters

▶ KEY TERM

Character entity—Character entities are special characters that are not represented in the HTML code as regular characters, but can be added to a page with small blocks of code. For example, the **&** symbol won't show up in the page if you add it from the keyboard as you would in a word processor. Instead, type **&** in your **HTML** and the browser will display the symbol as a regular ampersand when the page is viewed.

1 Select Characters and Symbols from the Insert Menu

This brings up the **Insert Character** dialog box, where you can select to add accented characters that aren't on the keyboard.

2 Select the Accent You Want to Apply and Click Insert

Click on the **Accent Lowercase** radio button and, from the drop-down list under letter, select the basic letter that you want. From the **Character** drop-down list, select the accent you want to apply and then click on **Insert**.

The character you selected is inserted into your page so that you can see it in the **Visual Editor**, but it is actually inserted as a character entity in your page. In my case, I selected *u* as the letter I wanted to accent using the grave accent.

3 Check the HTML Source for the Character Entity

Click on the **HTML Source View** tab at the bottom of the **Composer** window and scroll to the text in your page where you entered the accented character.

Notice that the code actually entered on your page is the character entity. In my case, it is **ù**.

If you use characters with accents, you really do *not* want to remember each character entity, so this is really a timesaver.

4 Insert the ® Symbol

Click on the headline at the end of the line and select **Characters and Symbols** from the **Insert** menu. Click on the **Common Symbols** radio button and, from the **Character** drop-down list, select a symbol (I use the ® symbol) and click on the **Insert** button.

You now have a special symbol added to your text, but it is in the font and size of the text in the line. The mark is also set on the baseline of the text, level with the bottoms of each character.

50

5 Set the ® Symbol to Superscript

Highlight the special symbol you just inserted into the page and, from the **Format** menu, select **Text Style**, **Superscript**.

The special symbol should now be smaller and line up with the tops of the characters in the line—not the bottoms.

51 Spell Check the Document

Misspellings on a web page are about the easiest way to make your page look unprofessional, and unprofessional sites don't attract viewers. If you do nothing else at all at the end of your work on a page, at the very least spell check your document.

1 Add a Misspelling to Your Page

Your page is probably perfect and doesn't have any misspellings, so for this task you need to select one character each in a few words and change them so that the word is misspelled.

2 Click on the Spell Check Icon

The **Spell Check** dialog box comes up and starts checking the page. The first thing you misspelled should show up in the **Misspelled Word** area at the top of the dialog box.

Before you do anything, be sure that you have the correct **Language** specified. By default, you get **British English** and **American English**, but you can download others if you need them.

From the dialog box, you can select a spelling from the **Suggestions** window. The word you select is added to the **Replace With** area directly above it. You can select to replace the word, or you can manually enter a word to replace the misspelled word and not use the suggested words. If the word is misspelled repeatedly, you can replace all instances of the word.

3 Add a Misspelled Word to Your Dictionary

If the word is not misspelled but the spell checker thinks it is, you can either ignore (or ignore all) instances of the word, or you can add the word to your personal dictionary, which will be available only to you on the machine you are working on and not in other copies of **Composer** on other machines.

The word has now been added to your personal dictionary, so anytime it comes up now in **Composer**, it won't show up as misspelled.

51

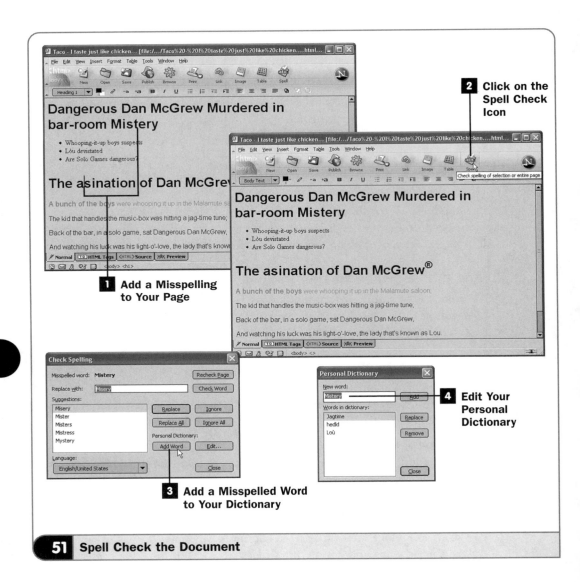

2 Click on the Spell Check Icon

1 Add a Misspelling to Your Page

3 Add a Misspelled Word to Your Dictionary

4 Edit Your Personal Dictionary

51 Spell Check the Document

4 Edit Your Personal Dictionary

With a misspelled word, click on the **Edit** button next to the **Add Word** button to edit your personal dictionary.

The **Personal Dictionary** dialog box comes up and shows the words you have added to the personal dictionary. You can add other words here, or delete words that you don't want in the dictionary any longer, such as terms that you only used for one project or personal names that you are not going to need in the future.

9

Organize Text with Tables and Rules

IN THIS CHAPTER:

Now that you have a feel for Netscape Composer's basic functions, you can start getting into the more advanced features to help you design your pages.

Using tables in Composer is going to be the basis of how you lock down the format of the page so that you can create more complex layouts. By default, as you have seen, Composer creates content in a single flow of content, just as a word processor would do. Maybe you've completed the chapter that uses GeoCities PageBuilder. You were able to use tables to line up text and images and to control how they looked on your page. If you haven't completed this yet, don't worry. You are going to work with tables now in Composer.

---

52   Insert a Table

✔ BEFORE YOU BEGIN	→ SEE ALSO
6 About Proper HTML Coding	**35** Add a Table
	48 Use the HTML Views

52

Inserting a table into your page is easy to do at any time, but if you plan ahead you can divide your work into two portions: design, where you think about how the page is going to look, and production, where you simply add content to the page.

Getting your existing content into a table is very easy, but you need to divide your content up into the units that you want to put in different places on the page. Effectively separating information is a skill you are going to use over and over to make your pages more informative and easy for the viewer to read.

1 Open a New Page in Composer

In this task, you are going to start with a new page and work with a table to design the page, and then you are going to copy the content from the existing page you have been working on.

2 Click on the Table Icon

This brings up the **Insert Table** dialog box. For every table, you must know how many columns and rows to have, how wide to make the table, and whether there is a border. There are other attributes of a table that you are going to use, but these are the ones that you have to do on every table.

The default table in **Composer** is set to produce two rows and two columns and to be 100% of the width of the element containing it, which is the page in this case. If you are inserting a table into another table cell—nesting the table—then that width is the width of the cell that contains the new table.

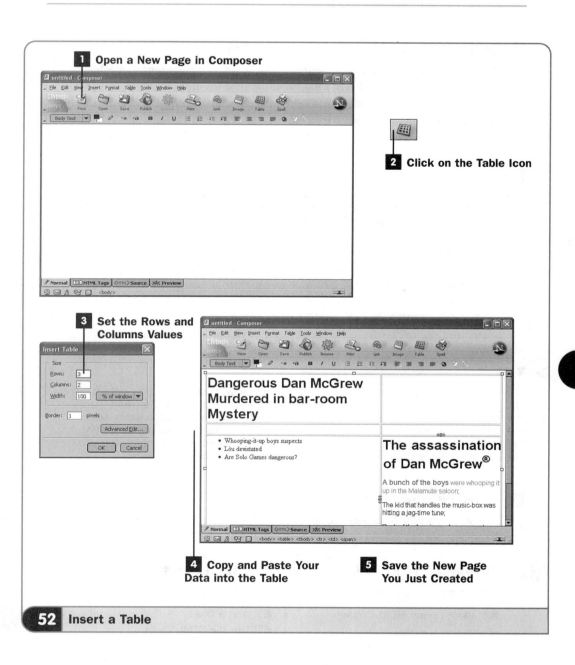

1 Open a New Page in Composer

2 Click on the Table Icon

3 Set the Rows and Columns Values

4 Copy and Paste Your Data into the Table

5 Save the New Page You Just Created

52 Insert a Table

3 Set the Rows and Columns Values

I will set the rows to 3 and the columns to 2 and click OK. This inserts the table into the page where you can begin to edit it.

▣ **Copy and Paste Your Data into the Table**

Open any page you have been working on, if you have content available. In my examples, I copy and paste the headline into the upper-left cell of the table. I also copy and paste the bulleted list into the bottom-left cell of the table. I even copy and paste the remaining text into the lower-right cell of the table. Tables are very flexible and can contain all kinds of content.

▶ **TIP**

HTML doesn't normally have ways to control format of a web page. To compensate for few native controls, web designers create page layout control with tables. You will use many tables as you design your pages. Experiment!

When you paste each item, the table resizes to accept that item. When you have content in only one cell in the first column, the second column might resize down to its smallest size to give as much room as possible for the content of the first column. If you insert content into an opposing cell, the table will balance itself. In my example, I click in the small, lower-right cell and paste, and the table resizes again to make both columns fit as best they can.

53

▶ **TIP**

When you copy and paste text, the styles might not follow from the original document. This is because the text styles, like the font styles, are carried in tags that wrap the format around the text. When you select items in the **Normal** view, you can easily select the contents of the tag, but in some cases you won't be able to select the formatting tags along with the content they contain. You need to be sure to check that what you paste matches what you copy, and be ready to reformat the text if necessary.

▣ **Save the New Page You Just Created**

Any work you do is important, so save it after any major change.

53 Customize Your Table for Effective Page Layout	
✔ **BEFORE YOU BEGIN**	→ **SEE ALSO**
6 About Proper HTML Coding	**35** Add a Table
	48 Use the HTML Views

When the table is inserted into the page, it is a container with no set boundaries, which means it is going to expand to fit any content inserted. This makes a great holder for the content. Keep in mind that you can section up your page to a point, but you have to work with the size and format of the table to force the table to "lock down" so that, as you add text, it shapes the content rather than having the content shape the table.

1 Click on a Resize Handle and Resize the Table

Click anywhere in your table and notice that the table gets small square resize handles on the sides and corners. Click on any resize handle and drag it in. See how it shapes your web page.

Note that the table resizes and the text in the table reflows to match the new widths of the columns that were automatically changed when the table width was reduced.

2 Click on the Delete Widget to Delete a Table Row

Click in any cell and delete the row by clicking on the delete *widget* that appears on the edge of the table cell.

▶ KEY TERM

Widget—A small and nonobtrusive piece of user interface in a program that enables you to change some property or execute some action more or less at the location of the change, rather than in a menu or a toolbar.

It is very easy to delete a row of cells. This happens most often when you create a table with more rows or columns than you end up using in your final layout.

53

3 Click on the Create New Row Below Widget to Create a New Row

Click in any cell, but avoid using the headline. Then create a new row by clicking on the **Create New Row Below** widget.

A new row appears. You can add a row above by clicking on the **Create New Row Above** widget. You can also add and delete columns in the same way with the widgets at the top of each selected cell. These abilities mean you can add new content by moving or deleting existing rows at will. You, not the software, are in control!

4 Select the Column

Click in any cell and then drag down across at least two cells below it to select the column. You must select at least two cells to let the software know you want a column, not just a cell or two.

Also, if you click and drag across two or more cells, you are selecting the cells—not their contents.

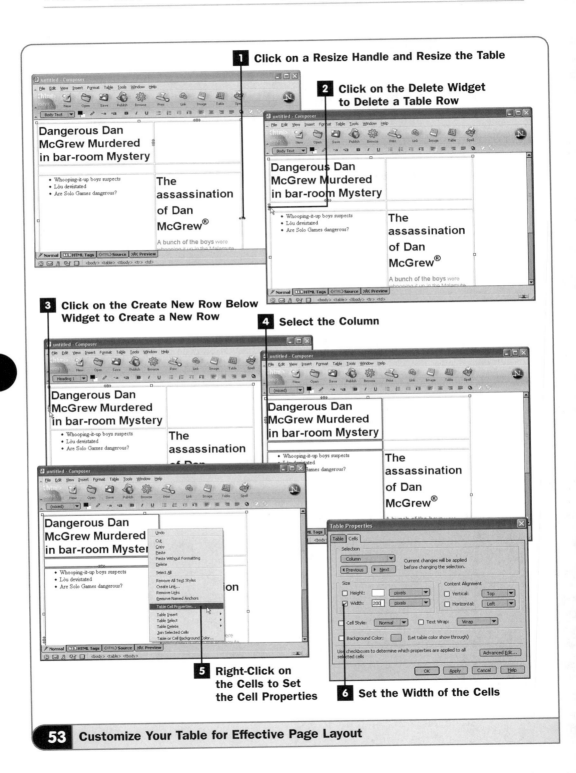

1 **Click on a Resize Handle and Resize the Table**

2 **Click on the Delete Widget to Delete a Table Row**

3 **Click on the Create New Row Below Widget to Create a New Row**

4 **Select the Column**

5 **Right-Click on the Cells to Set the Cell Properties**

6 **Set the Width of the Cells**

53

53   **Customize Your Table for Effective Page Layout**

5 Right-Click on the Cells to Set the Cell Properties

Right-click on the selected cells and select **Table Cell Properties** from the context menu, or go to the **Table** menu and select **Table Properties**.

The **Table Properties** dialog box appears and has two tabs that are loaded with attributes that you can apply to the table. On the **Table** tab of the dialog box, you can set the number of columns and rows, the width and height of the table, the border width of the table, and the spacing and padding of the cells, which enables you to add space around the edges of the tables. Padding adds space between the content and the edge of the cell, making more room around the edges of the table. Cell spacing makes the space between two cells wider.

The **Cells** tab of the dialog box has all the attributes you can assign to either individual cells or to groups of cells in columns or rows. You can modify your selection in the **Selection** area, which makes it easy to select a whole column or row if you haven't done so before you opened the dialog box. In the **Size** area, you can set the width and height of the selected cells.

The **Content Alignment** area enables you to control where the content in your cells lines up. The **Cell Style** drop-down box enables you to set the cell as a normal cell or a header cell (the difference between which is beyond the scope of this book). The **Text Wrap** is a handy drop-down box that enables you to adjust content that won't wrap or continue to the next line. You can select cells and can set column headings that won't resize, no matter what the user does on his screen. Experiment and enjoy the control you will have over your page format.

Want more customizations? The background color lets you set a color for the cells that is either the color of the page background or some other color to enable you to set a row or column off.

53

▶ TIP

The best way to figure out how to use **Cell Padding** and **Cell Spacing** is setting the padding to 10 or so. Now set the border width to 10 or 20. That is one change. Now set the spacing to 10 or so and the border width to 10 or 20. Observe the changes carefully.

6 Set the Width of the Cells

Set the **width** in the **Size** area of the **Cell** tab of the **Table Properties** dialog box to 200 pixels and then select the check box next to it. Click the OK button to apply the change and save the file.

The column with the headline should now be only 200 pixels wide, which should make it quite narrow compared to the right column with the text. Try other values and compare the effects.

54 Add Style to Your Table

✔ BEFORE YOU BEGIN	→ SEE ALSO
52 Insert a Table	**35** Add a Table
	48 Use the HTML Views

54

With the table sized and formatted correctly for your design, you can start to change the styles of the table to visually present your information.

■ Join the Headline Cell with the Adjacent Cell

Cells are good at containing bits of content. Sometimes you need to let important content fill an entire row. Let's use an example of a headline in a cell that needs to spread its wings across the row.

Click on the text with the headline, and then right-click and select **Join with Cell on Right** from the context menu.

Your headline now extends across the top of the entire table. You can also join cells vertically by selecting two or more cells by clicking and dragging across them and then selecting **Join Selected Cells** from the context menu.

There is a problem with the cell that you can't visually see in the editor right now, but you will see it in the browser if you view the page. Let's discuss what would happen if you had an existing column width restriction. Imagine in your last edits to the headline, you set the width of the column to 200 pixels. Here you have made the cell very wide so that it crosses the whole table and is a lot wider than 200 pixels. This is confusing for **Composer**, so it shows that the headline goes all the way across the table in the **Normal** view. To actually make the text stretch across the whole table, click on the cell. In the **Table Cell Properties** dialog box, remove the width property so that it can display correctly. So if you find conflicting results on your pages and in your tables, check for conflicting settings.

2 Select Table Cell Properties

Hold down the **Control** key and click on the text in the lower-right portion of the table. Select **Table Cell Properties** from the context menu.

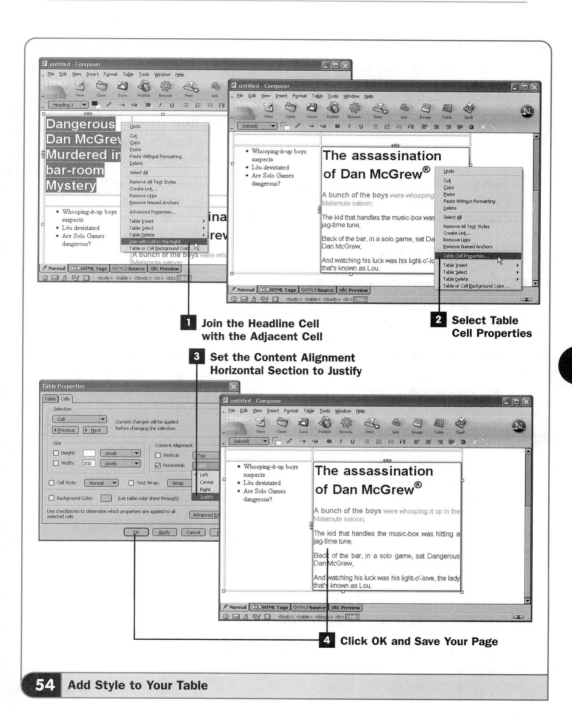

1 Join the Headline Cell with the Adjacent Cell

2 Select Table Cell Properties

3 Set the Content Alignment Horizontal Section to Justify

54

4 Click OK and Save Your Page

▶ **TIP**

When you want to select just one cell and not the contents of the cell, hold down the **Control** key as you click on the cell.

3 Set the Content Alignment Horizontal Section to Justify

In the **Table Properties** dialog box on the **Cells** tab, set the **Content Alignment Horizontal** section to **Justify** and click on the check box next to it.

Setting your text to justify makes the text go from one side of the cell to the other and spaces the words so that there is no ragged margin on the right side of the cell. This can make your text a little harder to read sometimes, but it sets the block of text as one single unit that will stand apart well from other text on the page.

4 Click OK and Save Your Page

Your text in the lower-right side of the table should be justified with each complete line extending across from each side of the cell to the other side of the cell. If you want to try changing more attributes in the **Cells** tab of the **Table Properties** dialog box, just click on the **Apply** tab as you work to see the changes applied to the table while keeping the dialog box open to keep making changes to the cell.

55

55	**Edit a Table**

✔ **BEFORE YOU BEGIN**	→ **SEE ALSO**
6 About Proper HTML Coding	**35** Add a Table
	48 Use the HTML Views
	52 Insert a Table
	53 Customize Your Table for Effective Page Layout
	54 Add Style to Your Table

Working with tables can be a little like building shelves for your books and realizing that you did the math wrong and ended up with more shelves than books. In a web page, though, this is easy to fix because you can rearrange the table by adding and subtracting and collapsing cells to make the table just right for the information.

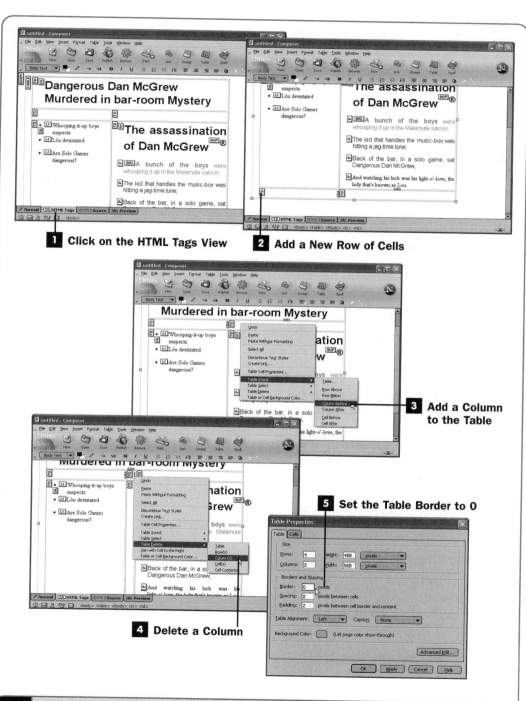

1 Click on the HTML Tags View

2 Add a New Row of Cells

3 Add a Column to the Table

5 Set the Table Border to 0

4 Delete a Column

55

55 Edit a Table

1 Click on the HTML Tags View

Note that there are now tags on the page that constitute the table. The outer-most **<table>** tag is just inside the **<body>** tag and represents the boundary of the table. Inside the table there are **<td>** tags for each cell. There is one **<th>** for the first cell, which indicates that it is a table header—a specialized sort of table cell that **Composer** adds by default.

2 Add a New Row of Cells

Click on the last **<p>** tag in the lower-right cell and press the Tab key. Maybe you're starting with a truly empty table. Place a **<p>** and **</p>** pairing in a cell.

When you press the tab at the end of a table rather than adding a space in the line, a new row of cells is added to the bottom of the table. This is the quickest way to add cells to a table and makes it easy to create a table that might be too small to start and then add as you need to every time that you get to the bottom of the table.

3 Add a Column to the Table

Click in an empty cell of the table. Right-click and select **Column Before** from **Table Insert** on the context menu.

A new column is added to the table before the cell you selected. Notice that the cell at the top that you have merged into one cell is not affected by your adding a new column.

4 Delete a Column

Click in the new column you just added, and then right-click and select **Column(s)** from **Table Delete** on the context menu.

The column you just added has been deleted. You can delete columns, rows, cells, the entire table, and the contents of cells at one time.

5 Set the Table Border to 0

Click anywhere in the table, and then right-click and select **Table Cell Properties** on the context menu. From the **Table** tab, set the border to 0 and click OK. This will cause the cell border to disappear, preserving your page layout without distracting lines.

Now that you have an idea of how tables work, you can hide the table border and start using tables as a layout tool. You'll notice that there is now a red border around the table cells. This is just a visual cue for you to know where the borders of the table cells are, but it won't show up on the page when you view it in the browser.

55

56 Use Horizontal Rules

✔ **BEFORE YOU BEGIN**

6 About Proper HTML Coding

For the most part, you don't need to use horizontal rules in your page if you learn to use paragraph styles and tables well. Having a break between two paragraphs with appropriate heading styles is the best way to separate two ideas. If you do need to use horizontal rules, though, you can easily do so in **Composer**.

1 Select Horizontal Line from the Insert Menu

Horizontal lines make important information stand out. One very important piece of content is the headline. Let's review horizontal lines by adding one after a headline. Click at the end of the headline in the first cell of the table and select **Horizontal Line** from the **Insert** menu.

A horizontal line has been added to the page directly below the headline.

2 Configure the Horizontal Line

The **Horizontal Line Properties** dialog box comes up. From here, you can set the width of the line, the height of the line, and set it to align left, center, or right. Feeling adventuresome? Try the 3D property for added effect.

There is no way to change a horizontal line into a vertical line in **HTML**.

56

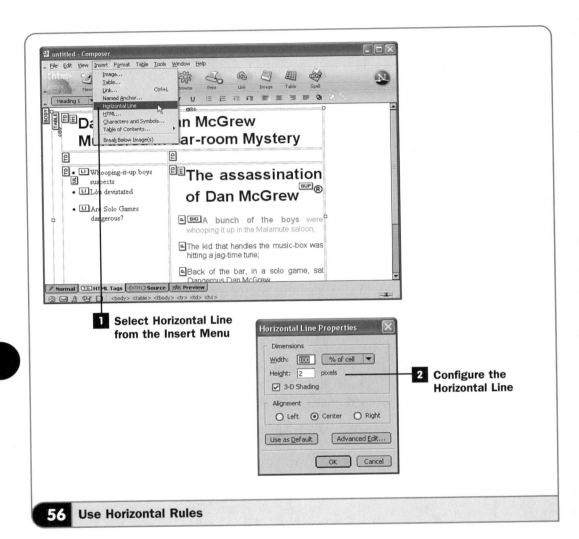

1 Select Horizontal Line from the Insert Menu

2 Configure the Horizontal Line

56 Use Horizontal Rules

10

Add Pictures, Video, Sound, and Special Effects to Your Website

IN THIS CHAPTER:

You have the tools to create basic web pages in **Netscape**. In this chapter, you are going to learn how to insert sounds, moving images (including **Flash** animations), and video into your pages. For the most part, your content should stand by itself and not need all the bells and whistles; but if the bells and whistles are the content you are trying to show off on your page (such as videos or songs) you'll need to know how to use them.

There are a lot of media file choices you can make for your site, but we won't cover all of them here because they change every month. The basic media types, though, are GIF and JPEG images; **animated GIF** files; **Flash** animations; **QuickTime** and **Windows Media Player** movies; and MP3, **Real Audio**, and **WAV** sound files.

GIF and JPEG (or JPG) files account, for all intents and purposes, for all the still pictures on the Web. **GIF** files are mainly used for images that need hard edges and have few colors (such as buttons and cartoons), whereas **JPEG** files are generally used for photographs and images without hard edges. In general, both image formats will work for most things, and most applications you use for graphics will produce either format. Try both sorts of images and stick with the format you like until you find a reason to use the other.

Animated GIF files are simply sets of **GIF** images that are played in sequence one after another like frames in a film. **Animated GIFs** are generally very short and small in area in the browser, because each frame of the animation adds download time. **GIF** animations don't have any sound.

Flash files are very slick animations that use a number of components, like sound and pictures. These animations can be programmed to have complex behaviors such as being able to link to other programs like a database. In other words, with **Flash** files, you have more than dancing penguins; you have a full-featured language that can make your website visually impressive and completely responsive to customer needs for information. **Flash** animations are created in **Macromedia Flash** or are generated at online services. To view a **Flash** animation, your viewers must have the **Flash plug-in** in their browsers. This is rarely a problem, though, because about 98% of browsers have the plug-in installed.

Apple QuickTime and **Microsoft Windows Media Player** are plug-ins that enable your viewers to view full-motion video on your page. Creating **QuickTime** or **Windows Media Player** video requires using one of many authoring tools, or bringing in video from a digital video or camera that can create **QuickTime** or **Windows Media Player** files. Your viewers will need to have either the **QuickTime** or **Windows Media Player** applications installed on their machines to view the videos.

MP3, **RealAudio**, and **WAV** sound files can be embedded into your pages or you can link to them. Sound files such as video clips can be very large, so you want to use them sparingly or have links to them so that you can let people choose to listen or not.

Whatever you do to add media to your pages, be judicious. The more you add to the page, the larger it gets, the longer it takes to download the page, and the more distracting it can become to the viewer. When you design, try to remember that you have to balance the cool stuff with your viewers' ability to wait for it to download and to tolerate your taste.

57 Add a Picture to Your Page

✔ BEFORE YOU BEGIN	→ SEE ALSO
25 Add Text and Graphics to the Page	**63** Add an Animated GIF to Your Page

In earlier tasks, you added images to your page. In this lesson, you are going to learn a little more about the way graphics files work, and what makes good graphics and what might not be as useful.

57

1 Select an Image

With the target page open in **Composer**, select **Image** from the **Insert** menu and click on the **Choose File** button to locate an image to insert.

The name of the image is placed in the **Image Location** area of the **Location** tab on the **Image Properties** dialog box. Below the filename is a check box marked **URL Is Relative to Page Location**. This check box tells **Composer** where the image file is located relative to the HTML file. If you uncheck the box, the full pathname to the file is added instead, which you do not want.

The **Tooltip** area enables you to add a short text that will appear on the browser screen if the user holds her cursor over the image. The **Alternate text** area enables you to add descriptive text for the image that is read by screen readers for the vision-impaired.

At the bottom of the dialog box is a small preview of the image with the height and width of the image.

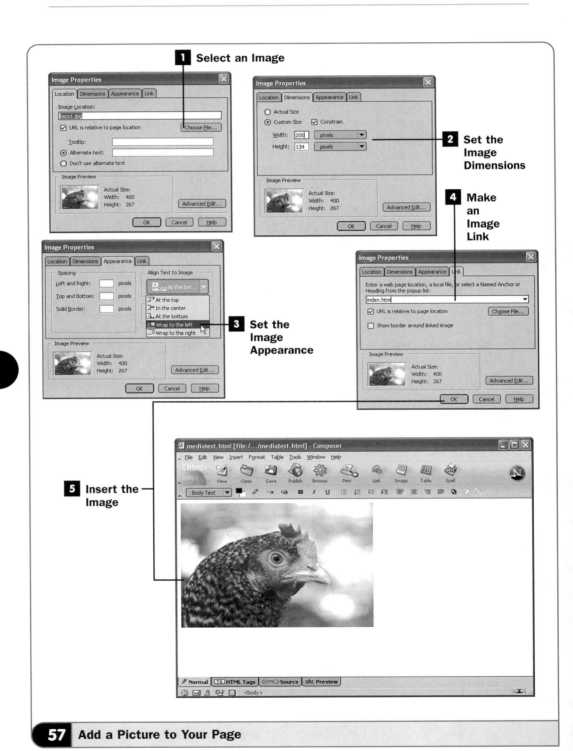

1 Select an Image

2 Set the Image Dimensions

3 Set the Image Appearance

4 Make an Image Link

5 Insert the Image

57

57 Add a Picture to Your Page

2 Set the Image Dimensions

Click on the **Dimensions** tab of the **Image Properties** dialog box.

In the **Dimensions** tab, you can set the size of the image. Setting the size of the image enables you to place an image that may be larger than you want it to appear in the browser. When you set the height and width, you will probably want to set the **Constrain** check box so that when you type in the size for one dimension, the other dimension will resize correspondingly. If you don't set the **Constrain** check box, the image will appear stretched.

3 Set the Image Appearance

Click on the **Appearance** tab of the **Image Properties** dialog box and set the image to align at the top in the **Align Text to Image** dialog box.

In the **Appearance** tab, you can set the spacing around the picture if you want to keep space between the image and the text that abuts the picture. In the **Align Text to Image** drop-down box, you can set the picture to align at the top of the line of text where it appears, in the center of the line of text, at the bottom of the line of text, or to wrap to the left or to the right.

Select the **Wrap to the Left** choice to allow the picture to be at the right of a block of text.

57

4 Make an Image a Link

Click on the **Link** tab of the **Image Properties** dialog box.

In the **Link** tab of the dialog box, you can set a link for the image so that when someone clicks on the image, it will behave just like a text link and go to another page. When you set an image as a link, usually it defaults to having a blue border around the image to indicate there is a link, which detracts from your layout. To remove the blue border, be sure that the **Show Border Around Linked Image** check box is unchecked—by default, it should be checked off in Composer.

5 Insert the Image

Click **OK** to insert the image into the page.

After you have inserted the image into the page, you can always get back to the **Image Properties** dialog box to change any of the attributes of the image.

▶ **TIP**

Use images carefully. Too many images that are too large are visually distracting, especially when they are set off by bright borders. Look at websites that work—and those that don't work. Work to create a flow between your words and your images such that nothing looks out of place.

---

58 | **Add Pictures to Tables**

✔ **BEFORE YOU BEGIN**	→ **SEE ALSO**
25 Add Text and Graphics to the Page	**52** Insert a Table
	55 Edit a Table
	57 Add a Picture to Your Page

58

After you have added a picture in **Composer**, you run into the same problems some have with the **Yahoo! PageBuilder**, a tool we cover in another chapter. The images added to the page are going to align with the text as though they are big letters in the flow of the paragraph. For some applications such as a newspaper or a magazine with text and pictures, images in these applications are going to be fine. However, if you want to create an album of photos or you want to present a number of images with captions, you probably will want to have absolute alignment over your images.

1 **Insert a Table**

Got a table handy for this task? If so, great. If not, let's add one. On the new line, insert a table with three columns and three rows. Make sure the border is set to **0** and the width of the table to **100%**.

Inserting a table gives you a way to create a grid for your page so that you can lay out anything you want, including pictures.

2 **Drag an Image into the Table**

Drag an image to the first cell of the table. By now, you should have a handy toolkit of images. If not, copy an image from a website.

The table resizes to fit the picture a little better.

3 **Enter a Caption**

Click in a cell next to the image and enter a caption for your image.

The table resizes as you type in the cell. If you want to lock down the table, you can do so with the table properties.

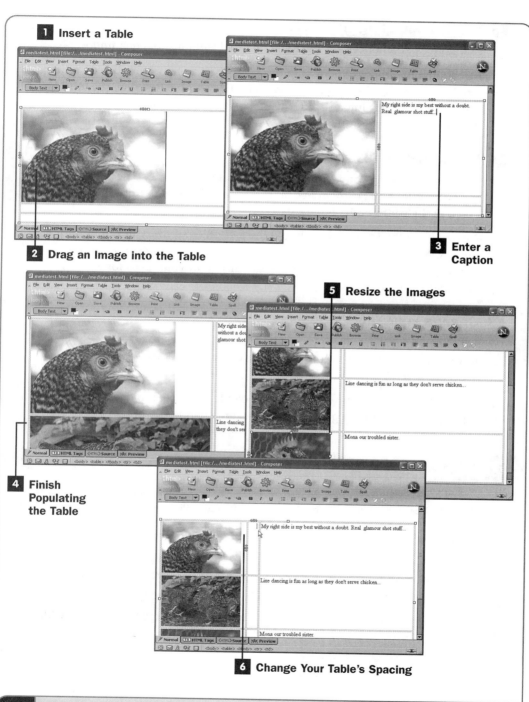

1 Insert a Table

2 Drag an Image into the Table

3 Enter a Caption

5 Resize the Images

58

4 Finish Populating the Table

6 Change Your Table's Spacing

58 Add Pictures to Tables

4 Finish Populating the Table

Add images to other cells in the table and add captions for each image.

As you add the images and text to the page, the table is going to keep resizing. If you have added an image that is larger than the first one, the table will resize to fit that image even if you have used the table attributes to set the width of the cells or the table.

5 Resize the Images

Click on each image and, while holding down the **Shift** key, click on the **resize handle** in the corner of each image and resize them until they take up much of the width of the table.

As you resize the images, you should see the table redraw again to fit the images. Now the text takes up most of the width of the table in response. Continue trying this and see how tables resize to fit your ideas for what is good placement and sizing.

6 Change your Table's Spacing

Redo the table so that the images and captions are separated by a column. Click in the column between the pictures and the captions—and press the spacebar several times.

As you add spaces to the center cell, the captions and the images are separated by a gutter to give the page a more open feel.

---

59 | Align Images Without Tables

✔ BEFORE YOU BEGIN	→ SEE ALSO
25 Add Text and Graphics to the Page	**57** Add a Picture to Your Page

---

Aligning images without using tables is more difficult and you are limited to what you can do with the built-in alignment commands.

To see how this works, you need to have an image and a large block of text with which to work.

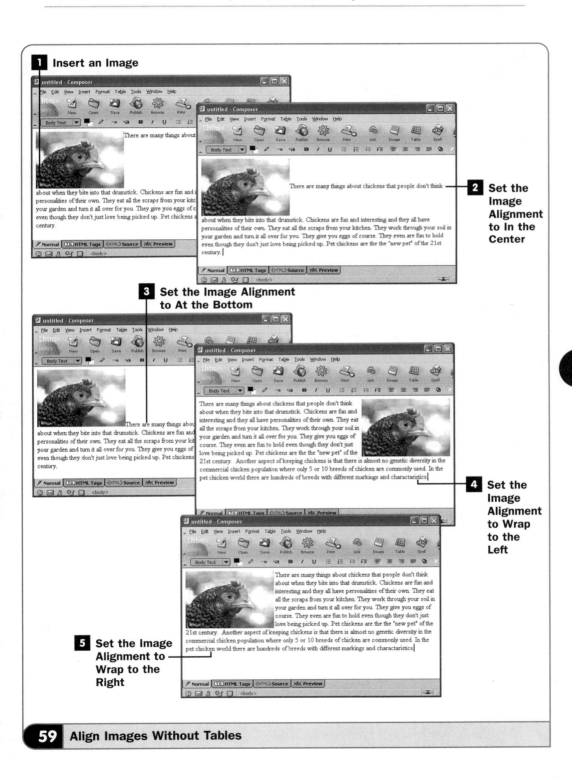

1 Insert an Image

2 Set the Image Alignment to In the Center

3 Set the Image Alignment to At the Bottom

4 Set the Image Alignment to Wrap to the Left

5 Set the Image Alignment to Wrap to the Right

59

59 Align Images Without Tables

1 Insert an Image

Insert one of your images into a page. In the **Image Properties** dialog box, when you insert the image, set the **Align Text to Image** on the **Appearance** tab to **At the Top**, click **OK**, and add a block of text.

The top of the image aligns with the top of the first line of text of the text block.

2 Set the Image Alignment to In the Center

Double click on the image and, in the **Image Properties** dialog box, set the **Align Text to Image** on the **Appearance** tab to **In the Center** and then click **OK**.

The vertical middle of the image aligns with the middle of the first line of text of the text block.

3 Set the Image Alignment to At the Bottom

Double-click on the image and, in the **Image Properties** dialog box, set the **Align Text to Image** on the **Appearance** tab to **At the Bottom** and then click **OK**.

The bottom of the image aligns with the bottom of the first line of text of the text block.

4 Set the Image Alignment to Wrap to the Left

The image now aligns to the left edge of the window and the text flows around the image.

5 Set the Image Alignment to Wrap to the Right

Double-click on the image and, in the **Image Properties** dialog box, set the **Align Text to Image** on the **Appearance** tab to **Wrap to the Right** and then click **OK**.

The image now aligns to the right edge of the window and the text flows around the image.

60 Add a Flash Animation to Your Page

✔ BEFORE YOU BEGIN	→ SEE ALSO
25 Add Text and Graphics to the Page	**57** Add a Picture to Your Page

Flash, as I mentioned before, is a really slick tool to add multimedia to your pages. You can build any animation you can imagine with video, audio, images, scripting, and even interactions with databases. Talking about how to create new **Flash** files is the subject of many other books; you might have even created some **Flash** files of your own. In this chapter, you are going to create a set of **Flash** navigation buttons, with an online service, and then insert the buttons into your page.

1 Open a Page and Go to http://www.FlashButtons.com

Open a page and open another browser window (**http://www.FlashButtons.com**).

FlashButtons.com is a site where you can use its servers to produce **Flash** buttons for your site. Like **GeoCities**, you can use the **FlashButtons** service for free by allowing it to show a small advertisement for its service on the menu, or you can subscribe to the service and not have any advertising.

60

2 Create a Navigation Bar at FlashButtons

Follow the instructions on **FlashButtons** to create a navigation bar. There are many templates to choose from. I selected **High Spy** for my button. Choose one that fits your fancy. Enter a name for each button and a link to the name of the page to which you want it to link. In the **Number of Buttons Per Line** text area, select the number of buttons for which you entered names and then click on the button marked **Click Here to Generate Your Free Navbar!**. On the next page, click on **Free Download** and save the file to the same location your page is in.

As you go through the process of creating your navigation bar, you can experiment with other styles and colors. You might also want to set the background color for the navigation bar to match the background of your site.

3 Copy the Navigation Bar Code

When **FlashButtons** takes all your choices and entries you have made and writes them to a Flash file, it writes the **HTML** code that you need to access the file to paste into your own page.

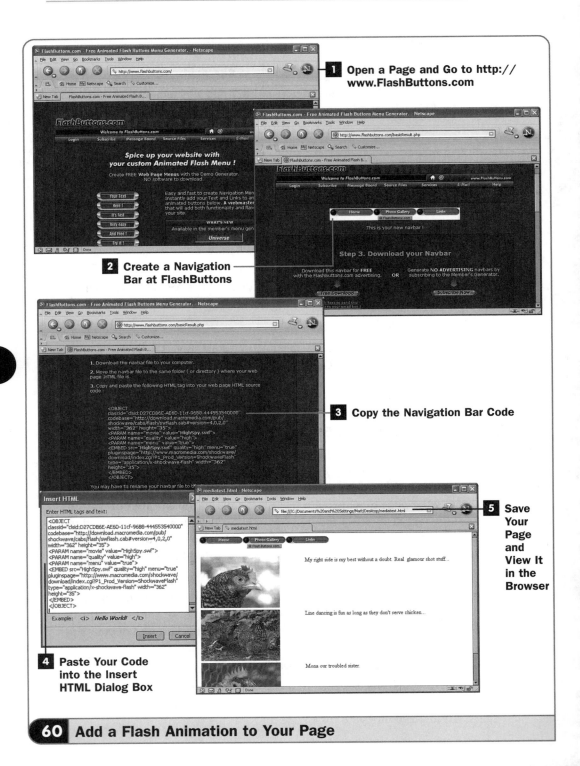

1 Open a Page and Go to http://www.FlashButtons.com

2 Create a Navigation Bar at FlashButtons

3 Copy the Navigation Bar Code

5 Save Your Page and View It in the Browser

4 Paste Your Code into the Insert HTML Dialog Box

60

60   Add a Flash Animation to Your Page

Scroll down the **FlashButtons** page to the block of code in step three on the page. Copy the code to your clipboard.

In my case, the **HTML** code looks like this:

```
<OBJECT classid="clsid:D27CDB6E-AE6D-11cf-96B8-444553540000" code-
base=
"http://download.macromedia.com/pub/
shockwave/cabs/flash/swflash.cab#version=4,0,2,0" width="362"
height="35">
<PARAM name="movie" value="HighSpy.swf">
<PARAM name="quality" value="high">
<PARAM name="menu" value="true">
<EMBED src="HighSpy.swf" quality="high" menu="true" pluginspage=
"http://www.macromedia.com/shockwave/
download/index.cgi?P1_Prod_Version=ShockwaveFlash" type=
"application/x-shockwave-flash" width="362" height="35">
</EMBED>
</OBJECT>
```

This is fairly complicated **HTML** code and it uses a few tags that you haven't seen. Good thing you don't have to worry about doing it by hand yourself.

60

4 Paste Your Code into the Insert HTML Dialog Box

In your **Composer** page, click where you want the navigation buttons to appear, select **HTML Code** from the **Insert** menu, paste your code into the **Insert HTML** dialog box, and press the **Insert** button.

Even though you can't see the inserted code and there is no real preview of the navigation bar in the page as you work in **Composer**, it will work when downloaded from your web server.

5 Save Your Page and View It in the Browser

Save your page and browse to it. Let's look at the navigation bar.

FlashButtons has its small advertisement there on the page below the menus. Some don't like to embed advertisements into their web pages. If you like the menu, you can always pay for the service and then regenerate the navigation bar without the advertisement.

Got problems? Browsers have a **view source** option among their menus. Compare the source coming from your web page with the source provided with your **Flash** button bar. Typos? Missing elements? Any small mistake can make big errors happen.

61 Add a Video to Your Page

✔ BEFORE YOU BEGIN	→ SEE ALSO
25 Add Text and Graphics to the Page	**57** Add a Picture to Your Page
	60 Add a Flash Animation to Your Page

Adding video to your page is much like adding a Flash animation to your page. You need to have a video source, like the **QuickTime** file that I took with my digital camera, and you need to use <OBJECT> and <EMBED> tags. However, you have to code the tags by hand.

For this task, you need to have the **QuickTime** plug-in installed in your browser and a **QuickTime** file that you can use from some source. If you don't have **QuickTime** installed, you can download it from **http://www.quicktime.com**.

You should also know how large the file is in height and width. If you need to get a **QuickTime** file, you can search on the Web for sites that have free video clips.

In this task, I am using a file called **biggirls.mov** (ahem…no…this is a movie of my chickens running around). You will need to find or save a movie of your own.

61

▶ **TIP**

There are a lot of resources on the Web for **QuickTime**. One of the better ones is obviously **Apple** itself. Try going to **http://www.quicktime.com**, and you will find many tutorials on all aspects of authoring and displaying **QuickTime**.

1 Add a Row of Cells to Your Table

Open one of your web pages in **Composer**, and press the **Tab** key to create a new row of cells. Click in the new last cell you just created and select **HTML Code** from the **Insert** menu.

2 Add the Code to Insert a QuickTime Movie

Click in the **HTML** window and type in the following information. (Where there is italics in this code, change the information for your own **QuickTime** file.)

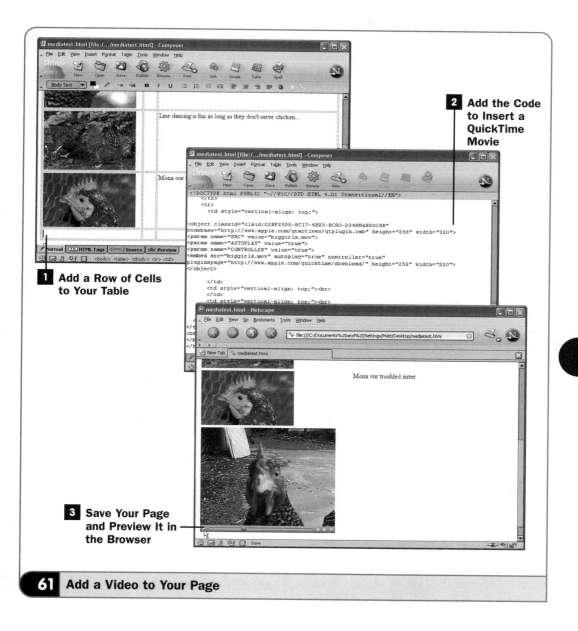

2 Add the Code to Insert a QuickTime Movie

1 Add a Row of Cells to Your Table

3 Save Your Page and Preview It in the Browser

61 Add a Video to Your Page

```
<object classid="clsid:02BF25D5-8C17-4B23-BC80-D3488ABDDC6B"
codebase="http://www.apple.com/qtactivex/qtplugin.cab"
height="256" width="320">
<param name="SRC" value="biggirls.mov">
<param name="AUTOPLAY" value="true">
<param name="CONTROLLER" value="true">
```

```
<embed src="biggirls.mov" autoplay="true" controller="true"
pluginspage="http://www.apple.com/quicktime/download/"
height="256" width="320">
</object>
```

This is the code for **<OBJECT>** and **<EMBED>** tags to show **QuickTime** on your page. You need to type it in exactly as it is here except for the height and width of the movie and the name. Remember that when you have the **<OBJECT>** and **<EMBED>** tags nested, you need to have the information in both tags, so the height, width, and source have to be entered twice.

You might want to experiment with turning the controller off so that the little controller bar is not visible. To do this, simply find the two locations where **"controller"** appears and set the value to **"false"** in both cases.

If you want the controller to be visible, you will need to increase the height 16 pixels more than the height of your movie. If you want to remove the controller, you will need to decrease the height of the movie by 16 pixels.

If you want the movie not to play when the page loads but to wait for some user interaction, find the two locations where **"Autoplay"** appears and change the values to **"false"**.

62

❸ Save Your Page and Preview It in the Browser

After you save your file in **Composer**, select the **Preview** tab. As before, compare the source with the content typed previously. Any small difference can make a large error in your results.

---

62 Add Sounds to Your Page

✔ BEFORE YOU BEGIN	→ SEE ALSO
25 Add Text and Graphics to the Page	**57** Add a Picture to Your Page
	60 Add a Flash Animation to Your Page
	61 Add a Video to Your Page

Adding sounds to your page can be done a few different ways. For the most part, there are sounds that you can play when the page opens at load time. Other sounds can be played when you link to them.

There are loads of sites with music on them on the Web. A quick search should find several sites with free sounds to download and use for this task. I am using a file called **klaxon.wav** as an example.

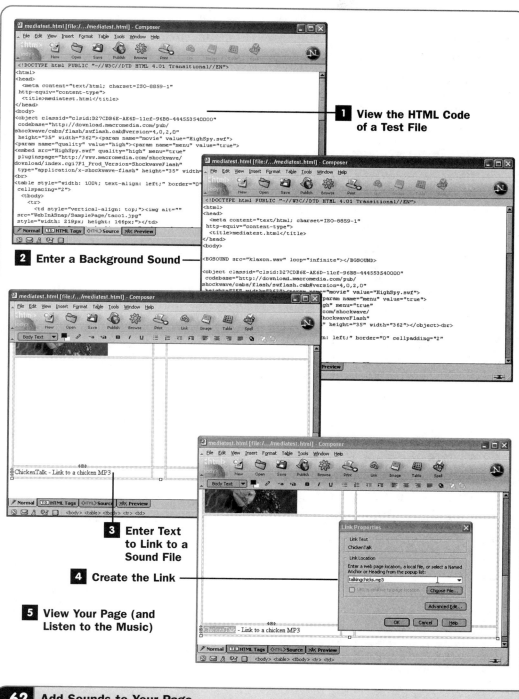

1 View the HTML Code of a Test File

2 Enter a Background Sound

3 Enter Text to Link to a Sound File

4 Create the Link

5 View Your Page (and Listen to the Music)

62

1 View the HTML Code of a Test File

Open a test page, put your cursor at the beginning of the page and select **HTML Code** from the **Insert** menu.

2 Enter a Background Sound

In the text area, add the following code and press **OK**. I am using **klaxon.wav**. Be sure to type your sound file's name in its place.

```
<BGSOUND src="klaxon.wav" loop="infinite">
```

The **<BGSOUND>** tag sets a background sound for the page when it loads. The **SRC** attribute points to a sound file for the tag to use. Setting the loop to **"infinite"** means that the clip is going to play over and over. (I recommend against playing any sounds over and over, by the way....)

You can try this technique with either **WAV** files or **MP3** files.

You might want to note that the **<BGSOUND>** tag doesn't work on all browsers. Test this line with your favorite browser. If it doesn't work, search your browser's online help for information on this browser directive.

62

3 Enter Text to Link to a Sound File

Create a new row of cells in which to work. Click in the first cell of the new row and enter text to create a link to connect to a sound file.

Enter some text that you can use for a link. In my case, I am going to link to an **MP3** file of my chickens talking, typical inane celebrity gossip at that.

4 Create the Link

Highlight the text you just created and right-click on the text to select **Make Link** from the context menu.

In the **Link Properties** dialog box, enter the name of your sound file to which you want to link and click **OK**.

5 View Your Page (and Listen to the Music)

Save your file and preview it in a browser. As always, check your typing (and your sound volume levels). You might even want to double-click on the copy sound file that is on your PC. This will test whether the sound file is corrupted and whether this sound file format is supported by your technology.

63 Add an Animated GIF to Your Page

✔ BEFORE YOU BEGIN	→ SEE ALSO
25 Add Text and Graphics to the Page	**57** Add a Picture to Your Page **60** Add a Flash Animation to Your Page **61** Add a Video to Your Page

Animated **GIF** files are about the easiest thing on the Web to use. All you need to do is find a source for them or create new ones of your own and then insert them like a regular image file.

Be careful when you select animated **GIF** files because a lot of them are very cartoon-like and repeat over and over, which can become annoying to your viewer.

One great source of animated **GIF** files is **http://www.animationfactory.com**. If you do a search for free animated **GIFs**, you will find many more sites than you have time to check out.

1 Insert Your Animated GIF

Select **Image** from the **Insert** menu and click on the **Choose File** button to locate an image to insert. Select an image and click **OK**.

2 Resize the Image

Click on the image and, while holding down the **Shift** key, click on the **resize handle** in the corner of the image and resize it.

You can make any changes to an animated **GIF** as you would for a regular image.

3 Preview Your Page (and Animation)

Save your file and preview it in the browser.

63

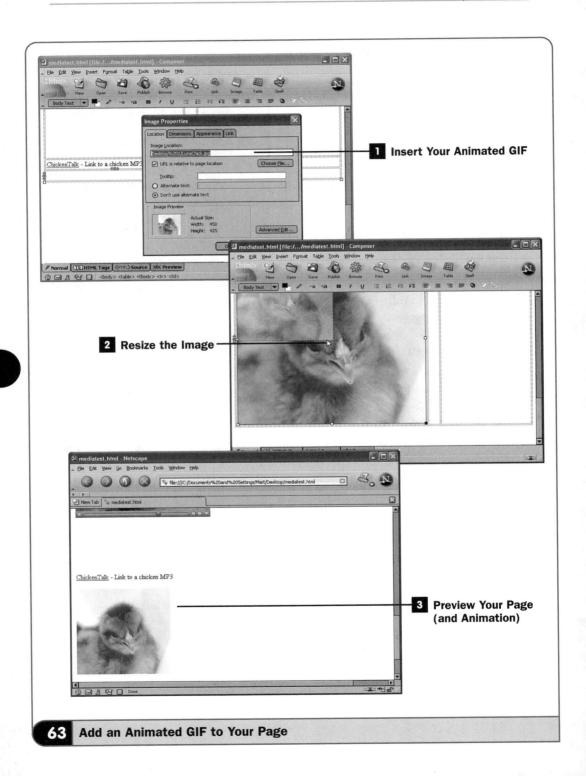

1 Insert Your Animated GIF

2 Resize the Image

3 Preview Your Page (and Animation)

63

63   Add an Animated GIF to Your Page

11

Build Web Forms

IN THIS CHAPTER:

You have seen forms everywhere you have been on the Web. If you have gone to a site that has a Search button on it, or visited a page and bought something, you have seen a form.

Communication from you to the viewer is easy—you know how to do that. Communication from your viewer to you, though, is where forms come in.

HTML uses forms to enable a viewer to enter information into a page and send it to you. Unfortunately, HTML only knows how to send information; it does not know how to capture that information on your side and do something with it so that you can actually use it. In this chapter, you will learn how to build forms and capture information viewers send to you. In this case, you will learn how to mail the contents of a form to yourself and how to create a response page for your viewer so that he knows the information he sent has gone somewhere.

▶ **TIP**

You will be creating a catalog form for ordering wine. You will notice that nowhere do we add a field for a credit card, and neither should you. Accepting credit cards is beyond the scope of this book. If you use the techniques we show you here for credit card information, your site is going to be vulnerable to security risks.

64

This form is designed for you to capture customer and order information for contacting the buyer. This is safe and serves as a way for you and your buyer to connect—it does not put any credit card information out over the Web.

64 About Forms

✔ **BEFORE YOU BEGIN**

🔳 6 About Proper HTML Coding

A **form** must have four things in HTML to do work:

- A <FORM> tag to enclose the elements of the form
- Form elements so that viewers can enter text or select from a set of choices
- Some way to tell the browser that the viewer is finished and ready to submit the form
- Some script or program on the server to capture the information the viewer has sent so that something can be done with it

To get an idea of how a form works, you are going to look at one and deconstruct it to see the different elements.

Open your browser and go to **http://www.ebay.com** and then click on **buy** from the menu along the top of the page.

You are probably familiar with **eBay.** To find what you want on a site where there are hundreds or thousands of pages changing every minute, you can either browse by category and go through a complicated tree of choices to find your Shaker ladder-back chair, or you can use the search function at the top of the page to look for your chair directly.

Type in **Shaker ladder-back chair** into the text area and click on the **Search** button.

Your results will look different each day because there are different sets of items for sale, but you will see that you have been given a list of chairs that are currently available.

To get here, you used a form that enclosed four form elements: the text area where you entered the search terms, a drop-down box that let you limit the search to a particular area of the site (such as furniture or antiques), a box that let you search in just the titles—the default—or in the titles and descriptions, and a **Search** button that submitted the information to the application that did the searches.

Each element has a tag. There are quite a few elements in HTML that you are able to use, but most are not used in every form. Those tags used will highlight interface properties like size and color and other options that will make the form stand out and be more useable.

65

---

65 **Create a Form**

✔ BEFORE YOU BEGIN	→ SEE ALSO
6 About Proper HTML Coding	**48** Use the HTML Views
	57 Add a Picture to Your Page

In this chapter, you are going to work in new pages. You can open existing ones, but for learning forms, there is a benefit to having little else on the page to cause confusion. Also, **Composer** doesn't have any tools to help you build forms, so you will have to do your first real hand-coding to add the forms to your page.

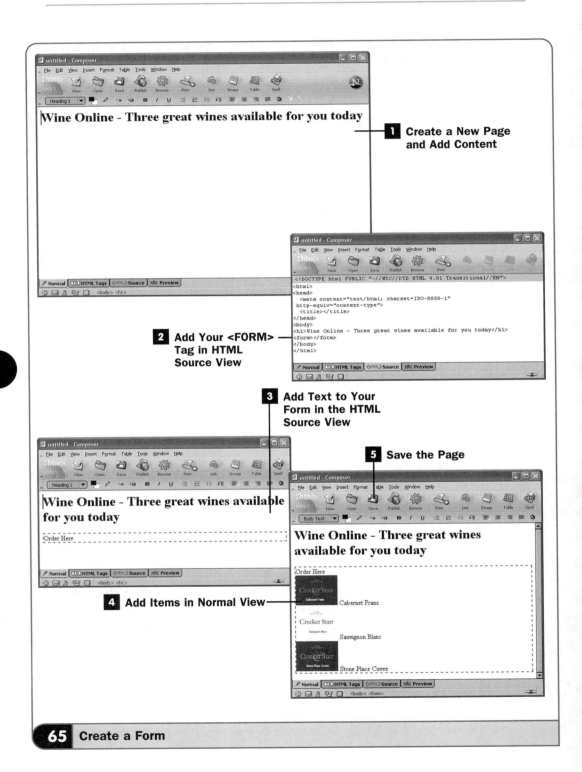

1 Create a New Page and Add Content

2 Add Your <FORM> Tag in HTML Source View

3 Add Text to Your Form in the HTML Source View

5 Save the Page

4 Add Items in Normal View

65

65 Create a Form

► **TIP**

We are going to build a small catalog form for a winery that enables the viewer to select the number of bottles of wine she wants and provide a shipping address and phone number so that we can call her back to get her payment information. You can build any sort of form you like, but the following examples are going to be wine related.

► **NOTE**

Remember, building a page that handles credit cards correctly and securely is beyond the scope of this book.

1 Create a New Page and Add Content

In **Composer**, create a new page and a headline so that you have some text on the page. Then set the text as **Heading 1** from the **Paragraph Format** choices in the **Format** toolbar and press **Return** to get a new line.

2 Add Your <FORM> Tag in HTML Source View

Click on the **<HTML> Source** tab to view the HTML for the page and then click in the line after the **<H1>** tag. Enter **<FORM></FORM>** to start and end your form.

Your code should look something like this:

```
<html>
<head>
<meta content="text/html; charset=ISO-8859-1"
http-equiv="content-type">
<title></title>
</head>
<body>
<h1>Wine Online - Three great wines available for you today</h1>
<form></form>
</body>
</html>
```

The beginning and end form tags contain your form markup and tell HTML where to look for form controls.

3 Add Text to Your Form in the HTML Source View

Click between **<FORM>** and **</FORM>** and type something (I typed **Order Here**) and then click on the **Normal** tab to view the page in the **Visual Editor**.

65

Note that the text you typed between the **<FORM>** and **</FORM>** tags is visible on the page and inside a dashed green box that shows you where the edges of the **HTML form** are.

Click on the **Normal** tab to view the page in the **Visual Editor**.

4 Add Items in Normal View

Click after the text you typed in step 3 and add other items as you wish. (I added a couple of images and pressed **Return** after each image to create two or three images one above the other. This will be my catalog of items for sale. I also added some text for each item and then clicked back on the **<HTML> Source** tab.)

This gives you the basics you need for the catalog. You have three things to buy and descriptions of each. In the **HTML Source** view, you can see the link for each picture where you see the image tag, **<IMG>**, and the descriptive text after each image.

5 Save the Page

Save the page. You now have the basic form and some items in the form, but you need to have form elements for the buttons and text you are going to capture. You will do that in the next task. But before you do, please select the **Preview** tab. This will give you a halfway error point check on all your typing. If you see HTML tags being displayed, you've mistyped something or have a missing end tag. I've been known to forget to slash my tags—that is, slash as in /.

---

66 Add Components to the Form

✔ **BEFORE YOU BEGIN**	→ **SEE ALSO**
6 About Proper HTML Coding	**48** Use the HTML Views
65 Create a Form	

Now you are going to add the elements to the form you created. I'm going to let the user specify how many bottles of wine she wants in my example. I'll also need to give the viewer a place to add her address so she will finally have the ability to send in her address and telephone numbers.

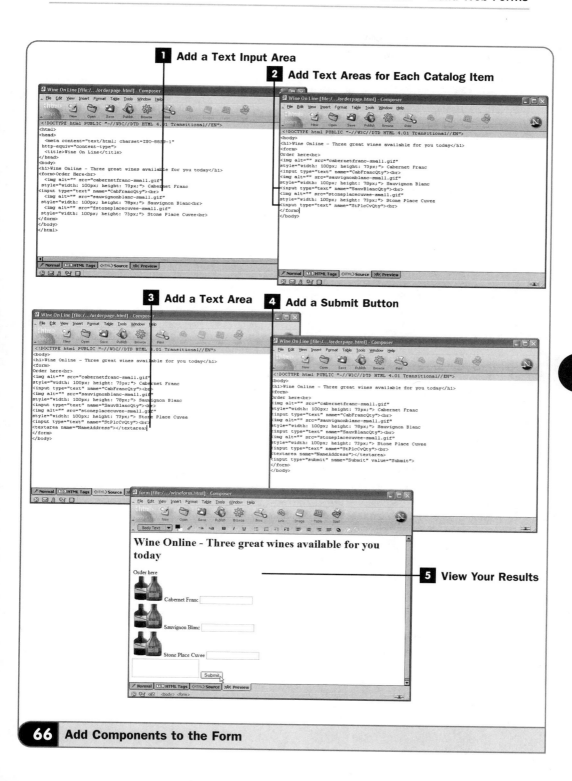

1 Add a Text Input Area

2 Add Text Areas for Each Catalog Item

3 Add a Text Area

4 Add a Submit Button

5 View Your Results

66

66 Add Components to the Form

1 Add a Text Input Area

Look at the **HTML Source View** and click after the description of the first item. We need to use a special word to represent this piece of information we will collect from the customer. I enter the following HTML code:

<input type="text" name="*CabFrancQty*">

This code adds a text input area to the form so that the viewer is able to enter the number of bottles of wine she wants. The type of the input being set to **"text"** tells HTML that the input area is a one-line entry box for text. Why did I use **CabFrancQty**? Why that's shorthand for Cabernet French wine bottle Quantity. I could have simply used **CheapStuff** (given my love of all things California), but remember: On all web pages, anything you type is viewable to the customer. You should type a nice name for the bottle quantity.

2 Add Text Areas for Each Catalog Item

Add text areas for the remaining items after each description.

The body of your code should look similar to this (the bold code is the portion you have added for the form):

```
<body>
<h1>Wine Online - Three great wines available for you today</h1>
<form>
Order here<br>
<img alt="" src="cabernetfranc-small.gif"
style="width: 100px; height: 73px;"> Cabernet Franc
<input type="text" name="CabFrancQty"><br>
<img alt="" src="sauvignonblanc-small.gif"
style="width: 100px; height: 78px;"> Sauvignon Blanc
<input type="text" name="SauvBlancQty"><br>
<img alt="" src="stoneplacecuvee-small.gif"
style="width: 100px; height: 73px;"> Stone Place Cuvee
<input type="text" name="StPlcCvQty"><br>
</form>
</body>
```

I want to let the users enter their addresses and phone numbers, so I'm going to add another form element.

3 Add a Text Area

Just before the end tag of the form, **</form>**, add a **text area**, which is different from a **text field** because it enables the user to add multiple lines of text instead of just one line. Add the following HTML code:

<textarea name="NameAddress"></textarea>

I chose the name for this information to be **NameAddress** so as to suggest what information I expect. In my previous example, I used a fancy name, made up of several words. It's also quite acceptable to use a simple name, something you're likely to remember a year later when you update the website.

▶ **TIP**

Names that are too complex or too simple can make website maintenance painful.

The body of the code should look something like this (the highlighted code is the portion you have added for the form):

```
<body>
<h1>Wine Online - Three great wines available for you today</h1>
<form>
Order here<br>
<img alt="" src="cabernetfranc-small.gif"
style="width: 100px; height: 73px;"> Cabernet Franc
<input type="text" name="CabFrancQty"><br>
<img alt="" src="sauvignonblanc-small.gif"
style="width: 100px; height: 78px;"> Sauvignon Blanc
<input type="text" name="SauvBlancQty"><br>
<img alt="" src="stoneplacecuvee-small.gif"
style="width: 100px; height: 73px;"> Stone Place Cuvee
<input type="text" name="StPlcCvQty"><br>
<textarea name="NameAddress"></textarea>
</form>
</body>
```

66

4 Add a Submit Button

Add the **Submit** button to the form so that the viewer can send the form. Just after the **textarea** end tag, add a **Submit** button. Add the following HTML code:

<input type="submit" name="Submit" value="Submit">

The body of the code should look something like this (the highlighted code is the portion you have added for the form):

```
<body>
<h1>Wine Online - Three great wines available for you today</h1>
<form>
Order here<br>
<img alt="" src="cabernetfranc-small.gif"
style="width: 100px; height: 73px;"> Cabernet Franc
<input type="text" name="CabFrancQty"><br>
<img alt="" src="sauvignonblanc-small.gif"
style="width: 100px; height: 78px;"> Sauvignon Blanc
<input type="text" name="SauvBlancQty"><br>
<img alt="" src="stoneplacecuvee-small.gif"
style="width: 100px; height: 73px;"> Stone Place Cuvee
<input type="text" name="StPlcCvQty"><br>
<textarea name="NameAddress"></textarea>
<input type="submit" name="Submit" value="Submit">
</form>
</body>
```

66

There are a load of other elements you could add, but this is a good start.

This completes most of the form. However, there is one more thing we need to do: which is to Add an *action*, which is a link to some service either on your own server or someone else's server that captures the content of the form and does something.

5 View Your Results

If the typing has gone well, you will see a beautiful form that has adequate text input boxes and a nice submit button. It is very important you review your results. One typo can ruin your form. Do you see any text in the form that shouldn't be there? That can indicate an extra carriage return has broken your HTML. Instead of interpreting the text as a closing tag, for example, the browser now interprets your half tag as text you want to display.

Also, review your graphics. In my example, I leave my graphics too wide to be readable. Also, I've used the same graphic for all three different types of wine. It's best that your quality review finds these problems early—before the customer!

Once you are satisfied with the results and have an accurate rendering of a form in HTML, it's time to move on and code what you want the form to do.

67 About FormBuddy

✔ **BEFORE YOU BEGIN**

6 About Proper HTML Coding

To process forms, you need to have a **form processor**. There are a number of ways to access one. Most professional sites use heavy-duty databases and application servers such as **ASP.NET**, **PHP**, and **ColdFusion**. You can also use scripts written in **Perl**. Both sets of alternatives are beyond the scope of this book because you need to be able to program in the different languages, which are much more complex than HTML. So, you are going to use one of the alternatives—a third-party form processor called **FormBuddy**, which is free but supported by placing ads on the page with your form.

In your browser, go to **http://www.formbuddy.com**. **FormBuddy.com** has a very good explanation of the service on the front page. From here you have options to sign up, view the **FAQs**, or get instructions to add FormBuddy to your site.

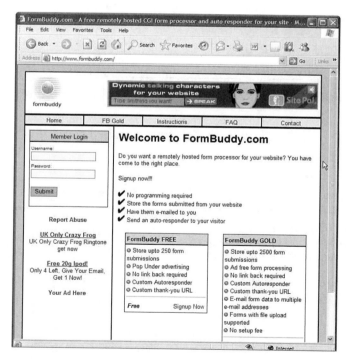

The FormBuddy front page.

We are going to set up the service in the next task.

67

The instructions on using **FormBuddy** fit on the first half of one single page. After you sign up for the service, you are going to copy this code and paste it into your page to enable the form to handle the data in the form.

The **FAQ** is very useful and, if you decide to use the service, it explains how to upgrade to the **FormBuddy Gold** service if you would like to eliminate the advertising that **FormBuddy's** free service adds to the page.

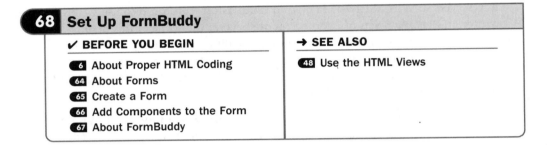

68 **Set Up FormBuddy**

✔ **BEFORE YOU BEGIN**

    6 About Proper HTML Coding
    64 About Forms
    65 Create a Form
    66 Add Components to the Form
    67 About FormBuddy

→ **SEE ALSO**

    48 Use the HTML Views

68

After you read the FAQs and instructions for FormBuddy, all you have to do is sign up for the service and follow the directions that are given.

1 Sign Up for FormBuddy

Sign up for **FormBuddy** by clicking on the option link you'd like to use. I am selecting the **Free** option. Read through the terms and then click on **I Agree**.

In the **User Registration** screen, enter your email address, click on the **Submit** button, and a confirmation email will be sent to you.

2 Confirm Your FormBuddy Account Registration

To confirm your registration, you have to click on the link sent in the email so that **FormBuddy** can figure out that you are a real person signing up for the service with an address and not an automatic service of some sort. Check the email account that you registered and click on the link to FormBuddy.com.

3 Set the Form Settings

Fill in the form and be sure to set the URL to your site correctly. For me, that would be **http://www.geocities.com/tacothechook**. You also have the choice of leaving the data on the server or emailing the data from the form to you. Select to have it emailed to you. You can always change that later if you want.

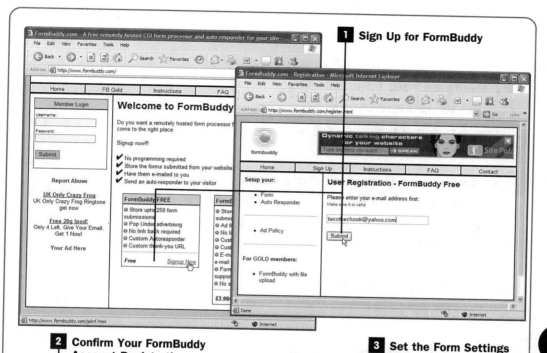

1 Sign Up for FormBuddy

2 Confirm Your FormBuddy Account Registration

3 Set the Form Settings

68

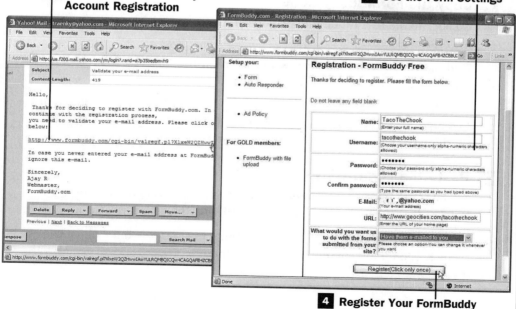

4 Register Your FormBuddy Settings

68 Set Up FormBuddy

For **FormBuddy** to work you have to have the same **URL** in the form as you have in the registration and that has to be the location where the page resides.

4 Register Your FormBuddy Settings

Click on the **Register** button.

Now **FormBuddy** is set up for you on the server and is ready to go.

---

69 Modify Your Form for FormBuddy

✔ BEFORE YOU BEGIN	→ SEE ALSO
6 About Proper HTML Coding 68 Set Up FormBuddy	48 Use the HTML Views

---

With **FormBuddy** ready and you all registered, you need to enter that information into the markup for the form that you are building so that it works when it is uploaded.

69

1 Copy the FormBuddy Code

Go back to the **FormBuddy** home page and click on the **Instructions** link on the right side of the page.

Find the **Your Form Must Start with the Following Lines of Code** section. Select the lines of code below the section and copy them.

FormBuddy uses the three hidden input tags to keep track of your data and to send it back to you, so it has to be entered exactly as it is here with your username and your **URL** entered in the appropriate places.

2 Paste the FormBuddy Code

In your form page in **Composer**, find the beginning <FORM> tag and highlight it. Then paste the text from the **FormBuddy** page that you just copied.

The body of your code should look something like this (the highlighted code is the portion that you pasted from **FormBuddy**):

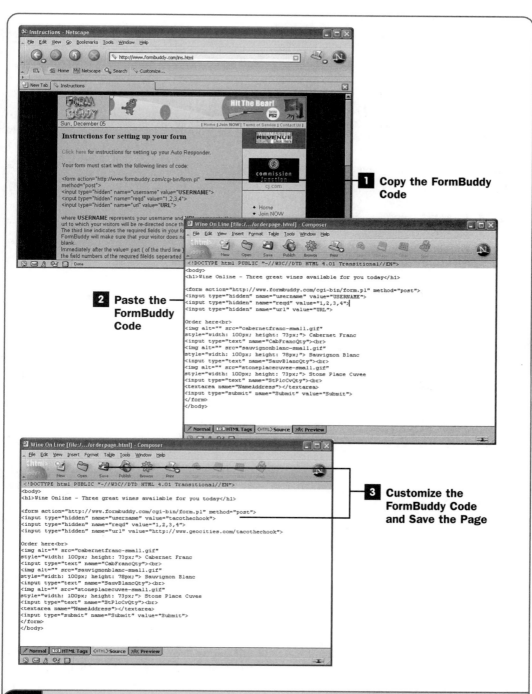

1 Copy the FormBuddy Code

2 Paste the FormBuddy Code

3 Customize the FormBuddy Code and Save the Page

69

69 Modify Your Form for FormBuddy

```
<body>
<h1>Wine Online - Three great wines available for you today</h1>

<form action="http://www.formbuddy.com/cgi-bin/form.pl"
method="post">
<input type="hidden" name="username" value="USERNAME">
<input type="hidden" name="reqd" value="1,2,3,4">
<input type="hidden" name="url" value="URL">

Order here<br>
<img alt="" src="cabernetfranc-small.gif"
style="width: 100px; height: 73px;"> Cabernet Franc <input
name="CabFrancQty" type="text"><br>
<img alt="" src="sauvignonblanc-small.gif"
style="width: 100px; height: 78px;"> Sauvignon Blanc <input
name="SauvBlancQty" type="text"><br>
<img alt="" src="stoneplacecuvee-small.gif"
style="width: 100px; height: 73px;"> Stone Place Cuvee <input
name="StPlcCvQty" type="text"><br>
<textarea name="NameAddress"></textarea><input name="Submit"
value="Submit" type="submit"></form>
</body>
```

70

3 Customize the FormBuddy Code and Save the Page

In the **FormBuddy** code on your page, change the **URL** to your own URL and
the **username** to the username you registered with **FormBuddy**. Be sure to
save the page.

My code for **FormBuddy** looks like this:

```
<form action="http://www.formbuddy.com/cgi-bin/form.pl"
method="post">
<input type="hidden" name="username" value="tacothechook">
<input type="hidden" name="reqd" value="1,2,3,4">
<input type="hidden" name="url" value="http://www.geocities.com/
tacothechook">
```

70 Set Up an Autoresponder

✔ BEFORE YOU BEGIN	→ SEE ALSO
6 About Proper HTML Coding	**68** Set Up FormBuddy
	69 Modify Your Form for FormBuddy

Your form is set to accept the input from the visitor to the site. You have the server at **FormBuddy** set to email the information to you. You have to upload the page to test it, which you are going to do in Chapter 12, "Publish Your Site." You have one more thing to do, though. You need to set up the **autoresponder** at **FormBuddy** so that your user will know you got the data from him. No one likes to have his email go off into a black hole. Once set up, the **autoresponder** will send an email to the address saved in the email text input field.

1 Enter a Text Area

Go to the **HTML Source View** of your page and find the end of the form tag, **</form>**. Add a break tag **
** and enter a **textarea** tag pair for your visitor's email.

The body of your code should look like this (the highlighted code is the portion that you need to add in this step):

```
<body>
<h1>Wine Online - Three great wines available for you today</h1>

<form action="http://www.formbuddy.com/cgi-bin/form.pl"
method="post">
<input type="hidden" name="username" value="tacothechook">
<input type="hidden" name="reqd" value="1,2,3,4">
<input type="hidden" name="url" value="http://www.geocities.com/
tacothechook">

Order here<br>
<img alt="" src="cabernetfranc-small.gif"
style="width: 100px; height: 73px;"> Cabernet Franc <input
name="CabFrancQty" type="text"><br>
<img alt="" src="sauvignonblanc-small.gif"
style="width: 100px; height: 78px;"> Sauvignon Blanc <input
name="SauvBlancQty" type="text"><br>
<img alt="" src="stoneplacecuvee-small.gif"
style="width: 100px; height: 73px;"> Stone Place Cuvee <input
name="StPlcCvQty" type="text"><br>
<textarea name="NameAddress"></textarea><input name="Submit"
value="Submit" type="submit">

<br>
<input type="text" name="e-mail"> E-mail address

</form>
</body>
```

70

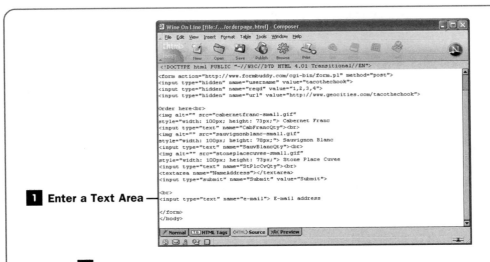

1 Enter a Text Area

2 Activate the Autoresponder
on the FormBuddy Page

70

3 Add a Subject and
Message for the
Autoresponder

4 Save Your File

70 Set Up an Autoresponder

2 Activate the Autoresponder on the FormBuddy Page

Save your page, go to the home page for **FormBuddy** in your browser, and log in to your account with your **username** and **password**. On the **Member Home Page**, click on the **Auto Responder** link on the menu on the left.

3 Add a Subject and Message for the Autoresponder

Enter a subject for the **autoresponder** email and, below that, type in a message that you want to send to the viewer.

This is the email that is going to go back to the user, so you want to thank him for his order or input, and give him some way to contact you if there is an issue.

4 Save Your File

Your page will now have a form so that your viewer can order from you or send input to you, and you have an **autoresponder** to send him a thank-you message. To view the form live, you need to upload it to your site and browse to it. You will cover that in Chapter 12.

70

12

Publish Your Site

IN THIS CHAPTER:

After you have built your pages in Composer, you need to upload the pages to your server. Composer uses a process called *File Transfer Protocol (FTP)* to move files across the Internet to your website. FTP is like HTTP, the protocol you use to browse and view web pages, but instead of enabling you to view pages, it lets you move files from your machine to a machine in a remote location over the Internet.

▶ **TIP**

Some free web servers (such as GeoCities) don't allow you to use FTP because it is part of the premium service. If you bought the premium service from GeoCities, you will be able to upload your files from Composer to your site without any trouble. If you are using the free service discussed in Chapter 4, "Getting Started Building Web Pages on GeoCities," you are going to have to use the GeoCities **File Manager** to upload your files or you are going to have to upgrade your account to one of the premium accounts at GeoCities. FTP is common, though, so knowing how it works will help you down the road.

71 Configure the Settings to Publish Your Site

✔ BEFORE YOU BEGIN	→ SEE ALSO
37 Use the File Manager	**36** Preview and Use the Easy Upload

71

Using **FTP** requires that you have an exact address on the Internet where you are supposed to send your files. You need to get this from your service provider. When you log into the support page, there is usually an entry in the FAQ that gives you all the information and even step-by-step instructions on how to set up different programs to use FTP to manipulate your site. In my case, I have upgraded my GeoCities registration to GeoCities Pro, which enables me to upload files via FTP.

Once upgraded, there is a link on the GeoCities home page to your FTP settings in the right column when you log in to your account.

In my case, the host is **ftp.geocities.com**, my username is **tacothechook**, and my password is whatever I used as my password when I originally set up the account.

The FTP settings for any site can be used in any program to connect with that server, so you don't need to use a GeoCities program such as **File Manager** to connect to your GeoCities site. You can use **Netscape Composer**, **Macromedia Dreamweaver**, **HomeSite**, **Microsoft FrontPage**, an FTP-only program such as **SmartFTP**, or even **Microsoft Internet Explorer** to upload your files to your website.

1 Write Down Your FTP Settings

Get your FTP settings from your service provider and write them down where you are going to remember them and have them ready.

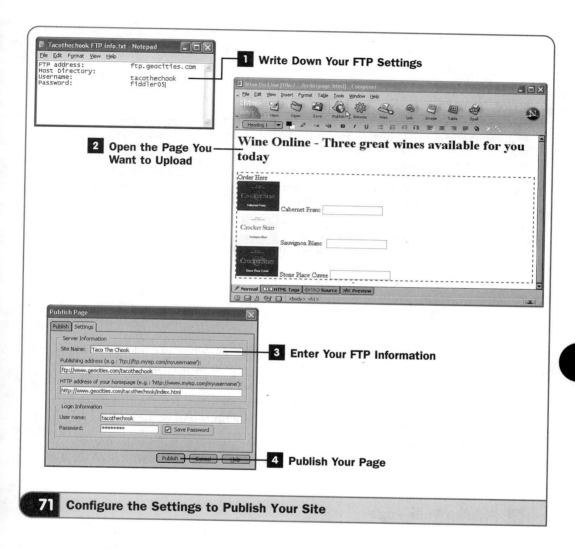

1 Write Down Your FTP Settings

2 Open the Page You Want to Upload

3 Enter Your FTP Information

4 Publish Your Page

71 Configure the Settings to Publish Your Site

2 Open the Page You Want to Upload

Open the page you want to upload and click on the Publish button on the Composition toolbar.

The Publish Page dialog box comes up on the Publish tab. You are going to use that in the next task. Click on the Settings tab.

3 Enter Your FTP Information

In the Site Name box, enter an easy name that will help you differentiate this site from others you create. In the Publishing Address box, enter the address of the *FTP* server. In the HTTP Address of Your Homepage box, enter the web address of your site. In the Login Information section, enter your username and password.

▶ KEY TERM

FTP—File Transfer Protocol is a web protocol much like HTTP (*Hypertext Transfer Protocol*) that moves information around the Web. The difference between the two is that HTTP opens a connection between the server and the browser, downloads the information (like a web page), and then closes the connection so that other browsers can access the server. FTP creates a connection and then leaves that connection open for a time to allow files to move to and from the server. This forces the server to focus on fewer dedicated connections at one time than on an HTTP server.

A simple example is a bartender (HTTP) who takes orders and delivers drinks, and then goes on to take another order, and so on. An FTP server is more like a barber who focuses on one thing until it is done and then accepts another customer.

The Site Name box is just plain language for "your site," so that in a list of several, you are easily able to pick the one you want without having to dig through a bunch of long addresses or cryptic names. You can call the site anything you want in this text box.

72

The Publishing Address box is where you enter the actual FTP address of your server. You can see an example in the dialog box in which the site is preceded by ftp:// (so my address, for example, would be **ftp://www.geocities.com/ tacothechook**). If you get an error when you publish, this is the first place to look to see whether you might have missed the ftp:// part of the address.

The HTTP Address of Your Homepage section is where you enter the home page of your site. In my case, that is **http://www.geocities.com/ tacothechook/index.html**.

■4 Publish Your Page

Click the **Upload** button. This uploads the page you are working on to the server address you specified. You are going to do more uploading in the next task, but you need to publish right now to save the settings for your FTP site.

---

72 Publish Your Page

✔ BEFORE YOU BEGIN	→ SEE ALSO
37 Use the File Manager	**36** Preview and Use the Easy Upload
71 Configure the Settings to Publish Your Site	

Setting up your FTP settings in the last task forced you to upload the file you were viewing at the time. You will upload the same file again in this task, but you'll use the **Publish** tab of the **Publish Page** dialog box, where you will get options on what you specifically want to upload and be able to choose from all the sites you have set up.

◼1 Click on the Publish Button on the Composition Toolbar

To start the publishing process from your page, click on the **Publish** button on the **Composition** toolbar.

◼2 Select the Site to Which You Want to Publish

Click on the drop-down list in the Site Name box and select the site to which you want to publish.

As you work on more and more sites or on only one part of a site, you can create as many sites as you like without having to type in all the details for each one every time.

▶ TIP

When you have larger sites you are working on, it can save you a lot of time and organization if you create "subsites" for each part of the site. For example, if you are creating a site for a winery, you might have a site that goes directly to the products folder of the website so that you don't accidentally change something in the calendar or administration areas of the site. If you have several folders for the different areas of the site, you are going to have several **index.html** pages, as well. If you keep the sites for each area separate, you are going to run less risk of overwriting one index file with the wrong one from a different folder.

72

◼3 Assign Titles and Filenames

Your title and filename should show up in the next two boxes.

You can assign new titles and filenames as you upload the files. If you have forgotten to add a title to your pages, you'll want to include one because some search engines use the title of the page to help rank pages in searches and to get information on what is on the page.

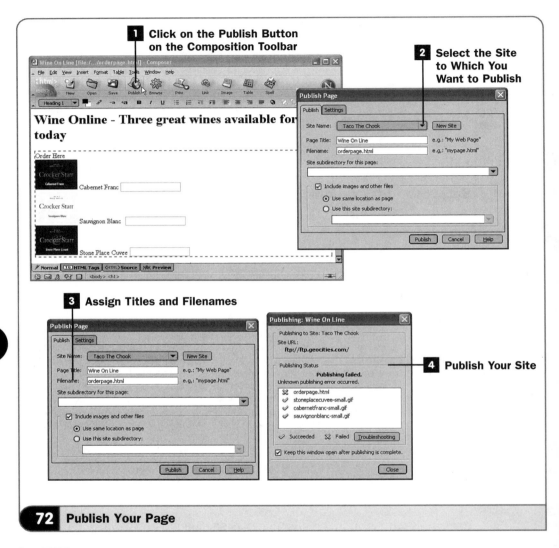

1 Click on the Publish Button on the Composition Toolbar

2 Select the Site to Which You Want to Publish

3 Assign Titles and Filenames

4 Publish Your Site

72 Publish Your Page

▶ TIP

Search engines and how they work is the topic of more than one entire book. One thing you can do to help your page get higher ratings is to title your pages with some content rather than just saying "hello." For instance, if you title your page "Welcome," you are going to appear with about 155,000,000 (just Googled to check that...) other websites. Instead, try to name your pages with a little information. So instead of **Welcome to Taco the Chook** on your home page, you might want to say, **Extraordinary Chickens in California—Taco the Chook,** which might give the search engines more to go on, and will give the viewer search results more information.

If you want to read more on search engines and how to make your pages more friendly toward them, you might want to check out *Search Engine Visibility* by Shari Thurow, published by New Riders.

Renaming the page as you upload works exactly like Save As does in the file menu except the file is saved to the remote file server.

The Site Subdirectory for This Page drop-down list lets you specify a directory on your site for the page to be loaded into. You add subdirectories to your site when you want to organize your page so that there is a separate part of your web address for each part. For instance, you might have a section of your site for products you sell. For that section, you would create a subdirectory on your site and in it you would put another index.html file so that the address for the Products part of your site would be something like **http://www.mysite.com/products** instead of **http://www.mysite.com/productspage.html**, which is harder to tell people over the phone and more difficult to remember.

The final section enables you to upload any images you might have on your page at the same time as the HTML file itself. When you insert a graphic into a page, you are really adding a link to the graphic and that graphic has to be on the site as well as the HTML page. If you upload them all at the same time, you will avoid problems such as forgetting all graphics you might have used—not that I have ever done that....

4 Publish Your Site

73

Click on the Publish button to begin the publishing process.

When you publish your pages, you get a dialog box that tells you which files uploaded and which didn't. When you are using a busy server, sometimes some files don't make it to the server, so checking this dialog box will tell you whether you need to upload files again.

---

73 Validate Your Site

✔ BEFORE YOU BEGIN	→ SEE ALSO
17 Organize Your Site's Content	**33** Use the HTML Editor
71 Configure the Settings to Publish Your Site	**48** Use the HTML Views
72 Publish Your Page	**51** Spell Check the Document

After you have your pages uploaded, you might think you are done, but you have one more important step. Web pages are not that difficult for the most part, but there are a few things that make them "break" that you'll want to catch right away. Doing a quick quality assurance test will ensure your pages are doing what you expect them to do.

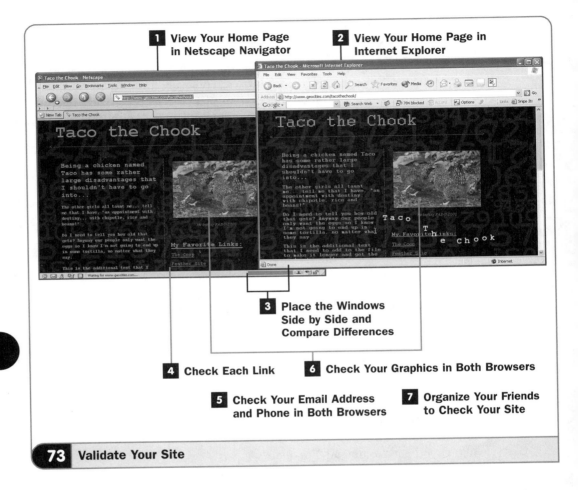

1 View Your Home Page in Netscape Navigator

2 View Your Home Page in Internet Explorer

3 Place the Windows Side by Side and Compare Differences

4 Check Each Link

6 Check Your Graphics in Both Browsers

5 Check Your Email Address and Phone in Both Browsers

7 Organize Your Friends to Check Your Site

73 Validate Your Site

73

We covered checking your page for misspellings earlier in Chapter 8, "Work with Text." The only thing that might be worse than misspelled words on your page is links to pages and graphics that are not in the right places in your site or that you have forgotten to upload.

Another thing you'll want to do is check your page in more than one web browser to see that the page looks the same or at least looks equally good in different browsers. Remember there are more browsers out there than the one or two that you like to use and they do not all display things the same way. Someone using **Netscape Navigator** on a Macintosh is probably going to have a different view of a page than someone using **Microsoft Internet Explorer** on Windows. Although you can't always make them the same, you can check to at least ensure that each user will have a similar experience, and that you will not have things on your page that work in only one browser.

Although it has been popular to author for one browser or another and then label the site as "**best viewed in whatever browser**," try to author for all the browsers you can. Usually, issues are pretty easy to fix after you know they exist.

■1 View Your Home Page in Netscape Navigator

Open **Netscape** and go to your site at your server and view your home page.

■2 View Your Home Page in Internet Explorer

Open **Internet Explorer** and go to your site at your server and view your home page.

■3 Place the Windows Side by Side and Compare Differences

Place the two windows side by side and notice the differences. As you move your cursor around in the **Internet Explorer** version of the page, you get the Yahoo! GeoCities banner that follows the cursor around. I added that to the page in the Yahoo! **PageBuilder**. In the **Netscape** page, there is no banner that follows the cursor like in **Internet Explorer**. The page is the same code, but the cursor-following banner is an **ActiveX control** that works in one browser and not in another.

You also notice the type looks different between the two browsers. In **Netscape**, the type for the body looks slightly smaller than it does in **Internet Explorer**. The headline "**Taco the Chook**" is quite different between the two browsers. The reason for the difference is that the code for the text has a typeface set in **Courier**, which is the name of the font on some machines; however, some machines have **Courier New** and not **Courier** installed. Small difference, but Netscape knows how to display the font when the exact font is not available. However, **Internet Explorer** doesn't know to try **Courier New** when it can't find **Courier** on the viewer's machine.

(To find the difference for yourself, go to the page in **Composer** and view the HTML source view. Check the top of the page and see what the font is set to in the source code. You can change the font by typing in the exact font name in the code where it says **Typeface = "Courier"** and changing that to **Typeface = "Courier New"** and resaving the file.)

When you check pages, you can find problems such as this early or at least know they are there before one of your site visitors points out the differences to you.

73

4 Check Each Link

In either **Internet Explorer** or **Netscape** (or your other favorite browser), click on the links under **My Favorite Links** one by one and make sure each goes to the correct site.

Links on the Web "rot" over time, which means that you might initially be able to link to pages, but over time, people who own those sites might stop working on them or change their web addresses, or the computers that host the files go down for some reason. You'll want to check your site every once in a while to be sure the links work.

5 Check Your Email Address and Phone in Both Browsers

In both browsers, scroll down and make sure your email address is correct. If you have a business, you might want to double-check the phone number you have on your page as well. No point in a business website if no one can reach you!

6 Check Your Graphics in Both Browsers

73

In both browsers, check that all your graphics are on the page and that they look as you intend them to look.

If the graphics were not uploaded with the page, you'll see a blank box with a red X in the corner in **Internet Explorer**, and a blank box with a small, multicolored icon in **Netscape**.

7 Organize Your Friends to Check Your Site

The final test after doing your own quality assurance is to ask a few of your friends to give the site a look. Invariably, people will find problems with your site, so getting your friends to look at the page before you call it "done" will almost always uncover a problem or two that you didn't catch.

PART IV

Manipulate Images and Share Them Online

IN THIS CHAPTER

13

The Basics of Using Photos and Graphics

IN THIS CHAPTER:

The Web is, above all, a visual medium. So when you build web pages, you'll need some way to get photos and graphics for your pages.

It's easy to get them into your PC using Windows XP. Whether you want to take pictures with a digital camera and import them into XP or use a scanner to get your prints into XP, it's easy to do. And you can also easily capture screenshots from your PC as well.

Not all graphics are suitable for the Web, though. So you'll also learn in this chapter how to make your pictures web friendly.

---

74 | Import Photos from a Digital Camera

✔ BEFORE YOU BEGIN	→ SEE ALSO
Just jump right in.	**77** Convert Between Image Formats
	78 Change Photo Resolution and Size
	139 Set Up and Take a Picture

74

Windows XP makes it extremely easy to import photos from a digital camera into your PC. Before you can import the photos, of course, you must first install the camera so that it works with your PC, and install the camera's software, if it has any. To do that, follow the camera's instructions.

In this task, you'll learn how to import photos into your PC using XP's built-in software. Many digital cameras also include software that lets you import photos, so you can instead use that software to do it. The quality of the camera's software varies widely, though, so you might want to use XP's built-in software instead of the software that ships with your camera.

1 Connect the Camera to Your Computer

Before you can transfer pictures to your PC, you must connect the camera to your computer. Unless you have a very old digital camera, connect it to the USB port and install it according to the camera's directions. After you've installed the camera, even after you disconnect it from the USB port, XP will automatically recognize the camera the next time you plug it in.

2 Run the Scanner and Camera Wizard

When you plug your camera into the USB port of your PC, the **Scanner and Camera Wizard** might start up automatically. If it doesn't, you can force the wizard to run by clicking the **Start** button, choosing **Control Panel**, choosing **Printers and Other Hardware**, selecting **Scanners and Cameras**, and then double-clicking the icon of your camera, such as the **Fujifilm FinePix A210**.

1 Connect the Camera to Your Computer

2 Run the Camera and Scanner Wizard

3 Choose the Pictures You Want to Copy

4 Choose a Destination and Name for Your Pictures

5 Copy the Pictures

6 Order Prints or Publish the Pictures Online

7 Work with the Pictures

74 Import Photos from a Digital Camera

The first screen of the wizard appears, telling you that the wizard is running. Click **Next**.

3 Choose the Pictures You Want to Copy

A screen appears, displaying all the pictures on your camera. There will be check marks in small boxes on the upper-right corner of each picture. When there is a check next to a picture, it means that you want to copy that picture to your PC. Uncheck any pictures that you don't want copied, and make sure that there are checks next to each picture that you do want to copy.

When you've selected all the pictures you want to copy, click **Next**.

4 Choose a Destination and Name for Your Pictures

The **Picture Name and Destination** page of the wizard appears. From here you will choose the folder where you want to copy the pictures and provide a base name for the pictures.

74

▶ **TIP**

By default, the photographs are placed in your **My Pictures** folder. If you want to place them in a different location, click the **Browse** button, choose the new location, and click **OK**.

You can also give your group of pictures a name. When you give the pictures a name, two things happen. First, a folder is created underneath the destination folder you chose. For example, if you store pictures in your **My Pictures** folder, and you give the pictures the name **Spring 04**, a new folder called **Spring 04** is created underneath your **My Pictures** folder and the pictures are stored in that new folder. Additionally, all the pictures are given the name **Spring 04**, and then ordered sequentially; for example, **Spring 04 001.jpg**, **Spring 04 002.jpg**, and so on.

▶ **TIP**

You have the option of copying the pictures from the camera to your PC and leaving them on the camera, or deleting the pictures from your camera after you copy them. To delete them after you copy them, enable the **Delete Pictures from My Device After Copying Them** check box. If the box isn't enabled, the pictures are not deleted from the camera after you copy them.

5 Copy the Pictures

Click **Next** when you've chosen a folder and name. The wizard now copies the pictures from your camera to your PC and shows you the progress as the pictures are copied.

6 Order Prints or Publish the Pictures Online

After the pictures are copied to your PC, the wizard gives you three options:

- Publish these pictures to a website.

- Order prints of these pictures from a photo-printing website.

- Nothing. I'm finished working with these pictures.

If you choose one of the first two options—publishing the pictures to a website or ordering prints from a photo-printing site—click **Next** and a new wizard will launch. You can first choose which of the pictures you want to publish or have developed from a photo-printing website.

▶ **NOTE**

If you've chosen to publish the pictures to a website, you'll be given a choice of a number of sites on which you can publish the pictures, and you then follow the wizard's instructions for publishing them. If you've chosen to order prints, you'll be given a choice of sites from which to order your prints, and can then follow the wizard's instructions for ordering prints.

7 Work with the Pictures

74

The last option offered by the wizard, the **Nothing** option, is confusing because it makes it sound as if after the pictures are copied, there's nothing you can do with them any longer. That is not the case, however. You can now view the pictures on your PC and use them in the same way you can use any other picture: by printing them, sending them to family and friends as email attachments, using them in newsletters, and so on. When you select the **Nothing** option and click **Next**, the final screen of the **Scanner and Camera Wizard** appears. On that screen, there is a link to the folder that contains your pictures—for example, **My Pictures\Spring 04**. If you want to immediately view and work with your pictures, click that link. If you want to work with the images later, click **Finish**. When you want to work with the images, open Windows Explorer and go to the folder, in this instance, **My Pictures\Spring 04**.

You can now work with the pictures as you can with any others. For more information about working with pictures, see **77 Convert Between Image Formats** and **78 Change Photo Resolution and Size**.

75   Scan In Photos

✔ BEFORE YOU BEGIN	→ SEE ALSO
Just jump right in.	**77** Convert Between Image Formats
	78 Change Photo Resolution and Size
	140 Use the Web to Get a Digital Picture

Scanning pictures with Windows XP is as easy as importing pictures with a digital camera. As with a camera, before you can scan pictures, you must first install the scanner so that it works with your PC, and install the scanner's software, if it has any. To do that, follow the scanner's instructions.

In this task, you'll learn how to scan pictures into your PC using Windows XP's built-in software. Many scanners also include software that lets you import scanned images, so you can instead use that software to do it. The quality of the software that comes with scanners varies widely, though, so you might want to use XP's built-in software instead of the software that ships with your scanner.

75

1   Connect the Scanner to Your Computer

Before you can scan pictures into your PC, you must connect the scanner to your computer. Unless you have a very old scanner, connect it to the USB port. After you've installed the scanner, even if you disconnect it from the USB port, Windows XP will automatically recognize the scanner the next time you plug it in.

2   Run the Scanner and Camera Wizard

When you plug your scanner into the USB port of your PC, the **Scanner and Camera Wizard** might start up automatically. If it doesn't, you can force the wizard to run by clicking the **Start** button, choosing **Control Panel**, choosing **Printers and Other Hardware**, selecting **Scanners and Cameras**, and then double-clicking the icon of your scanner, such as the **Hewlett-Packard ScanJet 4100C**.

The first wizard screen appears, telling you that the wizard is running. Click **Next**.

3   Select Your Scanning Preferences

The **Choose Scanning Preferences** screen appears, letting you choose whether you are scanning a color picture, a *grayscale picture*, or a black-and-white picture or text. Enable the button next to the option that best applies to the image you want to scan.

▶ KEY TERM

Grayscale picture—A black-and-white picture that has gradations of gray in it.

4 Preview Your Picture

Before actually performing the scan, you'll want to get a sense of its quality before proceeding. Click the **Preview** button, and the scanner will scan the picture and show you a preview of what the picture will look like.

If you're scanning a picture that is much smaller than the size of the scanner's image area, it might appear very small when you preview it. You can see a close-up of the picture by clicking the **Enlarge** button—the one just to the right of the **Preview** button. To see the picture in its normal size, click on the button to the right of it.

5 Customize Your Scanner Settings

If the preview looks too dim, too bright, does not have contrast, is fuzzy, or has some other problem with it, you can customize the scan settings. Click the **Custom Settings** button to open the **Advanced Properties** dialog box. From here you can change the brightness and contrast of the image, and change its resolution, which is measured in dots per inch (dpi). The higher the dpi, the higher the quality of the image (and the larger the picture file). The maximum dpi you can choose is determined by your scanner's capabilities.

Use the sliders to change the **Brightness** and **Contrast**, and the up and down arrows to change the **Resolution** (dpi). You can also change the **Picture Type** by selecting color, black-and-white, or grayscale from the drop-down list. As you make the changes, the sample image on the screen changes, so that you can see how your customizations will affect the picture.

▶ NOTE

As you make changes in the **Advanced Properties** dialog box, you'll see the effect your changes have on a sample image—a picture of daisies—not on your actual photo.

When you're done, click **OK**. You'll be sent back to the screen where you can preview your scan. Click the **Preview** button again to see how your scan will look. Click the **Custom Settings** button again if you're not yet happy with your scan, make changes, and preview the picture again. Keep doing this until you're satisfied with the scan. When you're satisfied with the preview, click **Next**.

75

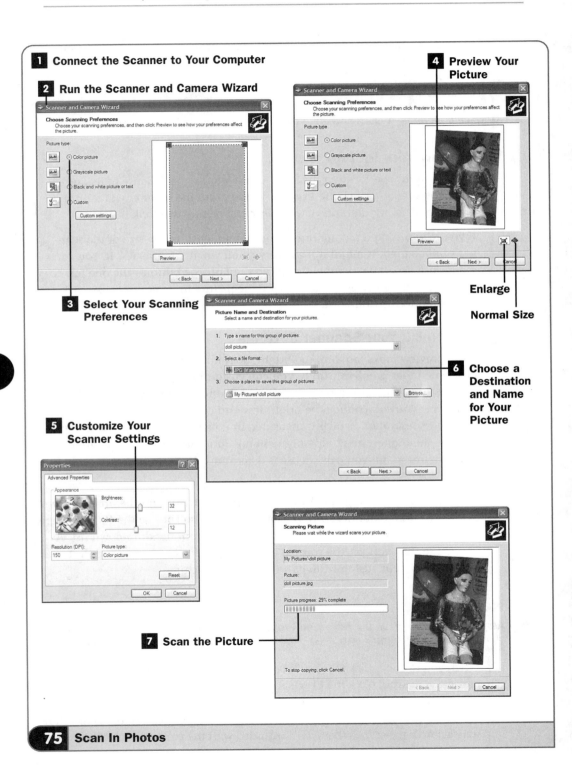

1 Connect the Scanner to Your Computer

4 Preview Your Picture

2 Run the Scanner and Camera Wizard

Enlarge

Normal Size

3 Select Your Scanning Preferences

6 Choose a Destination and Name for Your Picture

5 Customize Your Scanner Settings

7 Scan the Picture

75 Scan In Photos

6 Choose a Destination and Name for Your Picture

The **Picture Name and Destination** page of the wizard appears. From here you can name the picture and choose the folder where you want to store it.

▶ **TIP**

By default, the picture is placed in your **My Pictures** folder. If you want to place it in a different location, click the **Browse** button, choose the new location, and click **OK.**

You will also give your picture a name. When you give it a name, two things happen. First, a folder is created underneath the destination folder you chose. For example, if you store pictures in your **My Pictures** folder, and you give the pictures the name **doll picture**, a new folder called **doll picture** is created underneath your **My Pictures** folder, and your picture is stored in that new folder. Additionally, the picture is given the name **doll picture.jpg**.

7 Scan the Picture

Click **Next** when you've chosen a folder and name. The picture is now scanned, and you'll see the progress as the picture is scanned.

After the picture is scanned, the steps involved in using your pictures are exactly as described in steps 6 and 7 of **74** **Import Photos from a Digital Camera**, so turn to those steps for more details about how to work with your pictures after they're scanned in.

76

76 Capture a Screenshot

✔ BEFORE YOU BEGIN	→ SEE ALSO
Just jump right in.	**77** Convert Between Image Formats

If you need to capture a screen from your PC and use it on a web page, XP includes only a very primitive, awkward tool. To do it in XP, first press **Shift+Print Scrn**. That action captures the entire screen to the Windows XP Clipboard. Then you can open a graphics program such as Paint. (To open Paint, click the **Start** button, choose **All Programs, Accessories, Paint.**) When Paint opens, paste the screen from the Clipboard into it by choosing **Edit, Paste** from the menu. Now that the screen is in Paint, you can save it.

There are several problems with this process, though. When you save a screen this way, you can only save the *entire* screen—you can't save a portion of one. You also don't get a wide range of graphics formats to which you can save. And the whole thing is very awkward and kludgy.

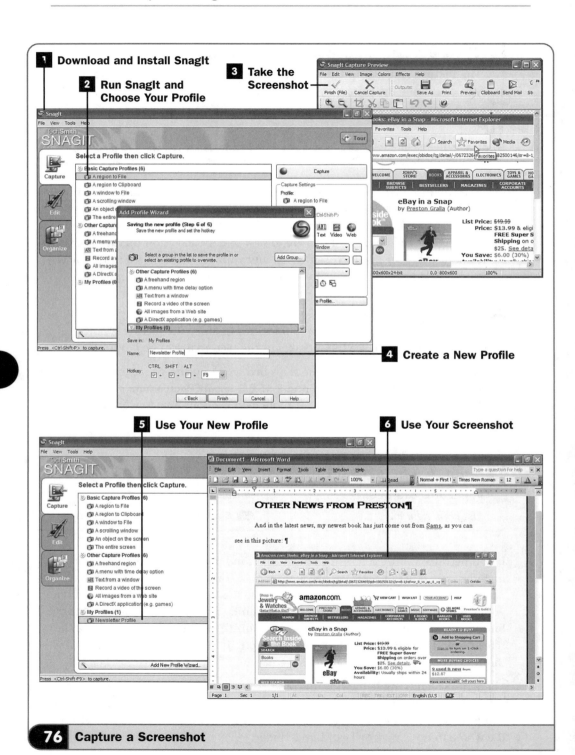

1 Download and Install SnagIt

2 Run SnagIt and Choose Your Profile

3 Take the Screenshot

4 Create a New Profile

5 Use Your New Profile

6 Use Your Screenshot

76 Capture a Screenshot

There's a better way. Use downloadable software to save screens. The best for the purpose is SnagIt, as you'll see in this task.

1 Download and Install SnagIt

Go to **www.snagit.com** and click the **Download** button at the top of the page. Follow the instructions for downloading and installing the program.

▶ **NOTE**

SnagIt is shareware, which means that you can try it out for free, but if you continue to use the program, you're expected to pay $39.95. You can pay directly on the website.

2 Run SnagIt and Choose Your Profile

Double-click the SnagIt icon on the desktop, or choose it from the **Start, All Programs** menu. When SnagIt runs, you'll see a list of what the program calls **Basic Capture Profiles**. Each profile allows you to do a different kind of screen capture. For example, the first one, **A Region to File**, lets you capture a portion of a screen and then save it as a file in a wide variety of graphics formats. **The Entire Screen** profile captures your entire screen to a file.

To find out the details about a profile, click it and look in the **Capture Settings** area on the right side of the screen for information about that profile. You'll see the following information for each profile:

76

▶ **NOTE**

A particularly useful feature of SnagIt is its capability to specify a delay time before the screen is captured (for example, if you want to arrange windows or menus before the screen is captured). To use it, click the **Timer Setup** icon (it looks like a stopwatch) at the bottom of the right side of the screen and fill in the form.

- **Hotkey**—The key combination you press to activate that particular profile. For a start, you use the same hotkey for each profile. To choose which profile to use when you press that hotkey, you first click the profile to highlight it. When you press that hotkey, you'll capture a screen using that profile. To capture a screen with a different profile, open SnagIt, highlight a different profile, and then press the hotkey. You can instead assign different hotkeys to different profiles. To assign a hotkey to a profile, right-click a profile, select **Set Hotkey** from the context menu, press the hotkey combination you want to use, and click **OK**.

- **Mode**—This setting determines whether you'll capture the image from the screen, the text from the screen, a video of several screens, or a website.

- **Input**—This setting determines what portion of the screen you'll capture: for example, the entire screen, only the currently active window, a rectangular portion of the screen, and so on.

- **Output**—This setting determines what happens when you capture the screen—do you send it to the printer, for example, or capture it as a file. If you do capture it as a file, you can set which file format the capture should be in.

- **Filters**—This option lets you apply a kind of filter to the screen capture—for example, you can change its resolution, add a border to it, add special effects to its edges (such as waves and fades), and so on.

- **Options**—Here you can choose your final options for the screenshot, such as whether to include the mouse pointer, and whether you should view your screenshot in a preview window before you save it.

After you look through the profiles, choose the one you want to use and then minimize the SnagIt window by clicking the **Minimize** button in the upper-right corner of the title bar.

76

③ Take the Screenshot

Arrange the screen in whatever manner constitutes the screenshot you want to capture (for example, a website). Press the SnagIt hotkey, which by default is **Ctrl+Shift+P**. If you've chosen to capture an entire screen or the current window, the **SnagIt Capture Preview** window appears, letting you preview your file. If you want to save the capture, click the **Finish (File)** button in the toolbar at the top of the window, navigate to the place on your hard disk where you want to save the file, give the file a filename, and click **Save**.

If you've chosen an option such as capturing a portion of the screen, a cropping tool appears, letting you define the portion of the screen you want to capture. After you stop dragging the area to crop, the **Capture Preview** window appears. Save the screenshot as explained in the previous paragraph.

④ Create a New Profile

To create a new profile, go back to the main SnagIt screen (the one that lists all the profiles). Click the **Add New Profile Wizard** button at the bottom of the list. A wizard runs, first asking you what type of capture mode you want to use. Make your selection and click **Next**. The wizard will walk you through every step of choosing all the options for a new profile—the options described in step 2 of this task.

In the final step, you'll be asked to name the profile and to choose a hotkey for it. Make sure that you choose a hotkey that isn't used by any other program or by Windows XP. Don't forget to give the profile a descriptive name, as well.

5 Use Your New Profile

To use your new profile, minimize the SnagIt window (click the **Minimize** button in the upper-right corner of the title bar) and go to the screen you want to capture. Press the hotkey you've defined for your new profile, and use SnagIt as outlined earlier in this task.

6 Use Your Screenshot

After you've saved your screenshot, you can use it as you would any other graphics file; for example, in a newsletter, in a report in a Word document, to send as an email attachment, and so on.

77 Convert Between Image Formats

✔ BEFORE YOU BEGIN	→ SEE ALSO
74 Import Photos from a Digital Camera	**78** Change Photo Resolution and Size
75 Scan In Photos	

Pictures come in a wide variety of image formats—there are literally dozens of them, including JPG, GIF, BMP, TIF, PCX, and many others. But when you post pictures on the Web, you can only use the JPG, GIF, or PNG format.

But what if you have a picture in a non-web-friendly format such as PCX and want to use it on the Web? You can convert the image from any format to a web-friendly one. That's what you'll learn in this task.

1 Download and Install IrfanView

The best way to convert files between different formats is to use the free program IrfanView, which lets you view graphics files, convert them between formats, and has some basic image-editing tools, as well. It's one of the best all-around graphics utilities you can find, and it's free to download and use.

To download it, go to **www.irfanview.com**, click the **Download** link, and follow the instructions for downloading. After you download it, follow the instructions for installing it.

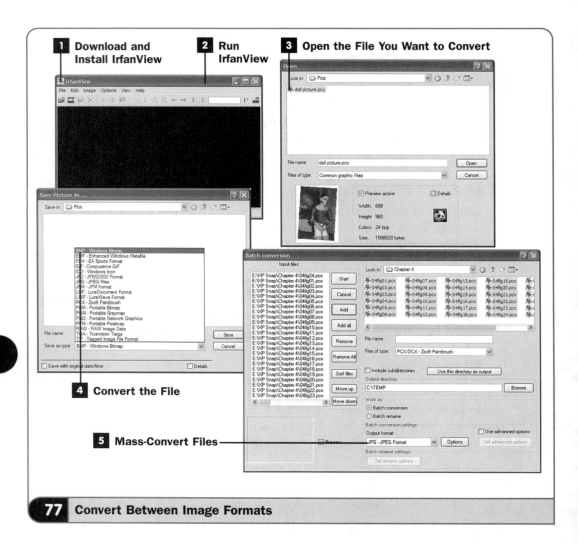

1 **Download and Install IrfanView**

2 **Run IrfanView**

3 **Open the File You Want to Convert**

4 **Convert the File**

5 **Mass-Convert Files**

77   **Convert Between Image Formats**

2 Run IrfanView

After you install IrfanView, open it by double-clicking its desktop icon, or by clicking the **Start** button, choosing **All Programs**, and then choosing **IrfanView** from the menu.

3 Open the File You Want to Convert

Choose **File**, **Open** from the menu, navigate to the folder that has the file you want to convert, and then double-click the file. IrfanView shows you a preview of the file in the **Open** dialog box, so it's easy to make sure that you've selected the correct file before you open it.

▶ **NOTE**

When you use IrfanView, if you want to see information about each file before you open it, such as the date it was created and the file size, enable the **Details** check box in the **Open** dialog box. You can then see that information about each file.

4 Convert the File

After you open the file, choose **File, Save As** from the menu. From the **Save As Type** drop-down list at the bottom of the dialog box, choose the file type you want to save the file as, such as JPG. (Again, remember that for the Web, you can only use graphics in JPG, GIF, or PNG.) Type a new name in the **File Name** text box if you want. Then click **Save**. Your file will now be converted to the new file type.

5 Mass-Convert Files

One of IrfanView's better features is its capability to convert an entire group of files from one format to another. To do it, open IrfanView and choose **File, Batch Conversion/Rename** from the menu. The **Batch Conversion** dialog box shows a list of all the graphics files in the selected folder. Navigate to the folder that holds the files you want to convert. Highlight all the files you want to convert and click the **Add** button. From the **Output Format** drop-down list, choose the file format to which you want to convert the files. Then click **Start** to convert the files.

78

78 Change Photo Resolution and Size

✔ BEFORE YOU BEGIN	→ SEE ALSO
74 Import Photos from a Digital Camera	**77** Convert Between Image Formats
75 Scan In Photos	**142** Make the Picture Web Friendly

Pictures of different *resolution*s and sizes are used for different purposes. For example, if you're going to have your digital pictures printed, you want them to be as high quality and in as high resolution as possible. But you don't use very high-resolution photos on the Web, because it will take too long to download.

▶ **KEY TERM**

Resolution—The quality of a picture, measured in *pixels*, which are small dots.

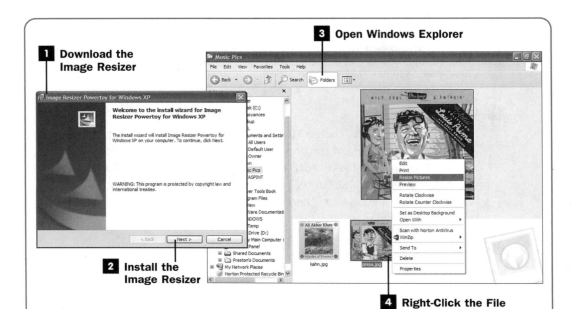

1 Download the Image Resizer

2 Install the Image Resizer

3 Open Windows Explorer

4 Right-Click the File You Want to Resize

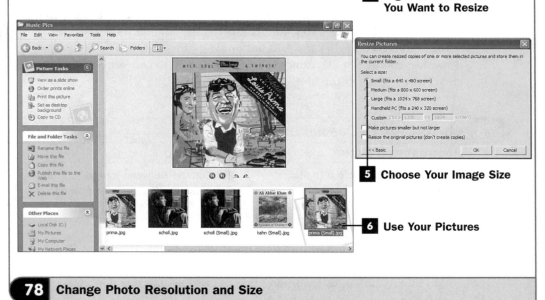

5 Choose Your Image Size

6 Use Your Pictures

78 **Change Photo Resolution and Size**

The solution? You can easily resize images and change their resolution so that you can use any picture for the Web, and make sure that it's at the right size.

1 Download the Image Resizer

The best tool for resizing images is free and available from Microsoft. It's called the **Image Resizer**, and it's one of a suite of free utilities that Microsoft calls **Microsoft Power Toys**. To find it, go to **www.microsoft.com/ windowsxp/pro/downloads/powertoys.asp**. Look in the list on the right side of the window for the **Image Resizer** utility. Click the **ImageResizer.exe** link to download the file, choose a folder location where you want to save it, and start the download.

2 Install the Image Resizer

After you download it, look for the file named **ImageResizerPowertoySetup.exe** in the folder where you saved it, and double-click it. This action launches an installation program. Click the **Next** button when the first screen appears and then follow the simple installation instructions.

▶ NOTE

Even though the link on the website calls the file **ImageResizer.exe**, the actual filename is **ImageResizerPowertoySetup.exe**.

78

3 Open Windows Explorer

The Image Resizer isn't a program that runs by itself. Instead, it integrates directly into Windows Explorer's right-click context menu. Open Windows Explorer and locate the file you want to resize.

4 Right-Click the File You Want to Resize

Right-click the file you want to resize. Choose **Resize Pictures** from the context menu to run the Image Resizer. Note that you can select multiple pictures and resize them all in a single operation. To select multiple pictures, **Ctrl+click** each file until you've selected all that you want to resize, right-click any of the files to open the context menu, and choose **Resize Pictures**.

5 Choose Your Image Size

The **Resize Pictures** dialog box appears, allowing you to change the picture size. You can choose any of the preset image sizes, or you can choose a custom size by selecting the **Custom** option and entering the size you want the image or images to be. After you make your selection, click **OK**. Keep in mind that if you resize a picture to make it larger than its original size, the quality of the resized picture will often not be very good—and might even be unusable. However, making a picture smaller will not adversely affect the picture quality.

▶ **NOTE**

It's not a good idea to select the **Resize the Original Pictures (Don't Create Copies)** option. If you choose that option, your original picture will be deleted, and if you don't like the new size of the picture, there's nothing you can do about it—you're stuck with it.

6 Use Your Pictures

The Image Resizer resizes the images and puts them in the same folder in which your original pictures are stored. The program labels the new pictures by appending their new size to the filename; for example, **(small)**. Keep in mind that the pictures won't look smaller in the thumbnail view in Windows Explorer, but the actual *file* is smaller. You can now use the resized image file in the same way you use any picture.

78

14

Performing Basic Image Tasks with Paint Shop Pro

IN THIS CHAPTER:

To build the best website, you need to have the best images. That doesn't mean you have to be a Michelangelo, or even be able to create your own pictures. But it does mean that you should have some basic skills in how to edit pictures so that they're as spiffy as possible when they're posted online. These pictures can range from a simple web button to an old black-and-white photo, or pictures from your child's recent birthday party.

In this chapter, you'll learn how to accomplish the most common image-editing tasks using Paint Shop Pro (PSP), which has an extremely powerful suite of tools, yet is relatively inexpensive and not as difficult to use as programs such as Photoshop. So you'll learn tasks such as displaying image information, zooming in and out, scrolling, magnifying an area so that you can perform detail work, protecting your photos with a copyright stamp, resizing an image, and changing the number of colors you can work with.

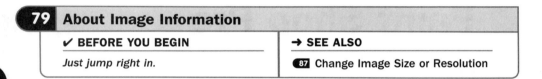

79 About Image Information

✔ BEFORE YOU BEGIN	→ SEE ALSO
Just jump right in.	**87** Change Image Size or Resolution

When needed, Paint Shop Pro can display information about the basic characteristics of an image—its file type, resolution, size, and data specific to the conditions under which it was taken. To display this information for any currently open image, change to that image first; then select **Image, Image Information** from the menu bar. The **Current Image Information** dialog box opens, containing three tabs, all loaded with information about the current image.

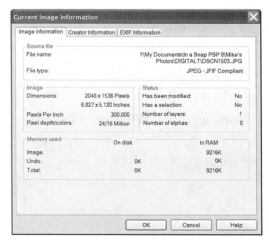

The Current Image Information dialog box.

On the **Image Information** tab, you'll find this data:

- **Source file**—Here you'll see the filename and file type (such as JPEG or TIFF).

- **Image**—The dimensions of the image are displayed in pixels and inches. The example shown here uses a resolution of 300 pixels per inch (ppi), resulting in a print size of 6.827"×5.120". These two values are interconnected; you'll learn more about changing resolution and resizing images in ⑩⑥ **About Size and Resolution**.

- **Status**—Here you can tell whether any changes have been made to the image, and whether it contains any current selections, layers, or *alpha channel* information.

▶ KEY TERM

Alpha channel—Data saved with an image for reuse when needed, such as selections, masks, and creator information.

- **Memory used**—If your computer resources are running low, you can look here to see how much memory your image editing is consuming.

The data on the **Creator Information** tab of the **Current Image Information** dialog box is entered by you and stored in the alpha channel of the image file. If you intend to publish your PSP image to public places, such as a personal web page, you can claim your copyright by typing copyright information and your name into this tab.

79

Many newer digital cameras are capable of saving additional data, such as the camera type, date the photo was taken, and shot conditions such as f-stop, shutter speed, and focal length. This data is stored in the image's Exchangeable Image File (EXIF) header. You'll find this data on the **EXIF Information** tab of the **Current Image Information** dialog box. Some of this data can be used by an EXIF-compatible printer to print your photo more accurately, with better color and brightness matching.

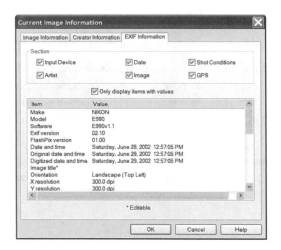

EXIF data may be stored with an image.

To make sure you don't lose this valuable EXIF data, save your image file using an EXIF-compatible program (PSP happens to be one) in an EXIF-compatible format (PSPImage or JPEG).

The **Overview** palette also displays some image information, because you might need to refer to it while considering changes to an image. Click the **Info** tab on the **Overview** palette to see the size of your image in pixels (useful to know, especially if you're working with the image zoomed in). You'll also see the pixel format listed—this is essentially the *color depth*. Some of Paint Shop Pro's features are not available unless an image is currently using 16 million colors, so looking here first can save you the trouble of looking for an option that you won't be able to select. On the **Info** tab, you'll also see the amount of memory being used—again, this is useful information to have if you're using an older computer with limited resources.

▶ KEY TERM

Color depth—The size of the image's current *color palette*, which contains the colors available for use in an image.

The Info tab of the Overview palette.

At the bottom of the **Info** tab, you can see the relative location of your mouse pointer as a pair of x (horizontal) and y (vertical) coordinates. In this coordinate system, {0, 0} is considered the upper-left corner of the image. The x value increases as you move the pointer to the right, and the y value increases as you move it down. When you're selecting a rectangular area of an image to be cut out or copied, the **Info** tab will also show you the selection's size in pixels and the relative locations of both the upper-left and lower-right corners of the selection.

▶ **TIP**

Before placing text or other data in a precise location within an image, display the **Info** tab of the **Overview** palette so that you can see the x and y coordinates as you work.

The data on the **Info** tab of the **Overview** palette also appears at the right end of the status bar. At the left end of the status bar, you'll find a brief description of any tool, toolbar button, or menu command you point to.

| Crop Tool: Click and drag to draw crop rectangle, then click Apply. Right-click to clear. | (342, 378) -> (1238, 1530) = (896 x 1152) [0.778] -- Image: 1536 x 2048 |

The Status toolbar displays vital information.

80

80 Zoom In and Out with the Zoom Tool

✔ BEFORE YOU BEGIN	→ SEE ALSO
Just jump right in.	**81** Zoom In and Out with the Overview Palette
	83 Magnify Your Work

Whether you're making changes to a photograph or some artwork you've created yourself, you must be able to view the image clearly to make precise changes. Typically, this means zooming in on some area that doesn't look right so that you can discern the problem, and later zooming back out again to see whether the change you made looks right when the image is viewed at its regular size. To zoom in on an image and back out again, use the **Zoom** tool and its **Tool Options** buttons.

▶ **TIP**

To zoom quickly, click the image with the **Zoom** tool. Right-click to zoom back out.

To zoom in on a particular area of an image, simply drag with the **Zoom** tool to select the area. The selected area is enlarged to fit the size of the image window.

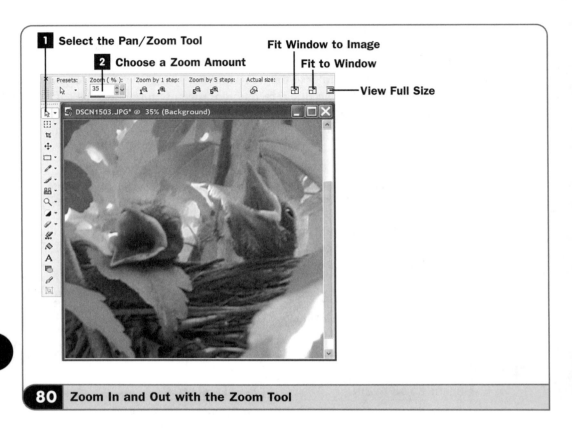

1 Select the Pan/Zoom Tool

2 Choose a Zoom Amount

Fit Window to Image

Fit to Window

View Full Size

80 Zoom In and Out with the Zoom Tool

1 Select the Pan/Zoom Tool

Click the **Pan** or **Zoom** button on the **Tools** toolbar.

▶ NOTE

You don't actually have to choose the **Zoom** tool if you simply want to use the controls on the **Tool Options** palette to zoom—so just click whichever button is currently displayed.

2 Choose a Zoom Amount

The **Tool Options** palette for the **Zoom** tool provides many ways in which you can zoom. To view an image at a particular zoom level (such as 50%), type that percentage in the **Zoom (%)** box.

▶ **TIP**

To zoom to 50%, 200%, 500%, or 1,000% *and increase the size of the image window to fit the available workspace*, click the **Presets** button, select a zoom amount, and click **OK**.

To zoom gradually, click either of the **Zoom by 1 Step** buttons—if you click the **1 Minus** button, you'll zoom out gradually; if you click the **Zoom Plus** button, you'll zoom in gradually.

To zoom in or out more quickly, click either of the **Zoom by 5 Steps** buttons. To view the image at 100% (actual size), click the **Actual Size** button.

▶ **TIP**

If your mouse has a scroll wheel, you can use it to zoom in and out: Roll the wheel up to zoom in or down to zoom out.

The image window can be larger or smaller than the image; to shrink the window so that it fits the image exactly, click the **Fit Window to Image** button. To enlarge the image to fit the size of the window, click the **Fit to Window** button instead. To enlarge the image to fit the available workspace, click **View Full Size**.

81

81	**Zoom In and Out with the Overview Palette**	
✔ **BEFORE YOU BEGIN**	→ **SEE ALSO**	
Just jump right in.	**80** Zoom In and Out with the Zoom Tool	
	83 Magnify Your Work	

In the last task, you learned how to zoom in or out using the **Zoom** tool and its buttons on the **Tool Options** palette. However, if the **Overview** palette is displayed, you can use it to zoom in and out without changing to the **Zoom** tool first.

▶ **TIP**

Another way you can zoom without changing to the **Zoom** tool first is to use the scroll wheel on your mouse (if it has one). Scroll the wheel forward to zoom in; scroll it backward to zoom out.

1 **Display the Overview Palette**

Choose **View, Palettes, Overview** from the menu bar, or press **F9**.

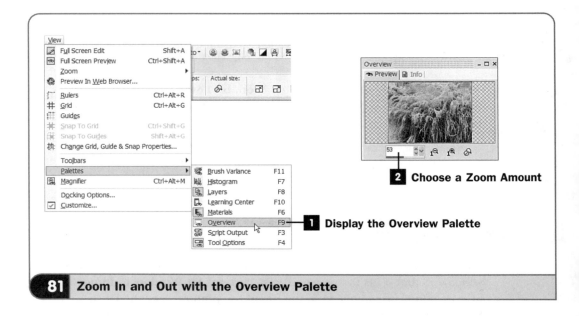

2 Choose a Zoom Amount

1 Display the Overview Palette

81 Zoom In and Out with the Overview Palette

82

2 Choose a Zoom Amount

To view an image at a particular zoom level (such as 50%), type a percentage in the **Zoom (Percent)** box.

To zoom gradually, click either of the **Zoom by 1 Step** buttons.

To view the image at 100% (actual size), click the **Actual Size** button.

▶ **NOTE**

You might have noticed the "do not" red slash/circle on the **Actual Size** icon and wondered, "Will this blow something up if I click it?" The answer is no—the symbol simply means, "no magnification," or 100% zoom.

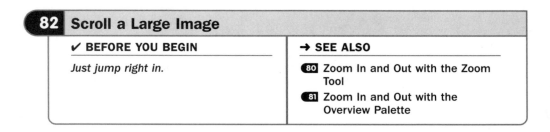

82 Scroll a Large Image

✔ BEFORE YOU BEGIN	→ SEE ALSO
Just jump right in.	**80** Zoom In and Out with the Zoom Tool
	81 Zoom In and Out with the Overview Palette

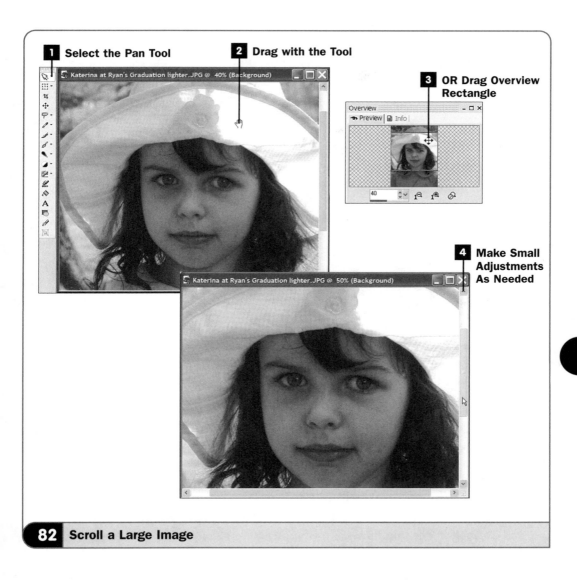

1 Select the Pan Tool

2 Drag with the Tool

3 OR Drag Overview Rectangle

4 Make Small Adjustments As Needed

82 Scroll a Large Image

If an image is being shown with a magnification larger than the image window can display, parts of that image will be obscured from view. If you need to make changes on a part of the image you can't currently see, you'll have to scroll to view it. To do that, use the **Pan** tool, the scrollbars, or the **Overview** palette.

1 Select the Pan Tool

Click the **Pan** button on the **Tools** toolbar.

2 Drag with the Tool

Click the mouse in the image window and drag with the hand pointer to display the portion of the image you want to view. For example, drag down to view a part of an image that's hidden just above the currently displayed portion.

3 OR Drag Overview Rectangle

You can also reposition the viewable portion of the image by dragging its rectangle within the **Overview** palette.

4 Make Small Adjustments As Needed

Click the scroll arrows on the horizontal/vertical scrollbars or press the arrow keys to move the viewable portion of the image by a small amount.

---

83 Magnify Your Work

✔ BEFORE YOU BEGIN	→ SEE ALSO
Just jump right in.	80 Zoom In and Out with the Zoom Tool
	81 Zoom In and Out with the Overview Palette

Some changes you'll want to make to an image will involve working in a small confined area. For example, perhaps you want to remove a small mole or other distraction from a person's face. To do that, you can use the Clone tool, but what if you can't see the area you want to fix all that clearly? You could zoom in, of course, but it might be nice to be able to view the changes as you make them, using a more zoomed-out view. Of course, there's always the **Overview** palette and its small image thumbnail, but your tiny changes might not be noticeable in that window. What you need is the ability to quickly zoom in on your work while still maintaining the big-picture view of your changes. To accomplish this task, you use the **Magnifier** palette.

1 Display the Magnifier Palette

Choose **View, Magnifier** from the menu bar or press **Ctrl+Alt+M**.

2 Magnify the Work Area

Move the mouse pointer anywhere over the image to magnify the area directly beneath the pointer.

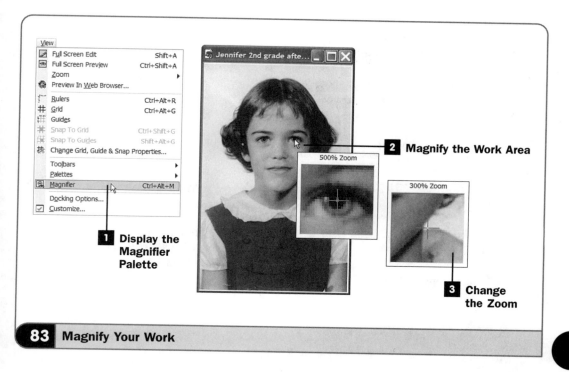

2 Magnify the Work Area

1 Display the
Magnifier
Palette

3 Change
the Zoom

83 Magnify Your Work

84

3 Change the Zoom

Change the zoom level of the **Magnifier** palette by pressing **Ctrl+plus** to zoom in or **Ctrl+minus** to zoom out.

84 Add Copyright Information

✔ **BEFORE YOU BEGIN**

87 Change Image Size or Resolution

Digimarc Corporation, a world leader in digital watermarking, in coordination with Paint Shop Pro's **Image, Watermarking, Embed Watermark** command, can provide you with a secure method of protecting your copyrighted images and tracking their use on the Web. The cost, however, is practical only for a profes- sional photographer. In this task, I'll show you a simple way to watermark your own images—for free! This method creates a copyright notice that you can embed softly within your own images.

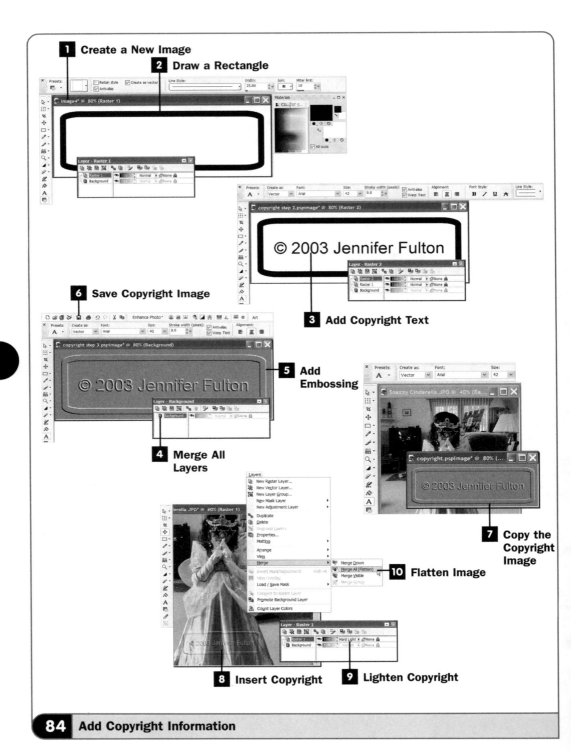

The photographs you take are already your property and protected by law. All you have to do to claim copyright over your photo is to place your © mark in some visible location. With a PSP image, you can place your © mark in the **Image Information** dialog box, but that notice can easily be stripped away, even though it's actually illegal for someone other than you (the claimant) to do so. This is where direct embedding of the copyright notice within the image itself comes in handy. Of course, you can't copyright just anything. For example, you can't copy an image off a web page, make changes to it, and then copyright the result.

▶ **TIP**

To make it easier to add a copyright to other images, record steps 7 to 10 as a script. You can then invoke the script during batch processing of new images, or within any open image.

1 Create a New Image

Start a new image by clicking the **New** button on the **Standard** toolbar. Set **Width** to 900, **Height** to 300, and **Units** to **Pixels**. Set the **Resolution** to 72 **Pixels/Inch**. Select **Raster Background**, with **Color Depth** at 16 Million Colors. Click the **Color** box, choose white, and click **OK**. Click **OK** again.

84

2 Draw a Rectangle

On the **Materials** palette, change the foreground color to **black** and the background color to **white**. On the **Tools** toolbar, click the **Preset Shape** tool. On the **Tool Options** palette, from the **Shape** list, select **Rounded Rectangle**. Enable the **Anti-alias** and **Create As Vector** check boxes, and disable **Retain Style**. Select the **#1 Solid Line Style** and set the **Width** to 25. In the image window, draw a rectangle that nearly fills the window. From the menu bar, choose **Layers, Convert to Raster Layer**.

3 Add Copyright Text

On the **Tools** toolbar, click the **Text** tool. On the **Tool Options** palette, choose **Arial** font, **42** point **Size**, and center **Alignment**. Set the background color to black. In the image window, click in the center of the rectangle. The **Text Entry** dialog box appears. Press and hold the **Alt** key and type **0169** on the numeric keypad to enter the copyright symbol (the © symbol). Type the year followed by your name. Click **Apply**.

▶ **NOTE**

The U.S. Copyright Office states that official notice of copyright must contain the word *copyright* or the circle-C symbol, the year the work was first published, and the claimant's name. The use of the copyright notice does not require advance permission from, or registration with, the Copyright Office.

If necessary, you can adjust the position of the text by dragging it. You'll want to center the text within the rectangle. When you're done, choose **Layers, Convert to Raster Layer** from the menu bar.

4 Merge All Layers

Choose **Layers, Merge, Merge All (Flatten)** from the menu bar to flatten the image so that you can add embossing.

5 Add Embossing

Choose **Effects, Texture Effects, Emboss** from the menu bar. The **Emboss** effect changes the copyright notice to a mostly gray image with raised text. The edge of the rounded rectangle appears raised as well.

84

6 Save Copyright Image

Click the **Save** button. Type **copyright** in the **File Name** box. Select **Paint Shop Pro Image** from the **Save As Type** list. Click **Save**.

7 Copy the Copyright Image

When it comes time for you to attach a copyright notice to an original image, open the **copyright.pspimage** file. Resize the copyright notice to fit the image you want to watermark by choosing **Image, Resize**, entering new dimensions, and clicking **OK**. When the copyright notice is the correct size, click the **Copy** button on the **Standard** toolbar.

8 Insert Copyright

Open any image you want to copyright. Choose **Edit, Paste, As New Layer** from the menu. The copyright notice is placed on its own layer, on top of the image. Use the **Move** tool if needed to reposition the notice.

▶ **TIP**

Place the copyright over an important part of the image—something that cannot be cropped out without ruining the photo.

9 Lighten Copyright

On the **Layer** palette, select the copyright layer. (It will be on the top of the list because it was the layer most recently created.) Click the **Blend Mode** list and choose **Soft Light**.

▶ **TIP**

If the copyright fades away too much, select **Hard Light** instead. Lighten the effect even more by adjusting the copyright layer's opacity by dragging the **Opacity** slider in the **Layer** palette to the left.

10 Flatten Image

Choose **Layers, Merge, Merge All (Flatten)**. The copyright notice is now permanently "embedded" in the image file. Save the image.

---

85 Share Images Using Email

✔ BEFORE YOU BEGIN	→ SEE ALSO
78 Change Photo Resolution and Size	119 About Online Photo Services
	122 Share Images Using an Online Service in Adobe Photoshop Elements
	123 Print Images Using an Online Photo Service in Adobe Photoshop Elements

85

One reason you take the time to clean up digital photographs or to create your own art in Paint Shop Pro is so that you can share your work with friends and family. If you have a connection to the Internet, sharing your images by attaching them to email messages is a simple process.

If you have Photo Album, you can also use it to send images using email. Photo Album has the advantage here because it can compress images on the fly, making them smaller and thus easier to send electronically. To send images using Photo Album, select the images to send by clicking them in the **Album View** window, and then click the **Email** button on the toolbar. An email message with the images compressed and attached is automatically created for you to address and send.

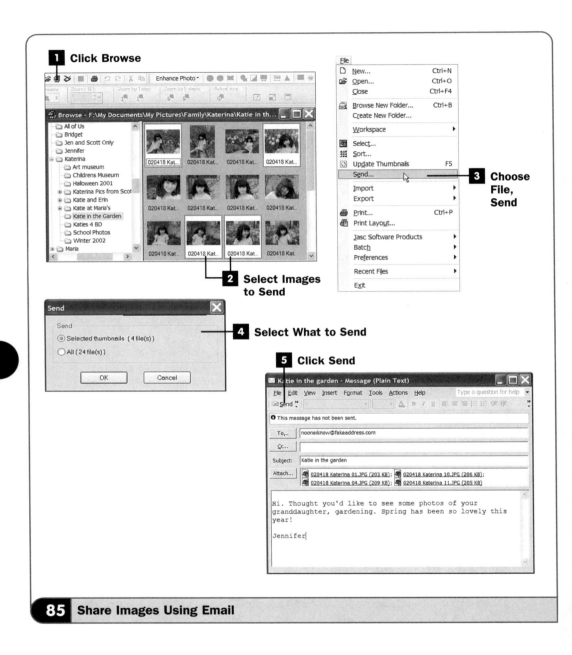

85   Share Images Using Email

▶ **NOTE**

To send images by email using PSP or Photo Album, your computer must have a MAPI-compatible email program installed such as Outlook, Outlook Express, Eudora, or Pegasus Mail. AOL, Yahoo!, and Hotmail mail programs will not work.

1 Click Browse

Click the **Browse** button on the **Standard** toolbar. The **Browser** appears.

2 Select Images to Send

Select the folder that contains the images you want to send. If you don't want to send all the images in the folder, click the first image and then press and hold **Ctrl** as you click each additional image you want to send.

▶ **TIP**

If you want to send all the images in the current folder, skip step 3.

3 Choose File, Send

Choose **File, Send** from the main menu. The **Send** dialog box opens.

4 Select What to Send

Choose either **Selected Thumbnails** (to send only the images you've selected) or **All** (to send all the images in the current folder). Then click **OK**.

5 Click Send

An email message with the images attached is automatically created. Notice the list of image files that have been attached to this message. Address the email message in the usual manner and click **Send** to send it on its way.

86

86 About Size and Resolution

✔ BEFORE YOU BEGIN	→ SEE ALSO
78 Change Photo Resolution and Size	**87** Change Image Size or Resolution **88** Change the Working Area Without Affecting Image Size

Two of the most common changes you'll make to an image are to adjust its size and to change its resolution. By *size*, I'm referring to an image's dimensions when printed, not its size onscreen. An image's *resolution* is determined by the number of pixels (dots) per inch.

To compute an image's print size, Paint Shop Pro looks at the number of pixels in an image and their relative size (the number of pixels per inch). Take a look at the first figure here, which depicts an image that's 10 pixels wide by 5 pixels high, using an imaginary scale of 16 pixels per inch. Based on the size of these pixels, the printed image will be about 1.6" wide by .81" high.

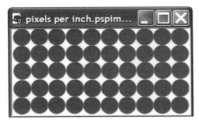

An image that's 10 pixels wide by 5 pixels high.

To compute the resolution of an image, you simply count the number of pixels per inch (ppi). Luckily, PSP does that for you, and you can view the print size and resolution of an image in the **Image Information** dialog box (choose **Image, Image Information** from the menu bar). The print size is listed as **Dimensions** and the resolution as **Pixels per Inch**. If you never plan to print a certain image, the image won't need a high resolution (a great number of pixels). But for you to print an image, you need the highest number of pixels you can get—the more the better. You must have an image resolution of 300ppi (pixels per inch) to create a high-quality print using an outside lab; for home printing, 200ppi usually does just fine.

▶ NOTE

High resolution (over 200 pixels per inch) is unnecessary for an image destined to be displayed on a computer monitor or a television screen because NTSC standard TV resolution is 72 dots per inch and computer screen resolutions average 102 pixels per inch.

An image's print size and its resolution are interdependent; changing one without changing the other will affect the image's print quality. Reducing resolution while maintaining the same print size, for example, decreases the number of pixels per inch and, as you can imagine, inflates the size of each pixel. If the pixels become too large, a mosaic effect called *pixelation* might distract you from seeing the image as a whole. Look at the first figure showing the 10×5 rectangle. If you change the size of the pixels and make them twice as big (as shown in the second figure), you'll get a much larger rectangle, but the pixels will be much more apparent. When printed, the rectangle might look more like a mesh of dots than a solid rectangle, which is probably not the effect you're going for. The same is true of any graphic image: Make the image larger without increasing the number of pixels (resolution), and the pixels will become bigger and more evident in the final print.

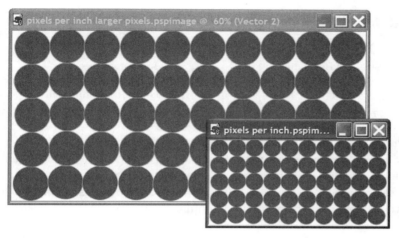

Enlarging the pixels increases the image size while decreasing its quality.

Suppose that, instead of changing the size of the pixels, you maintain their relative size, but double their number. Once again, you'll also double the print size, although the print quality will remain the same, as shown in the third figure.

86

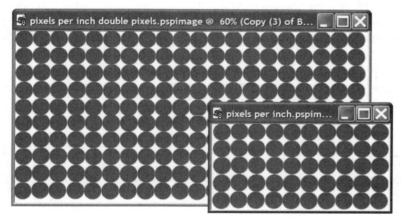

You can also enlarge an image without sacrificing quality by adding to the number of pixels.

▶ **NOTE**

To increase the size of an image without changing its resolution, use the **Image, Resize** command to resample it. See **87 Change Image Size or Resolution**.

87 | Change Image Size or Resolution

✔ BEFORE YOU BEGIN	→ SEE ALSO
86 About Size and Resolution	**75** Scan In Photos
	88 Change the Working Area Without Affecting Image Size

As you learned in **86** **About Size and Resolution,** an image's size is tied directly to the number of pixels in the image as well as the relative size of the pixels. When you create images with a digital camera, or scan printed images with a scanner, you choose the resolution you want to use—for instance, 300 pixels per inch. The resolution you choose also determines the resulting print size. For example, an image that's 2,048 pixels wide by 1,536 pixels tall (the typical dimensions of an image taken with a 3MP camera), whose resolution is 300 pixels per inch, will print at 6.827" by 5.120".

So what do you do if you want your image to print at a larger size, but remain at 300dpi? In other words, what do you do if you want to increase its size without inflating the size of pixels? The answer is, you ask PSP to *resample* the image. When resampling is employed, either to increase an image's print size or its resolution, new pixels are inserted between existing ones. The colors for these new pixels are determined by a process that *samples* the values of surrounding pixels and uses estimated values in between. Resampling can also be used when reducing an image's print size or resolution. In such a circumstance, pixels are removed from an image, and the colors of the remaining pixels are determined through sampling of all the original colors and approximating their blended values.

▶ KEY TERM

Resample—The process of creating new pixels based on the value of surrounding pixels.

Because resampling is based on best-guess estimation, using it to change an image's size or resolution by more than 20% often produces poor results. You can resize or change an image's resolution without resampling by telling Paint Shop Pro that you want to maintain the relationship between the size and the resolution. In this manner, you can double an image's print resolution by cutting its print size in half. The image will contain as many pixels as it did before, but the pixels will be smaller, and there will be more of them per inch. Onscreen, you won't see any change at all.

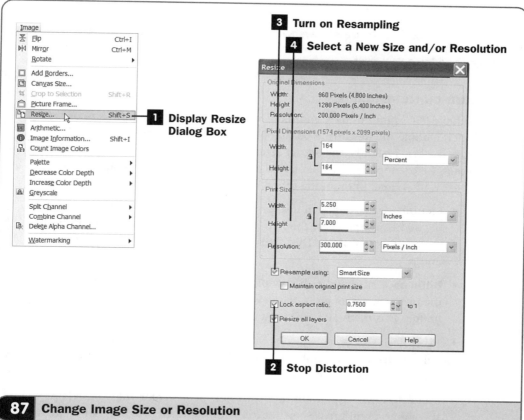

3 Turn on Resampling

4 Select a New Size and/or Resolution

1 Display Resize Dialog Box

2 Stop Distortion

87 Change Image Size or Resolution

▶ **TIP**

One fast way to remove moiré patterns, fuzziness, and spots from an image is to scan the image at 600dpi and then reduce its resolution to 300dpi *while maintaining its print size.*

1 Display Resize Dialog Box

Choose **Image, Resize** from the menu bar or press **Shift+S**. The **Resize** dialog box appears.

2 Stop Distortion

If you do not want the image distorted during the resizing process, select the **Lock Aspect Ratio** option to turn it on.

If the image contains multiple layers, and you want all the layers resized to the same size, enable the **Resize All Layers** option as well.

▶ **NOTE**

If you don't choose the **Resize All Layers** option, only the current layer or active selection is resized. Leaving this option disabled is a handy way to resize a selection or an image copied to a new layer.

3 Turn on Resampling

To have PSP estimate colors for pixels when you change the print size or resolution, enable the **Resample Using** option and select a sampling formula from the list. Typically, the **Smart Size** option works best because it determines the appropriate formula based on the image's unique requirements. Here's a brief description of the other formulas:

• **Bicubic**—Estimates each new pixel's color value based on the values of the 16 nearest pixels to the new pixel's location relative to the original image, in a 4×4 array. This method is best used when enlarging an image.

• **Bilinear**—Estimates each new pixel's color value based on the values of the four nearest pixels to the new pixel's location relative to the original image. This method is best used when reducing an image.

• **Pixel Resize**—Copies the color value of each new pixel from the exact value of its nearest neighbor. Fast and dirty, with often poor results including jagged edges and stair-step effects.

• **Weighted Average**—Estimates each new pixel's color value based on the values of all the pixels that fall within a fixed proximity of the new pixel's location relative to the original image. Here, the pixel residing in the same proportionate location in the original image as that of the new pixel in the resized image is given the extra "weight" when estimating the new color value. This method is best used when reducing the size of an image.

▶ **NOTE**

To avoid resampling an image, turn off the **Resample Using** option and change either the **Height/Width** or **Resolution** values in the **Print Size** area of the **Resize** dialog box. If you increase the **Resolution** without resampling, for example, the image will be resized smaller.

4 Select a New Size and/or Resolution

If you know what size you want the final image to be, type a value in the **Print Size Width** box; the **Height** value changes proportionately (or vice versa).

You can also change an image's size by adjusting its pixel dimensions. For example, if you want the image to be twice as big, select **Percent** from the **Pixel Dimensions** list and type **200** in the **Width** and **Height** boxes. This changes the number of pixels without affecting their size (assuming **Resample** is on).

To change the resolution, type a value in the **Resolution** box. Altering resolution in this manner does not change the image's print size, unless you entered new print dimensions earlier. Because the **Resample Using** option is selected, new pixels are created as needed to meet your print size and resolution requirements.

88	Change the Working Area Without Affecting Image Size
✔ BEFORE YOU BEGIN	→ SEE ALSO
86 About Size and Resolution	87 Change Image Size or Resolution

Each image begins with a *canvas*—essentially the image background. The benefit of thinking of an image's background layer as a canvas is that it helps you conceive how that layer can be stretched to change the size of the area on which you can paint. For a newly imported digital photo, the image is "painted," if you will, to fill the canvas. You can expand the background layer (the canvas) of an image such as a photograph, for example, to make room for a frame, and then fill the new area with color or texture. Or you might simply want to expand the canvas to create more room in which to add a clip from another image, an object, or some text.

▶ KEY TERM

Canvas—In PSP, the canvas is the geometric platform that provides the coordinate system for every image, and to which the background layer is attached.

When you expand the canvas for an image, you expand the background layer. If you've already created other layers in the image, all those layers are expanded by the same amount. If the background layer is transparent, any extra space you create is filled with transparent pixels. You can choose to fill the extra space in the background layer with a color you select.

1 Display Canvas Size Dialog Box

Choose **Image, Canvas Size** from the menu bar. The **Canvas Size** dialog box is displayed.

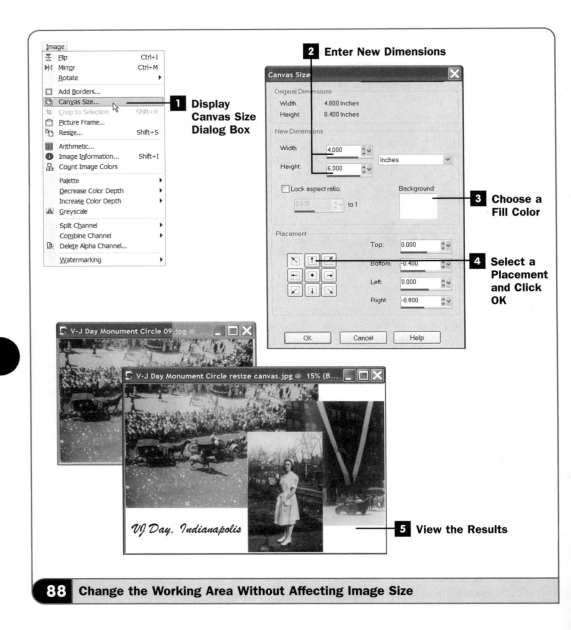

88 Change the Working Area Without Affecting Image Size

2 Enter New Dimensions

If you want the image to retain its ratio of height to width after stretching the canvas, enable the **Lock Aspect Ratio** option.

To change the aspect ratio to fit a specific format—such as 1.33 to 1 for a standard television screen—enter the aspect ratio you want in the box.

▶ **NOTE**

You can reduce the canvas size of an image. If you do, all the layers are reduced in size, but data is not removed from the non-background layers—it's just placed off the canvas where it is not seen in the final image.

Select a unit of measure such as inches or pixels from the **New Dimensions** list box. Then type values in the **Width** and **Height** boxes. If you've selected **Lock Aspect Ratio**, any change you make to the **Width** value is reflected proportionately in the **Height** value, and vice versa.

3 Choose a Fill Color

If the background is not transparent, you can choose a color to fill the extra canvas space. Click the **Background** color picker and select a color. You can also click anywhere in the image to pick up that color with the dropper.

4 Select a Placement and Click OK

To choose how you want the new canvas space distributed, click a **Placement** button. The button you click indicates where the image should appear in relation to the new canvas areas. If you click the center button, for example, the new canvas space is distributed around the image evenly; if you click the upper-left corner button, the image is placed there and the new canvas areas are inserted along the bottom and to the right. Click **OK**, and the canvas is expanded as directed by your selections.

89

5 View the Results

In the sample figure, the canvas was expanded to the right and along the bottom, text was added, and several new images were pasted into the image to fill the new space.

89 Change Color Depth

✔ BEFORE YOU BEGIN	→ SEE ALSO
Just jump right in.	77 Convert Between Image Formats
	78 Change Photo Resolution and Size
	86 About Size and Resolution

One of the key factors affecting the size of an image file is the maximum number of colors it can include. If you're working on an image to be shared over the Internet, small file size is often a high priority. One way you can reduce a file's size is to reduce its color depth. Of course, reducing the number of colors in an image's palette can also reduce its quality because a limited number of colors are used instead of a full spectrum.

▶ **NOTE**

A 16-million-color image might not actually contain 16 million colors, even though it is capable of doing so. Reducing the color depth for images that are generally monochromatic to start with might not appreciably reduce the quality but will shrink the file sizes considerably.

Because some commands are available only for grayscale images or for those that use 16 million colors, you might sometimes find yourself temporarily *increasing* an image's color depth. This won't, however, improve the resolution of a low-resolution image—increasing an image's color palette simply makes more colors available for use; it does not tell PSP where to use them in an image to boost detail and clarity.

If file size is your main priority, you can *compress* an image into GIF, JPEG, or PNG format (for example), a process that also reduces its color palette a bit more scientifically than the method discussed here. You can also convert an image to grayscale to reduce its color depth.

89

▶ **TIP**

If you're curious about how many colors your image is currently using, choose **Image, Count Image Colors**. To check the current color depth, look at the right end of the status bar.

1 **Display Increase/Decrease Color Depth Menu**

Choose **Image, Increase Color Depth** from the menu bar to increase the number of colors in an image; choose **Image, Decrease Color Depth** to reduce the number of colors instead.

2 **Select Color Depth**

Select the color depth you want from the menu that appears. If you're increasing color depth, the image is not changed, but more colors become available for you to use.

If you're reducing the color depth, a dialog box appears, allowing you to choose how Paint Shop Pro will narrow the color palette and adjust image colors. Continue to step 3.

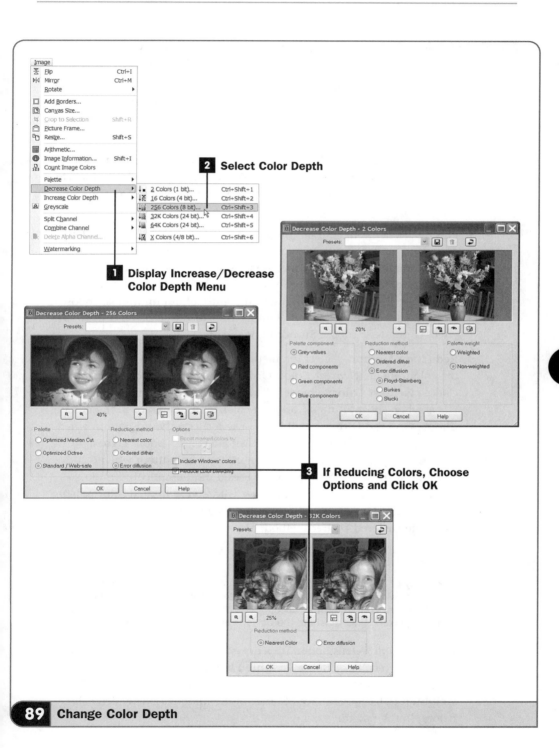

2 Select Color Depth

1 Display Increase/Decrease Color Depth Menu

3 If Reducing Colors, Choose Options and Click OK

89

89 Change Color Depth

▣ If Reducing Colors, Choose Options and Click OK

If you're reducing colors in an image, select how you want PSP to choose the colors for the palette by selecting options in the dialog box that appears. (The dialog box you see depends on which color depth option you selected in step 2.) Here are some choices you might encounter—select one of the following and click **OK**:

- **Palette Component**—When reducing an image to two colors (black and white), you must tell Paint Shop Pro how to choose which pixels to change to white: based on their gray values, or their red, green, or blue components.

- **Palette**—When reducing an image to 16 or 256 colors, use the **Palette** options to tell PSP how you want it to select the optimal range of colors for the image's palette. To select the most common colors used in the image, choose **Optimized Median Cut**. To choose the most common color in each of several small quadrants throughout an image, choose **Optimized Octree**. To make the image appear the same on a wide variety of computers, choose **Standard/Web-safe**.

- **Reduction Method**—Select the method you want PSP to use to reduce the color palette: **Nearest Color**, **Ordered Dither**, or *Error Diffusion*. Choose **Nearest Color** to have PSP choose the nearest color in the color wheel when substituting an original color for a new color in the palette. Choose **Ordered Dither** to tell PSP to use a checkerboard pattern when working with two colors to create a blended color. Choose **Error Diffusion** if you want PSP to use a more random pattern when color blending with two colors. Because it uses a mathematical formula, **Error Diffusion** (when used in images with a very limited color palette) can sometimes generate artifacts in a color blended area, more so than using the **Ordered Dither** method.

89

▶ KEY TERM

Error Diffusion—Any of several mathematical techniques that attempt to compensate for large error values (differences between the intensities of an original pixel and its replacement in a reprocessed image) by dividing this difference into parts and distributing it to neighboring pixels, thus masking the obvious inaccuracy.

- **Palette Weight**—This option appears only when you're reducing an image to two colors. Choose **Weighted** to balance out the color palette with an even number of light, dark, and medium tones. Choose **Non-weighted** to let the balance of tones in the image decide which colors belong in the palette.

- **Boost Marked Colors By**—To use this option in 16 or 256 color images, select an area whose colors you want to favor, enable the **Optimized Median Cut** reduction method, and set a relative boost factor between 1 and 10.

- **Include Windows' Colors**—If you intend to use the image exclusively within a Windows program such as PowerPoint, enable this option to include the Windows standard palette of 32 colors in the image palette.

- **Reduce Color Bleeding**—As the **Error Diffusion** reduction method moves from left to right across an image substituting colors, a loss of color integrity might occur, with colors becoming too blended and more muted. Enable this option to prevent this from happening to your image.

89

15

Retouching a Photograph with Paint Shop Pro

IN THIS CHAPTER:

A photograph used to be a permanent record of a singular moment in time. With digital imaging, however, a photograph can be improved, enhanced, and even fundamentally changed to hide the "truth" of the original moment it captured. Through retouching, you can repair minor flaws such as scratches and holes and remove distortion caused by the camera lens or high file compression. You can even improve a human subject, removing red eye, erasing freckles and blemishes, and whitening teeth. In this chapter, I'll teach you how to use Paint Shop Pro's (PSP's) tools and filters to retouch your photographs and make them as good as new (or even better!).

---

90   About Removing Scratches, Specks, and Holes

✔ BEFORE YOU BEGIN	→ SEE ALSO
74 Import Photos from a Digital Camera	**91** Remove Scratches Automatically
75 Scan In Photos	**92** Repair Scratches Manually
	93 Remove Specks and Spots
	94 Repair Holes and Tears

90

It's not uncommon for photographs to acquire small scratches, spots, holes, and tears, even if the photos are not very old. If a photograph is not stored flat with its surface protected from damage, the photo might easily develop surface defects. PSP offers many tools you can use to repair these scratches and other small anomalies:

▶ **TIP**

Like most changes you can make to an image, you can limit your retouching to either a layer or a selection.

- **Automatic Small Scratch Removal.** If scratches are small, use this command to get rid of them quickly. See **91** **Remove Scratches Automatically**.

- **Scratch Remover Tool.** This tool gives you precise control over how scratches, cracks, and small specks are removed. See **92** **Repair Scratches Manually**.

- **Clone Brush Tool.** This tool allows you to remove defects by cloning or copying parts of an image over tops of holes, tears, scratches, or specks. It's perfect for making large repairs that the other tools and filters cannot handle easily. You can also repair large holes, tears, and scratches using a technique that borrows data from the undamaged parts of an image. See **94** **Repair Holes and Tears**.

- **Despeckle.** Does your photograph have a lot of tiny single-pixel dots on it? Use this filter to remove them—no matter their color. See **93** **Remove Specks and Spots**.

- **Salt and Pepper.** Large black or white specks that the **Despeckle** command misses can easily be removed with this filter. See **93** **Remove Specks and Spots**.

- **Noise Filters.** To remove a general scattering of dots or *noise* from a photograph, use any one of these filters: **Edge Preserving Smooth**, **Median**, or **Texture Preserving Smooth**. See **93** **Remove Specks and Spots**.

▶ KEY TERM

Noise—A random pattern of pixels that gives an image a grainy texture. Digital still cameras have the same picture-taking electronics as digital video cameras, so the noise that generally cancels itself out when viewed at 30 frames per second can't be ignored on a frozen frame.

▶ NOTE

Many of the tools you might use to remove scratches, specks, and holes require that your image be either grayscale or have a full color depth of 16 million colors.

91

91 **Remove Scratches Automatically**	
✔ **BEFORE YOU BEGIN**	→ **SEE ALSO**
74 Import Photos from a Digital Camera **75** Scan In Photos	**92** Repair Scratches Manually **94** Repair Holes and Tears

Printed photographs are fragile by nature and are easily scratched, especially if they are not stored in protective sleeves. The scanning process can actually enhance scratches by introducing halos around them, making them even more noticeable—especially in lower-resolution scans—than they were on the print. By using the **Automatic Small Scratch Removal** command, you can easily remove small, line-shaped scratches across the surface of an image. By its nature, this command is not terribly aggressive at removing scratches, so it's fairly safe to use on just about any image without worrying about introducing fuzziness and unwanted patterns.

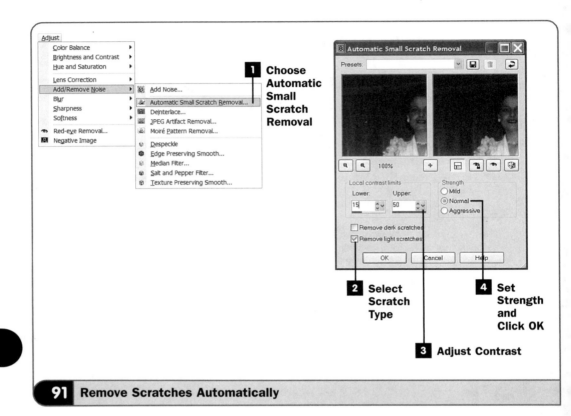

91

91 Remove Scratches Automatically

▶ NOTE

For scratches the **Automatic Small Scratch Removal** command won't get rid of, try removing them manually with the **Scratch Remover** or **Clone Brush** tools. See **92** **Repair Scratches Manually**.

1 Choose Automatic Small Scratch Removal

Choose **Adjust, Add/Remove Noise, Automatic Small Scratch Removal** from the menu. The **Automatic Small Scratch Removal** dialog box opens.

▶ TIP

To prevent details from being lost in areas that do not contain scratches, select the scratched area before choosing this command.

2 Select Scratch Type

Select the type of scratches you want to remove—dark scratches from a light background, light ones from a dark background, or both.

3 Adjust Contrast

By default, PSP sets the **Lower** contrast level to 0% and the **Upper** level to 50%. (PSP assumes that neighboring pixels with a contrast difference greater than 50% are intentional and not accidental.) PSP then seeks out line-shaped areas that contrast with surrounding pixels by that amount and removes them. To narrow this range, adjust the **Lower** and **Upper** limits.

▶ **NOTE**

If scratches remain while the contrast limits are set to 0 and 50, PSP cannot identify and remove them with this tool; you should try something else.

4 Set Strength and Click OK

Adjust the **Strength** as needed. For example, you might change the setting from **Normal** to **Aggressive** to have PSP be less discriminating in identifying scratches, or to **Mild** to have PSP be more careful. Click **OK** to apply the changes.

▶ **TIP**

Before clicking **OK**, check the image to make sure that no details have been accidentally erased.

92

92	**Repair Scratches Manually**
✔ **BEFORE YOU BEGIN**	→ **SEE ALSO**
90 About Removing Scratches, Specks, and Holes	**91** Remove Scratches Automatically
	94 Repair Holes and Tears

When a photograph contains large scratches or tears, you can remove them quickly using the **Scratch Remover** tool. You use this tool to trace all or part of a scratch or tear—if the tear isn't straight, you might have to apply the tool several times in small sections. As you drag with the tool on the image, you'll see a small rectangle bordered by two "gutters"; the pixels inside the two gutters are used to calculate the color of the pixels that will replace those inside the rectangle, covering up the tear. Proper placement of the rectangle and its two gutters is critical to achieving success. It'll be easier if you zoom in so that you can see the edges of the defect completely, and then drag as narrow a rectangle as possible around the tear so that fewer good pixels are "caught" within its boundaries and replaced.

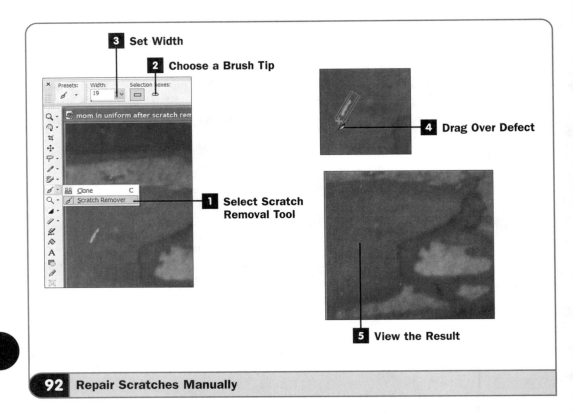

3 Set Width

2 Choose a Brush Tip

4 Drag Over Defect

1 Select Scratch Removal Tool

5 View the Result

92 Repair Scratches Manually

The **Scratch Remover** tool offers a choice of two tool tips: a rectangle with 90-degree corners, and a flattened hexagon. Use the pointy-ended hexagon when removing scratches close to the edge of some other object; doing so enables you to get in close without actually capturing any of that neighboring object's pixels.

▶ **TIP**

The **Scratch Remover** tool works by copying colors from surrounding pixels and applying them to the defect area in a random pattern. As a result, this tool works best on areas that are smooth, with no background pattern or texture. If the background of your image is not smooth, use the **Clone Brush** tool to remove the scratches instead.

1 **Select Scratch Removal Tool**

Select the **Scratch Removal** tool on the **Tools** toolbar.

▶ **NOTE**

The **Scratch Removal** tool works only on single-layer images. If you've just scanned in or imported a digital photo, it should have only one layer, so the tool will work just fine. If the image contains more than one layer, however, you must flatten it first or use the **Clone Brush** tool.

2 **Choose a Brush Tip**

On the **Tool Options** palette, click the brush tip you want to use. When working near the boundary of another object, select the pointy-ended tip; otherwise, choose the tip with square corners.

3 **Set Width**

Set the **Width** to a value just greater than the width of the scratch or tear you're trying to remove.

The idea is to capture a few good pixels on either side of the tear to create a good sample, but not so many that the sample becomes distorted. If you're not sure what **Width** to set, select the scratch first with the rectangle **Selection** tool and judge its size using the coordinates shown on the status bar.

92

4 **Drag Over Defect**

Click just above the beginning of the tear and drag down so that the "gutters" capture pixels on either side of the tear. Don't let the tear itself fall into the gutter (keep it within the rectangle), or the result will make the tear look bigger.

▶ **TIP**

If a tear meanders like a fickle snake throughout your image, you do not have to try to capture the entire tear with one motion. Instead, divide a large tear into smaller repair sections, and sew up the tear one section at a time.

5 **View the Result**

As you can see, the **Scratch Remover** tool easily removes the scratch, leaving a natural-colored patch. By repeating this process in an image, all the scratches and tears can be easily removed.

Sometimes, even when you adjust the **Width** correctly, because of nearby dust specks or a faded background, the **Scratch Remover** continues to create a bad-looking repair. In such a case, try a different tool such as the **Clone Brush**.

93 Remove Specks and Spots

✔ BEFORE YOU BEGIN	→ SEE ALSO
90 About Removing Scratches, Specks, and Holes	**94** Repair Holes and Tears

Noise can creep into your images in the most innocuous ways—after scanning a newspaper image, capturing an image with a video camera or grabbing it from live video, taking a long exposure with a digital camera (*CCD noise*), over-sharpening an image, or simply letting an image accumulate everyday dust and dirt. You'll notice noise the most in the shadows or the flat, nontextured, non-patterned areas of an image.

▶ KEY TERM

CCD noise—Random distortions introduced into a photo by a digital camera's CCD chip—its principal light detector. CCD noise happens most often during long exposures or at high ISO settings (film speed), and is magnified when "electronic zoom" is used to simulate a close-up of a subject taken at a distance. This type of noise mostly affects the shadow areas of an image, within the red and blue channels.

Paint Shop Pro provides many filters you can use to remove noise from an image. **Despeckle** removes nearly black or nearly white single pixel specks, and thus has limited use. The **Salt and Pepper** filter removes specks of the size you specify, whose brightness varies dramatically from that of surrounding pixels. **Salt and Pepper** is great at removing general noise and small specks of dust and dirt from old photographs. The **Median** filter is similar to **Salt and Pepper** except that it changes *all pixels* to match the median brightness of their neighbors, and not just the specks. This task shows you how to use the **Salt and Pepper** and **Median** filters. The **Median** filter works faster than the **Salt and Pepper** filter because it's less discriminating but it often causes detail to be lost. You might want to try both the **Salt and Pepper** and the **Median** filter on an image and compare the results.

▶ NOTE

To use the **Despeckle** filter, choose **Adjust, Add/Remove Noise, Despeckle**. The filter works automatically, removing single, very dark, or very light specks.

1 Choose a Filter

Choose **Adjust, Add/Remove Noise** from the menu bar, and then choose either **Salt and Pepper Filter** or **Median Filter**. Here, I'll try both filters on an old photo that has acquired some small specks.

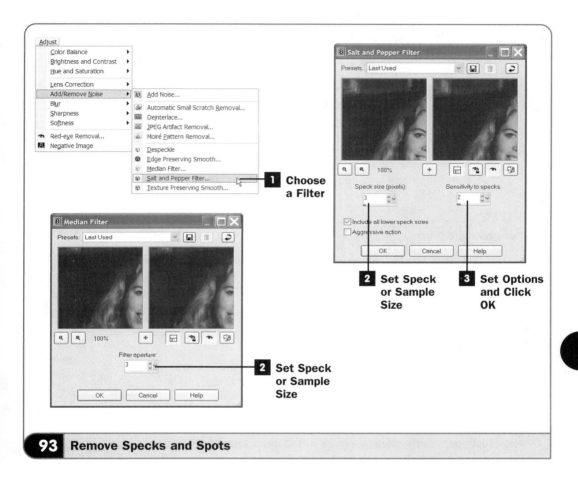

1 Choose a Filter

2 Set Speck or Sample Size

3 Set Options and Click OK

2 Set Speck or Sample Size

93 Remove Specks and Spots

93

▶ **TIP**

To prevent loss of detail, first select the areas of your image that contain noise, and then choose the filter. Only the area you selected will be affected by the filter.

2 **Set Speck or Sample Size**

In the **Salt and Pepper Filter** dialog box, adjust the size of the specks you want to remove by changing the **Speck size** value. To remove specks this size and smaller, enable the **Include All Lower Speck Sizes** check box.

In the **Median Filter** dialog box, adjust the area to sample for brightness differences by changing the **Filter aperture** value. Each pixel in the selection or layer is compared to the brightness of its many neighbors and is adjusted accordingly.

3 Set Options and Click OK

The **Median** filter has no other options, but in the **Salt and Pepper Filter** dialog box, you can also set the **Sensitivity to specks**. This value tells PSP how different an area must be from surrounding pixels to be considered a speck; higher values tell PSP that an area doesn't have to be that different from its neighbors to be a speck. Enable the **Aggressive Action** check box to have PSP change the brightness of specks more drastically than it would normally. Click **OK** to apply the filter.

After using the **Median** filter, you will probably have to sharpen the image.

▶ NOTE

If you compare the images, you'll see that both filters did a pretty good job at eliminating the small white specks in my red sweater and black pants, and in the shadows of the fireplace. The **Median** filter, however, has blurred the image too much. Compare the results in the Color Gallery section in this book.

94

94 Repair Holes and Tears

✔ BEFORE YOU BEGIN	→ SEE ALSO
90 About Removing Scratches, Specks, and Holes	**93** Remove Specks and Spots

---

Because of their fragile nature, photographs are easily bent, torn, and scratched—especially when they are not stored properly. In earlier tasks, you learned how to repair small tears and to remove specks of dust and such, but what do you do if there are a lot of tears, holes, and maybe even old foldlines, and the image is simply in sad shape?

One way in which you can cover up flaws is to use the **Clone Brush** to copy pixels from an undamaged area. The problem with this method, however, is that unless it's done carefully, the **Clone Brush** often leaves an unnatural, easily detectable pattern. In this task, you'll learn an alternative method that's both fast and foolproof.

1 Duplicate the Background Layer

Open the image you want to repair and then click the **Duplicate Layer** button on the **Layer** palette. Name the duplicate layer **Shifted**.

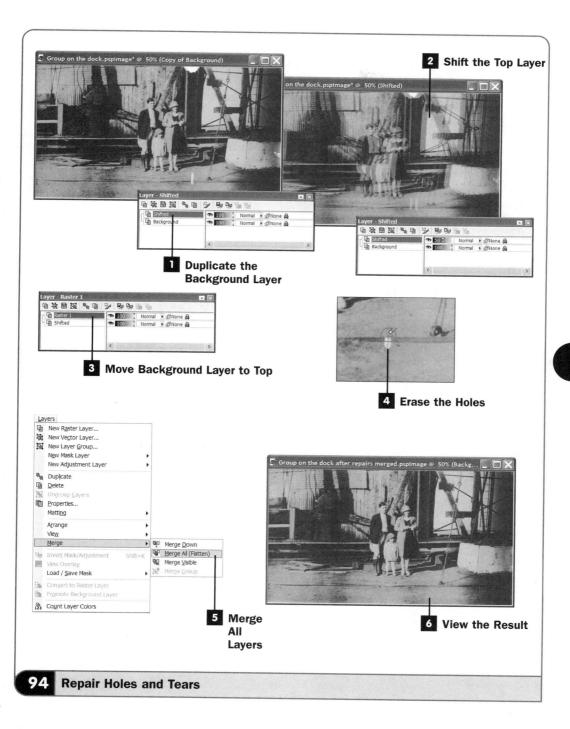

2 Shift the Top Layer

1 Duplicate the Background Layer

3 Move Background Layer to Top

4 Erase the Holes

5 Merge All Layers

6 View the Result

94 **Repair Holes and Tears**

2 Shift the Top Layer

In the **Layer** palette, change the **Opacity** of the **Shifted** layer to 50%. This lets you see the **Background** layer content while you're moving the **Shifted** layer. You're going to use pieces of the **Shifted** layer to cover the holes on the **Background** layer. Click the **Move** tool on the **Tools** toolbar and slowly drag the **Shifted** layer up, down, right, or left, until the torn area on the **Background** layer is covered by content from the **Shifted** layer.

▶ NOTE

In this example, we wanted to repair the tear just below and to the right of the family, and the hole along the right edge, so we've moved the **Shifted** layer to the right.

3 Move Background Layer to Top

In the **Layer** palette, reset the **Opacity** of the **Shifted** layer to 100%. To be able to move the **Background** layer to the top, you must first promote it to a full raster layer. Select **Layers, Promote Background Layer** from the menu. This changes the name of the **Background** layer to **Raster 1**. Now drag the bottom **Raster 1** layer to the top of the layer stack.

94

▶ NOTE

After dragging the **Raster 1** layer to the top of the layer stack in step 3, the photo will look as it did originally—tears, holes, and everything.

4 Erase the Holes

Click the **Eraser** tool on the **Tools** toolbar. On the **Tool Options** palette, adjust the **Size** value so that the eraser is slightly bigger than the defect. Soften the edge a bit by setting **Hardness** to 50 and **Density** to 80. Then drag over the defect with the eraser, revealing the **Shifted** layer beneath.

5 Merge All Layers

After erasing all the holes and tears, merge the layers into one by choosing **Layers, Merge, Merge All (Flatten)**.

6 View the Result

After erasing the holes and tears using the **Eraser** tool, I followed up with the **Clone Brush** to fill the ghastly tear at the top of the image. Then I merged all layers.

▶ TIP

If your image has large tears you don't want to fix this way, use the **Clone Brush**.

95 | Correct Red Eye

✔ BEFORE YOU BEGIN	→ SEE ALSO
Just jump right in.	98 Awaken Tired Eyes

When used properly, a camera flash can help lighten shadows and illuminate an otherwise dark image. Unfortunately, using a flash might sometimes have unintended effects, such as *red eye*. In nonhuman subjects such as dogs or cats, the result might be "glassy eye" rather than red eye. No matter; you remove it in the same way: with PSP's **Red-eye Removal** command.

This task explains how to remove red eye in Paint Shop Pro; however, you can also remove red eye using Photo Album, if you have that program. Open the image in the **Image View** window, zoom in on the eye you want to fix, click the arrow on the **Red Eye** button, and choose **One Click Removal**. The pointer changes to a circle cross-hair—center this cursor on the red area of the eye and click. If you would rather paint the red out manually, click the arrow on the **Red Eye** button and choose **Red Eye Brush**. Adjust the width of the brush by selecting **Brush Width** from the **Red Eye** menu. Then drag over the red to paint the pupil black. If you have to repaint part of the iris, change the brush color by choosing the **Brush Color** command from the **Red Eye** menu. To paint the glint back in, choose **Highlight Brush** from the **Red Eye** menu and click the pupil.

95

▶ KEY TERM

Red eye—An effect caused when a camera flash is reflected by the retina at the back of the eye. It isn't an optical illusion; you're actually photographing a fully illuminated retina in its natural color—bright red.

▶ TIP

When you're shooting your photograph, you can avoid giving your subjects red eye by separating the flash unit from the camera (if possible), or telling your subjects to not look directly at the camera. Some cameras have a red-eye reduction feature, which causes the flash to go off several times. The first series of flashes at lower intensity cause the pupil to contract, thus blocking the reflection, whereas the final flash at full intensity illuminates the subject for the picture.

1 Choose Adjust, Red-eye Removal

Choose **Adjust, Red-eye Removal** from the menu bar. The **Red-eye Removal** dialog box appears.

As you make adjustments, the corrections appear in the right preview pane of the **Red-eye Removal** dialog box.

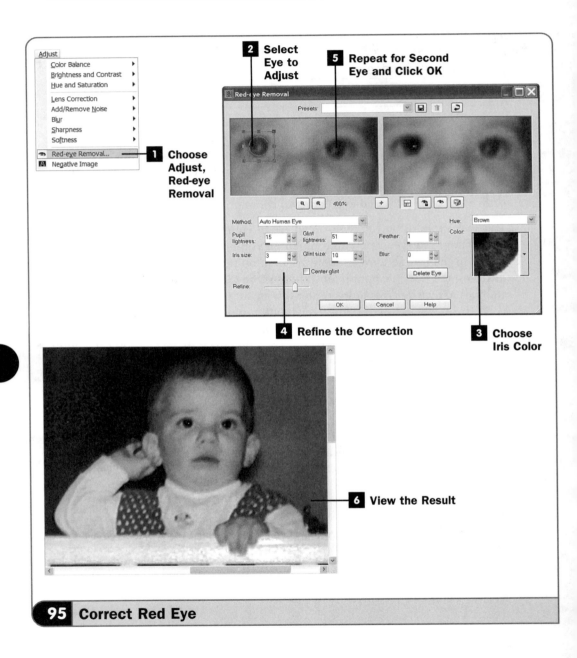

95 **Correct Red Eye**

2 Select Eye to Adjust

Zoom in on the eye you want to adjust using the **Zoom In** and **Select Area** buttons. Change the portion of the image shown in the right preview by dragging if needed.

Open the **Method** list and choose **Auto Human Eye** if you're adjusting a human eye, or **Auto Animal Eye** if you're adjusting a cat, dog, or other animal eye. In the left preview window, click in the absolute center of the *pupil*. A circle-guide appears; drag this guide until it touches the outer rim of the *iris*. For an animal, select only the pupil.

If the pupil shape is not perfectly round, you might have better luck selecting it manually. Choose **Freehand Pupil Outline** from the **Method** list and draw around the pupil, or choose **Point-to-Point** and click along the pupil's edge.

▶ KEY TERM

Pupil—The black center of the eye that adjusts in size based on the amount of ambient light.

Iris—The colored part of the eye; typically brown, blue, or green.

3 Choose Iris Color

For a human eye, open the **Hue** list and choose the person's actual iris color. Then open the **Color** list and choose the variation of that eye color that matches the person's natural color. For an animal, choose a variation from the **Color** list only.

4 Refine the Correction

To adjust how much of the guide circle is painted with the iris color, drag the **Refine** slider. If you drag with the **Refine** slider all the way to the right, PSP paints a whole, round iris, even if it overlaps part of the eyelid. By dragging toward the left, you can prevent part of the eyelid from being painted. You might move the **Refine** slider to the left in a half-opened eye.

Adjust **Pupil lightness**, **Glint lightness**, **Glint size**, and **Iris size** as needed. Position the *glint* in the center of the pupil by enabling the **Center glint** check box. Add a **Feather** to the outside of the pupil or **Blur** the outer edge of the iris if desired by specifying values in these fields.

▶ KEY TERM

Glint—A tiny reflection of light that appears on the pupil.

5 Repeat for Second Eye and Click OK

Repeat steps 2 through 4 to select and correct the pupil of the second eye and then click **OK** to apply the correction.

95

6 View the Result

The red eye is gone, and with a bit of sharpening, we're left with a cute baby just waking up from his nap.

---

96 Remove Freckles and Minor Blemishes

✔ BEFORE YOU BEGIN	→ SEE ALSO
80 Zoom In and Out with the Zoom Tool	**97** Whiten Teeth
81 Zoom In and Out with the Overview Palette	**98** Awaken Tired Eyes

---

96

Almost everyone has certain...cosmetic distinctions that help identify and even glamorize a person. However, if they're the temporary kind, you might not want a permanent record of them. Sometimes a perfectly good photograph is marred by minor distractions such as a few blemishes, a mole, a cold sore, or a few wrinkles just beginning to show. Is it vain to want to fix nature? Perhaps, but don't let that stop you—especially when it's so easy.

You can use the **Clone Brush** to paint away minor defects in a photograph by copying good pixels from some other area. But the process is tedious and often easily detectable. In this task, you'll use a quicker method.

1 Duplicate Background Layer

Open the image you want to repair and then click the **Duplicate Layer** button on the **Layer** palette. Name the new layer **Unblurred**.

2 Blur Background Layer

Change to the **Background** layer and select **Adjust, Blur, Blur More** from the menu.

▶ TIP

To see the blurred **Background** layer, hide the top layer temporarily by clicking its eye button on the **Layer** palette.

For very large images such as those at 1048×1478 resolution, the **Blur More** filter might not do enough to blur the layer. In such cases, try the **Gaussian Blur** filter (**Adjust, Blur, Gaussian Blur**).

1 Duplicate Background Layer

2 Blur Background Layer

3 Erase Blemishes

4 Merge All Layers

5 View the Result

96

96 Remove Freckles and Minor Blemishes

3 Erase Blemishes

On the **Layer** palette, change to the **Unblurred** layer; click the **Eraser** tool. Adjust the **Size** value so that the eraser is slightly bigger than the blemish you want to remove. Soften the edge a bit by setting **Hardness** to 50 and **Density** to 80. Then click the blemish with the eraser, revealing the blurred layer beneath.

4 Merge All Layers

After erasing all the minor imperfections, merge the layers into one by choosing **Layers, Merge, Merge All (Flatten)**.

5 View the Result

There, that's better. We didn't erase the detail and character of the face, just improved it a bit. Look for this in the Color Gallery section in this book.

---

97 Whiten Teeth

✔ BEFORE YOU BEGIN	→ SEE ALSO
80 Zoom In and Out with the Zoom Tool	**96** Remove Freckles and Minor Blemishes
81 Zoom In and Out with the Overview Palette	**98** Awaken Tired Eyes

97

There are many products on the market that you can use to whiten your teeth: gels, toothpastes, whitening strips, and bleaches, but none work as fast and as effectively as digital editing. It's not vanity to want to improve mother nature; in our culture today, a great importance is placed on having clean, white teeth, and if a photo will be used in a resumé or to advertise a product, you'll want to give the best impression you can by making sure that your subject looks his or her best.

Whitening teeth is tricky, however; you don't want the effect to look obvious and artificial. You'll want to avoid the temptation to use *pure white* to paint over all your teeth, which results in a picket-fence effect that can look genuinely scary. The technique explained here uses the **Dodge** tool, which selectively lightens the brightness of the pixels over which it passes. You must be cautious, however, so that you don't burn out the color and create a fake whiteness.

▶ TIP

I always get good results with the **Dodge** tool, but if you don't like its effects, try selecting the teeth, choosing **Adjust, Color Balance, Red/Green/Blue**, and increasing the **Blue** value.

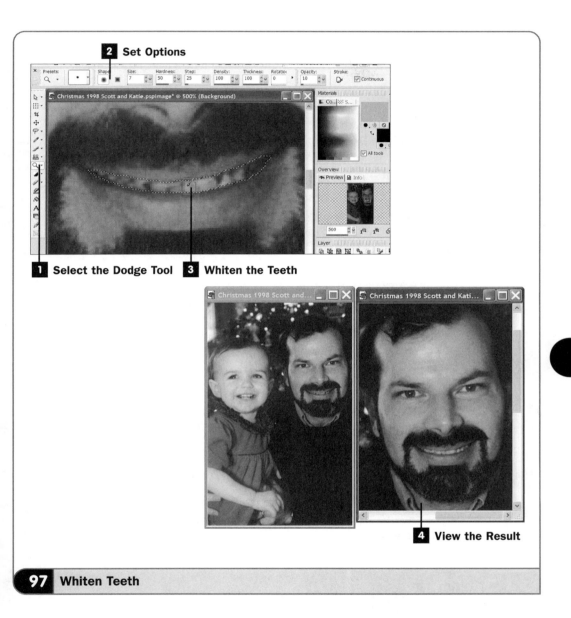

2 Set Options

Christmas 1998 Scott and Katie.pspimage* @ 500% (Background)

1 Select the Dodge Tool   3 Whiten the Teeth

Christmas 1998 Scott and...   Christmas 1998 Scott and Kati...

97

4 View the Result

97 Whiten Teeth

1 Select the Dodge Tool

Zoom in on the teeth so that you can see them clearly, and then select the **Dodge** tool on the **Tools** toolbar.

▶ **TIP**

To isolate the effects of the **Dodge** tool, select the teeth before beginning. You might want to select the gums as well.

2 **Set Options**

Adjust the **Size** of the **Dodge** tool in the **Tool Options** palette so that the brush tip is just larger than the teeth. Set **Opacity** to 10 or so, **Density** to 100, and **Hardness** to 50.

If you want to prevent over-lightening the teeth and burning them out, select the **Continuous** option. This option prevents the brush from lightening pixels more, even if you pass over them more than once.

3 **Whiten the Teeth**

If the **Continuous** option is not turned on, position the brush tip over the first tooth and click once. The tooth should get just a bit lighter. Click again to lighten a bit more, or move to the next tooth. Repeat until all the teeth are whiter. If the **Continuous** option is set, drag over the teeth to lighten—they will only be lightened up to the **Opacity** amount you select, even if you brush over them several times.

98

▶ **TIP**

Remove any remaining imperfections (such as uneven color or spots on the teeth) with the **Clone Brush.**

4 **View the Result**

Compare the original (on the left) to the whitened version; you can see that the teeth on the right look better, and yet still natural. Look for this image in the Color Gallery section.

---

98 **Awaken Tired Eyes**

✔ **BEFORE YOU BEGIN**	→ **SEE ALSO**
80 Zoom In and Out with the Zoom Tool	**95** Correct Red Eye
81 Zoom In and Out with the Overview Palette	**96** Remove Freckles and Minor Blemishes
	97 Whiten Teeth

They say that the eyes are the window to the soul. It must be true, because if a woman has dark circles under her eyes, we think she looks tired (even if the dark circles are a natural skin condition). By slightly lightening the skin under the eyes, you can take years off a face and brighten a person's outlook. And it's simple to do, using the **Change to Target** tool.

Redness in the eyes caused by chlorine in swimming pools can also make them look tired. To whiten the eyes, select the white parts and choose **Adjust, Hue and Saturation, Hue/Saturation/Lightness.** Then change the color to white by setting **Hue** to –180 and **Saturation** to –100. Then adjust the **Lightness** value to achieve a lighter, yet still natural, white (try 18 to 25).

▶ **TIP**

If your subject is looking into the sun, her pupils might be quite small, making her look tired and sleepy. To widen the pupils, use the **Red-eye Removal** command as described in **95 Correct Red Eye.** Move **Refine** to the far right to prevent changes to the iris, and then set **Iris Size** to 1 or 0 to make the pupil as big as you like.

1 Select Change to Target Tool

Select the **Change to Target** tool on the **Tools** toolbar.

2 Set Options

On the **Tool Options** palette, open the **Mode** list and select **Lightness.** Set the **Size** to the width of the area you want to lighten. Set **Hardness** to 50 and **Opacity** to 10.

98

3 Select a Light Pixel

Press the **Ctrl** key and use the eyedropper to click a skin pixel close to the eye that's fairly light. The **Change to Target** tool uses this pixel's lightness value to lighten the skin you paint over.

▶ **TIP**

If you're lightening a large area of skin, change the source pixel from time to time for a more natural look.

4 Lighten Skin Under the Eyes

Drag the **Change to Target** over the dark patches under the eye, changing the pixels there to the same lightness value as the pixel you clicked with the eyedropper in step 3.

▶ **TIP**

If you have trouble using the **Change to Target**, try creating a copy of the image on a duplicate layer and making your changes to the copy. You can then use the **Opacity** setting to control the amount of the changes you see.

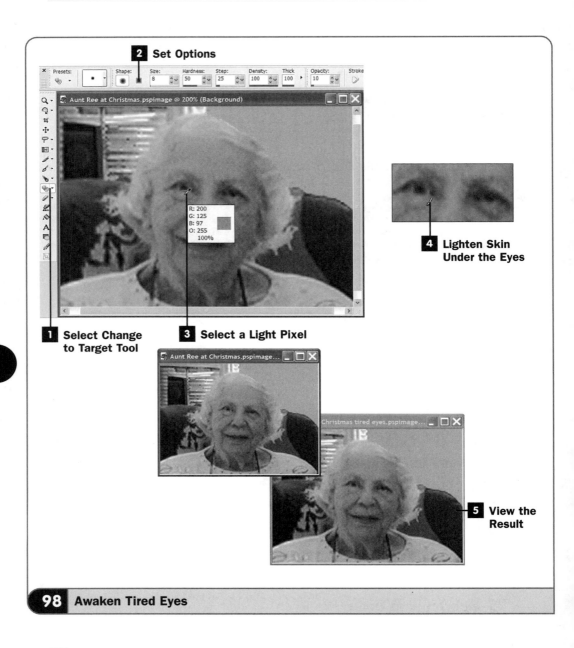

2 Set Options

4 Lighten Skin Under the Eyes

1 Select Change to Target Tool

3 Select a Light Pixel

98

5 View the Result

98 Awaken Tired Eyes

5 View the Result

The final result (on the right) is very natural looking. With lighter patches under her eyes, Aunt Ree looks less tired, and it's easier to see how truly loving, humorous, and wonderful she is.

16

Performing Basic Image Tasks with Adobe Photoshop Elements

IN THIS CHAPTER:

As explained in Chapter 14, "Performing Basic Image Tasks with Paint Shop Pro," to build the best website you need to have the best images. That doesn't mean you have to be a Michelangelo, or even be able to create your own pictures. But it does mean that you should have some basic skills in how to edit pictures so they're as spiffy as possible when they're posted online. These pictures can range from a simple web button to an old black-and-white photo, or pictures from your child's recent birthday party.

So in this chapter, you'll learn how to accomplish the most common graphics tasks to help with your website, using Adobe Photoshop Elements.

99   About Image Information

✔ BEFORE YOU BEGIN	SEE ALSO
Just jump right in.	**107** Change Image Size or Resolution

99

When needed, the **Editor** can display information about the basic characteristics of an image—its file type, resolution, size, and data specific to the conditions under which it was taken. To display this metadata (so-called because it's stored at the top of the image file) for any image open in the **Editor**, select **File, File Info** from the menu bar. A dialog box opens, loaded with information about the current image.

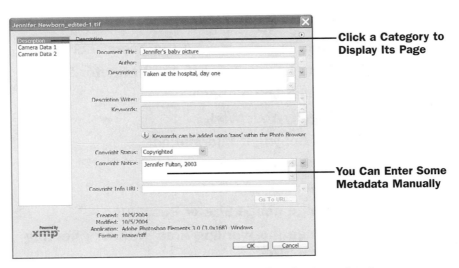

Click a Category to Display Its Page

You Can Enter Some Metadata Manually

The File Info dialog box contains lots of information about your image.

On the left, you'll find a list of categories of information stored within the image file. Click a category to display its page of information. For example, click the **Camera Data 1** category to find out what the flash setting was when you took this photograph. Some metadata can be entered by you, simply by clicking inside any of the white boxes. For example, you might enter your name under **Author** or type in a **Copyright Notice**. Metadata you can view but not change is shown in gray. This kind of metadata is typically EXIF data that your camera recorded when the image was taken, such as shutter speed and f-stop.

You can also change some of this metadata through the Organizer. For example, if you click the **Description** category on the left, you'll see the text caption you entered in the Organizer (shown here as the **Description**) and any tags or collection markers you attached to the image (shown here as **Keywords**). The metadata you enter manually is stored in the *alpha channel* of the image. Metadata you enter through this dialog box is permanently saved *only* if you store the image in PSD, TIFF, PNG, GIF, or JPEG format. At the bottom of the **Description** page, you'll find basic information about the image, such as the file date, modified date, and file type.

▶ **NOTE**

You can also view and change a file's metadata on the **Metadata** palette within the **File Browser**. In the **Editor**, choose **File, Browse Folders** to display the browser. In the Organizer, you can view an image's metadata on the **Properties** pane. Choose **Window, Properties** from the Organizer menu; then click the **Metadata** button at the top of the **Properties** pane.

99

▶ **NOTE**

Some metadata, such as an image's size and resolution, is added or changed by Photoshop Elements when you edit an image and save changes. So even if you have an image that started out as a scan of a printed photo, there might be information for you to view in the File Info dialog box.

▶ **KEY TERM**

Alpha channel—Data saved with an image for reuse when needed, such as selections, masks, and creator information.

You can add a copyright notice on the **Description** page by changing the **Copyright Status** drop-down list to **Copyrighted**, and typing your copyright text in the **Copyright Notice** text box. You can add your web page address in the **Copyright Info URL** box. Note, however, that copyright data such as this is of limited use because anyone with a program capable of reading image metadata can change or remove it. Better to protect your images with a copyright that can't be removed—see **104** **Add Copyright Information** for help.

As I mentioned earlier, metadata your digital camera recorded when the shot was taken—such as the camera type, date the photo was taken, and shot conditions such as f-stop, shutter speed, and focal length—can be found on the **Camera Data 1** and **Camera Data 2** pages in the **File Info** dialog box. Some of this data can be used by an EXIF-compatible printer to print your photo more accurately, with better color and brightness matching. To make sure you don't lose this valuable EXIF data, save your digital camera file using an EXIF-compatible program (Photoshop Elements just happens to be one), in an EXIF-compatible format (Photoshop PSD or JPEG).

▶ **NOTE**

If you use the **Save for Web** command to compress an image for use on the Web, as part of its compression process, the **Editor** will strip all EXIF metadata from the image. So you'll definitely want to save your compressed image as a *copy*, and save your original image and your changes in a PSD-formatted file.

Also on the **Camera Data 2** page, you'll find the image's current size in pixels, resolution, and ICC color profile (listed here as **Color Source**). By the way, you can change an image's size and resolution as needed (see **107 Change Image Size or Resolution**).

In the Organizer, the **Properties** pane can provide you with further information about the currently selected image. To display the **Properties** pane, click the **Show or Hide Properties** button on the **Options** bar, or choose **Window, Properties**. Although the **Properties** pane also displays EXIF data, it includes other information that you won't find in the **File Info** dialog box. In the **Properties** pane, you'll find information about where the image is stored, its file date, text caption, audio caption, and any notes you attached on the **General** tab. Markers you might have attached to an image are listed on the **Tags** tab. The file date, modified date, import date, and related information can be found on the **History** tab, and EXIF and other metadata is located on the **Metadata** tab. To display a condensed version of the metadata, select the **Brief** option; to display all the metadata, select the **Complete** option instead.

▶ **TIP**

The **Properties** pane normally appears over the top of the thumbnails in the catalog. Drag it by its title bar to move it out of the way, or park it in the **Organize** bin by choosing **Window, Dock Properties in Organize Bin**. Select this command again to make the **Properties** pane "float" in the work area once more.

▶ **TIP**

You can display the **Properties** pane while using **Date View**, but you can't dock it because the **Organize** bin is not displayed.

► **TIP**

You can resize the **Properties** pane to make its data easier to read. Just drag a side or corner to resize.

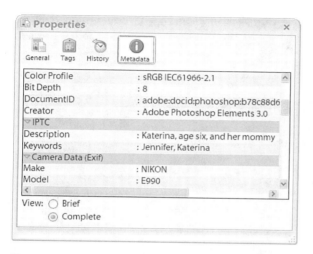

The Properties pane enables you to access image information from within the Organizer.

100

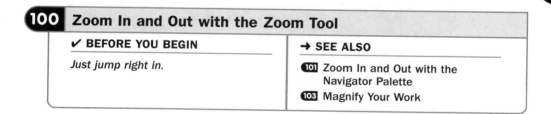

100 **Zoom In and Out with the Zoom Tool**

✔ BEFORE YOU BEGIN	→ SEE ALSO
Just jump right in.	**101** Zoom In and Out with the Navigator Palette
	103 Magnify Your Work

Whether you're making changes to a photograph or some artwork you've created yourself, you must be able to view the image clearly to make precise changes. Typically, this means zooming in on some area that doesn't look right so that you can discern the problem, and later zooming back out again to see whether the change you made looks right when the image is viewed at its regular size. To zoom in on an image and back out again, use the **Zoom** tool.

1 **Select the Zoom Tool**

Open an image in the **Editor** and then click the **Zoom** tool in the **Toolbox**.

1 Select the Zoom Tool

Zoom In
Zoom Out

2 Choose a Zoom Amount

3 Or Click to Zoom

4 Or Zoom to a Set Size

100 Zoom In and Out with the Zoom Tool

2 Choose a Zoom Amount

The **Zoom** tool provides many ways in which you can zoom. To view an image at a particular zoom level (such as 50%), select the current percentage in the **Zoom** box on the **Options** bar, type a new percentage, and press **Enter**. You can also use the slider on the **Zoom** box to select a zoom amount by dragging the slider left or right.

▶ **TIP**

When you're zooming an image in or out to any percentage, you can change the size of the image window to fit the image, up to the available workspace, by first enabling the **Resize Window to Fit** option on the **Options** bar. To allow the image window to expand below free-floating palettes that might be in the workspace, enable the **Ignore Palettes** option. (To temporarily hide free-floating palettes, press **Tab**; press **Tab** again to make them reappear.) To zoom all open image windows by the same amount, enable the **Zoom All Windows** option. This option works only if you zoom using the **Zoom In** or **Zoom Out** buttons, and not the **Zoom** slider.

▣ Or Click to Zoom

You can zoom by a predetermined amount toward a particular point within an image. First, click the **Zoom In** or **Zoom Out** button on the **Options** bar to determine the direction of the zoom. Then click the point you want to zoom in on (or away from) within the image window.

To zoom in on a particular area of an image, simply drag with the **Zoom** tool to select the area you want to see up close. The selected area is enlarged to fit the size of the image window.

▣ Or Zoom to a Set Size

100

To view the image at 100% (based on roughly 72 pixels per inch [ppi], or optimum screen resolution), click the **Actual Pixels** button on the **Options** bar. You can also double-click the **Zoom** tool in the **Toolbox** to view the image at 100%. Assuming that a user's screen resolution is the same as yours, this option displays an image in the same size it will look on somebody else's screen.

To zoom the image as large as possible to fill the workspace, click the **Fit on Screen** button. You can also double-click the **Hand** tool in the **Toolbox** to fit the image to the workspace, and center the image within the window.

To zoom the image to the approximate magnification it will be when you print it (based on the current image resolution), click the **Print Size** button.

▶ **TIP**

To zoom in and out without actually selecting the **Zoom** tool first, press and hold **Ctrl+Spacebar** and click the image to zoom in. Press and hold **Alt+Spacebar** and click the image to zoom out.

101 Zoom In and Out with the Navigator Palette

✔ BEFORE YOU BEGIN	→ SEE ALSO
Just jump right in.	100 Zoom In and Out with the Zoom Tool
	103 Magnify Your Work

In the preceding task, you learned how to zoom in and out using the **Zoom** tool and its options. However, if the **Navigator** palette is displayed, you can use it to zoom in and out without changing to the **Zoom** tool first.

▶ TIP

If you're working on multiple images and have tiled them in the **Editor** window, you'll want to use the **Navigator** palette to zoom, rather than the **Zoom** tool, which might untile the windows.

1 Display the Navigator Palette

Open an image in the **Editor**. If the **Navigator** palette is not displayed, choose **Window, Navigator** from the menu bar.

2 Enter a Zoom Amount

To view an image at a particular zoom level (such as 50%), select the current zoom percentage shown in the box on the left side of the palette. Then type a new zoom percentage and press **Enter**.

3 Or Adjust Zoom Slider

You can also drag the slider on the **Navigator** palette to zoom. Drag the slider to the left to zoom out; drag it to the right to zoom in.

▶ TIP

To zoom by a predetermined amount, click either of the **Zoom** buttons, located on either side of the slider. The minus button zooms out, whereas the plus button zooms in.

1 Display the Navigator Palette

2 Enter a Zoom Amount

3 Or Adjust Zoom Slider

102

101 Zoom In and Out with the Navigator Palette

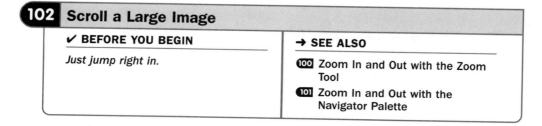

102 Scroll a Large Image

✔ BEFORE YOU BEGIN	→ SEE ALSO
Just jump right in.	**100** Zoom In and Out with the Zoom Tool
	101 Zoom In and Out with the Navigator Palette

If an image is being shown with a magnification larger than the image window can display, parts of that image will be obscured from view. If you want to make changes on a part of the image you can't currently see, you'll have to scroll to view that part of the image. To do that, use the **Hand** tool, the scrollbars, or the **Navigator** palette.

4 Make Small Adjustments

3 Or Drag Navigator Rectangle

1 Select the Hand Tool   **2** Drag with the Hand Tool

102

102 Scroll a Large Image

1 Select the Hand Tool

Open an image in the **Editor** and click the **Hand** tool in the **Toolbox**.

▶ TIP

A quick way to activate the **Hand** tool without actually clicking it in the **Toolbox** is to simply hold the **Spacebar** as you drag inside the image window.

2 Drag with the Hand Tool

Click the mouse in the image window and drag with the hand pointer to display the portion of the image you want to view. For example, drag down with the **Hand** tool to view a part of an image that's hidden just above the currently displayed portion.

3 Or Drag Navigator Rectangle

You can also reposition the viewable portion of the image by dragging the red rectangle within the **Navigator** palette. (If the **Navigator** palette is not displayed, choose **Window, Navigator** from the menu bar.) The rectangle encompasses the portion of the image you're actually seeing in the work-space; when it frames the entire thumbnail, you're actually seeing the entire image.

▶ TIP

The **Navigator** palette has several advantages over the other scrolling methods. Most notably, you can scroll quickly in the direction you want, and you can see what you're about to do before you do it.

▶ TIP

To scroll to a particular point within an image, click that point in the image preview shown on the **Navigator** palette. The red rectangle moves to center itself on that point, and the image is scrolled by that same amount.

▪4 Make Small Adjustments

Click the scroll arrows on the horizontal/vertical scrollbars or press the arrow keys on the keyboard to move the viewable portion of the image by a small amount.

103

103 Magnify Your Work	
✔ **BEFORE YOU BEGIN**	→ **SEE ALSO**
Just jump right in.	**100** Zoom In and Out with the Zoom Tool
	101 Zoom In and Out with the Navigator Palette

Some changes you'll want to make to an image will involve working in a small confined area. For example, perhaps you want to remove a small mole or other distraction from a person's face. To do that, you can use the **Clone Stamp** tool, but what if you can't see the area you want to fix all that clearly? You could zoom in, of course, but it might be nice to be able to view the changes as you make them using a more zoomed-out view. Of course, there's always the **Navigator** palette and its small image thumbnail, but your tiny changes might not be noticeable in that window. What you need is the ability to quickly zoom in on your work while still maintaining the big-picture view of your changes. To accomplish this task, you use a duplicate image window.

103 Magnify Your Work

1 Open a Second Window

> ▶ **NOTE**
>
> If you don't want to open a second window on an image, you can quickly zoom in and out of an already open image window by pressing **Ctrl+Spacebar** and clicking the image window to zoom in, or pressing **Alt+Spacebar** and clicking the image window to zoom back out.

1 Open a Second Window

Open an image in the **Editor** and increase the zoom so that the area you want to work on is magnified and easy to see. To open a second window that displays the same image, choose **View, New Window for *XXX***, where XXX is the name of the image file.

2 Arrange the Two Windows

Click the **Automatically Tile Windows** button (the four-tiny-squares button at the right end of the **Shortcuts** bar) or choose **Window, Images, Tile** from the menu to arrange the two windows on top of the other. Drag the border of the first window so that you can see the area you want to work on comfortably. Then drag the border of the second window so that it doesn't take up too much room in the workspace (the second window will be smaller). You can use the first window as the work window, and the second, smaller window as a magnifier window.

▶ **TIP**

To create a larger working area, hide the **Palette** bin and the **Photo** bin temporarily by clicking their buttons on the **Status** bar.

▶ **TIP**

To save time, instead of resizing the second (smaller) window and then zooming it, click the window, click the **Zoom** tool, and on the **Options** bar, enable the **Resize Window to Fit** option. Then drag the window to the exact small size you need.

103

3 Change the Zoom

Change the zoom level of the second window so that the entire image fits within its boundaries: Click the second image window to make it active, click the **Zoom** tool, and use the **Option** bar to adjust the zoom. You should now have two windows: one window that's larger and zoomed in on the portion of the image you want to work on, and a second window that's fairly small, which depicts the image in its entirety.

Here, you can see an old photo of a woman and her mother. Like most old photos, it had some spots and scratches that needed repair. So, I zoomed in on the woman's mother's face and began work with the **Healing Brush** tool. To make sure that the changes I made to her face were subtle, I opened a second window so that I could view the photograph in its entirety as I worked.

104 Add Copyright Information

✔ **BEFORE YOU BEGIN**

99 About Image Information

If you plan to share images that you create and photographs you have taken, you should consider copyrighting them. All the photographs you take are already your property and are protected by law. It is not necessary to fill out any forms or contact the U.S. Copyright Office before copyrighting your images. Still, the government isn't going to compensate you if someone steals your work, and because it's easy to protect your images against unauthorized use, why not do so?

▶ **NOTE**

If you are a professional photographer, consider purchasing the digital watermarking plug-in provided by Digimarc Corporation. This plug-in provides a secure method of protecting your copyrighted images and tracking their use on the Web. However, because of the costs involved, this solution is not practical for most casual users.

104

▶ **NOTE**

A typical copyright includes the word *copyright* or the © symbol, the year the work was first published, and the claimant's name.

The Editor provides two ways to protect your work. The first method involves typing a copyright notice in the **File Info** dialog box, as discussed in **99** **About Image Information**. The notice becomes a part of the file's metadata, and most graphics editors such as Photoshop and Photoshop Elements can read this metadata and display the copyright on the image's title bar when the image is opened. There are a lot of programs (including the Editor) that can not only view an image's metadata, but allow the user to change it as well. So, if you add a copyright notice in this manner, keep in mind that it's a simple public notice, and that it can be easily removed or altered.

The best way to protect your work is to add a notice that can't be removed because it's part of the image itself. To copyright your images in this manner, you'll create a copyright file that you can copy into each image you want to protect against misuse. To create the copyright file, you'll type the text you want to use for the copyright and apply the **Emboss** filter to give it a raised appearance. After pasting the copyright into an image you want to mark, you'll use the **Soft Light** blend mode to make the copyright see-through, like a watermark. Finally, you'll merge all the layers together, blending the copyright text with the image pixels permanently. This is the image copy you should share online because it can't be altered to look like it was created by someone else. A key here is to make sure that you place the copyright in an integral part of the image so that it cannot be cropped away and the rest of the image used anyway.

① Create a New Image

In the Editor, choose **File, New, Blank File** from the menu bar or click the **New** button on the **Shortcuts** bar to display the **New** dialog box. Type **Copyright** in the **Name** box. Set the **Width** to **900** and **Height** to **300** pixels. Set **Resolution** to **300ppi**, or whatever resolution you typically use for images you share or use online. Set the **Color Mode** to **RGB Color**. From the **Background Contents** list, select **white**. Click **OK** to create the new file.

② Add Copyright Text

Select the **Type** tool on the **Toolbox**; choose a font and size and a dark **Color**. Click in the image and type the copyright text: Hold down the **Alt** key and type **0169** on the numeric keypad to enter the copyright symbol (©), and then type the year and your name.

③ Create a Border

Click the **Rectangular Marquee** tool on the **Toolbox**. Draw a selection just inside the image border. Choose **Select, Inverse** to invert the selection. You now have a selection along the outer edges of the copyright image.

Select the **Background** layer on the **Layers** palette. Click the **Paint Bucket** tool on the **Toolbox**. Fill the selection with black.

104

④ Merge Layers

Merge the layers together by choosing **Layer, Flatten Image**. The two layers are merged into a single layer called **Background**.

⑤ Add Embossing and Save

To give your copyright a raised appearance, apply the **Emboss** filter. Choose **Filter, Stylize, Emboss**. The **Emboss** dialog box opens. Typically, the default settings work just fine for this purpose, but you can adjust the settings if you don't like the look. Click **OK**.

Click the **Save** button to save the image in PSD format. Use the filename **Copyright.psd**.

⑥ Paste Copyright

In the **Copyright** image you just created, choose **Select, All** and then **Edit, Copy** from the menu bar to copy the entire image to the clipboard.

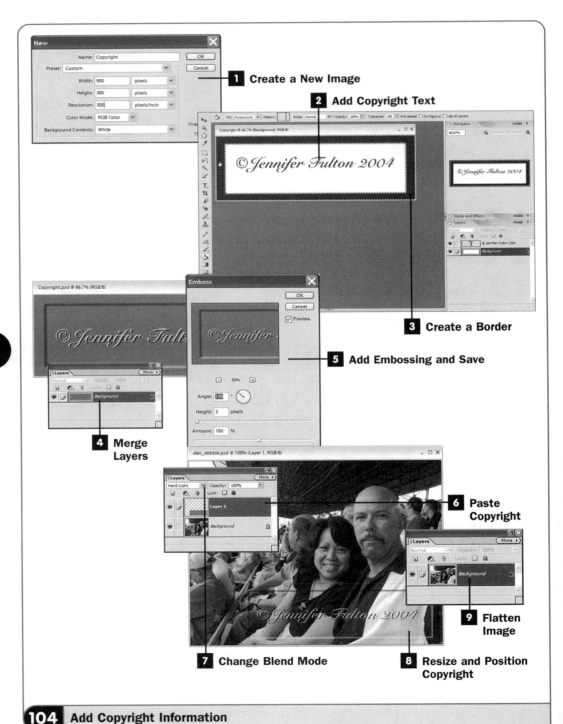

1 Create a New Image

2 Add Copyright Text

3 Create a Border

4 Merge Layers

5 Add Embossing and Save

6 Paste Copyright

7 Change Blend Mode

8 Resize and Position Copyright

9 Flatten Image

104

104 Add Copyright Information

Open an image you want to copyright. Save this image in Photoshop (*.psd) format. Then select **Edit, Paste** to paste the copyright data onto a new layer in the image.

7 Change Blend Mode

Change the blend **Mode** of the copyright layer to **Hard Light**. The copyright is now transparent.

8 Resize and Position Copyright

Click the **Move** tool on the **Toolbox**. On the **Options** bar, enable the **Show Bounding Box** option. Click and drag the copyright to move it into a good position on the image.

▶ NOTE

You'll want to position the copyright over some important part of the image that would be impossible to crop out, and yet not obscure the image so much that it's no longer enjoyable to look at. Balance your need to protect with your need to share.

You can resize the copyright as well by dragging a corner handle. Make sure that you enable the **Maintain Aspect Ratio** option on the **Options** bar so that the text does not become distorted.

104

▶ TIP

To apply a quick copyright to an image, type some text and apply the **Clear Emboss** effect. The result is a lot more subtle than what's shown here, and it may be easier to remove as a result, but it's quick and incredibly easy.

9 Flatten Image

When you're satisfied with the image, save the PSD file. Then merge the layers together by choosing **Layer, Flatten Image** and resave the result in JPEG or TIFF format, leaving your PSD image unflattened so that you can return at a later time and make different adjustments if you want. For example, you might return to the PSD file and resize it or change its resolution to fit your current sharing situation.

With the TIFF or JPEG image flattened, your copyright notice cannot be easily removed from the image, and you can share it online without worry. To copyright another image, keep your **Copyright.psd** file open and repeat steps 6–8.

105 Share Images Using Email

✔ BEFORE YOU BEGIN	→ SEE ALSO
78 Change Photo Resolution and Size	**119** About Online Photo Services
	122 Share Images Using an Online Service in Adobe Photoshop Elements
	123 Print Images Using an Online Photo Service in Adobe Photoshop Elements

If you have an Internet connection and use Microsoft Outlook, Outlook Express, or Adobe Email Service, you can send anything you create in Photoshop Elements to anyone who has an email address. Even if you don't use a compatible email client, you can still use the **Organizer** to prepare your items for sending using email. After you've shown Photoshop Elements and your email client how to find and recognize each other, you can select what you want to send from the Organizer catalog or open an image in the Editor, decide who to send it to, add a message, and give the order to **Send**. And you can do all this without shutting down or minimizing the Editor or the Organizer window and switching to your email program. You do all the work in Photoshop Elements, and the application then hands off the message to your email client to process and send.

105

In addition to individual pictures, you can send creations such as slideshows, photo albums, postcards, and calendars. You also can include sound and video files with your photos, but not with creations. In addition, only one creation can be included in an email message, and you can't send it with any other item type.

1 Select Items to Send

In the Organizer catalog, select one or more items to send. To select contiguous items, click the first item; then press and hold the **Shift** key while you click the last item in the group. To select noncontiguous items, click the first item; then hold the **Ctrl** key while you click each additional item. Remember that you can send a mix of images, audio files, and video files, but you can only send an individual creation by itself. Blue borders around the thumbnails indicate the selected items.

▶ TIP

You might want to send a group of related images, such as the photos from a recent family outing. Use the **Find** feature to display them in the catalog. When only these items are displayed, press **Ctrl+A** to select them all. If the catalog is sorted by batch or folder, click the gray bar above a group to select every item in the group.

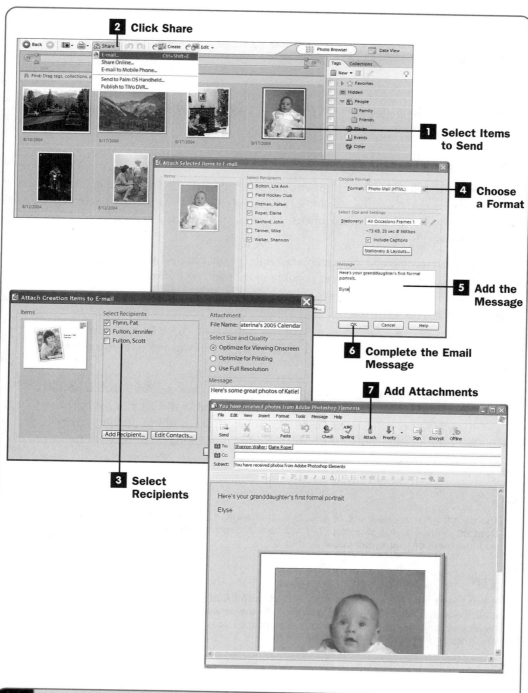

2 Click Share

1 Select Items to Send

4 Choose a Format

5 Add the Message

105

6 Complete the Email Message

7 Add Attachments

3 Select Recipients

105 Share Images Using Email

▶ **TIP**

You can send an image from within the Editor by saving it first and then choosing File, Attach to Email. The Attach to Email dialog box appears.

▶ **TIP**

To send a creation immediately after making it, click the **Email** button in the last step of the wizard.

2 **Click Share**

When the items you want to send are selected, click the **Share** button on the Options bar. From the menu that opens, select **Email**. The **Attach Selected Items to Email** dialog box opens. The items you selected to send are displayed on the left.

Because some email systems place limits on the file sizes they will handle, try to send small files whenever possible so that you do not exceed that limit.

3 **Select Recipients**

In the **Select Recipients** section of the dialog box, check one or more of the names in your Contact Book to identify those you want to receive the message.

If a recipient's name doesn't appear on this list, click the **Add Recipient** button to add the name to your **Contact Book**—and to the list you see in the **Attach Selected Items to Email** dialog box. If you want to update a recipient's listing, click the **Edit Contacts** button and change that person's name or email address.

▶ **TIP**

You do not have to designate recipients at this stage. If you haven't added people to the **Contact Book** yet, just skip step 3. You'll have a chance later to add them using the address book of your email client in step 6.

▶ **TIP**

If you forgot an item you wanted to send, click the **Add** button at the bottom left. In the dialog box that appears, you can sort through the entire catalog listing, or narrow the display by selecting a tag or collection. Select the items to add to those already selected for sending, and click **OK**.

4 Choose a Format

If you're sending images, audio files, or video files, open the **Format** list and choose a format for the email message you are going to send. If your recipients all have HTML mail service that enables them to receive photos embedded in their messages, select **Photo Mail (HTML)**. Open the **Stationery** list and select a background for the email message, or click the **Stationery and Layouts** button and select a design you can customize. Choose a stationery on the first page of the wizard that appears, click **Next Step**, and set options to customize the stationery (such as photo size and layout). Click **Enter Message Here** to type a personal message. Click **Done** to return to the **Attach Selected Items to Email** dialog box. If you have previously added **Captions** to your selected items through the **Organizer**, you can enable the **Include Caption** check box to include that caption below its item in the message. A typical caption explains or identifies the item, such as **Cousin Mary at Yawning Gap**.

▶ **NOTE**

Aware that viruses are often planted in graphic files, some email systems strip the illustrations from HTML mail and send them as attachments instead. This ensures that the graphics are not automatically opened along with the message. Should you receive such a message, make sure that it's from someone you trust before you open the attachments.

105

To combine the selected pictures and video items into an automated slideshow that can be played on the recipient's computer, select **Simple Slideshow (PDF)**. The pictures and video files are packaged as an Adobe Acrobat **PDF** file; recipients can open the file in Acrobat or the Adobe Reader and scan through them one by one. Type a **File Name** for the file. Adjust the quality of the resulting slideshow by selecting a **Size**.

Among the creations you can make through the Organizer is a custom slideshow that can include sound and other forms of multimedia. You can create such a slideshow separately and attach it to a message, but you cannot do so using the email wizard.

If any recipients have text-only email service, select the **Individual Attachments** option. Enable the **Convert Photos to JPEGs** option to have the Organizer compress the attachments using JPEG compression and the **Size** you choose. If you don't choose this option, the items are attached uncompressed. The items are prepared and attached to the resulting email message, rather than embedded in it. If you're sending video or audio files, they are normally sent as attachments.

If you are sending a creation, it will be converted to PDF format before sending. You will have to enter a **File Name** for the resulting file and set a **Size and Quality** option.

5 Add the Message

If you want to include a message to the people who are receiving the selected items, type it in the **Message** text box. This entry will become the text block of the email message.

6 Complete the Email Message

Click **OK**. Items are prepared for sending, the message is created, and it opens in your email program. The format of the email message form should be very familiar to you; you are now in your email client's native format.

At this point, you can do anything the email program allows, including adding or subtracting recipients and editing the message text. Because your email client's address book is undoubtedly more complete than your Photoshop Elements **Contact Book**, you can add names from your address book to the **To** or **CC** line in the email message form.

7 Add Attachments

If any items you selected were not embedded in the email message or attached for you, you can attach them yourself. Follow the steps for adding attachments using your particular email client. For example, both of the Outlook programs have an **Attach** button. Click it to select the files to attach.

▶ NOTE

Photoshop Elements generates its own subject line. You might want to take this opportunity to replace it with something more personal.

---

106 About Size and Resolution

✔ BEFORE YOU BEGIN	→ SEE ALSO
78 Change Photo Resolution and Size	**107** Change Image Size or Resolution

Two of the most common changes you'll make to an image are to adjust its size and to change its resolution. By *size*, I'm referring to an image's dimensions when printed, not its size onscreen. An image's resolution is determined by the number of pixels (dots) per inch.

To compute an image's print size, the Editor looks at the number of pixels in an image and their relative size (the number of pixels per inch). Take a look at the first figure here, which depicts an image that's 10 pixels wide by 5 pixels high, using an imaginary scale of 4 pixels per inch. Based on the size of these pixels, the printed image will be about 2.5" wide by 1.25" high.

▶ **TIP**

You can display an image onscreen in the same size it will be when printed by clicking the **Zoom** tool on the **Toolbox** and clicking the **Print Size** button on the **Options** bar. To display the image in the size it will appear on a user's screen set to the same screen resolution as you, click the **Actual Pixels** button instead.

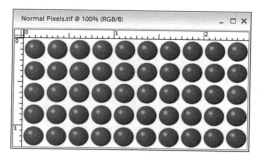

Figure 1: An (imaginary) image that's 10 pixels wide by 5 pixels high.

106

To compute the resolution of an image, you simply count the number of pixels per inch. Luckily, Photoshop Elements does that for you, and you can view the image size (such as 2048×1536 pixels), resolution (such as 300dpi), and print size (such as 6.827"×5.12", which is calculated by taking the image size and dividing it by the resolution) of an image in the **Image Size** dialog box choose **Image, Resize, Image Size** from the menu bar). You'll learn how to use this dialog box to change the size or resolution of an image in **107** **Change Image Size or Resolution**.

If you never plan to print a certain image, the image won't need a high resolution (a great number of pixels) to look good onscreen. But to print an acceptable image, you need the highest number of pixels you can get—the more the better. You must have a print resolution of 200–300 dots per inch (dpi) to create a high-quality print using your home printer; for prints sent off to a lab, 150dpi usually does just fine.

▶ **NOTE**

High resolution (more than 200ppi) is unnecessary for an image destined to be displayed on a computer monitor or a television screen because NTSC standard TV resolution (transposed to the average monitor size) is 72dpi, and computer screen resolutions average 102ppi. (Just so you know, the theoretical resolution for HDTV—high-definition—is 162ppi.)

An image's print size and its resolution are interdependent; changing one without changing the other affects the image's print quality. For example, maintaining the same number of pixels in an image while trying to force it to print in a larger print size decreases the number of pixels per inch and, as you can imagine, inflates the size of each pixel to compensate. If the pixels become too large, a mosaic effect called *pixelation* might distract you from seeing the image as a whole.

Imagine for a moment that the first figure represents all the pixels in an image whose total resolution is 10×5 pixels. As shown in the second figure, if you change the size of the pixels to make them twice as big (in this case, by keeping the same number of pixels while increasing the print size), you'll get a much larger rectangle, but the pixels will be much more apparent. When printed, the rectangle might look more like a mesh of dots than a solid rectangle, which is probably not the effect you're going for. The same is true of any graphic image: If you print the image at something larger than its native print size without also increasing the number of pixels (the image resolution), the pixels will become bigger and more evident in the final print. This is what can happen if you choose to rescale an image on the fly, using options in the **Print Preview** dialog box (in the Editor) or the **Print Selected Photos** dialog box (in the Organizer).

106

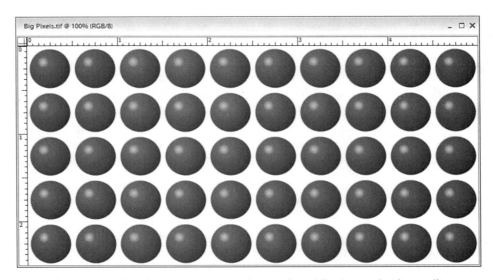

Figure 2: Enlarging the pixels increases the image size while decreasing its quality.

Suppose that, instead of changing the size of the pixels, you maintain their relative size but double their number. In other words, you double an image's resolution (increase the number of pixels) from 150 to 300ppi, for example, while also doubling the print size of an image. The print quality will remain the same because the pixels will remain the same size, but you'll get a much bigger print, as shown here by comparing the first figure (10×5 pixels) with the third figure (20×10 pixels). The sizes of the pixels are the same in both figures, but the second one is bigger because it has twice as many pixels. Don't need a larger print size, but want better quality? Just increase the resolution (number of pixels) while maintaining the same print size. If you compare Figure 2 to Figure 3, that's exactly what I've done. The images are the same size, but Figure 3 has more pixels and, therefore, more detail and better quality.

▶ **NOTE**

Just because you increase resolution on an image, you do not necessarily increase quality. Obviously, you can't add detail that wasn't there in the original image, so when you increase resolution (using resampling to add pixels and improve print quality), you do so at a possible loss of background detail.

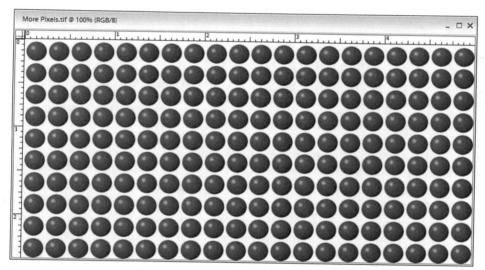

Figure 3: You can enlarge an image, and perhaps improve print quality, by increasing the number of pixels.

106

▶ **TIP**

To increase the size of an image without changing its resolution, resample it. Resampling uses one of a choice of five complex mathematical formulas to compute the color and brightness of new pixels added to an image to increase its size. See **107** **Change Image Size or Resolution**.

▶ **TIP**

You do not have to use resampling when *reducing* the resolution or print size of an image, although you might because the resampling process mathematically decides which pixels to remove from the file.

107 Change Image Size or Resolution

✔ BEFORE YOU BEGIN	→ SEE ALSO
106 About Size and Resolution	**75** Scan In Photos
	108 Change the Working Area Without Affecting Image Size

As you learned in **106** **About Size and Resolution,** an image's size is tied directly to the number of pixels in the image as well as the relative size of the pixels. When you create images with a digital camera or scan printed images with a scanner, you choose the resolution you want to use—for instance, 300ppi. The resolution you choose also determines the resulting print size. For example, an image that's 2048 pixels wide by 1536 pixels tall (the typical dimensions of an image taken with a 3 megapixel camera), whose resolution is 300ppi, will print at 6.827" by 5.120".

▶ **NOTE**

To calculate the print dimensions of an image yourself, take the image size in pixels and divide it by the number of pixels per inch. To display an image in its print size, click the **Zoom** tool on the **Toolbox** and then click the **Print Size** button on the **Options** bar. To view an image's size in pixels, resolution, and print size, display the **Image Size** dialog box by choosing **Edit, Resize, Image Size.**

So what do you do if you want to print your image at a different size—larger or smaller—while maintaining or even increasing its resolution to, say, 300dpi? Answer: You use resampling. When you use *resampling* to increase an image's print size and/or its resolution, new pixels are inserted between existing ones. The Editor determines the colors for these new pixels by sampling the color value of each surrounding pixel, calculating a value within the sample range, and assigning that value to that new pixel. Conversely, when you reduce an image's print size, resampling removes pixels from the image and then adjusts the colors of the pixels remaining in the image by approximating the blended color values of the pixels that were removed.

▶ **KEY TERM**

Resampling—The mathematical process applied during image resizing that evaluates the content of the pixels in the image in order to calculate the value of new pixels (when enlarging) or neighboring pixels (when reducing), and which reinterprets the result to minimize loss of detail.

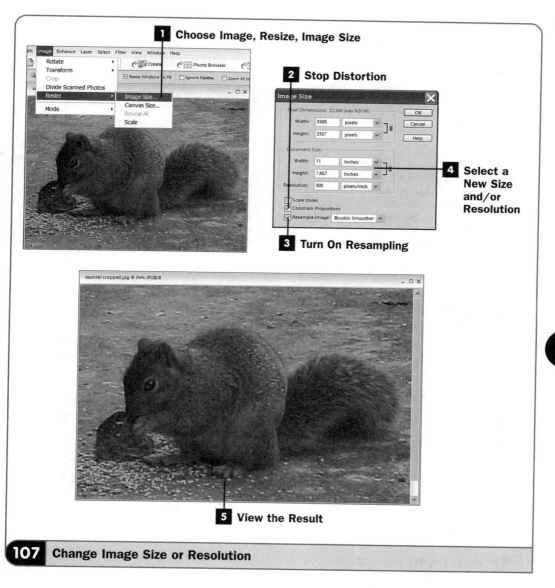

1 Choose Image, Resize, Image Size

2 Stop Distortion

4 Select a New Size and/or Resolution

3 Turn On Resampling

5 View the Result

107 Change Image Size or Resolution

Because resampling is based on best-guess estimation, using it to change an image's size or resolution by more than 20% often produces poor results. You can resize or change an image's resolution without resampling by telling the **Editor** that you want to turn resampling off, and therefore maintain the relationship between the size and the resolution. In this manner, you can double an image's print resolution by cutting its print size in half (the image will contain as many pixels as it did before, but the pixels will be smaller, and there will be more of them per inch). Onscreen, you won't see any apparent change at all.

▶ **TIP**

One fast way to remove **moiré patterns**, fuzziness, and spots created when you scan an image is to scan at 600dpi and then reduce its resolution to 300dpi *while maintaining its print size.*

▶ **TIP**

If you want to print an image in some size other than its normal print size, you can "rescale" the image on the fly when you print it. If you print an image in a larger size than normal, however, the resolution is decreased proportionately to compensate (pixels are not added). If the resulting resolution falls below acceptable levels of quality, you'll see a warning, so that you can choose a different print size. Regardless, with this method, the original resolution and print size of the image are left unchanged. If you get the warning, it's best to abandon printing and then resize and resample the image to the print size you want, by following the steps in this task.

107

1 **Choose Image, Resize, Image Size**

In the Editor, open the image you want to resize or whose resolution you want to, and save it in Photoshop (*.psd) format. Then choose **Image, Resize, Image Size** from the menu bar. The **Image Size** dialog box appears.

2 **Stop Distortion**

If you want to make sure that the image is not distorted during the resizing process, enable the **Constrain Proportions** check box.

If you've applied a **Layer Style** to the image and want the pattern of that style to be resized as the image is resized, enable the **Scale Styles** option as well. Note that the **Scale Styles** option does not affect the size of patterns formed by **Effects**, so you might want to apply such embellishments after resizing the image.

3 **Turn On Resampling**

To have the Editor mathematically re-evaluate and re-render the content of the image when you change its print size or resolution, enable the **Resample Image** option and select a sampling formula from the list. Here's a brief description of the formulas:

▶ **TIP**

Why would you ever choose *not* to resample an image? When you make your image larger or smaller, the rescaling process can introduce artifacts or patterns that resampling can eliminate. However, in smoothing out any possible artifacts or unwanted patterns, resampling after you resize can result in loss of detail, especially in the background or in small areas. So limit the number of times you resample an image to *once*; if you have detail in the background you don't want to risk losing, do not resample.

- **Bicubic**—Estimates each new pixel's color value based on the values of the 16 pixels nearest to the new pixel's location relative to the original image, in a 4×4 array. This method is best used when enlarging an image.

- **Bicubic Smoother**—Similar to the Bicubic formula, except that the tendency of Bicubic resampling to create halos around highly contrasting edges is reduced. Best used when enlarging an image.

- **Bicubic Sharper**—Similar to the **Bicubic** formula, except the edges are sharper with even higher contrast. Best used when reducing the size of an image.

- **Bilinear**—Estimates each new pixel's color value based on the values of the four pixels nearest to the new pixel's location relative to the original image. This method is best used when reducing an image.

- **Nearest Neighbor**—Estimates each new pixel's color value based on the values of all the pixels that fall within a fixed proximity of the new pixel's location relative to the original image. Here, the pixel residing in the same proportionate location in the original image as that of the new pixel in the resized image is given the extra "weight" when estimating the new color value. This method is best used when reducing the size of an image, but only for those images with edges that have not been antialiased.

107

▶ **NOTE**

To avoid resampling an image, disable the **Resample Image** option and change either the **Height/Width** or **Resolution** values in the **Document Size** area of the **Image Resize** dialog box. Just keep in mind that if you increase the **Resolution** without resampling, the image will be resized smaller.

4 **Select a New Size and/or Resolution**

If you know what size you want the final image to be, type a value in the **Document Size Width** box; the **Height** value changes proportionately (or vice versa).

You can also change an image's size by adding or removing pixels. When you add pixels while maintaining the same resolution, you make the image bigger. For example, if you want the image to be twice as big, in the frame marked **Pixel Dimensions**, for either **Width** or **Height**, type **200** in the text box, and from the adjacent drop-down list, choose **Percent**. This increases the number of pixels without affecting their size (assuming that **Resample Image** is on).

To change the resolution, type a value in the **Resolution** box. Altering resolution in this manner does not change the image's print size unless you entered new values for **Document Size** earlier. Click **OK**. Because the **Resample Image** option is selected, new pixels are created as needed to meet your print size and resolution requirements.

▶ **TIP**

Because resampling often leaves an image a bit fuzzy, it's best to follow up by treating your resampled image to an **Unsharp Mask**.

5 **View the Result**

108

After you're satisfied with the result of the resizing process, make any other changes you want and then save the final image in JPEG or TIFF format, leaving your PSD image with its **layers** (if any) intact so that you can return at a later time and make different adjustments if you want.

Even though I increased the size of this photo by quite a lot (from 5"×7" to 11"×7.857"), the quality (resolution) was maintained because I selected **Bicubic Smoother** resampling.

---

108 **Change the Working Area Without Affecting Image Size**

✔ BEFORE YOU BEGIN	→ SEE ALSO
86 About Size and Resolution	**107** Change Image Size or Resolution

---

Each image has a *canvas*—essentially the image background. The benefit of thinking of an image's **background layer** as a canvas is that it helps you conceive how that **layer** can be stretched to change the size of the area on which you can paint, draw objects, and insert text. For a newly imported digital photo, the image is "painted," if you will, to fill the canvas. You can expand the background layer (the canvas) of an image such as a photograph, for example, to make room for a frame, and fill the new area with color and apply a filter, style, or effect. Or you might simply want to expand the canvas to create more room in which to add a clip from another image, an object, or some text.

▶ **KEY TERM**

Canvas—The working area of an image, as defined by the image's outer dimensions.

When you expand the canvas of an image, you add new pixels around its edges. Every photo imported from a digital camera or scanner has a background layer. When you use the **Canvas Size** command, the extra pixels are given the color you select. If an image has no background layer—for example, if you created the image using the **File, New** command and made the bottom layer transparent, or you converted the original **Background** layer to a regular layer using the **Layer, New, Layer from Background** command—then the new pixels are made transparent. Every layer above the base layer—whether it's a background layer or a regular layer—is expanded by the same amount.

If you shrink the canvas, data on the lowest layer outside the canvas area is discarded. However, data in the upper layers is simply hidden and not removed. Because this data on upper layers is only hidden, you can reposition that data as needed to display what you want.

108

1 **Choose Image, Resize, Canvas Size**

In the **Editor**, open the image whose canvas size you want to adjust, and save it in Photoshop (*.psd) format. Choose **Image, Resize, Canvas Size** from the menu bar. The **Canvas Size** dialog box is displayed.

2 **Enter New Dimensions**

The current dimensions of the image are displayed at the top of the **Canvas Size** dialog box. If you want to simply *add* a certain amount to the outer dimensions of the image, enable the **Relative** option. If the option is disabled, the dimensions you enter reflect the *total* width and height of the image.

▶ **NOTE**

You can reduce the canvas size of an image. If you do, although all the layers are reduced in size, data is not removed from the upper layers—it's just placed off the canvas where it is not seen in the final image. You can then use the **Move** tool to move the data on these nonbackground layers to display exactly the portion you want. Data from the bottom layer is clipped and cannot be retrieved. But if you increase the canvas size later on (even after saving and closing the image), you'll see that the data on upper layers is now visible again.

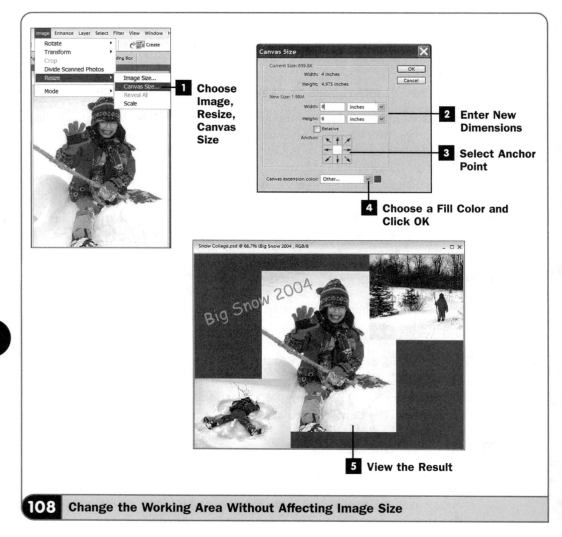

1 Choose Image, Resize, Canvas Size

2 Enter New Dimensions

3 Select Anchor Point

4 Choose a Fill Color and Click OK

5 View the Result

 Change the Working Area Without Affecting Image Size

In the **New Size** pane, select a unit of measure such as inches or pixels from one of the drop-down lists next to the **Width** and **Height** boxes (the other will change automatically). Then type values in the **Width** and **Height** boxes.

3 Select Anchor Point

Normally, the anchor point is in the center of the **Anchor** pad. This means that the added canvas is placed equally around the image. If you want to add canvas to just one side of the image, you can tell the Editor where to position the image in relation to the canvas by clicking the appropriate arrow on the **Anchor** pad. For example, to add canvas only on the left side of the image, click the → arrow, located to the right of the center white button. This action tells the Editor to position the image in the right-center position and to place the additional canvas width to the left. To add space to the left and below the image, click the arrow (located in the upper-right corner of the **Anchor** pad) instead.

4 Choose a Fill Color and Click OK

If the bottom layer of the image is not a **Background** layer, the added canvas will be transparent. If the bottom layer is the **Background** layer, the added canvas will be opaque. You can choose a color to fill the extra canvas space. Open the **Canvas Extension Color** list and select an option such as **Background** (which applies the current **background color**). If you choose **Other**, the **Color Picker** appears, and you can choose a color from it. With the **Color Picker** displayed, you can also click anywhere in the image to pick up that color with the dropper.

108

▶ **TIP**

To display the **Color Picker** without choosing **Other** from the **Canvas Extension Color** list, just click the box to the right of the list.

5 View the Result

After expanding the image canvas, make any other changes you want and then save the final image in JPEG or TIFF format, leaving your PSD image with its layers (if any) intact so that you can return at a later time and make different adjustments if you want.

In the sample figure, the canvas was expanded around the central image, text was added, and several new images were pasted into the new space, creating a photo collage of a snowy day. Look for this image in the Color Gallery.

109 Change Color Mode

✔ BEFORE YOU BEGIN	→ SEE ALSO
Just jump right in.	**77** Convert Between Image Formats
	78 Change Photo Resolution and Size
	106 About Size and Resolution

One of the key factors affecting the size of an image file is the maximum number of colors it can include. If a file is theoretically capable of including a large number of colors—even though it may actually contain very few—the file's size will be large to ensure that capacity. If you're working on an image to be shared over the Internet, small file size is often a high priority. One way you can reduce a file's size is to change its **color mode**—the number of colors an image can contain, even if it doesn't actually contain that many. However, reducing the number of colors an image can use might lead to striation and patchiness in areas you think should be a single, solid color.

A full-color image in RGB color mode generally does not actually contain all 16 million-plus colors that standard video cards support. (For RGB color mode, each color channel—Red, Green, and Blue—must be capable of "counting" to 256 for each pixel. 256×256×256=16,777,216.) To reduce the file size in a color image, the **Editor** gives you the option of switching to an Indexed color mode similar to the encoding scheme for GIF images. With an Indexed color mode, the entire image uses only 256 colors, although these colors are selected from all the 16,777,216 hues the standard video card produces. If your image is black and white, or black and white plus gray, there are other modes you can use to make your image file even smaller. How perceptible the difference is, when changing to a lower color mode, depends on the image you're working with. For this reason, the Editor makes it possible for you to sample different color reduction modes, enabling you to choose the least detrimental mode for your image.

▶ **NOTE**

Because some commands are available only for images that use RGB or grayscale mode, you might sometimes find yourself temporarily *increasing* an image's color mode (from grayscale to RGB, for example). This won't, however, improve the resolution or quality of a low-resolution image—increasing an image's color palette simply makes more colors available for use; it does not tell the Editor where to use them in an image to boost detail and clarity.

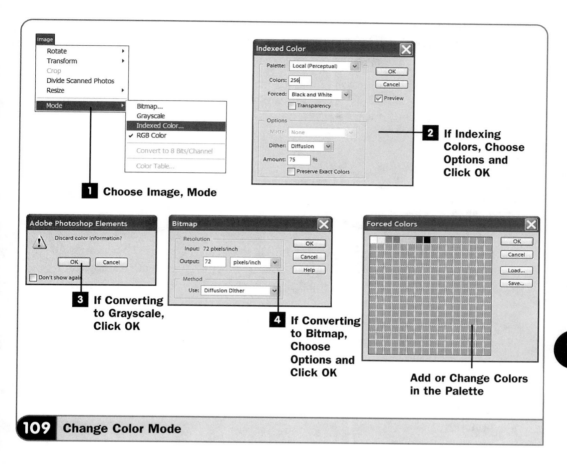

1 Choose Image, Mode

2 If Indexing Colors, Choose Options and Click OK

3 If Converting to Grayscale, Click OK

4 If Converting to Bitmap, Choose Options and Click OK

Add or Change Colors in the Palette

109 Change Color Mode

If file size is your main priority, you can *compress* an image into GIF, JPEG, or PNG format (for example), a process that also reduces its color palette a bit more scientifically than the method discussed here. You can also convert an image to grayscale to reduce its color palette.

1 Choose Image, Mode

In the Editor, open the image you want to convert, and save it in Photoshop (***.psd**) format. Choose **Image, Mode** from the menu bar. Select the color mode you want to convert to from the submenu that appears:

- **Bitmap**—1-bit color in black and white; suitable for images in black and white only, with no gray tones.

- **Grayscale**—8-bit color in 256 shades of gray.

- **Indexed Color**—8 bits per pixel, in 256 colors, selected from the entire color gamut. Perfect for use with GIF images.

- **RGB**—24-bit color, with 8 bits per color channel. Here, 24 bits are used to encode the color value for each pixel. Compare to **Indexed Color**, which uses 8 bits per pixel, and you'll understand why RGB images provide the most detail.

▶ **NOTE**

Technically speaking, the number of *bits* (binary digits) required for an image to encode the color value for one pixel is the base-2 logarithm of the maximum number of colors. In other words, 2 raised to that power equals the maximum number. It takes 8 bits to encode up to 256 values, and 24 bits to encode up to 16,777,216 values—thus the arithmetic behind the phrase *24-bit color*.

If you're increasing color depth, the image itself is not changed, but more colors become available for your use. If you're reducing color depth, a dialog box appears from which you must choose options. Continue to step 2, 3, or 4.

2 If Indexing Colors, Choose Options and Click OK

109

If you're reducing colors in an image with **Indexed Color** mode, select how you want the Editor to choose the colors for the palette by choosing from various options in the dialog box that appears. Before you begin making selections, enable the **Preview** option so that you can see how your selections affect the actual image. From the **Palette** list, choose one of the following options:

▶ **NOTE**

If the image already uses 256 colors or fewer, the **Palette** option is automatically set to **Exact**, which means that all colors in the image are added to the palette. You do not have to make a selection.

- **System (Mac OS)** uses the 256 color palette developed for the first color Macintosh computers. Select this palette to generate small files best displayed on Macs.

- **System (Windows)** uses the 256 color palette developed for Windows 3.0, which has been used as the backup palette for 8-bit color mode ever since.

- **Web** uses a 216 color palette (the last 40 index values are reserved) recommended for use in generating images for web pages because these are the 216 values that Mac and Windows have in common. Choosing this option ensures that the image will appear the same on both a Windows and a Mac computer.

- **Uniform** calculates 216 colors from equidistant positions in the RGB color gamut by rotating color index values from all white to all black. This setting ensures that your image uses colors sampled from throughout the image's color spectrum.

- The three **Local** options direct the Editor to create a palette based solely on the colors found in the currently open image.

- The three **Master** options instruct the Editor to create a palette based on the colors found in all the images currently open in the Editor.

  Among the **Local** and **Master** options, **Adaptive** instructs the Editor to select 256 colors that are mathematically most similar to the colors in the original image.

  Perceptual takes the 256 colors generated by the **Adaptive** algorithm and alters the selections slightly to favor colors that the human eye would tend to notice if they were changed—typically throwing away more colors in areas with the least amount of contrast, while favoring colors in areas with high contrast because the eye would notice that more.

  Selective takes the 256 colors refined by the **Perceptual** algorithm and then weights the values to more closely resemble the **Web** spectrum, while also favoring broad areas of color within the image.

  109

- Select **Custom** to make changes to any colors in the palette that the Editor is currently preparing to adopt. When the **Color Table** dialog box appears (which looks similar to the **Forced Colors** dialog box shown here), double-click the color in the palette you want to change. Select a new color from the **Color Picker** dialog box and click **OK**. To add a color to the palette, click an empty spot and then select a color to add. Repeat for any other palette colors you want to change or add, and click **OK** when finished. You're returned to the **Indexed Color** dialog box.

- Choose **Previous** to load the previously used custom color palette. Use **Previous** to convert a series of images to Indexed color mode, using the same color palette.

After selecting a **Palette** option in the **Indexed Color** dialog box, you can set additional options as well. To reduce your file size even further, set **Colors** to a value lower than 256 (to reduce file size *significantly*, select a value lower than 128).

The options in the **Forced** list instruct the Editor to override some or all of its palette color choices and to include specific color values, some of which you can choose yourself from the **Forced Color** dialog box that appears. These "forced" choices may or may not be represented in the actual image, but they are included in the image's palette:

- **Black & White** forces the Editor to include pure black and pure white as two of the colors in the palette.

- **Primaries** forces the Editor to include the first eight colors of the old IBM Extended Graphics palette: red, green, blue, cyan, magenta, yellow, black, and white. This allows a large measure of downward compatibility (if you really need it) with some of the first images ever produced for display on PCs.

- **Web** forces the Editor to include the entire 216-color web palette (essentially the same as choosing **Web** from the **Palette** list).

- Choose **Custom** to change or add colors to the palette. Double-click a palette color. Select a new color from the **Color Picker** dialog box and click **OK**. To add a color, click an empty spot, select a color, and click **OK**. Repeat for any other palette colors you want to add or change and click **OK** when finished.

109

If the image has transparency but you don't want to retain it, disable the **Transparency** option. Then select from the **Matte** drop-down list a color to change the transparent pixels to. Semitransparent pixels are blended with the color you choose to make them fully opaque. You can choose **Foreground Color**, **Background Color**, **White**, **Black**, **50% Gray**, or **Netscape Gray** (a lighter gray) from the list, or select your own color by choosing **Custom** from the **Matte** drop-down list and using the **Color Picker** that appears to select a color to use. To choose a color from the image, just click in the image with the **Eyedropper** tool. If you choose **None** from the **Matte** drop-down list, semitransparent pixels are simply changed to fully opaque ones and are not blended with anything. Transparent pixels are made white.

If the image contains transparent pixels and you want to retain them, enable the **Transparency** option. If the image contains semitransparent pixels, open the **Matte** list and choose a color to blend with them to make them fully opaque.

To reduce the side effects caused by using a smaller number of colors than the original image contained, select the dither pattern you prefer from the **Dither** list:

- **Diffusion** instructs the Editor to apply an *error diffusion* algorithm, which blends dissimilar colors by dividing the differences between them mathematically and spreading that difference to neighboring pixels, hiding the transition. When you make this choice, enter the relative percentage of error diffusion in the **Amount** text box. Enable the **Preserve Exact Colors** option to instruct the Editor not to dither any colors it encounters in the original image whose values exactly match any of those in the current reduction palette.

► **KEY TERM**

Error diffusion—Any of several mathematical techniques that attempt to compensate for large error values (differences between the intensities of an original pixel and its replacement in a reprocessed image) by dividing this difference into parts and distributing it to neighboring pixels, thus masking the obvious inaccuracy.

- **Pattern** applies a geometric dithering pattern, which might be noticeable in photographic images but is permissible in more patterned images such as original drawings.

- **Noise** scatters dithered pixels randomly.

- **None** turns off diffusion and causes the Editor to substitute the closest color in the palette for any color not in the palette.

► **NOTE**

Because it uses a mathematical formula, error diffusion (when used in images with a very limited color palette or large blocks of color, such as comics art) can sometimes generate artifacts in a color-blended area, more so than using an ordered dither method such as **Pattern**.

To finalize your choices, click **OK**.

3 If Converting to Grayscale, Click OK

When you're converting a color image to various hues of gray (grayscale), click **OK**; if the image has multiple layers, you'll be asked whether you want to flatten all layers before proceeding. Click **Merge**.

► **NOTE**

If the color layers currently in the image use blend modes other than **Normal** to create its current appearance—especially if that appearance depends on how the *color* of one layer interacts with the *colors* of the layers beneath it—these effects will probably be completely lost if the image is flattened while converting it to grayscale. To preserve the layers and their blend modes, click **Don't Merge** in step 3.

4 If Converting to Bitmap, Choose Options and Click OK

When converting an image to pure black-and-white (**Bitmap** mode), the Editor could simply make relatively dark pixels black and the relatively light ones white. However, the result might not be desirable, so you might want to apply dithering.

First, let the Editor convert your image to grayscale by clicking **OK**. It's easier for the Editor to convert grays to black-and-white than to convert colors directly to black and white. If there are multiple layers, the Editor warns you to flatten them first; click **OK** to have it do that and continue. In the **Bitmap** dialog box that appears, in the **Resolution** area, make sure that your image is set for the resolution of your output device. At first, this is set to the image's current resolution. To ensure best appearance, you might have to adjust resolution—and thus, size—accordingly. For onscreen use, choose 72ppi; for printing, choose 150–300dpi. Altering this setting resizes the image, both in print and onscreen.

In the **Method** area, choose how you want the Editor to apply dithering. The **50% Threshold** option applies no dithering whatsoever—light pixels are made white, and dark ones are made black. The **Pattern Dither** option applies a geometric dithering pattern, which might be adequate if your original image is a simple drawing—such as a corporate logo—rather than a photograph. **Diffusion Dither** applies an error diffusion pattern, distributing vast differences in brightness value over wider areas—which is generally more appropriate for photographs.

109

To finalize your choices, click **OK**.

After changing the color mode of your image, make any other changes you want and then save the final image in JPEG or TIFF format, leaving your PSD image with its layers (if any) intact so that you can return at a later time and make different adjustments if you want.

▶ **TIP**

If you're curious about what color mode your image is currently using, simply look at the title bar, after the image filename.

17

Retouching a Photograph with Photoshop Elements

IN THIS CHAPTER:

Although a photograph is an accurate record of a specific moment in time, there's no particular reason why you have to "remember" the flaws your camera captured as well: the slightly yellow teeth, the blotchy skin, the wrinkles, and the wind that blew everyone's hair out of place. Using the Editor's tools, you can erase these flaws or simply make them less noticeable. For example, you can remove red eye, wrinkles, freckles, and minor blemishes. You can even whiten teeth and awaken tired eyes. In this chapter, you'll learn how to perform these and other digital tricks while maintaining the essential loveliness and inner beauty of your subjects, so that when you post the pictures online, the world will see them as you know they truly are.

In this chapter, you'll learn to do more as well—you'll see how you can repair and restore old photographs, or new ones that have been damaged. You'll learn how to remove scratches and specks and to repair tears, stains, and even holes. When you're finished, you might look at the results and decide the old homestead never looked better and that Uncle Ben was a surprisingly handsome guy.

110

110 About Removing Scratches, Specks, and Holes

✔ **BEFORE YOU BEGIN**	→ **SEE ALSO**
74 Import Photos from a Digital Camera	**111** Remove Scratches
75 Scan In Photos	**112** Remove Specks and Spots
	113 Repair Minor Holes and Tears
	114 Repair Major Holes and Tears

It's not uncommon for photographs to acquire small scratches, spots, holes, and tears, even if the photos are not very old. If a photograph is not stored flat with its surface protected from damage, the photo can easily develop surface defects. The Editor offers many tools you can use to repair these scratches and other small anomalies:

▶ **TIP**

Like most changes you can make to an image, you can limit your retouching to either a layer or a selection.

- **Spot Healing Brush**—If scratches or spots are small, use the **Spot Healing Brush** to get rid of them quickly. The **Spot Healing Brush** samples pixels at the outer edge of the brush tip and uses them to replace the pixels under the center of the tip. In this way, the tool can be used to repair spots and small scratches. The **Spot Healing Brush** can also be set to sample all pixels under the brush tip, creating a blended patch for the center of the tip. In this way, the tool can be used to repair a textured area. See **111 Remove Scratches**.

- **Clone Stamp**—This tool enables you to remove defects by cloning (copying) good parts of an image over top of small tears, scratches, spots, or stains. For example, if there's a small hole in someone's dress, you can copy a good part of the dress to make the repair. See **113 Repair Minor Holes and Tears**.

- **Healing Brush**—Works like the **Clone Stamp** tool in that it copies pixels from a good area of an image. However, unlike the **Clone Stamp**, the **Healing Brush** *blends* the good pixels with existing pixels in the repair area, thus hiding the repair by matching the texture of the repair area. Use this tool instead of the **Clone Stamp** when you're cloning into an area with a texture, such as grass, wood, or a sweater. See **111 Remove Scratches**.

- **Smudge tool**—Uses either the current foreground color or the color under the brush tip at the beginning of a stroke to blend into existing pixels as you drag. This is sort of like finger painting. Use this tool to work color into damaged areas, fix some stray hairs, or soften a bad makeup job by smudging it.

- **Blur tool**—Softens hard edges to reduce contrast. Often, you can soften the impact of a defect by using this tool to blur the contrast between it and an unpatched area.

- **Brush tool**—Yes, you can even paint in a repair when needed. The trouble here is you're painting solid-colored pixels that do not blend well with the natural randomness of the pixels in a photo, so use this technique sparingly. I have used a very tiny **Brush** tool with a dark grayish purple to paint in eyelashes on occasion.

110

In addition to tools, the Editor provides the digital retouching artist with many useful filters to help make repairs:

- **Despeckle, Median, and Reduce Noise**—To remove a general scattering of dots or *noise* from a photograph, use one of these three filters (see **112 Remove Specks and Spots**). The **Reduce Noise** filter is also helpful in removing noise caused by photographing in low light without a flash.

- **Dust & Scratches**—To remove small spots in a localized area, apply the **Dust & Scratches** filter. The **Dust & Scratches** filter is also good at repairing small scratches. Contrast at the edges of objects is preserved (see **111 Remove Scratches**).

▶ KEY TERM

Noise—A random pattern of pixels that gives an image a grainy texture. Digital still cameras have the same picture-taking electronics as digital video cameras, so the noise that generally cancels itself out when viewed at 30 frames per second can't be ignored in a frozen frame (single image).

▶ **NOTE**

Many of the tools you might use to remove scratches, specks, and holes require that your image use either **Grayscale** or **RGB Color** mode.

▶ **NOTE**

All filters work on the current layer. Because these retouching filters work by either reducing contrast between pixels or blurring edges, it's best to make a selection first before applying any of the filters listed here or to copy the area you want to repair to its own layer. That way, important contrast (along the edges of objects, for example) is preserved and the detail in your photo won't be lost.

111	**Remove Scratches**	
✔ **BEFORE YOU BEGIN**		→ **SEE ALSO**
110 About Removing Scratches, Specks, and Holes		**113** Repair Minor Holes and Tears

111

This small photo has been around since the 1940s and has had plenty of opportunity to acquire dust spots, scratches, and other flaws. Such a picture is a good candidate for a progressive approach: Start with a tool such as the **Dust & Scratches** filter to remove thin, short scratches and scattered dust spots in a small area. Then, move up to the **Healing Brush** to remove longer and wider scratches.

Like any old photo, there's typically several different ways to go about repairing the damage. In this task, you'll learn a method that's best applied when you have several small scratches and dust spots in the same area. If your photo has spots but no scratches, you can still use the method described here, but if the spots are in an area that's fairly even in tone, you'll want to see **112** **Remove Specks and Spots** for an alternative method that might work better. If your photo has isolated spots, scratches in areas of detail, or small tears and stains, see **113** **Repair Minor Holes and Tears**.

1 **Choose Dust & Scratches Filter**

Open an image in the **Editor** in **Standard Edit** mode and save it in Photoshop (***.psd**) format. Zoom in on an area of dust spots—it's easier to work with an enlarged view.

Using the **Lasso** tool, select an area that contains thin scratches or dust spots. Your selection will help contain the effect of the filter so that you don't lose important detail. Keep this area as small as possible while still including as many spots and scratches as you can. Choose **Filter, Noise, Dust & Scratches**. The **Dust & Scratches** dialog box appears.

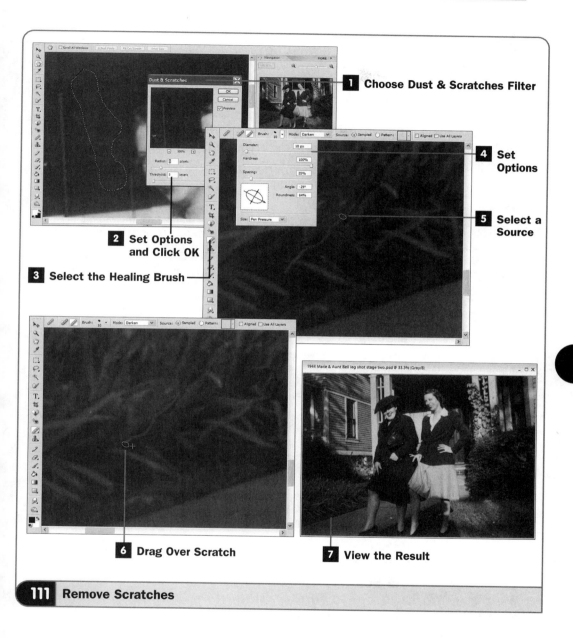

1 Choose Dust & Scratches Filter

4 Set Options

5 Select a Source

2 Set Options and Click OK

3 Select the Healing Brush

6 Drag Over Scratch

7 View the Result

111

111 Remove Scratches

2 Set Options and Click OK

The **Dust & Scratches** filter works by searching out pixels that contrast greatly with their neighbors and reducing this contrast, essentially removing the dust or scratch by camouflaging it. The **Radius** setting controls the area over which the filter searches for such differences. The larger the radius, the larger the area and the larger the spots the filter will correct. Ideally, you want to set the **Radius** to roughly the same size as the scratches or spots you're trying to remove.

You control the level of correction with the **Threshold** setting. If **Threshold** is set to a low value, the spot or scratch must contrast a lot with neighboring pixels before it will be removed. As you raise the **Threshold** little by little, you'll remove more spots at the risk of possibly losing some detail. When you find the right balance between the settings, click **OK** to apply them.

▶ **NOTE**

If you enable the **Preview** check box in the **Dust & Scratches** dialog box, the effects of your current settings appear on the actual image. If necessary, repeat steps 1 and 2 to select another area with spots and scratches and remove them. Assuming that most of the spots and scratches in the image are grouped in smallish areas, you can use this method to remove the majority of the spots and scratches in a photo in just a few minutes.

▶ **TIP**

To remove the next set of spots, select them, and then reapply the **Dust & Scratches** filter using the same settings. Unless these spots or scratches are really different in size, the original settings should work fine on this new selection. To reapply the last filter you used, with the exact same settings, press **Ctrl+F**, or choose that filter from the very top of the **Filter** list, where it will continue to appear until you use a different filter.

3 Select the Healing Brush

When you have wider or longer scratches that seem to resist the **Dust & Scratches** filter, turn to the **Healing Brush** tool. Because the **Healing Brush** blends the cloned pixels with original pixels at the repair site, it preserves the original shading and texture of the picture while it overlays a repair. Thus, you should use the **Healing Brush** rather than the **Clone Stamp** whenever you want to repair scratches in a textured area, such as grass or wood. Select the **Healing Brush** from the **Toolbox**.

4 Set Options

On the **Options** bar, open the **Brush** palette and adjust the brush **Diameter** to the size of the scratch you're trying to repair. I typically reduce the **Roundness** setting to flatten the brush tip and adjust the **Angle** to match the scratch.

Enable the **Sampled** option. Because the scratch is lighter than the cloned pixels will be, select **Darken** from the blend **Mode** list. Set any other options as desired.

▶ NOTE

With the **Aligned** option enabled, the relationship between the source point and the place where you begin cloning is maintained throughout the entire cloning procedure, regardless of how many times you stop and start. With **Aligned** disabled, pixels are always copied beginning at the original source point, and moving in the same direction you drag. If you begin a new stroke, the pixels are copied beginning at the original source.

5 Select a Source

Press **Alt** and click the image to establish the source for the repair. I typically click very near the scratch so that the cloned pixels will match the repair area closely.

6 Drag Over Scratch

Drag the brush over the scratch to remove it. As you move the brush, the source point (the crosshair) moves with it. Pixels are copied from the source and blended with existing pixels, completing the repair. Because you selected **Darken** blend mode, the cloned pixels replace the source pixels completely if they are darker than the scratch. Repeat steps 3 to 6 to repair any remaining scratches.

112

7 View the Result

After removing the scratches and small spots grouped in the same area, make any other changes you want, and save the PSD file. Then resave the file in JPEG or TIFF format, leaving your PSD image with its layers (if any) intact so that you can return at a later time and make different adjustments if you want.

After less than five minutes, I had easily removed the majority of the spots and faint scratches on this photo. There are a few larger spots that remain, and I'll use the **Spot Healing Brush** described in the next task to remove them.

---

112 Remove Specks and Spots

✔ BEFORE YOU BEGIN	→ SEE ALSO
110 About Removing Scratches, Specks, and Holes	**113** Repair Minor Holes and Tears **114** Repair Major Holes and Tears

---

Dust, scratches, and other "age spots" aren't the only kinds of damage a picture can suffer. Digital cameras and cell phone cameras can add their own kinds of spottiness in the form of *CCD noise*. This kind of noise, which occurs in a digital camera when you take a long exposure or overextend the digital zoom, takes the form of graininess or colored specks in areas that should be fairly uniform. Cell phone cameras introduce a certain level of noise naturally, simply because of the low quality of their images. Noise can also appear in scans of halftone images printed in a newspaper or magazine, in still images captured from video, or in images recorded under low-light conditions.

▶ **KEY TERM**

CCD noise—Random distortions introduced into a photo by the CCD chip in a digital camera, cell phone camera, or scanner—its principal light detector. In a digital camera or cell phone camera, CCD noise happens most often during long exposures or at high ISO settings (film speed), and is magnified when electronic zoom is used to simulate a close-up of a subject at a distance. In a scanner, CCD noise happens naturally (mostly in darker tones), but especially at low scanning resolutions. This type of noise usually affects the shadow areas of an image, in the red and blue channels.

Three noise filters can help eliminate these specks. The **Median**, **Despeckle**, and **Reduce Noise** filters can easily remove the random pattern of dots caused by noise, regardless of the cause. Because it tends to average out the tones in a selection (changing pixels to the same average level of brightness as their neighbors), the **Median** filter is often a good choice when the noise affects large areas that are supposed to be even in tone—like the patch of sky in this example. The **Despeckle** filter blurs pixels to smooth out areas of low contrast, leaving areas of high contrast (which are typically the edges of objects in a photo) untouched. The **Despeckle** filter is lousy at removing dust and speck type spots, but is good at removing low-contrast noise in a large area while preserving your edges.

The **Reduce Noise** filter again looks for pixels that contrast with their neighbors, and in a manner similar to **Median**, reduces their contrast by averaging out their brightness. Unlike **Median**, the **Reduce Noise** filter also evens out color by averaging the hue of each pi XEl with that of its neighbors. And like **Despeckle**, the **Reduce Noise** filter preserves the contrast along edges in your photo. After removing general noise (tiny specks that occur in a random pattern over a wide area), you'll learn how to use the **Spot Healing Brush** to remove spots that occur in isolated areas.

▶ **NOTE**

To remove small spots in a specific area, it's typically best to use the **Dust & Scratches** filter rather than the **Median** filter because the **Median** filter tends to remove not only spots but detail as well, as it averages out the tone in a selection. The **Dust & Scratches** filter removes small spots in an area without removing detail; however, in some situations, such as areas of even tone that contain specks or spots caused by age, the **Median** filter can do a better job.

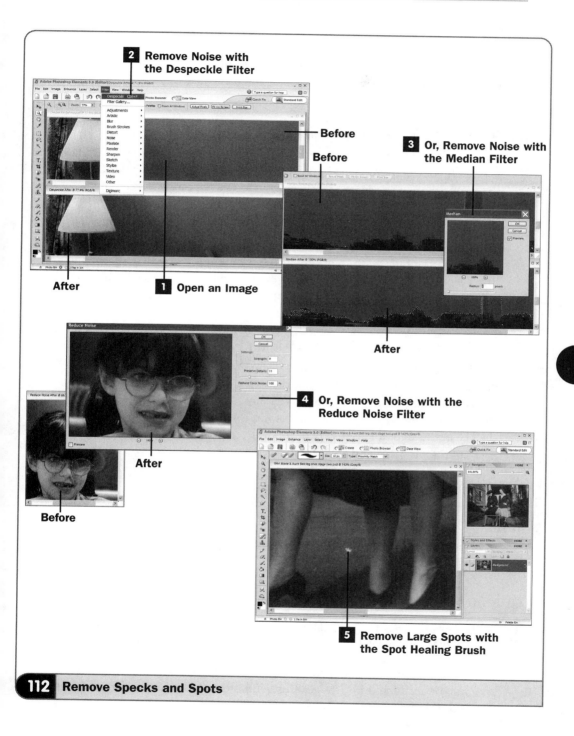

2 Remove Noise with the Despeckle Filter

Before

Before

3 Or, Remove Noise with the Median Filter

After

1 Open an Image

After

4 Or, Remove Noise with the Reduce Noise Filter

After

Before

5 Remove Large Spots with the Spot Healing Brush

112

112 Remove Specks and Spots

1 Open an Image

Open an image in the **Editor** in **Standard Edit** mode and save it in Photoshop (*.psd) format. Then remove noise using any of the three **Noise** filters.

2 Remove Noise with the Despeckle Filter

To remove low-contrast noise from a photo, choose **Filter, Noise, Despeckle**. Although you could make a selection first, because **Despeckle** works only on low-contrast areas to remove noise, your edges will be preserved so there's typically no need to isolate the filter with a selection. The **Despeckle** filter works automatically, so you'll be able to judge its effectiveness right away.

This photo was taken to record the new paint job in our bedroom. Despite the sunshine coming through the window, the resulting photo had a lot of noise throughout. The **Despeckle** filter did a pretty good job of removing this low-contrast noise. I applied the filter multiple times to remove the noise completely, and yet the edges were preserved.

3 Or, Remove Noise with the Median Filter

To apply the **Median** filter to an area of similar tone, first select the portion of the image you want to change. If necessary, on the **Layers** palette, change to the layer that contains the data to change. Then use your favorite selection tool to select the area that contains the noise you want to remove. Because the sky in this example is nearly a uniform color, I selected it with a few clicks of the **Magic Wand** tool. Zoom in on the image so that you can see your changes clearly. Choose **Filter, Noise, Median**. The **Median** dialog box appears.

▶ **TIP**

The **Median** filter averages out the brightness of neighboring pixels, so make sure that you do not include high-contrast edges in your selection because you might lose that detail after applying the filter.

▶ **TIP**

Enable the **Preview** check box in the **Median** dialog box so that you can see how the changes you make to the filter's settings affect the selected area in the image window.

Adjust the **Radius** value to a setting that removes the noise without removing too much natural texture. The **Radius** defines the area in which neighboring pixels are examined, to calculate an average value for the central pi XEl. Typically, a low value such as **2** or **3** is sufficient. Click **OK** to apply the filter.

112

I used the **Magic Wand** to select the sky in this nighttime photo of the Washington Monument. The low-light conditions caused the noise, but it was easily removed using a low **Radius** setting in the **Median** dialog box.

4 Or, Remove Noise with the Reduce Noise Filter

The **Reduce Noise** filter combines the best of the **Despeckle** and **Median** filters, so it's a good one to try in their place. Choose **Filter, Noise, Reduce Noise**. The **Reduce Noise** dialog box appears.

First, lower the **Preserve Details** value or you won't see any effect. This value controls how much contrast a pi XEl must have with its neighbor before its brightness is lowered to bring it more in line with the "neighborhood average." Increase this value to preserve your edges; lower it to reduce noise even more. **Strength** controls the **Median** effect on qualifying pixels—in other words, the amount that a pi XEl's brightness might be changed. To change pi XEl hue values in a manner similar to the way the **Strength** value adjusts pi XEl brightness, increase the **Reduce Color Noise** value. The effect of your selections on the image appears in the large preview window on the left. When you're satisfied, click **OK** to apply the filter.

5 Remove Large Spots with the Spot Healing Brush

112

The **Noise** filters are great, but they do nothing to large spots on a digital image. The **Dust & Scratches** filter does a wonderful job of removing such spots, especially when they are grouped together, but you must be careful to apply the filter to a small area or you'll lose detail. To remove spots that are isolated or larger than a small dot, use the **Spot Healing Brush**.

You don't have to make a selection first; the effect is controlled by the size of your brush tip. Zoom in so that you can see the spot you want to remove, and then select the **Spot Healing Brush** on the **Toolbox**. On the **Options** bar, select a brush tip and adjust its **Size** to something slightly larger than the size of the spot you want to repair. Set the **Type** option to **Proximity Match**. This option analyzes the pixels around the edges of the brush to create a patch for the repair. Click the spot to remove it. Here, I returned to the 1940s photo and removed several large-to-medium spots with quick clicks of the **Spot Healing Brush**.

▶ TIP

If the area the spot is in has a definite texture, you can replicate that texture to a degree and create a more convincing patch than with the **Proximity Match** option. Just enable the **Create Texture** option on the **Options** bar instead, which analyzes all the pixels under the brush tip for both color and tone, and then uses that sampling to create a similar pattern.

When you're satisfied with the results of the **Noise** filters and the **Spot Healing Brush**, make any other changes you want and save the PSD file. Then resave the file in JPEG or TIFF format, leaving your PSD image with its **layers** (if any) intact so that you can return at a later time and make different adjustments if you want.

---

113   Repair Minor Holes and Tears

✔ BEFORE YOU BEGIN	→ SEE ALSO
110 About Removing Scratches, Specks, and Holes	**114** Repair Major Holes and Tears

---

Even cute pictures from the past are vulnerable to damage. Sometimes the damage is minor but annoying, such as a thin crease, small tear, scratch, spot, or stain. As you learned in **111** **Remove Scratches**, you can use the **Dust & Scratches** filter to remove thin scratches and small specks in the same general area, in one quick step. You also learned how to use the **Healing Brush** to clone data and texture from one area of a photo, repairing wider scratches in the process. In **112** **Remove Specks and Spots**, you learned that you can use the **Median** filter to remove larger specks within a selected area and use the **Spot Healing Brush** to remove isolated, large specks.

Sometimes the damage to the image is too much for the **Healing Brush** to correct. Although the **Healing Brush** works in a manner similar to the **Clone Stamp**, it *blends* copied pixels with those in the area you're repairing, and sometimes, blending is not what you want. For example, if you're repairing a tear that's fairly white, the **Healing Brush** blends the copied pixels (taken from an intact part of the picture) with the whiteness of the tear, creating an almost ghostlike effect. The same thing happens if you use the **Healing Brush** to repair a large hole; the whiteness of the hole will interfere with the cover-up job you're trying to achieve. In this task, you'll learn how to use the **Clone Stamp** effectively to clone missing data back into a photo. In **114** **Repair Major Holes and Tears**, you'll learn an alternative technique that's quick and effective at filling in missing information. In this task, you'll also learn how to use the **Smudge** tool to blend out small blemishes and the **Sponge** tool to swab off stains.

▶ NOTE

In some situations, you can use the **Brush** tool to daub over small blemishes—if you can achieve an exact color match. Select the **Brush** tool on the **Toolbox** and press **Alt**; when the brush tip changes to an **Eyedropper**, use it to pick up the color you need from the image. Because the **Brush** delivers a solid bit of color, the patch often stands out from the blended pixels around it. The secret to using the **Brush** on a photo is to use it sparingly, with as small a tip as possible, and lower the **Opacity** setting.

1 Smudge Out Spots

2 Choose the Clone Stamp

4 Hide the Tear or Crease

3 Select a Source

Sponge Tool

Burn Tool

5 Lighten or Darken Stain

6 Blend Stain Edges

Before

7 View the Result

113 Repair Minor Holes and Tears

1 Smudge Out Spots

Open an image in the **Editor** in **Standard Edit** mode and save it in Photoshop (*.psd) format. Select the **Smudge** tool from the **Toolbox**. In the **Options** bar, select a soft brush in a **Size** that will cover the spot you want to erase. Set other options as desired; because the first spot I wanted to correct was a dark spot on light-colored skin, I chose the **Lighten** blend **Mode** because it uses only pixels lighter than the spot to complete the repair.

▶ **TIP**

Because the **Smudge** tool blends pixels into existing ones, I typically use a **Strength** setting at 100% to cover the spot completely. In cases where the spot is hardly there and I want to retain its color, I lower the **Strength** value.

▶ **TIP**

Instead of smudging a color from the surrounding area, the **Finger Painting** option uses the current foreground color to smudge into the areas over which you drag. Although this is a fun option for playing around, it has limited use in photo repair because the color you'll want to use to cover up a spot is typically right next to the spot itself and so you can just smudge it over.

113

Click a bit away from your spot and drag with the **Smudge** tool toward the spot. This action picks up nearby colors and blends them over the spot's color. Repeat this step to blend out other spots. If there are light spots in dark areas, change the **Mode** setting to **Darken** and click to correct those areas. Change the **Mode** to **Normal** to correct less-noticeable spots, such as lighter spots on a light background or dark dust specks on a darker background.

2 Choose the Clone Stamp

Select the **Clone Stamp** tool from the **Toolbox**. Select a soft brush tip and set the **Size** just a bit larger than the flaw you want to repair. Because tears and creases are lighter than surrounding pixels, select the **Darken** blend **Mode**. That way, if your brush tip is a bit larger than the crease or tear in some spots, you won't replace good pixels with cloned ones because only light pixels are replaced with this mode. Enable the **Aligned** option, and set **Opacity** to 100% to fully replace the tear.

With the **Aligned** option enabled, the relationship between the source point and the place where you begin cloning is maintained throughout the entire cloning procedure, regardless of how many times you stop and start. That makes the **Aligned** option perfect for repairing a crease or large tear—the repair will match surrounding pixels perfectly. With **Aligned** disabled, pixels are always copied beginning at the original source point and moving in the same direction that you drag. If you begin a new stroke, the pixels are copied beginning at the original source point.

3 Select a Source

Press and hold the **Alt** key. Click in the image near the crease or tear to specify the source point—the "good pixels" you want the tool to clone to fix the flaw.

▶ TIP

Because the **Clone Stamp** adjusts the source point as you drag, it allows for differences in color and tone as you drag over the tear or crease. The disadvantage is that the tool picks up and duplicates any flaws it encounters. This is why selecting your source point is important. As a rule, select the source as physically close to the flaw as you can. Doing so helps ensure that the pixels you use to repair the flaw match as closely as possible to the surrounding pixels. As the tear or crease changes direction, adjust the source point as well (by pressing **Alt** and clicking the image again) so that you can continue to match objects perfectly.

4 Hide the Tear or Crease

Click at the beginning of the tear or crease and drag slowly down the crease. The pixels you sampled in step 3 are copied over the flaw as you drag. As you work, the source point (marked by a crosshair) moves with the brush tip.

5 Lighten or Darken Stain

Removing stains on color images can be tricky, but for grayscale images, it's fairly straightforward. The center of the stain will probably be lighter, especially if it's a water stain like the one shown here. To darken the pixels, select the **Burn** tool on the **Toolbox**. On the **Options** bar, adjust the **Size** of the tool to the width of the stain's *interior*. Set the **Range** to **Highlights** and the **Exposure** rate to a low value, such as **30%**. This setting prevents you from darkening the pixels too quickly. Brush over the stain's interior, darkening the lightest pixels. To darken the midtones as well, change the **Range** setting to **Midtones** and brush over the interior again.

If the interior of the stain is darker than the surrounding area, use the **Dodge** tool instead, because it lightens pixels. Set the **Range** to **Shadows** and then to **Midtones** to lighten the pixels in the center of the stain.

6 Blend Stain Edges

To hide the repair, use the **Sponge** tool to desaturate the pixels around the edge of the stain, where they are typically darker. This tool helps blend the edge of the stain with surrounding pixels. Change to the **Sponge** tool by

113

clicking its icon on the **Options** bar. Select a soft brush tip and choose a **Size** that's slightly larger than the dark edge of the stain. Choose **Desaturate** from the **Mode** list. Lower the **Flow** to **50%** or less, so that the tool will lower the pixels' saturation slowly and not overdo the repair. Brush the tool over the edge of the stain, desaturating the pixels.

▶ TIP

You can also use the **Sponge** tool to saturate pixels, which you might do in a color image that's faded over time. Use the **Sponge** tool after adjusting for any color shifts in the image, which also occurs as photographs get older.

▶ TIP

If the stain has occurred on a color photograph, the simplest method is to clone over the stain with good data (if available). If not, isolate the stain by selecting it and copying it to a new layer. Then you can try several methods for changing its color to the color it should be. You can invert the layer colors (**Filter**, **Adjustments**, **Invert**) and blend the result with the image layer by changing the copy layer's blend **Mode** to **Color**. Or you can colorize the layer (**Enhance**, **Adjust Color**, **Hue/Saturation**), enable the **Colorize** option, and adjust the **Hue** slider to change the color. Lower the **Lightness** value as well, because stains are darker than surrounding pixels.

114

7 View the Result

This photo of three elderly aunts braving a snow storm was apparently stored in someone's pocket. It has many creases, spots, specks, and a few water stains. It took a little while to repair the damage, but as you can see, the result is a great improvement.

114 Repair Major Holes and Tears	
✔ **BEFORE YOU BEGIN**	→ **SEE ALSO**
110 About Removing Scratches, Specks, and Holes	**113** Repair Minor Holes and Tears

Photoshop Elements has retouching tools that can take care of most of the small defects in an old photo. They will even take care of some of the larger ones. But once in a while, a picture is missing a big chunk. At some time in the past, it might have been torn or have been mounted in an album with plastic tape (a sworn enemy of photo preservation). The photo might be missing a corner or have holes in it from being mounted on a bulletin board.

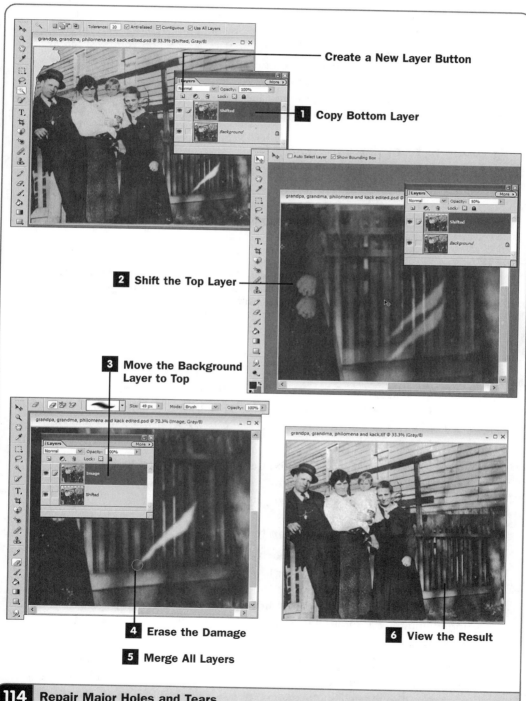

Create a New Layer Button

1 Copy Bottom Layer

2 Shift the Top Layer

3 Move the Background Layer to Top

4 Erase the Damage

5 Merge All Layers

6 View the Result

114

Repairing this kind of damage has the same purpose as using the **Clone Stamp** or the **Healing Brush** to repair smaller areas: The goal is to replace the bad section of a photo with a good section of the photo. However, when you must repair a large damaged area, using the **Clone Stamp** or **Healing Brush** to copy data is not only tedious (you have to move the source often to hide what you're doing) but often leads to poor results despite your best efforts. In this task, I show you a rather tricky approach to filling in big gaps in your photo.

1 Copy Bottom Layer

Open an image in the **Editor** in **Standard Edit** mode and save it in Photoshop (***.psd**) format. On the **Layers** palette, drag the layer onto the **Create a New Layer** button or select **Layer, Duplicate** to create a duplicate of the original **Background** layer. Rename this new layer **Shifted**.

▶ TIP

114

If the good information you want to use to repair the hole or tear is located in another image, open that image, and adjust its size and resolution to match the image you want to repair. Choose **Select, All,** and then choose **Edit, Copy.** Change to the image you want to repair, and choose **Edit, Paste** to paste the image with the good data onto a new layer. Rename this new layer **Shifted.**

2 Shift the Top Layer

On the **Layers** palette, change the **Opacity** of the **Shifted** layer to **50%**. This setting lets you see the **Background** layer as you shift the top layer. You're going to use good pieces of the **Shifted** layer to cover the holes and tears in the **Background** layer.

Click the **Move** tool on the **Toolbox**. Click the **Shifted** layer in the image and slowly move it left, right, up, or down until its good portion covers up the area on the **Background** layer that you want to fill in.

3 Move the Background Layer to Top

In the **Layers** palette, reset the **Opacity** of the **Shifted** layer to 100%. Convert the **Background** layer to a regular layer (a process also known as "simplifying") by choosing the **Background** layer in the **Layers** palette and choosing **Layer, New, Layer from Background.** Name the converted layer **Image.** Simplifying the background layer enables you to move its position in the layer stack.

Click the newly created **Image** layer in the **Layers** palette and drag it above the **Shifted** layer. The **Shifted** layer is now on the bottom, with the **Image** layer on top. Notice that the hole in the original image is noticeable once again.

4 Erase the Damage

On the **Layers** palette, select the **Image** layer. In the **Toolbox**, select the **Eraser** tool. In the **Options** bar, set the **Mode** option to **Brush**, select a soft-edged brush, and adjust its **Size** to fit the size of the hole or tear. Set **Opacity** to **100%**.

Start brushing over the damaged area, erasing the top image layer to reveal the undamaged area of the **Shifted** layer under it.

5 Merge All Layers

If the shifted data happens to line up with another hole or tear, you can repeat step 4 to repair that damage as well. If not, you'll need to merge the layers, and then repeat steps 1 to 4 to repair any other damaged areas. To merge the layers, choose **Layer, Flatten Image**.

6 View the Result

After you've made all necessary repairs to the holes and tears, make any other changes you want, such as removing small spots and creases. Save the PSD file, and then resave the file in JPEG or TIFF format, leaving your PSD image with its layers (if any) intact so that you can return at a later time and make different adjustments if you want.

This old photo of my grandparents and aunt has been through a lot, as you can see. There was a tear in the middle and in one corner; small specks and spots adorned various areas, and it had lost its tone. To repair the damage, I borrowed a good spot in the fence and, following the steps in this task, repaired it. I repeated the process to fix the missing section in the upper-left corner. After merging all layers, I adjusted the contrast and used the **Spot Healing Brush** on the specks. The result, as you can see, is much improved.

115

115 Correct Red Eye

✔ BEFORE YOU BEGIN	→ SEE ALSO
Just jump right in.	118 Awaken Tired Eyes

When used properly, a camera flash can help lighten shadows and illuminate an otherwise dark image. Unfortunately, using a flash might sometimes have unintended effects, such as *red eye*. In nonhuman subjects such as dogs or cats, the result might be "glassy eye" rather than red eye. No matter; you remove it in the same way: with the **Editor's Red Eye Removal** tool.

► **KEY TERM**

Red eye—A reddening of the pupil caused by a reflection of the intense light from a camera flash against the retina in the back of the subject's eyes.

► **TIP**

When you're shooting your photograph, you can avoid giving your subjects red eye by separating the flash unit from the camera (if possible), or by telling your subjects to not look directly at the camera.

► **TIP**

Some cameras have a red eye reduction feature, which causes the flash to go off several times. The first series of flashes at lower intensity causes the pupil to contract, thus blocking the reflection, while the final flash at full intensity illuminates the subject for the picture. Just be sure to warn your subject not to move until the second flash goes off.

115

1 **Zoom In on Eye**

Open an image in the Editor in either **Quick Fix** or **Standard Edit** mode, and save it in Photoshop (*****.psd**) format. Zoom in on the first eye you want to correct so that you can see it better. To zoom in, click the **Zoom** tool in the **Toolbox**. Then select a **Zoom** amount on the **Options** bar or click the **Zoom In** button on the **Options** bar and drag a rectangle within the image around the eye you want to see more closely.

2 **Click Red Eye Removal Tool**

Click the **Red Eye Removal** tool in the **Toolbox**.

3 **Set Options**

If the *pupil* of the eye you want to correct is larger in area than 50% of the *iris*, change the **Pupil Size** setting on the **Options** bar to the correct ratio. If the **Pupil Size** ratio is way off, the Editor might not remove all the red eye, or it might paint in too much of the iris color, making the iris larger than it should be.

► **KEY TERM**

Pupil—The black center of the eye that adjusts in size based on the amount of ambient light.

► **KEY TERM**

Iris—The colored part of the eye; typically brown, blue, or green.

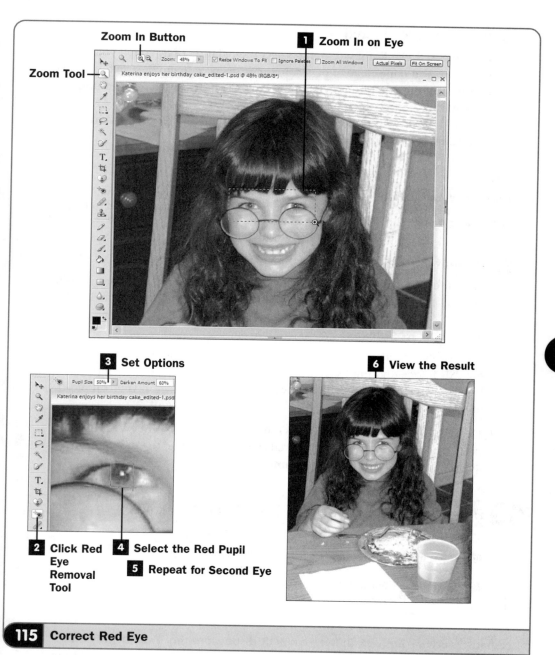

Zoom In Button

1 Zoom In on Eye

Zoom Tool

3 Set Options

6 View the Result

2 Click Red Eye Removal Tool   **4** Select the Red Pupil

5 Repeat for Second Eye

115

115 Correct Red Eye

Typically, you won't have to adjust the **Darken Amount** on the **Options** bar. However, if the pupil is not darkened enough after you apply the **Red Eye Removal** tool, you can try the tool again after increasing the **Darken Amount**.

4 Select the Red Pupil

Drag the **Red Eye Removal** tool to select the red area of the pupil you want to correct. You don't have to be terribly precise because only red pixels will be affected; on the other hand, you don't want to select too big an area and accidentally remove the red from pixels you don't want to change. After you drag, red pixels within the selected area are changed to black or the iris color, depending on the **Pupil Size** you've set.

▶ **TIP**

Instead of dragging to select the area to change, you can click anywhere within the red area of the pupil. Red pixels contiguous to the pi XEl you clicked are changed to black. If one method doesn't work for you, try the other and you might get better results.

5 Repeat for Second Eye

Scroll the image if necessary so that you can see the second eye. Drag again to select the red area. The red pixels within that area are changed to black.

6 View the Result

116

After you're satisfied with the result, make any other changes you want to the PSD image and then save it. Resave the result in JPEG or TIFF format, leaving your PSD image with its layers (if any) intact so that you can return at a later time and make different adjustments if you want.

This photo of a young "Hermione Granger" at her Harry Potter birthday party was marred only by a bit of red eye. Lucky for me, the problem was quickly fi XEd with the **Red Eye Removal** tool.

---

116   **Remove Wrinkles, Freckles, and Minor Blemishes**

✔ **BEFORE YOU BEGIN**	→ **SEE ALSO**
100 Zoom In and Out with the Zoom Tool	**117** Whiten Teeth
101 Zoom In and Out with the Navigator Palette	**118** Awaken Tired Eyes

---

Almost everyone has certain...er...cosmetic distinctions that help identify and even glamorize a person. However, if they're the temporary kind, you might not want a permanent record of them. Sometimes a perfectly good photograph is marred by minor distractions such as a few blemishes, a mole, a cold sore, or a few wrinkles just beginning to show. Is it vain to want to fix nature? Perhaps, but don't let that stop you—especially when it's so easy to eliminate them.

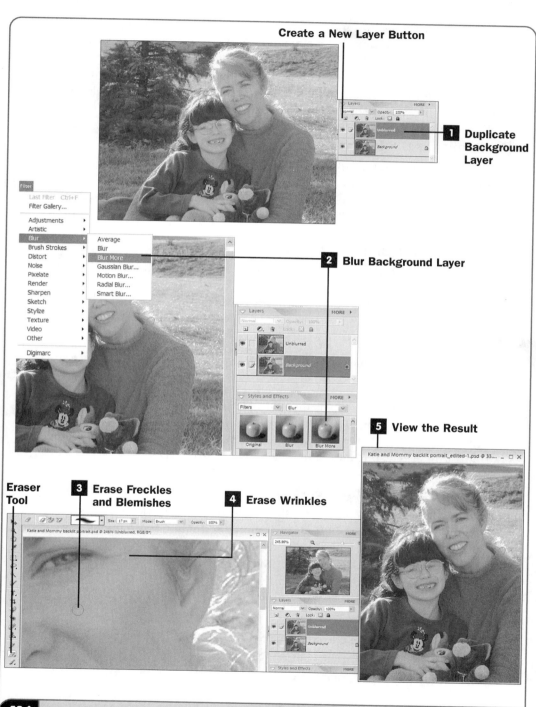

Create a New Layer Button

1 Duplicate Background Layer

2 Blur Background Layer

5 View the Result

Eraser Tool

3 Erase Freckles and Blemishes

4 Erase Wrinkles

116

You can use the **Clone Stamp** tool to paint away minor defects in a photograph by copying good pixels from some other area. For some very minor problem areas, you might try the **Spot Healing Brush** discussed in **111 Remove Scratches** and an upcoming Tip. But in either case, the process is tedious and often easily detectable unless the tools are used sparingly. In this task, you'll use a quicker method that involves one of the blur filters.

1 Duplicate Background Layer

Open an image in the **Editor** in **Standard Edit** mode, and save it in Photoshop (*.psd) format. Then drag the **Background Layer** onto the **Create a New Layer** button on the **Layers** palette (to create a copy of it), or select **Layer, Duplicate Layer**. Name the new layer **Unblurred**.

2 Blur Background Layer

Change to the **Background** layer and select **Filter, Blur, Blur More** from the menu or double-click the **Blur More** icon on the **Filters** list of the **Styles and Effects** palette. The **Background** layer is blurred just a bit.

116

▶ **TIP**

To see the blurred **Background** layer, hide the top layer temporarily by clicking its eye button on the **Layers** palette.

For very large images such as those at 1048×1478 resolution, the **Blur More** filter might not do enough to blur the layer. In such cases, try the **Gaussian Blur** filter (choose **Filter, Blur, Gaussian Blur**) or double-click the **Gaussian Blur** icon in the **Filters** list of the **Styles and Effects** palette.

3 Erase Freckles and Blemishes

On the **Layers** palette, change to the **Unblurred** layer. Click the **Eraser** tool on the **Toolbox**. On the **Options** bar, select a soft round brush. Adjust the **Size** value so that the eraser is slightly bigger than the blemish you want to remove. Click the freckle or blemish with the eraser, which erases that spot, revealing the blurred layer beneath.

▶ **TIP**

Another way you can remove blemishes and freckles quickly is to blend them away with the **Spot Healing Brush** tool. Set the **Size** so that the brush includes the clean area of skin around the blemish or freckle, set **Type** to **Proximity Match**, position the pointer over the blemish or freckle, and click to blend it away.

4 Erase Wrinkles

Change the **Size** value on the **Options** bar to resize the **Eraser** tool so that it's just wider than the wrinkles you want to remove. Then drag the **Eraser** over any wrinkles to erase the wrinkle, revealing the blurred wrinkle on the **Background** layer.

5 View the Result

After you're satisfied with the image, save it in its PSD format. Merge the layers together by selecting **Layer**, **Flatten Image** and save the result in JPEG or TIFF format, leaving your PSD image unflattened so that you can return at a later time and make different adjustments if you want.

This photo of me and my daughter is just wonderful, but the small blemish and the wrinkles just beginning to show on my face made the photo less than perfect for me. A bit of blur and a few minutes with the **Eraser**, and I'm the person I see when I look in the mirror. Add a bit of judicious cropping and some work at removing the reflections from my daughter's glasses, and I have a portrait worthy of my living room wall.

117

117 Whiten Teeth

✔ BEFORE YOU BEGIN	→ SEE ALSO
100 Zoom In and Out with the Zoom Tool	**116** Remove Wrinkles, Freckles, and Minor Blemishes
101 Zoom In and Out with the Navigator Palette	**118** Awaken Tired Eyes

There are many products on the market you can use to whiten your teeth—gels, toothpastes, whitening strips, and bleaches—but none work as fast and as effectively as digital editing. It's not vanity to want to improve Mother Nature; in our culture today, a great importance is placed on having clean, white teeth, and if a photo will be used in a resumé or to advertise a product, you'll want to give the best impression you can by making sure that your subject looks his or her best.

Whitening teeth is tricky, however; you don't want the effect to look obvious and artificial. You'll want to avoid the temptation to use *pure white* to paint over all your teeth, which results in a picket-fence effect that can look genuinely scary. The technique explained here uses the **Dodge** tool, which selectively lightens the brightness of the pixels over which it passes. You must be cautious, however, so that you don't burn out the color and create a fake whiteness.

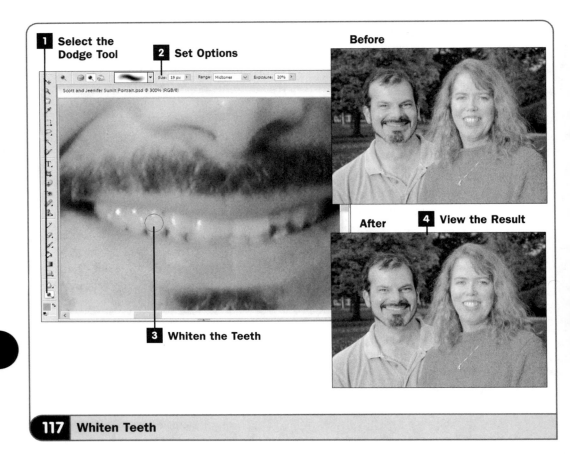

1 Select the Dodge Tool

2 Set Options

Before

Scott and Jeenifer Sunlit Portrait.psd @ 300% (RGB/8)

After   **4** View the Result

3 Whiten the Teeth

117

117 Whiten Teeth

▶ **TIP**

I always get good results with the **Dodge** tool, but if you don't like its effects, try selecting the teeth, choosing **Enhance**, **Adjust Color**, **Color Variations**, choosing **Highlights**, and clicking the **Increase Blue** and **Lighten** buttons.

1 Select the Dodge Tool

Open an image in the **Editor** in **Standard Edit** mode, and save it in Photoshop (***.psd**) format. Zoom in on the teeth so that you can see them clearly, and then select the **Dodge** tool in the **Toolbox**.

▶ **TIP**

To isolate the effects of the **Dodge** tool, select the teeth before beginning. You might want to select the gums as well (if they are reddish and irritated) so that you can lighten them too.

▶ **TIP**

Instead of using the **Dodge** tool to whiten teeth, you can try selecting them, choosing **Enhance**, **Adjust Color**, **Adjust Hue/Saturation**, and then increasing the lightness in the **Master** channel and decreasing the saturation in the **Yellow** channel.

2 Set Options

On the **Options** bar, choose a soft round brush. Adjust the **Size** of the **Dodge** tool so that the brush tip is about the size of one tooth. Set the **Range** to **Midtones** so that you affect only the midtones, and set **Exposure** to about **20%** so that you don't lighten the teeth too fast and accidentally burn out the color.

3 Whiten the Teeth

Position the brush tip over the first tooth and click once. The tooth should get just a bit lighter. Click again to lighten a bit more, or move to the next tooth. Repeat until all the teeth are whiter. You can also drag the brush over the teeth.

Remove any remaining imperfections (such as uneven color or spots on the teeth) with the **Clone Stamp** tool.

117

4 View the Result

When you're satisfied with the result, make any other changes you want and save the PSD file. Resave the result in JPEG or TIFF format, leaving your PSD image with its layers (if any) intact so that you can return at a later time and make different adjustments if you want.

In this portrait, the golden light of sunset made our teeth look yellowish. A few minutes with the **Dodge** tool fi XEd that easily. Compare the original (on the left) to the whitened version; you can see that the teeth on the right look better, and yet still natural. I also used the technique discussed in **116** **Remove Wrinkles, Freckles, and Minor Blemishes** to freshen my face a bit. The last things to address are the circles under my husband's eyes, caused mostly by the low angle of the sun. To fix that problem, I'll follow the steps in the next task, **118** **Awaken Tired Eyes**. Look for the final result in the Color Gallery.

(118) Awaken Tired Eyes

✔ BEFORE YOU BEGIN	→ SEE ALSO
(100) Zoom In and Out with the Zoom Tool	(115) Correct Red Eye
(101) Zoom In and Out with the Navigator Palette	(116) Remove Wrinkles, Freckles, and Minor Blemishes
	(117) Whiten Teeth

They say that the eyes are the window to the soul. It must be true because if a woman has dark circles under her eyes, we think she looks tired (even if the dark circles are a natural skin condition). By slightly lightening the skin under the eyes, you can take years off a face and brighten a person's outlook. And it's simple to do, using the **Dodge** tool.

Redness in the whites of the eyes caused by chlorine in swimming pools or lack of sleep can also make your subject look tired. To whiten the eyes, you'll remove the redness gradually and lighten them a little using the **Color Variations** command. One final thing that can make eyes look tired is a lack of sharpness. Eyes that are in sharp focus have a distinctive twinkle that makes their owner look alert, interesting, and beautiful. Eyes such as these invite a viewer to look a moment longer at the subject. To fix a problem with slightly out-of-focus eyes, you'll oversharpen a copy of the image on a new layer and use a mask to reveal only the sharpened eyes.

1 Select the Dodge Tool

Open an image in the Editor in **Standard Edit** mode, and save it in Photoshop (***.psd**) format. Zoom in on the eyes so that you can see them clearly, and then select the **Dodge** tool in the **Toolbox**.

2 Set Options

On the **Options** bar, choose a soft round brush. Adjust the **Size** of the **Dodge** tool so that the brush tip is about the size of the area you want to lighten. In this case, I adjusted the size so that the brush was the same size as the crease under one eye.

Set the **Range** to **Shadows**, and **Exposure** to about **20%** so that you don't lighten the under-eye area too fast and accidentally burn out the color.

▶ TIP

If you'd like more control over the **Dodge** tool, try duplicating the image layer and performing your lightening on the copy layer. You can then adjust the **Opacity** of the copy layer to lower the effect of the lightening if you accidentally apply too much.

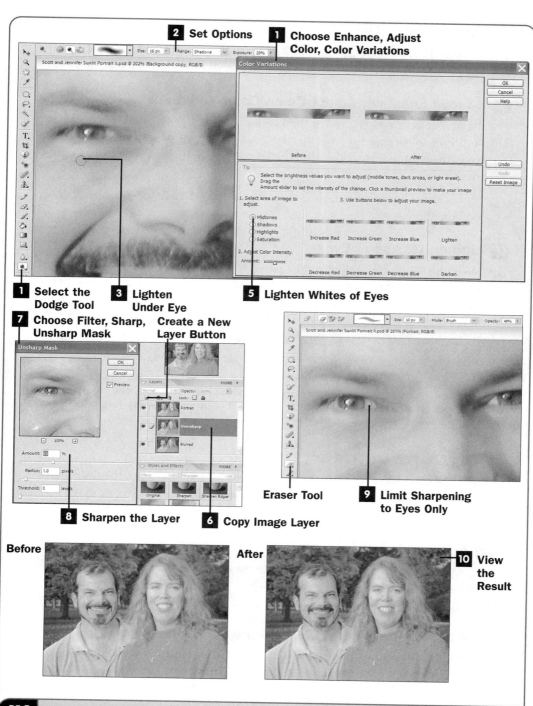

2 Set Options **1** Choose Enhance, Adjust Color, Color Variations

1 Select the Dodge Tool

3 Lighten Under Eye

5 Lighten Whites of Eyes

7 Choose Filter, Sharp, Unsharp Mask

Create a New Layer Button

118

8 Sharpen the Layer

6 Copy Image Layer

Eraser Tool

9 Limit Sharpening to Eyes Only

Before

After

10 View the Result

118 Awaken Tired Eyes

3 Lighten Under Eye

Drag the brush over the area you want to lighten. In my case, I dragged the brush carefully over the under-eye crease. Repeat this step for the second eye.

4 Choose Enhance, Adjust Color, Color Variations

If your subject's eyes are red or tired looking, select the white area of both eyes using your favorite selection tool. (I used the **Magic Wand** tool to select the whites of each eye, and the **Lasso** to snag any parts that didn't get selected.)

Choose **Enhance, Adjust Color, Color Variations**. The **Color Variations** dialog box appears.

5 Lighten Whites of Eyes

Select the **Midtones** option in the lower-left corner of the dialog box so that you affect only the midtones in the image, and then click the **Decrease Red** button to remove the redness from the eye area. Click the **Lighten** button to make the whites a little whiter. The **After** image at the top of the dialog box reflects the changes you're making. When you're through, click **OK**.

118

▶ **NOTE**

You can click the buttons in the **Color Variations** dialog box more than once to apply the same change multiple times. For example, you could click the **Decrease Red** button twice if your subject's eyes are particularly reddish.

6 Copy Image Layer

To sharpen the eyes of your subject, drag the image layer onto the **Create a New Layer** button on the **Layers Palette** (to create a copy of it), or select **Layer, Duplicate Layer**. Name the new layer **Oversharp**.

▶ **NOTE**

My original image is on a layer called **Portrait**; the **Blurred** layer at the bottom was added so that I could remove some wrinkles, blemishes, and the like. See **116 Remove Wrinkles, Freckles, and Minor Blemishes**.

7 Choose Filter, Sharp, Unsharp Mask

With the **Oversharp** layer selected, choose **Filter, Sharpen, Unsharp Mask** from the menu or double-click the **Unsharp Mask** icon on the **Filters** list of the **Styles and Effects** palette. The **Unsharp Mask** dialog box appears.

8 Sharpen the Layer

In the **Unsharp Mask** dialog box, zoom in on one of the eyes, and then adjust the settings for the filter until the eye is sharp and crisp. I typically leave the **Threshold** at a low value, set the **Radius** to somewhere between 1 and 2, and then play with the **Amount** until I get the effect I want. Check the other eye in the preview window of the dialog box (by dragging the image in the preview), and when you're satisfied with the look, click **OK**.

To make the eyes really sharp, reapply the **Unsharp Mask** settings one or two more times by choosing **Filter, Unsharp Mask**.

▶ **TIP**

Because the **Oversharp** layer is below the image layer, you won't see the effects of the sharpening on your actual image at first. To view the sharpening, on the **Layers** palette, click off the eye icon on the image layer to hide that layer temporarily.

9 Limit Sharpening to Eyes Only

The effect right now is a too-sharp image, and we wanted to limit the effect to just the eyes. On the **Layers** palette, drag the **Oversharp** layer below your image layer. The sharpness will appear to go away, but really it's just hidden by the image layer above it.

118

▶ **TIP**

If your image is on the Background layer, you'll have to convert it to a regular layer before you can drag the **Oversharp** layer underneath it in the layer stack. To do that, select the **Background** layer on the **Layers** palette, and choose **Layer, New, Layer from Background**.

To reveal the sharpened eyes, click the **Eraser tool** on the **Toolbox**. On the **Options** bar, select a small, soft brush. On the **Layers** palette, select the image layer. Then erase just the eyes, revealing the oversharpened layer below.

10 View the Result

After you're satisfied with the result, make any other changes you want, and save the PSD file. Resave the result in JPEG or TIFF format, leaving your PSD image with its layers (if any) intact so that you can return at a later time and make different adjustments if you want.

Although I had brightened our teeth and done some other minor retouching to this portrait of my husband and me, the circles under my husband's eyes and the tired look in both our eyes still bothered me. So I lightened the creases under his eyes and whitened both of our eyes just a bit, and then sharpened the eyes. Finally, I used the **Spot Healing Brush** to remove some shininess on our faces, ending up with a very special portrait. Look for this final result in the Color Gallery.

118

18

Build an Album and Post Pictures on an Online Service

IN THIS CHAPTER:

The long-running comic strip *Blondie* often depicts the Bumstead family looking through a photo album and commenting on some disreputable relative. In the twenty-first century, the photo album easily could be electronic, and the Bumsteads could share photos online with all their relatives, including the disreputable ones.

Online photo albums are a great way to share photos with others, but they're also a great way for you to keep your own photos as well. When they're online, no matter where you are, they're within reach. And you can easily print the photos, and order photos from the online photo service as well. Your friends and relatives can do the same.

This chapter shows you how to build and use online photo services with ease. There are many online photo services you can use, but in this chapter we'll concentrate on how you can use a publishing wizard built directly into Windows XP to create an online photo album in MSN Groups, as well as how to use tools built directly into Adobe Photoshop Elements to create photo albums on the Ofoto site, jointly created by Adobe and Kodak. There are also other online photo sites worth trying, including **www.shutterfly.com** and **www.flickr.com**.

119

119	**About Online Photo Services**

✔ BEFORE YOU BEGIN	→ SEE ALSO
74 Import Photos from a Digital Camera	**122** Select an Online Photo Service in Adobe Photoshop Elements
75 Scan In Photos	

In the same way digital photography has forever changed the way we take pictures, use our cameras, and even think about photography, online photo services have changed the way we use and think about photo albums, and share photographs with others.

Photo albums are no longer a physical object that only you have alone, that gets yellow over time, and that can only be viewed at your convenience. When you create an album online, you send out the URL to others, and they can view the album whenever they want. You and your visitors can print any photo they want on their own printers, or if they want it printed on photo stock, they can order prints online as well.

▶ **TIP**

If you print a lot of photos, consider investing in a photo printer. They can cost as low as $100, but will print out high-quality photos on photo stock.

Because of their many benefits, and the popularity of digital photography, online photo services have become increasingly popular. And there are many to choose from. These are the kinds of things they enable you to do:

- Scroll through thumbnails of all the photos in an album. When you do this, you can easily view many photos on a page, as you can see in the nearby figure, showing a photo album on Shutterfly.com. You can then see full-size images of any photo you want.

Here's how an online album looks on Shutterfly.com. From here, you can see larger images of each picture, order them, and print them.

- Print any photo directly to your printer.

- Reorganize your album by reordering and deleting photographs, and adding new photographs.

- Add captions to photographs.

- View photographs as a slideshow.

- Create multiple albums. You might have an album for a family trip you took to Hawaii, another for wedding photographs, and so on.

- Some services, such as **www.flickr.com**, allow other people to comment on your photographs.

As you'll see in the rest of this chapter, creating an online photo album is exceptionally easy, and can be accomplished with a minimum of mouse clicks. It's easier, in fact, than manually building photo albums the old-fashioned way.

After you've built an album, to share it with others, you send out the URL, and then your visitors can view and use your album as well. They won't be able to edit the album by adding or deleting photos, and some services let you have control over whether they can buy photographs.

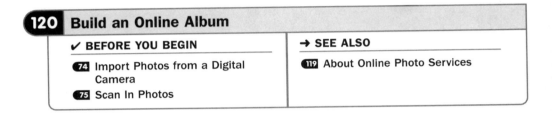

120

If you're looking for the absolute easiest way to create an online photo album, use the **Web Publishing Wizard** built into Windows XP. When you use it, you'll create a photo album on Microsoft's MSN site. You'll get 3MB of storage space for your photos. The wizard will walk you through the free registration process. If you want more storage, you can pay $20 for a year to get 30MB of space.

1 Select the Folder with Pictures You Want to Publish

Open Windows Explorer and navigate to the folder that has the pictures you want to publish on the Web. To use the wizard to publish your pictures, the folder must be designated as a Photo Album folder. You'll know the folder is a Photo Album folder if the **Print Pictures** option appears in the **Tasks** list on the left side of the screen.

▶ NOTE

You must be connected to the Internet to complete the wizard and publish your photos, so make sure you're connected before starting the wizard.

If the folder is not a Photo Album folder, it's easy to turn it into one. Select **View, Customize This Folder** from the menu and click the Customize tab. From the **Use This Folder File As a Template** drop-down list, select **Photo Album** and click **OK**.

1 Select the Folder with Pictures You Want to Publish

2 Select Publish This Folder to the Web

3 Select the Pictures to Publish

4 Select MSN Groups

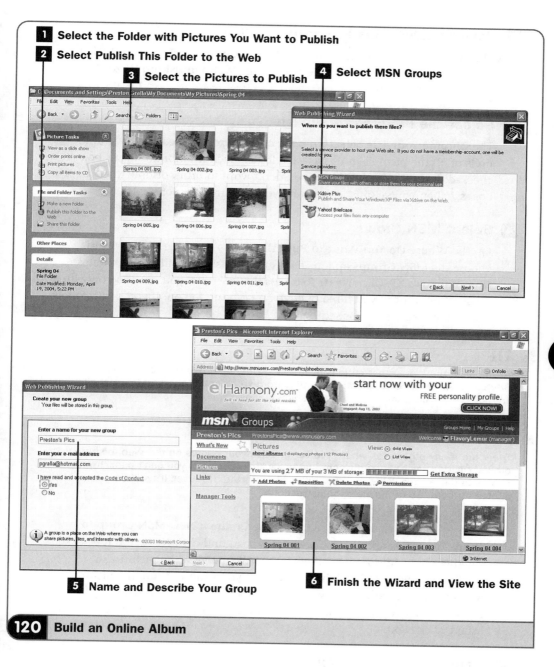

5 Name and Describe Your Group

6 Finish the Wizard and View the Site

120 Build an Online Album

2 Select Publish This Folder to the Web

Click the **Publish This Folder to the Web** link in the **Tasks** list on the left side of the window. The Welcome page of the **Web Publishing Wizard** appears. Click **Next**.

3 Select the Pictures to Publish

The **Change Your File Selection** page of the wizard appears, with thumbnails of all the pictures in the selected folder. Each thumbnail has its box checked. If there are any photos you don't want to print, disable their check boxes. When you've finished making your picture selections, click **Next**.

4 Select MSN Groups

On the **Where Do You Want to Publish These Files** page of the wizard, choose the **MSN Groups** option. That's the best site for publishing photos from Windows XP. Click **Next**. To access the MSN site, you must log on with a Passport account. If you already have an account, log on. If you don't, follow the online instructions for setting up a Passport account.

120

▶ **TIP**

You'll notice there are other options available, including **Xdrive Plus** and **Yahoo! Briefcase**. These services let you store files from your computer on an Internet site, but are not specifically photo sites for publishing photos.

▶ **NOTE**

There are many other sites where you can publish your photos on the Web to share with others, such as **www.shutterfly.com** and **www.flickr.com**. But you can't publish your photos to those sites using the **Web Publishing Wizard**. However, it's still easy to publish photos to them. Go to the sites for instructions.

After you log in to the MSN site, click the **Create a New MSN Group to Share Your Files** option on the wizard screen and click **Next**. You'll be asked whether you want to allow others on the Web to view the pictures, or whether you want to keep them private. If you want to share the pictures with others, click **Shared**. If you want to keep the pictures private, click **Personal**. When you've made your choice about how the files should be published, click **Next**.

5 Name and Describe Your Group

On the **Create Your New Group** wizard page, type a name for your group, type your email address, select the **Yes** radio button indicating you've read and understand the code of conduct, and click on **Next**.

On the next screen that appears, type a description of your group. This description will be used when others are searching and looking for groups on MSN. If you want to list your group in the **MSN Directory**, select the **Yes** radio button. Doing this makes it easier for others to find your photo site. When you're done, click **Next**.

6 Finish the Wizard and View the Site

A screen appears, giving you the web address of your photo site. You don't have to write it down, though, because it will be emailed to you at the address you used for your Passport account.

You'll be asked whether you want to add the site to your Internet Favorites. If you want to do this, select **Yes**; if not, select **No**. Then click **Next**.

A screen reminds you where your pictures can be found on the Web; click **Next**. The following screen gives you basic information about your photo site; click **Next** again.

Another screen asks whether you want to resize your pictures, and if so, what size you want them to be (small, medium, or large). Unless there is a specific reason you want to resize your images—for example, if they are very large, and it will take a long time for people to download them to view them when they visit your site—don't resize the pictures, and so don't check any boxes. If you resize them, click the **Yes** box and select your preferred picture size.

Click **Next**. The wizard now uploads your pictures to the MSN site. After they're uploaded, you'll get confirmation. Click **Next**; from the final page of the wizard, click **Finish**. Your photos are now available for anyone to see. Just email the web address for your MSN site to someone, and he can view all your pictures online in his browser.

121

121 Select an Online Photo Service in Adobe Photoshop Elements

✔ BEFORE YOU BEGIN	→ SEE ALSO
119 About Online Photo Services	122 Share Images Using an Online Service in Adobe Photoshop Elements
	123 Print Images Using an Online Photo Service in Adobe Photoshop Elements

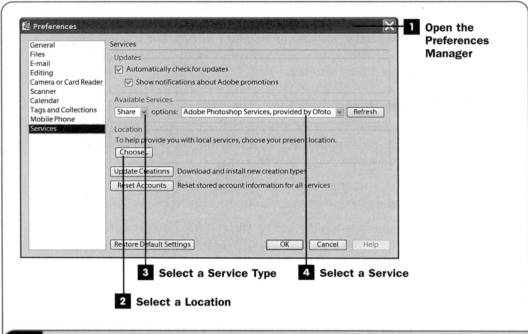

121

121 Select an Online Photo Service in Adobe Photoshop Elements

Using Adobe's associations with various providers, Photoshop Elements offers a way to take advantage of online imaging services. For example, you can upload images to a printing service associated with Photoshop Elements. The service prints the images and mails the prints back to you—just as if they had come from the photo print shop down the street, and you don't have to leave home to take them or pick them up. You could also have your image printed on a t-shirt, cup, magnet, greeting cards, or postcards (see **123 Print Images Using an Online Photo Service in Adobe Photoshop Elements**). In North America, Adobe has partnered with Kodak Ofoto to provide you with fast, professional, Kodak-quality prints.

Another option some services offer (including Ofoto) is to post your images on the World Wide Web where your friends and relatives can see them (see **122 Share Images Using an Online Service in Adobe Photoshop Elements**). In North America, your only choice for either of these services is Adobe Ofoto. If you travel abroad, however, update your services list to find a local service that can deliver your prints, for example. In addition, you might want to download the latest creation types and set up the Organizer to notify you of sales and promotions.

▪ Open the Preferences Manager

Make sure your Internet connection is active. From the **Organizer's** main menu, select **Edit, Preferences, Services**. If you are starting from the **Editor**, select **Edit, Preferences, Organize & Share**. Then click **Services** from the list on the left. The **Preferences** dialog box opens with the **Services** page selected.

▪ Select a Location

Click the **Choose** button in the **Location** frame. The **Choose Location** dialog box appears. Select your country from the **Country** list and click **OK**. This selection lets Photoshop Elements know where you live so it can provide a list of service providers best suited to your current printing and sharing needs.

▪ Select a Service Type

Based on the location you selected in step 2, the **Available Services** list includes applicable online service options for which you can set up preferences. To locate an online service that can host a display of your images your friends and family can visit, select the **Share** option from the first drop-down list.

▪ Select a Service

Open the **Options** list (the second drop-down list). A list of available services for the service type you chose in step 3 appears. Select a service from those listed.

Repeat steps 3 and 4 for each online service type you want to use. For example, select **Print** from the **Available Services** list to select an online print service. When you're finished selecting the specific service you want to use for each online service type, click **OK** to close the **Preferences** dialog box and save your selections.

▶ NOTE

From time to time, Adobe adds service providers to the list of online service providers associated with Photoshop Elements. To make sure your provider list is up to date, click the **Refresh** button in the **Preferences** dialog box. To have Adobe automatically check for new services and other updates to the program, enable the **Automatically Check for Updates** option at the top of the dialog box.

▶ NOTE

If you want to be notified from time to time about promotions related to your online services, enable the **Show Notifications About Adobe Promotions** option. A **Notification** icon appears on the status bar when there's a promotion; click this icon to view the promotion details.

121

▶ **NOTE**

To update your program with the latest creation types supported by your online service, click **Update Creations**.

122	**Share Images Using an Online Service in Adobe Photoshop Elements**

✔ **BEFORE YOU BEGIN**	→ **SEE ALSO**
121 Select an Online Photo Service in Adobe Photoshop Elements	**123** Print Images Using an Online Photo Service in Adobe Photoshop Elements

You can use email to quickly send messages and photos to friends and family members. But emailed pictures must be small enough to travel through the Internet mail system without being rejected by an email server. Small files, particularly if they're compressed for transmission, often leave much to be desired in terms of quality. An additional problem with email is that not everyone has an email connection at home, and many people rely on the service they have available at work. Receiving your pictures on office email systems does not always go over well with employers.

An alternative is to post your pictures on the World Wide Web by way of an online service such as Adobe Ofoto. There, you can display pictures in larger sizes and higher resolution. Your recipients can check out your images at times convenient to them; using a web browser to view images is much easier for most people than dealing with an email client.

▶ **NOTE**

This task also assumes you have chosen Ofoto as your preferred share service (see **121** **Select an Online Photo Service in Adobe Photoshop Elements**). If you've chosen a different share service, the steps will be similar to those shown, but not exactly the same.

1 Select the Images

In the Organizer, before you choose the images you want to share, review each one and edit it to look its best. You might also want to give each a text caption to help identify and explain it when people visit your online gallery.

Display your images in the catalog. To select a single image, click it. To select multiple images, click the first one; then press and hold the **Ctrl** key as you click each additional thumbnail. To select a range of contiguous images, click the first image, press and hold the **Shift** key, and then click the last image of the group.

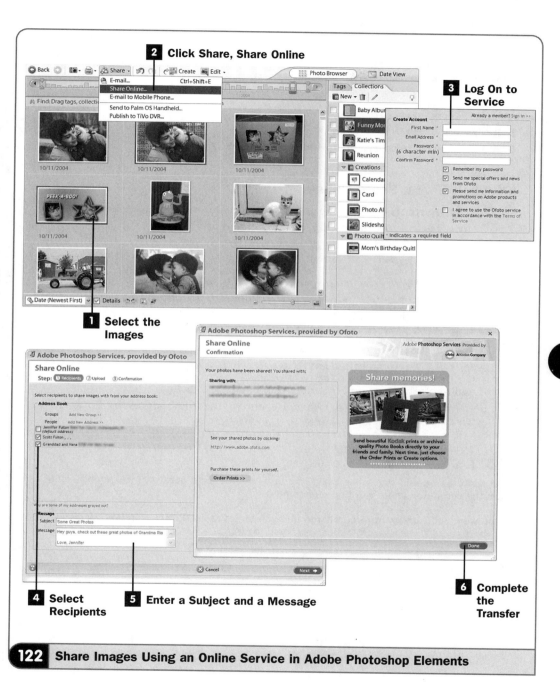

2 Click Share, Share Online

3 Log On to Service

1 Select the Images

4 Select Recipients

5 Enter a Subject and a Message

6 Complete the Transfer

122

122 Share Images Using an Online Service in Adobe Photoshop Elements

▶ **TIP**

If the images are grouped by date or folder, you can click the gray bar above a group to select the entire group.

▶ **WEB RESOURCE**

http://www.ofoto.com

Visit the Ofoto site for special offers, which often include free prints.

2 Click Share, Share Online

On the **Shortcuts** bar, click **Share**. From the menu that opens, select **Share Online**. The **Adobe Photoshop Services** dialog box appears.

3 Log On to Service

If this is your first time using the service, you'll be asked to set up an account. Enter the required information and select additional options (such as automatic notification of sales and other offers). Read the **Terms of Service** by clicking its link, and enable the check box to indicate you agree with the terms. Enable the **Remember My Password** check box to have the Organizer enter this data for you the next time you use this service.

If you're already an Ofoto member and you asked that your password be remembered, skip to step 4. Otherwise, enter your email address and password now. Click the **Next** button at the bottom of the dialog box.

122

▶ **NOTES**

Your Ofoto account is accessible using the email address and password you supply—only from the computer where you first registered it.

If you want your password remembered and you forgot to indicate that initially, select the **Remember My Password** option when you log in.

4 Select Recipients

On the **Step 1 Recipients** screen, a list of people in your **Contact Book** appears on the left. Enable the check boxes in front of the persons with whom you want to share these photos. You can also order prints of the shared photos for each person you selected—just click the **Click Here to Also Send Prints** check box to the right of their names. If you chose this option, a few extra pages in the wizard appear so that you can select the number of prints and their sizes. See **123** **Print Images Using an Online Photo Service in Adobe Photoshop Elements**.

To add a new address to the **Contact Book**, click the **Add New Address** link, enter the address data, and click **Next** to return to this screen. If a person's name is grayed out, you must complete her information by clicking **Edit** to the right of her name, entering the rest of the email and address data, and clicking **Next** to return.

▶ **TIP**

If you simply have the email notification sent to you, you can use the addresses already in your email client's address book to forward the message onto your friends and relations.

▶ **TIP**

If you want to see your own online photos, add your own email address to the address list and select your name as one of the recipients in step 4.

5 Enter a Subject and a Message

Type a **Subject** and a **Message** in the email notification form near the bottom of the dialog box. Click **Next**.

6 Complete the Transfer

To make each invitee join Ofoto and sign in to view the images, enable the **Require Friends to Sign In to View Your Album** option. Without this option, anyone who knows the link to your web page can view your photos. Click **Next** to upload the images.

After the images are uploaded, the **Confirmation** screen appears, displaying the list of names with whom you shared the photos, and a link to the website.

If you ordered prints, the **Confirmation** screen will include an order summary. Click the **Print This Confirmation** button to print a copy of this page.

Click **Done**. The wizard closes, and you return to the catalog. Recipients will receive email invitations to look at your images.

123

---

123 Print Images Using an Online Photo Service in Adobe Photoshop Elements

✔ BEFORE YOU BEGIN	→ SEE ALSO
Just jump right in.	**122** Share Images Using an Online Service in Adobe Photoshop Elements

If you don't have a photo printer or a printer capable of printing on photo paper, you can still make wonderful, high-quality photo prints directly from the Organizer, *right now*. Using your Internet connection, you can link directly from the Organizer to an online service, upload your images, have the service print the images (perhaps with professional corrections), and ship you the results—in some cases, by next-day air!

Before printing, however, you should prepare your images properly. Select each image in the Organizer, send it to the Editor, save the file in PSD format, and make any necessary improvements to the image's color, contrast, saturation, and sharpness. Resize the image as needed to ensure that its print size matches the size you want to use when printing, and that it has a high-enough resolution to produce a good quality print. Finally, save a copy of your image in a shareable format you can upload to an online service, such as TIFF or JPEG.

123

▶ NOTE

To complete this task, you need a working Internet connection—dial-up is fine, broad-band is better. This task also assumes that you have chosen Ofoto as your preferred print service (see **121 Select an Online Photo Service in Adobe Photoshop Elements**). If you've chosen a different print service, the steps will be similar to those shown here, but not exactly the same.

▶ NOTE

You can print a creation already saved to the catalog using an online service by simply following the steps given here. You can also print a creation after creating or editing it by clicking the **Order Online** button on the **Step 5: Share** page of the **Creation** Wizard. Certain creation types (such as a slideshow) cannot be uploaded to an online service for printing.

1 Select Images to Print

After you've prepared each image for printing, in the Organizer, press **Shift** and click the first image in the group you want to upload for printing, and then click the last image in the contiguous group. Alternatively, click the first image, press **Ctrl**, and click each additional image you want to upload for printing.

▶ TIP

Organizer uploads for printing all currently displayed images. If you want to display a group of related images, such as all the images from your last vacation, use the **Find** bar first. If the catalog is sorted by batch or folder, you can click the gray bar above a group to select all the items in that group. With either of these two methods, you might also end up selecting video, audio, and creation files, but they'll be automatically exclud-ed from the print job.

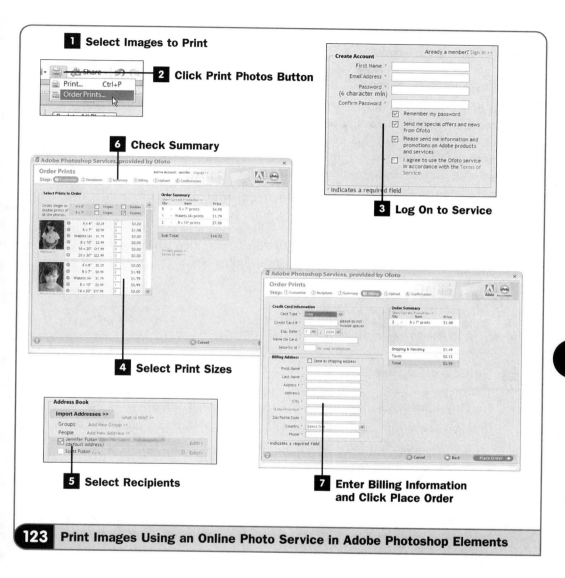

1 Select Images to Print

2 Click Print Photos Button

6 Check Summary

3 Log On to Service

4 Select Print Sizes

5 Select Recipients

7 Enter Billing Information and Click Place Order

123

123 Print Images Using an Online Photo Service in Adobe Photoshop Elements

▶ **WEB RESOURCE**

http://www.ofoto.com

See Ofoto for special offers, which often include free prints.

2 Click Print Photos Button

Click the **Print Photos to a Local Printer or Online Service** button on the **Shortcuts** bar, and click **Order Prints** from the menu that appears. You can also select **File, Order Prints** from the menu. The **Adobe Photoshop Services** dialog box appears.

3 Log On to Service

If this is your first time using the service, you'll be asked to set up an account. Enter the required information. Read the **Terms of Service** by clicking its link and enable the check box to indicate you agree with the terms. Enable the **Remember My Password** check box to have the Organizer enter this data for you the next time you print using this service.

If you're already an Ofoto member and requested that your password be remembered, skip to step 4. Otherwise, enter your email address and password now. If you want your password remembered and you forgot to indicate that initially, select the **Remember My Password** option when you log in. Click the **Next** button at the bottom of the dialog box.

▶ **NOTE**

Your Ofoto account is only accessible using the email address and password you supply—from the computer where you first registered it.

123

4 Select Print Sizes

The **Order Prints** process is organized like a wizard, with the current step number highlighted at the top of the dialog box; click **Next** to continue to the next part of the order process or click **Back** to return to a previous step.

Here, the first step is to enter the quantities for the various print sizes you want next to the image thumbnails that appear on the left. A running total based on your current selections appears in the **Order Summary** frame. Use the scroll bars to select print sizes for each image. At the bottom of the listing, enable the **Zoom and Trim** option to let Adobe Photoshop Services (Ofoto) trim your images as needed to fit the print sizes you select. Click **Next** to continue.

▶ **TIP**

A green icon appears next to each print size that's appropriate for a particular image based on its image size and resolution. A red icon indicates that the image does not have a high-enough resolution to support that print size; selecting one of these print sizes will result in a less-than-quality print.

▶ **TIP**

To order single or double prints for all images in either 4"×6" or 5"×7" size, enable the appropriate **Single** or **Double** check box at the top of the image list on the left.

▶ **TIP**

Even if you plan on shipping these prints to multiple people, enter only the total you want each person to receive. Later, when you select recipients, this total will be increased accordingly.

5 Select Recipients

On the **Step 2 Recipients** screen, choose where you want your prints delivered. A list of people you've previously sent photos to appears on the left. Enable the check box in front of the person to whom you want these prints delivered. If you select more than one person, your order is duplicated that many times so that each person receives the number of prints you choose in step 4.

To add a new address, click the **Add New Address** link, enter the address data, and click **Next** to return to this screen. If a person's name is grayed out, you must complete his information by clicking **Edit** next to his name, entering the rest of the address data, and clicking **Next**. To replace the address listing with the data already stored in your Organizer Contact Book, click the **Import Addresses** button.

6 Check Summary

On the **Step 3 Summary** screen, verify the **Order Details**. Select how you want the photos shipped from the **Ship Via** list. The cost of shipping your prints using this method is calculated and added to your total, displayed on the right. Verify this total and click **Next** to continue.

7 Enter Billing Information and Click Place Order

On the **Step 4 Billing** screen, enter your **Credit Card Information**. Enter a **Billing Address**, or enable the **Same As Shipping Address** check box to ship the prints to the same address listed in the Address Book. Click the **Place Order** button to upload the images and place your order with the online service.

After the images are uploaded, the **Confirmation** screen appears, displaying your order number and an order summary. Click the **Print This Confirmation** button to print a copy of this page. You'll also receive an email message confirming your order and providing a delivery date.

Now simply wait for your selected delivery service to deliver your prints!

123

PART V

Make Money Building Auctions on eBay

IN THIS CHAPTER

19

How to Sell on eBay

IN THIS CHAPTER:

You've got something you want to sell, and you believe the world wants to buy it. eBay offers one of the world's easiest ways to sell, with a minimum of effort.

In this chapter, you learn how to create your first auction listing. You learn how to do everything including finding items to sell, choosing a title and category, writing a description, choosing the right bidding price, adding pictures, and more. By the end of the chapter, you'll have learned how to create a listing, and you'll see it live online.

124 About Selling on eBay

✔ BEFORE YOU BEGIN	→ SEE ALSO
Just jump right in.	**161** Set Up an eBay Store
	171 About Selling Cars and Vehicles

For many people, there's no quicker way to make money than to sell on eBay. Trudge up to your attic, find some items that are doing little more than gathering dust, fill out some forms, and wait for the money to start coming in.

Well, it's not quite that easy for most of us, but the truth is that it *can* be easy to sell and make money on eBay, and it is a great way to get some extra spending money.

Don't expect, though, to start selling and making a living on eBay. Many people do it, but frequently they already have a physical store, are selling in some other way, or have slowly built up to a full-time income over time.

Before you can sell on eBay, you have to register as a seller. Simply registering on the site isn't good enough; you must specifically register as a seller. To register, click the **Sell** button at the top of any eBay page, and from the page that appears, click the **Seller's Account** link. Registration is straightforward, but you are asked for credit card or debit card information and bank account information so eBay can be guaranteed to collect seller fees from you.

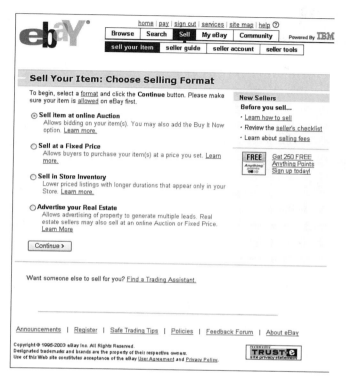

After you register to sell on eBay, selling your item is easy: Start by filling out a form on the Sell Your Item page.

If you don't want to provide credit card or debit card information to eBay, you can instead become **ID verified**. This classification of user lets you sell on eBay, allows you to buy using eBay's **Buy It Now** feature, and lets you bid above $15,000. You'll have to pay a $5 fee, however.

▶ KEY TERM

ID verified—An eBay certification that allows you to sell on eBay, use eBay's **Buy It Now** feature, and bid above $15,000 for an item. It costs $5. However, if you provide credit card or debit card information to eBay, you don't need to become ID verified to do all that.

▶ WEB RESOURCE

http://pages.ebay.com/services/buyandsell/idverify-login.html
To get ID verified, go to this site and follow the directions.

Selling an item requires a good deal of preparation. You need to know how much you want to charge, how you'll ship the goods, and how much shipping will cost. You also have to prepare a description of the item and probably take photographs of it. But as you'll see in the rest of this chapter, a little bit of work will pay big dividends.

125 | About Finding Items to Sell

✔ BEFORE YOU BEGIN	→ SEE ALSO
124 About Selling on eBay	**126** About Banned Items

If you get serious about making money at auctions, you're going to need a way to find inexpensive goods you can sell. The first place to look, obviously, is in your house, attic, and garage. But if you're going to get more serious, you need to find other sources. Here is a rundown of the best sources.

School and Church "White Elephant" Sales

Schools and churches frequently hold fund-raisers. Often, the most popular parts of these fund-raisers are "white elephant" sales in which people donate items to be sold. You can find items of surprisingly high quality—everything from clothing to books, toys, and software. You'll find very low prices here. Make sure to come early, though, because within an hour after the sale opens, the best items are often gone.

Garage, Yard, Block, and Tag Sales

In the spring and fall, people hold garage, yard, and tag sales (*tag sales* mean the same thing as garage and yard sales) in which they clean out their garages and houses and sell what they no longer want. They're great places to find treasures of all kinds. Come early to get the best selection. Come late to get the best deals because, at the end of the day, sellers often simply allow people to haul away what hasn't yet been sold. But keep in mind that what is left at the end often is the dregs of the sale.

Departing College Students

Every spring, students leave college to go back home or to leave for summer vacation. They often sell things before they go, and they often sell them dirt cheap. Check areas near universities around the time that students leave, and look on college bulletin boards at that time of year for notices of sales as well.

Auction Sites

Surprise! Auction sites are good places to buy things to sell. But only do this if you're a smart bidder, and if you do your homework. You'll need to be able to sell things for a much higher price than you buy them for if you're going to turn a profit.

▶ TIP

Newspaper and Internet classified ads are great places to buy things inexpensively that you can then sell at auctions. And they're also good places to find out about flea markets and other similar kinds of places where you can buy inexpensive collectibles and goods. So check out the classified ad section of your local newspaper, both in print and online.

Estate Sales

Estate sales are excellent places for finding collectibles to sell at online auctions. Estate sales advertise in the newspapers, so make a habit of checking the newspaper—both in print and online—for them.

You should show up several hours before an estate sale is set to open and give your name. Sometimes you must have your name on a list to get in. Then come back when the sale opens to find the best items.

Depending on how long the sale lasts, you might or might not be able to buy items discounted. You might be able to get discounts a day or two after the opening.

Flea Markets and Swap Meets

Other great sources of sellables are flea markets and swap meets. Many flea markets are held on a regularly scheduled basis (weekly, monthly, biannually, or annually), so find out the schedules for those held in your area. Both flea markets and swap meets are generally advertised in newspapers, so check your local papers.

As with other types of sales, get there early; the best deals are usually gone within a few hours of the opening. If you find a regular seller at a flea market who often has goods you're interested in buying, get a business card or contact information from him. That way, you can get in touch without having to go to the flea market and can get his best items before he puts them up for public sale.

Bric-a-Brac Stores

Bric-a-brac stores are places that are often just one step above a yard sale and are filled with a variety of used items for sale. Depending on the store and its location, a bric-a-brac store can be an excellent place to find items to sell at online auctions.

125

▶ **TIP**

Look for bric-a-brac stores in inexpensive neighborhoods because stores in more costly neighborhoods won't sell things inexpensively.

---

126   **About Banned Items**

✔ **BEFORE YOU BEGIN**	➔ **SEE ALSO**
125 About Finding Items to Sell	124 About Selling on eBay

126

eBay is a wide-open market that connects buyers and sellers. But that doesn't mean you can sell anything you want. Normal laws apply—for example, you can't sell illegal drugs on eBay, or any other item banned by law.

In addition, eBay bans a variety of items and restricts some items from being sold. The consequences for violating this policy can result in disciplinary action taken by eBay. You might simply get a warning and have violating items taken off the site. But you can also be temporarily or indefinitely suspended from the site as well. So it's worth your while to ensure that you don't sell any banned or prohibited items.

eBay has three categories of potentially problematic items:

- **Prohibited**—These items cannot be sold on eBay.

- **Questionable**—These items can be sold only under certain specific conditions—for example, eBay bans the sale of batteries with mercury in them but allows other kinds of batteries to be sold.

- **Potentially infringing**—These items might violate copyrights, trademarks, or other legal rights. For example, academic versions of software, such as Microsoft Office, can be sold only by an authorized educational reseller, an educational institution, a student, or a faculty member but by no one else.

eBay has some very complicated regulations covering questionable and potentially infringing items, so the best way to know whether any items on those lists might be prohibited is to check eBay's rules online. Head to http://pages.ebay.com/help/policies/items-ov.html for the complete list and details.

Here's the list of problematic items, by category.

Prohibited Items

▶ **KEY TERM**

Prohibited item—An item that cannot be sold on eBay for any of a variety of reasons, such as that it violates state or federal laws.

- Alcohol
- Animals and wildlife products
- Catalog and URL sales
- Counterfeit currency and stamps
- Counterfeit items
- Credit cards
- Drugs and drug paraphernalia
- Embargoed goods and goods from prohibited countries
- Firearms
- Fireworks
- Government IDs and licenses
- Human parts and remains
- Links
- Lock-picking devices
- Lottery tickets
- Mailing lists and personal information
- Plants and seeds
- Postage meters
- Prescription drugs and devices
- Recalled items
- Satellite and cable TV descramblers
- Stocks and other securities
- Stolen property
- Surveillance equipment

126

- Tobacco
- Travel

Questionable Items

▶ KEY TERM

Questionable item—An item that can be sold only under certain specific conditions—for example, eBay bans the sale of batteries with mercury in them but allows other types of batteries to be sold.

- Artifacts (from archeological digs, graves, and historical locations)
- Autographed items
- Batteries
- Catalytic converters and test pipes
- Compilation and information media
- Contracts and tickets
- Electronics equipment
- Event tickets
- Food
- Freon and other refrigerants
- Hazardous materials
- Imported and emission-noncompliant vehicles
- International trading—buyers
- International trading—sellers
- Items intended for mature audiences
- Medical devices (for example, those that require prescriptions, among others)
- Offensive material
- Pesticides
- Police-related items
- Presale listings
- Slot machines
- Used airbags

126

- Used clothing

- Warranties

- Weapons and knives

- Wine

Potentially Infringing Items

▶ **KEY TERM**

Potentially infringing item—An item that might violate copyrights, trademarks, or other legal rights. For example, academic versions of software, such as Microsoft Office, can be sold only by an authorized educational reseller, an educational institution, a student, or a faculty member, but by no one else.

- Academic software

- Anticircumvention policy

- Authenticity disclaimers

- Beta software

- Bootleg recordings

- Brand-name misuse

- Comparison policy

- Contracts and tickets

- Downloadable media

- Encouraging policy

- Faces, names, and signatures

- Item description and picture theft

- Importation of goods into the United States

- Misleading titles

- Mod chips, game enhancers, and boot discs

- Movie prints

- OEM software

- Recordable media

- Replica and counterfeit items

126

- Promotional items
- Unauthorized copies

▶ WEB RESOURCE
http://pages.ebay.com/help/community/png-items.html
For details about eBay's banned items, visit this website.

---

127 **Determine Your Selling Price and Estimate Your Selling Fees**

✔ **BEFORE YOU BEGIN**

124 About Selling on eBay

Selling on eBay can be a form of entertainment—but it's entertainment in which you get paid, rather than in which you do the paying. And perhaps for you it's not entertainment, but a way to make money.

Before you put an item up for auction, you should know how much money, at a minimum, you expect to make. So you'll need to know the minimum price at which you'll sell an item, and you also need to know the fees you'll have to pay eBay to list the item. Then just do the math: Take your minimum selling price, subtract the eBay fees, subtract how much money you spent to buy the item (if any), and you'll come up with your minimum profit. If people bid above your minimum selling price, you'll get even more profit. But to be conservative, assume the minimum selling price. Here's how you can figure out your minimum selling price and your eBay fees:

1 Do a Web Pricing Search

Price comparison sites such as PriceGrabber at **www.pricegrabber.com** and MySimon at **www.mysimon.com** scour the Internet for you and find the lowest price on new items. This way, you'll know how much the item is currently selling for at online retailers. Keep in mind that if you're selling a used item, the price you can expect to get will be below what you find on sites such as PriceGrabber.

▶ NOTE
If you register with PriceGrabber and tell it where you live, it uses that information to calculate whether you have to pay tax when buying the item online (if you buy, even online, from a store in the same state, you have to pay tax) and estimates shipping fees.

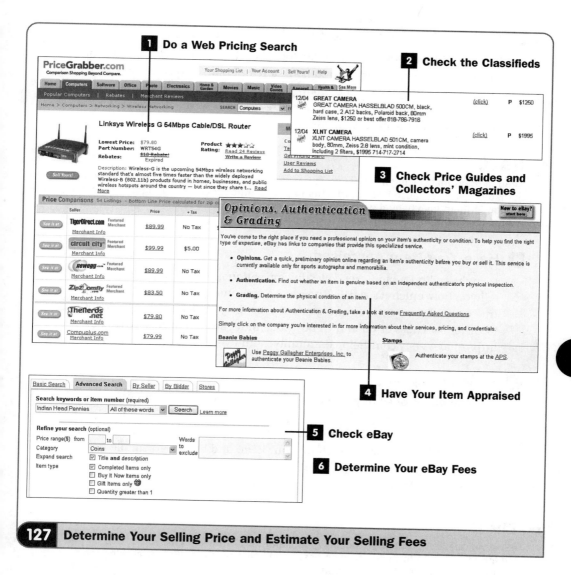

1 Do a Web Pricing Search

2 Check the Classifieds

3 Check Price Guides and Collectors' Magazines

4 Have Your Item Appraised

5 Check eBay

6 Determine Your eBay Fees

127   Determine Your Selling Price and Estimate Your Selling Fees

2 Check the Classifieds

Many people sell used items in classified ads in newspapers and online, and the want ads are a great place to find the going price for used goods. Check your local newspaper, or head to online classified sites such as recycler.com. Also check out the online classified site of your local newspaper.

3 Check Price Guides and Collectors' Magazines

Pricing guides are usually available for collectibles and specialty items; find them at your local library or at a bookstore or online bookstore. These resources should give you a ballpark estimate of what you might be able to sell an item for. Collector's magazines are useful as well, often more for the classifieds than the articles themselves.

▶ **NOTE**

Keep in mind that pricing information in books and magazines is necessarily somewhat outdated. That's because it takes months to put together books and magazines, so information in them lags behind what's happening online. Still, they're worth checking out for a start on pricing information.

4 Have Your Item Appraised

If you're selling a big-ticket collectible or antique, pay an appraisal service to tell you how much it's worth. The service can authenticate that your item is a true collectible or antique and grade it according to its quality. Check your local Yellow Pages or go to the eBay page that lists appraisal services at http://pages.ebay.com/help/community/auth-overview.html.

127

5 Check eBay

The best gauge of what your item will sell for is how much the same or similar items have already sold for on eBay. To do that, search for completed auctions. From the top of any eBay screen, click the **Search** tab and then click **Advanced Search**. Do a search for your item, and be sure to enable the **Completed Items Only** check box. That way, you'll see all the completed auctions, which lists the final selling prices.

▶ **TIP**

eBay members are a helpful, friendly group, and they often will give you advice on pricing information. Go to the discussion boards and chat areas in eBay by clicking the **Community** tab at the top of any eBay page and then entering the chat or discussion boards. Look for the specialized chat or discussion board that matches the item you're about to sell.

6 Determine Your eBay Fees

eBay fees can vary tremendously, depending on how you list your item. eBay has two kinds of fees—those you are required to pay and optional fees you can pay if you want special treatment of your listing.

You have to pay two kinds of required fees—an *insertion fee* and a *final value fee*. On every item put up for bid, an insertion fee is charged, regardless of whether the item sells. Final value fees are charged only for items that actually sell. In both instances, fees are charged on a sliding scale—the higher the price of the item, the more you pay.

▶ KEY TERMS

Insertion fee—The basic fee charged for every item you put up for sale on eBay. You're charged this fee regardless of whether the item sells.

Final value fee—The fee you pay only if your item sells on eBay. If the item doesn't sell, you're not charged this fee.

Reserve price—A secret price you set for the item you're selling; if the bids don't reach that price, you don't sell the item.

The following table lists insertion fee costs. They are based on the minimum price you set for the item you're selling, the *reserve price* you set, or the opening bid.

eBay Insertion Fees

Starting Price, Opening Value, or Reserve Price	Insertion Fee
$0.01–$9.99	$0.30
$10.00–$24.99	$0.55
$25.00–$49.99	$1.10
$50.00–$199.99	$2.20
$200.00 and up	$3.30

The next table lists the final value fees you'll pay. They're based on the final selling price of the item.

eBay Final Value Fees

Closing Value	Final Value Fee
$0–$25	5.25% of the closing value
$25–$1,000	5.25% of the initial $25 ($1.31), plus 2.75% of the remaining closing value balance ($25.01–$1,000)
Over $1,000	5.25% of the initial $25 ($1.31), plus 2.75% of the initial $25–$1,000 ($26.81), plus 1.50% of the remaining closing value balance ($1,000.01–closing value)

127

If you want to give extra visibility to your auction, you can pay for a variety of other options, such as adding boldface to your title for $1. The third table lists the eBay optional fees. For more information about what each of these fees buys, go to http://pages.ebay.com/help/sell/fees.html.

eBay Optional Upgrade Fees

Listing Upgrade	Listing Upgrade Fee
Home Page Features	$99.95 (single quantity) or $199.95 (quantity of two or more)
Featured Plus!	$19.95
Highlight	$5.00
Item Subtitle	$0.50
Bold	$1.00
Listing Designer	$0.10
Gallery	$0.25
Gallery Featured	$19.95
List in Two Categories	Double the insertion and listing upgrades fees (excluding Scheduled Listings and Home Page Features)
10-Day Duration (the longest listing duration available)	$0.10
Scheduled Listings	$0.10
Buy It Now	$0.05
Gift Services	$0.25

128

128 About the eBay Sell Your Item Page

✔ BEFORE YOU BEGIN	→ SEE ALSO
127 Determine Your Selling Price and Estimate Your Selling Fees	**129** Start the Sell Form and Choose a Category
	130 Write the Title and Description
	132 Choose Pricing, Duration, and Location
	133 About Dutch Auctions
	136 Set Payment and Shipping Options
	137 Review and Post Your Auction

You create an eBay auction listing by filling out a series of step-by-step forms, as you'll see throughout the rest of this chapter. Before you do that, though, you must make sure you've done the following:

- **Register as a seller**—Until you register, you can't sell. For details, go to **124** **About Selling on eBay**.

- **Decide on your minimum bid and selling fees**—To learn how to set these prices, go to **127** **Determine Your Selling Price and Estimate Your Selling Fees**.

- **Assemble your art**—Pictures help sell, so you should use art in your auctions. Use a digital camera or scanner to create a digital image file you can upload to your listing. For more information, see **134** **Add Pictures to Your Auction**.

Continue >

After you've done all that, you're ready to create your auction. You'll do it by filling out five pages of information about the item you want to sell. Not uncommonly, you'll have to move back and forth between those pages. For example, while you're in the **Pictures & Details** page, you might suddenly decide to rewrite your title and therefore want to go back to the **Title & Description** page. When you have to do that, use the **Back** and **Continue** buttons rather than your browser's **Back** and **Forward** buttons. If you use your browser's **Back** button to move back to a previous page, it will likely appear as if you've lost all the information you've filled in because the form will be blank. You haven't really lost the information, though—click the **Refresh** link at the top of each **Sell Your Item** form page to have your information automatically fill in.

129 | Start the Sell Form and Choose a Category

✔ BEFORE YOU BEGIN	→ SEE ALSO
127 Determine Your Selling Price and Estimate Your Selling Fees	**130** Write the Title and Description
128 About the eBay Sell Your Item Page	**131** Format Your Description with eBay's HTML Editor
	132 Choose Pricing, Duration, and Location
	134 Add Pictures to Your Auction
	136 Set Payment and Shipping Options

129

You've done your preparation and are finally ready to sell your first item on eBay. The first step, and in some ways the most important step, is to create a title and choose a category. You can easily overlook the importance of this step, and you might be tempted to rush through it quickly. But it's worth your while to spend some time doing this because, if you choose the wrong category or don't write a descriptive title, no one will ever find your auction and it's unlikely anyone will bid on it.

1 Get to the Sell Your Item Form

To get to the **Sell Your Item** form, click the **Sell** button at the top of any eBay page. If you want help before filling out the form, click the **Learn How to Sell** link. You can also get live help by chatting with an eBay customer service representative by clicking the **Live Help** button.

2 Choose Your Selling Format

The first step in filling out the **Sell Your Item** form is to choose the kind of auction you want to create. You have four choices:

- **Sell Item at Online Auction**—This is the most common type of auction. It lets you create an auction in which people bid on your item. If you want, you can use the **Buy It Now** option, which allows people to bid or buy the item at a fixed price you set.

- **Sell at a Fixed Price**—In this type of auction, there is no bidding. Buyers purchase your item(s) at a fixed price you set. (This is the format you choose if you want to sell something using the **Buy It Now** feature.)

- **Sell In Store Inventory**—Select this option if you have an eBay store and want to sell items in it. For more information, see **Chapter 23, Starting an eBay Business**.

- **Advertise Your Real Estate**—Select this option if you're selling real estate.

When you've chosen your selling format, click the **Continue** button at the bottom of the page.

3 Choose Your Main Category

The **Main Category** is the top-level category under which your auction will be listed—the categories people see on the left side of the main eBay page. Scroll through the list and click the main category that most closely matches the item you want to sell.

129

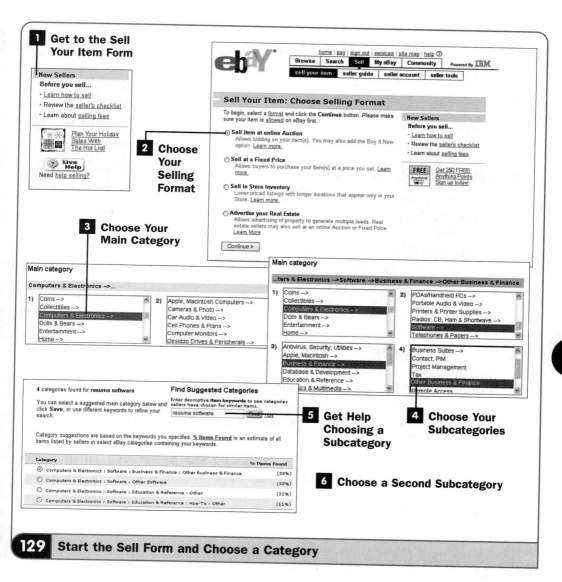

1 Get to the Sell Your Item Form

2 Choose Your Selling Format

3 Choose Your Main Category

4 Choose Your Subcategories

5 Get Help Choosing a Subcategory

6 Choose a Second Subcategory

129

129 Start the Sell Form and Choose a Category

4 Choose Your Subcategories

When you choose the main category, a list of subcategories appears in the box next to the main category list box. Select the subcategory that most closely matches your item.

▶ **NOTE**

You'll notice that some subcategories have small arrows next to them, whereas others don't. If a subcategory has an arrow next to it, that means there are further subcategories below it from which you must choose. If no arrow appears, you've reached the lowest level of subcategory and that is where your item will be listed.

Further subcategories might appear in boxes on the page. Continue to select subcategories until you reach the final, most specific one.

5 Get Help Choosing a Subcategory

Selecting the right category and subcategories can be more difficult than it appears—at the subcategory level in particular, it's not always obvious which option you should choose. eBay can give you suggestions for which subcategory to choose. In the **Find Suggested Categories** section of the **Sell Your Item** form, enter keywords that describe the item you want to sell and click **Find**. A page appears that gives you several suggestions for which subcategory to choose. Click the radio button next to the one you want to use and click **Save**.

130

6 Choose a Second Subcategory

You can pay extra to have your item listed in two subcategories instead of one. This doubles its exposure and makes it more likely to get bids. Your insertion fee and most listing upgrade fees are doubled. But your final value fee does not change (the final value fee is the same as if you had listed the item in a single category).

To choose a second subcategory, select it from the **Choose a Second Category** section at the bottom of the **Sell Your Item** form.

When you're done, click the **Continue** button. You are brought to the **Title & Description** page, as described in 🔳 **Write the Title and Description**.

---

130 **Write the Title and Description**

✔ BEFORE YOU BEGIN	→ SEE ALSO
🔳 Start the Sell Form and Choose a Category	🔳 Format Your Description with eBay's HTML Editor

---

More than anything, what sells your item is its title and description. The title draws attention to your auction, and after people are on the auction page, the description you've written for the item should be so appealing that they end up bidding.

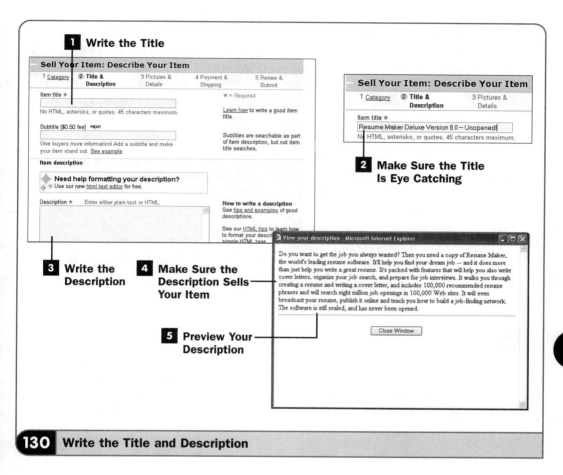

1 **Write the Title**

Sell Your Item: Describe Your Item

| 1 Category | 2 Title & Description | 3 Pictures & Details | 4 Payment & Shipping | 5 Review & Submit |

Item title ★

No HTML, asterisks, or quotes. 45 characters maximum.

★ = Required

Learn how to write a good item title.

Subtitle ($0.50 fee) NEW!

Give buyers more information! Add a subtitle and make your item stand out. See example

Subtitles are searchable as part of item description, but not item title searches.

Item description

◆ **Need help formatting your description?**
◆ Use our new html text editor for free.

Description ★   Enter either plain text or HTML.

How to write a description
See tips and examples of good descriptions.

See our HTML tips to learn how to format your descri
simple HTML tags.

Sell Your Item: Describe Your Item

| 1 Category | 2 Title & Description | 3 Pictures & Details |

Item title ★

Resume Maker Deluxe Version 8.0 – Unopened

No HTML, asterisks, or quotes. 45 characters maximum.

2 **Make Sure the Title Is Eye Catching**

3 **Write the Description**

4 **Make Sure the Description Sells Your Item**

View your description - Microsoft Internet Explorer

Do you want to get the job you always wanted? Then you need a copy of Resume Maker, the world's leading resume software. It'll help you find your dream job -- and it does more than just help you write a great resume. It's packed with features that will help you also write cover letters, organize your job search, and prepare for job interviews. It walks you through creating a resume and writing a cover letter, and includes 100,000 recommended resume phrases and will search eight million job openings in 100,000 Web sites. It will even broadcast your resume, publish it online and teach you how to build a job-finding network. The software is still sealed, and has never been opened.

Close Window

5 **Preview Your Description**

130

130 **Write the Title and Description**

That's the theory, anyway. In this section, you learn how to fill in the title and description—and get tips on how to write titles and descriptions that sell.

1 **Write the Title**

If you haven't started to fill out the **Sell Your Item** form yet, back up to **129** **Start the Sell Form and Choose a Category** to learn how to begin the process of creating an auction listing.

In the **Item Title** text box of the **Sell Your Item** form, type the title for the item you want to sell; this is what people see when they browse through categories or do a search, so choose the title with care. You have a limit of 45 characters, so make every word count.

2 Make Sure the Title Is Eye Catching

Selecting a title can be the single most important thing you'll do to ensure that your item sells. Literally millions of items are for sale on eBay, and if your auction doesn't have a title that's both clear and catches people's attention, you won't sell your item—or, if you do, it'll be for less money than it otherwise would have sold.

If your title doesn't catch the eyes of people browsing or searching the site and doesn't include specific, accurate information about what you're selling, you won't hook the buyers. So, be sure to write an eye-catching title. For details, go to **156** **About Writing Effective Ad Copy**.

▶ **TIP**

The words in titles are used when people search through eBay looking for an item to buy. So the title should include as many descriptive keywords as possible. That way, your auction will be found by the most people. Above all, make sure you're including adjectives that describe exactly what you're selling. Are you selling a real elephant or an elephant statue?

130

3 Write the Description

In the **Item Description** text box, type your description. This is the hardest part for most people. You must be as descriptive as possible, so bidders have as complete an understanding of what's for sale as possible. But you also have to do a bit of selling here to give bidders a reason to want to buy, and you don't want to mislead in any way.

Be as complete as you can when describing the item—this is an instance when more is better. Because bidders can't physically examine the goods you're selling, they're going to spend a lot of time reading your words. Take care to use words that describe the physical condition of what you're selling, such as *poor, fair, good, new,* and so on. (Again, be absolutely accurate here and don't try to shade the truth in your favor; otherwise, you'll have some very unhappy buyers and will get a bad reputation as well.)

▶ **TIP**

eBay lets you use HTML in your description. HTML is the language of the Web and lets you use different fonts and colors and add backgrounds, pictures, graphics, and more. Auctions that use HTML are much more eye catching and appealing than plain-text auctions. But if you go crazy adding too many fonts, pictures, and colors, you'll turn off potential bidders. For more information about how to use HTML to create an auction, turn to **157** **Jazz Up Text and Headlines with HTML** and **158** **Colorize and Change Fonts and Add Effects with HTML**. Also, **131** **Format Your Description with eBay's HTML Editor** shows how you can use HTML without knowing how to code.

4   Make Sure the Description Sells Your Item

Your auction page is your online storefront. In the same way that a store must be appealing and its goods put nicely on display, your description must be laid out nicely and clearly and should be enticing enough that people want to buy what you're selling. Follow this advice, and you'll go a long way toward writing the best descriptions to help sell your items at auctions:

- **Be comprehensive in your description**—The more details you provide, the more likely someone is to bid on what you have up for sale. Make sure to list all the item's features, especially anything that makes it unique. You're not limited in how much space you use for your description, so feel free to use the space.

- **Be enthusiastic in your description**—If you're not excited about the item you have for sale, how do you think the bidder will feel? You want to impart a sense of enthusiasm and energy in the description you write.

- **Accurately portray the condition of the item you're selling**—Don't try to hide the fact that your item has flaws or defects, or that it has been used. The buyer will find out the truth and, if you've been inaccurate in your portrayal of the item, might ask for her money back. In any event, you're more likely than not to get negative feedback, which will hurt your eBay reputation. On the other hand, don't dwell solely on the item's defects—you mainly want to point out what's good about it.

- **Stress the benefits of the item you're selling, not just its features**— Let's say you're selling a Palm digital organizer. If you were going to stress only its features, you might write **Comes with 15MB RAM**. That's not much of a sell. If, instead, you write **It will store your entire yearly schedule, address book, all your to-do lists, your expense accounts, and more in its 15MB of RAM**, you're stressing its specific benefits. You're more likely to get bidders when you can sell them on the benefits of the item you have for sale.

- **Start off your description with a bang**—If you don't grab potential bidders in your first sentence, you're going to lose them. That's the time to stress the benefits of what you have for sale, its uniqueness, its special features, and anything else you can think of that will make people want to buy it.

- **End your description with a summarizing sales pitch**—The last words of a listing can be the primary thing people remember after reading your listing, and it's probably the last thing they'll read before making

130

a bid. Because of that, you want to ensure that the end of your description sums up the item and stresses all its benefits with enthusiasm.

- **Anticipate questions that potential buyers might have about the item**—Stand back for a moment and imagine yourself as a buyer of what you have for sale. What questions do you think a buyer would ask about it? What more might she want to know? Now include the answers to those questions in your description.

- **Include brand names, manufacturer, years of manufacture, and other similar information**—Some collectors collect everything imaginable. You might not realize it, but collectors might specialize in the precise brand or manufacturer of what you have for sale. It's important to include these details in your descriptions.

5 Preview Your Description

Before moving on to the next step, preview your description by clicking the **Preview your description** link. When you're satisfied with what you've written, click the **Continue** button at the bottom of the screen.

131 ▶ **TIP**

Click the **Back** button at the bottom of the **Sell Your Item** form page (not your browser's **Back** button) to back up through the pages of the **Sell Your Item** form if you decide to make changes to earlier selections you've made. Click the **Continue** button to advance through the pages of the form.

---

131 **Format Your Description with eBay's HTML Editor**

✔ **BEFORE YOU BEGIN**	→ **SEE ALSO**
130 Write the Title and Description	**157** Jazz Up Text and Headlines with HTML
	158 Colorize and Change Fonts and Add Effects with HTML
	159 About Including HTML on eBay Auction Pages

Plain text doesn't sell. On eBay, where potential buyers have short attention spans, you need colors, fonts, and formatting to draw them in and keep them focused on your auction.

You have to use HTML to format your text for display on the eBay site, but eBay includes a nifty HTML text editor that lets you format your text without knowing a single HTML command. Here's how to use it:

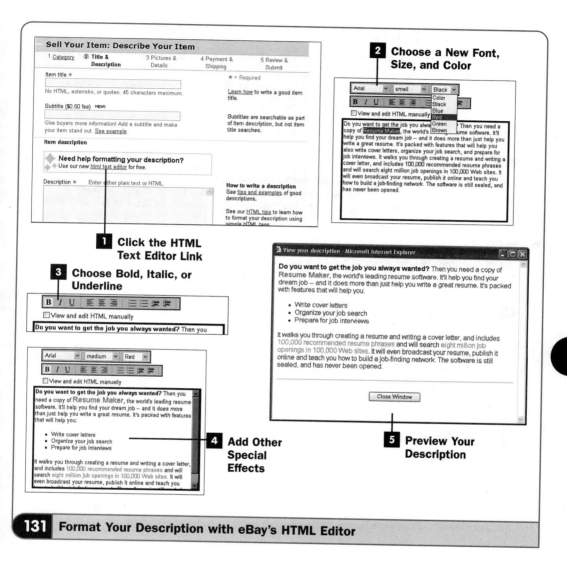

1 Click the HTML Text Editor Link

2 Choose a New Font, Size, and Color

3 Choose Bold, Italic, or Underline

4 Add Other Special Effects

5 Preview Your Description

131

131 Format Your Description with eBay's HTML Editor

1 Click the HTML Text Editor Link

If you haven't begun to fill out the **Sell Your Item** form yet, back up to **129** **Start the Sell Form and Choose a Category** to learn how to begin the process of creating an auction listing; continue with **130** **Write the Title and Description**.

Just above the **Description** text box on the **Sell Your Item** page, click the **HTML Text Editor** link. After a few seconds, the HTML Editor appears just above the description.

2 Choose a New Font, Size, and Color

Highlight the text you want to change, and then from the drop-down lists in the HTML Editor, select a new font, a new font size, and a new color. Note that you can change the format of individual words and letters or entire sections of the description—you don't have to change them all to be the same size, font, and color.

▶ TIP

When using fonts, sizes, and colors, be careful that you don't mix too many different sizes, colors, and fonts. If you do, you'll end up with the "ransom note effect," making your text look like a patched-together amalgamation, which is very difficult to read.

▶ NOTE

The default font in your descriptions is **Arial** in the **Small** size. If you want to use the **Arial Small** size, there's no need to reformat your text.

3 Choose Bold, Italic, or Underline

131

Bold, italic, and underlined formats can add emphasis to text. Choose the text you want to have those formats, and click the **Bold**, **Italic**, or **Underline** button in the HTML Editor. Don't overuse these effects because if you do, you'll only make your description more difficult to read. Use these formatting options only to highlight key words, sentences, or phrases.

4 Add Other Special Effects

The HTML Editor lets you use other effects, such as bulleted lists, numbered lists, centered text, indented text, or flush left or flush right text. Highlight the text to which you want to add these special effects, and then click the appropriate button in the HTML Editor. Once again, use these special effects with care so you don't make your description unreadable.

5 Preview Your Description

When you're done modifying the text in your description, click the **Preview Your Description** link and view the description in the window that appears. Click **Close Window** to close the window and return to the **Sell Your Item** page. Keep editing the text with the HTML Editor until you're happy with the results. When you are, click **Continue**.

▶ **TIP**

Click the **Back** button at the bottom of the **Sell Your Item** form page (not your browser's **Back** button) to back up through the pages of the **Sell Your Item** form if you decide to make changes to earlier selections you've made. Click the **Continue** button to advance through the pages of the form.

---

132 | **Choose Pricing, Duration, and Location**

✔ BEFORE YOU BEGIN	→ SEE ALSO
129 Start the Sell Form and Choose a Category	**133** About Dutch Auctions
130 Write the Title and Description	**134** Add Pictures to Your Auction
	135 Choose Auction Extras
	136 Set Payment and Shipping Options
	137 Review and Post Your Auction

Now we get to the heart of your auction—choosing your pricing, the duration of your auction, and other important details. The title and description draw people's attention and get them interested. But your pricing and other important details help determine whether they bid, and if they do, what their bidding prices will be.

132

1 **Choose the Duration of Your Auction**

If you haven't begun to fill out the **Sell Your Item** form yet, back up to **129** **Start the Sell Form and Choose a Category** to learn how to begin the process of creating an auction listing; continue with **130** **Write the Title and Description**.

From the **Duration** drop-down list in the **Sell Your Item** form, choose 1, 3, 5, 7, or **10** days. If you choose **10** days, you have to pay an extra $0.10 for the listing.

The most common auction length is seven days, and for most auctions, that's the best choice. However, three-day auctions can create a sense of excitement and urgency that you can't get in a seven-day auction. A title that contains the words "Must Sell! 3 DAYS!" or "Fast Sale! 3 DAYS ONLY!" can go a long way toward drawing in bidders who smell a good deal in the making.

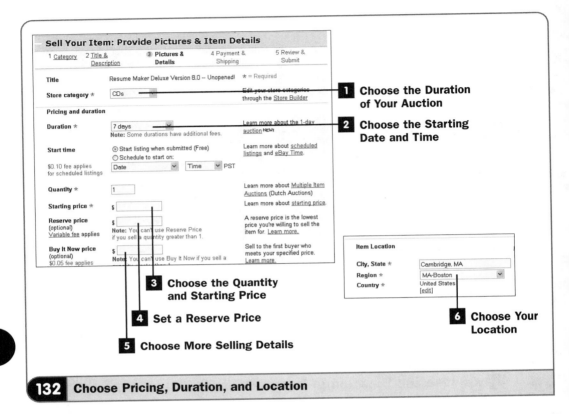

Sell Your Item: Provide Pictures & Item Details

1 Category   2 Title & Description   3 Pictures & Details   4 Payment & Shipping   5 Review & Submit

| Title | Resume Maker Deluxe Version 8.0 -- Unopened! | * = Required |

Store category *   CDs   ▾   Edit your store categories through the Store Builder   **1** Choose the Duration of Your Auction

Pricing and duration

Duration *   7 days   ▾   Note: Some durations have additional fees.   Learn more about the 1-day auction NEW!   **2** Choose the Starting Date and Time

Start time   ⦿ Start listing when submitted (Free)   ○ Schedule to start on: Learn more about scheduled listings and eBay Time.

$0.10 fee applies for scheduled listings   Date ▾   Time ▾ PST

Quantity *   1   Learn more about Multiple Item Auctions (Dutch Auctions)

Starting price * $ _____   Learn more about starting price.

Reserve price (optional) $ _____   A reserve price is the lowest price you're willing to sell the item for. Learn more.
Variable fee applies   Note: You can't use Reserve Price if you sell a quantity greater than 1.

Buy It Now price (optional) $ _____   Sell to the first buyer who meets your specified price. Learn more.
$0.05 fee applies   Note: You can't use Buy It Now if you sell a

Item Location

City, State *   Cambridge, MA
Region *   MA-Boston   ▾
Country *   United States [edit]

3 Choose the Quantity and Starting Price

4 Set a Reserve Price

5 Choose More Selling Details

6 Choose Your Location

| 132 | Choose Pricing, Duration, and Location |

2 Choose the Starting Date and Time

From the **Start Time** section, select the starting date and starting time for your auction. If you want the auction to start immediately after you finish filling out the form, enable the **Start Listing When Submitted** radio button. If you want to specify a starting date and time, enable the **Schedule to Start On** radio button and then choose the date and time from the drop-down list boxes. Choosing a starting date and time costs an additional $0.10, but it can be well worth that extra money because the time you begin and end your auctions can have a big effect on whether you have bidders and how high they bid.

Why is that? Why should one time be any better than another for an eBay auction? It's because of the existence of auction *sniper*s and those who like to bid close to the end of the auction to get the best possible deal. Many bidders haunt auction sites, checking which auctions are in the process of closing, or are near closing, and then they bid.

▶ KEY TERM

Sniper—Someone who bids at the last possible second at the end of the auction, in order to get the item at the lowest possible price.

So what does this have to do with when your auctions begin and end? You want your auctions to end at the time when you have the greatest possible audience. If your auction ends at a time when there is the greatest audience, the most people possible will notice your auction's closing, so you'll have the most bidders.

▶ NOTE

When choosing the time you want your auction to begin and end, keep in mind that the eBay clock, which shows the current time on the site and time stamps auctions, is set to Pacific Standard Time (PST).

The United States spans four time zones, so you should pick a time for your auction to end when the maximum number of people are likely to be logged on to the Internet at the eBay auction site. It should be after work hours—most people don't spend a lot of time bidding on auctions during work (or at least they shouldn't, if they want to keep their jobs). Your auction should end enough after work for people to come home and get online. Given that, you'd want your auction to end sometime after 6:30 p.m. PST, which is 9:30 p.m. EST. It shouldn't end too late on the East Coast because you'll lose a lot of bidders.

132

▶ TIP

It's best for your auction to end sometime between 6:30 p.m. and 8:30 p.m. PST—that's the time when you'll get the greatest number of active bidders.

Knowing when your auction should end will determine when it should begin. Auctions end a set number of days after you create your listing—for example, three, five, or seven days (which is your choice, as explained in step 2). Auctions end at the exact time you created them. So be sure to specify a start time that's the same time you want your auction to end.

Now you have a good sense of the best time to start and end your auctions. But how about the day of the week?

No great surprise here: Weekends are good. Consider either starting or ending your auctions on a weekend, when people have more free time than they do on weekdays. If you do, adjust the starting and ending time accordingly. If you're starting or ending on a Saturday, for example, don't set the time for the evening when people might be out for dinner or entertainment. I'd suggest early afternoon EST. That way, you'll get East Coasters before they go out for the evening, and you'll still get West Coasters during the early afternoon.

Sunday late afternoons or evenings are good times, too, and I suggest starting or ending your auction earlier than you might for workday auctions. Often on Sunday nights, people want to get to bed earlier than they do during the rest of the week to be rested before the week starts. From about 3:00 p.m. to 7:00 p.m. PST on Sunday is a good start/end time.

▶ **TIP**

Don't end your auctions on a holiday. That's when people often travel or spend time with their families and are less likely to visit auction sites, so you'll get fewer bidders.

3 Choose the Quantity and Starting Price

In the **Quantity** text box, enter the number of items you have to sell. If you are selling more than one item, you can sell using a *Dutch auction* format.

132

▶ **KEY TERM**

Dutch auction—An auction in which multiple items are up for sale. All the winning bidders on the items in a Dutch auction pay the same price for the items, the lowest successful bid.

In the **Starting Price** text box, enter the price at which you want people to start bidding in your auction. You learned in **127 Determine Your Selling Price and Estimate Your Selling Fees** how to decide on what price you should get for an item. That doesn't mean, though, that that's the starting price you should decide on—it only means that it's the price you can expect to get. If you set the starting price too high—at your expected final selling price, for example—you can scare away bidders. Many auctions typically start with very low selling prices, as a way to get people to bid.

The starting price determines the minimum *bidding increment*. If you set a minimum bid of $1, for example, the minimum bidding increment is $0.05; if you set a minimum bid of $5, the minimum bidding increment is $0.25. The higher the minimum bid, the more money you'll get for each subsequent bid. The following table lists the bidding increment for each price range.

▶ **KEY TERM**

Bidding increment—The amount of money you must add to the current bidding price for your bid to be considered valid. The higher the minimum initial bid, the higher the bidding increment. For example, a minimum initial bid of $1 has a bidding increment of $0.05, whereas a $5 minimum initial bid has a bidding increment of $0.25.

eBay Bidding Increments

Starting Price	Bidding Increment
$0–$1	$0.05
$1–$5	$0.25
$5–$25	$0.50
$25–$100	$1
$100–$250	$2.50
$250–$500	$5
$500–$1,000	$10
$1,000–$2,500	$25
$2,500–$5,000	$50
$5,000+	$100

When setting your minimum bid, balance the need to draw people into the auction against ensuring you get a fair price for what you're selling. A low minimum price will draw more bidders, but then each subsequent bid won't be much higher than the minimum bid. A higher minimum price might scare away bidders, but then each subsequent bid will be a larger jump above the minimum bid.

132

▶ NOTE

When you create an auction, you must choose a starting price. eBay won't let you complete your form unless you include a starting price.

4 Set a Reserve Price

You have the option of setting a *reserve price*—a price under which you're not willing to sell the item. Why not simply set the starting price as your reserve price? Because that's likely to scare away potential buyers—typically you need to set a low price if you want to get people to start bidding.

You have to pay an extra fee if you set a reserve price. You're only charged that fee if the item doesn't sell—if it does sell, the fee is refunded to you. The fee you pay depends on the reserve price you set. Items up to $24.99 are charged $0.50; those between $25 and $99.99 are charged $1; and items $100 and up are charged up to 1% of the reserve price, with a maximum fee of $100.

5 Choose More Selling Details

If you want your item to be a Buy It Now item that can be bought at a fixed price rather than through the auction format, type a set price for the item in the **Buy It Now price** box. You'll be charged $0.05 if you list an item with the **Buy It Now** option.

▶ **TIP**

You can use the **Buy It Now** feature only if you are selling a single item; you can't use it for multiple-item auctions.

You can also choose to make your auction a private one. In a *private auction*, bidders' IDs can't be seen by others. You might choose this option if you are selling very high-priced items and are worried that bidders don't want others to know that they are willing to spend a great deal of money. Or you might use it if you are selling some types of adult-related material and worry that bidders will not want it known that they are bidding on this type of material.

132 ▶ **KEY TERM**

Private auction—An auction in which bidders cannot see the IDs of other bidders. The only one who knows who is bidding is the seller.

6 Choose Your Location

You must fill in the city, state, and country where you live (or from which you will be shipping the item at the close of the auction). You can also choose your region, which increases the exposure of your auction. When you choose a region, your item is listed in the region listings on eBay. There's no extra charge for this, so you should do it. However, if you don't want your auction listed in the region auctions, select **Do Not List Regionally** from the **Region** drop-down box.

When you're finished selecting auction pricing and duration information, you're ready to add pictures and other auction extras, so don't click **Continue** yet. Only click **Continue** after you've added pictures (if you want to add them) and chosen auction extras. For information, see **134 Add Pictures to Your Auction** and **135 Choose Auction Extras**.

▶ **TIP**

Click the **Back** button at the bottom of the **Sell Your Item** form page (not your browser's **Back** button) to back up through the pages of the **Sell Your Item** form if you decide to make changes to earlier selections you've made. Click the **Continue** button to advance through the pages of the form.

133 About Dutch Auctions

✔ BEFORE YOU BEGIN	→ SEE ALSO
132 Choose Pricing, Duration, and Location	**134** Add Pictures to Your Auction
	135 Choose Auction Extras
	136 Set Payment and Shipping Options
	137 Review and Post Your Auction

Most items on eBay are sold in the traditional online auction manner: A single item is put up for sale and people bid against one another to buy it.

But what if you've gone to a liquidator and gotten a great deal on 25 sets of high-quality computer speakers? As you can see from this chapter, it takes a good deal of work to create a single auction. Imagine having to create that auction 25 times. And then imagine having to track each of those individual auctions. If you're selling goods in volume, it simply wouldn't be worth your while to conduct your auctions in this one-off fashion.

A much better bet, when you have multiple items to sell, is to sell them at a Dutch auction—that is, you sell multiple items at one single auction. That way, you create the auction once and track only a single auction. Dutch auctions are particularly well suited for those who are trying to make a living by selling on eBay or who want to get a substantial side income from eBay.

You create a Dutch auction in the same way you do any other auction. But when you fill out the **Quantity** field in the **Sell Your Item** form, as detailed in **132** **Choose Pricing, Duration, and Location**, you instead choose to sell multiple items, rather than a single one.

You can sell multiple items at a Dutch auction in two formats: the online-auction format and the fixed-price format. Here's what you need to know about each:

- **Online-auction format**—When you choose this format, you set a starting price and people bid above it, just as they do in a traditional auction. Bidders specify the number of items they want to buy, as well as their price. All the winning bidders pay the same price, though: the lowest successful bid. Suppose you are selling 10 items, and the bids of the top 10 bidders ranged from $34.50 to $41. All 10 items would be sold for $34.50.

- **Fixed-price format**—When you choose this format, you set a selling price and whoever wants to buy the item can buy it at that price. If you set a selling price of $35 for your items, no bidding would take place, and whoever wanted to buy one or more of your items would pay $35. A **Buy It Now** icon appears in the listing.

133

Which format you choose depends on your specific circumstances. The online-auction format has a bigger upside as well as a bigger downside—if a bidding war breaks out, you'll be in the money, but if you get unenthusiastic bidders, you won't get much for your goods. The fixed-price format is better suited when you have a good idea of what the items will sell for and want to move them quickly.

▶ **NOTE**

If you want to be able to sell using Dutch auctions, you must have a **feedback rating of 30 or above** and be registered on eBay for **14 days** or more. Alternatively, you can be **ID Verified**.

134 Add Pictures to Your Auction

✔ BEFORE YOU BEGIN	→ SEE ALSO
128 About the eBay Sell Your Item Page	**138** About Digital Pictures and eBay
129 Start the Sell Form and Choose a Category	
130 Write the Title and Description	
131 Format Your Description with eBay's HTML Editor	
132 Choose Pricing, Duration, and Location	

134

A picture is worth a thousand words—and helps you sell the goods. It's a simple fact that when you include a picture in your auction, the item has a better chance of selling—and selling for more money—than if no picture is included.

eBay makes including pictures in your auctions easy. However, if you want to get the most out of your auction pictures, turn to Chapter 20, "Power Tips for Handling Digital Auction Pictures."

1 Take a Picture

You'll need a picture of your item, and the picture has to be in a digital format. Use a digital camera, a regular camera, or a scanner to get your picture in a digital format:

- **Take a photograph using a digital camera**—Digital cameras are an excellent way to get pictures into your computer. They store pictures on their own hard disks or memory sticks. After you take the pictures, you transfer them to your computer.

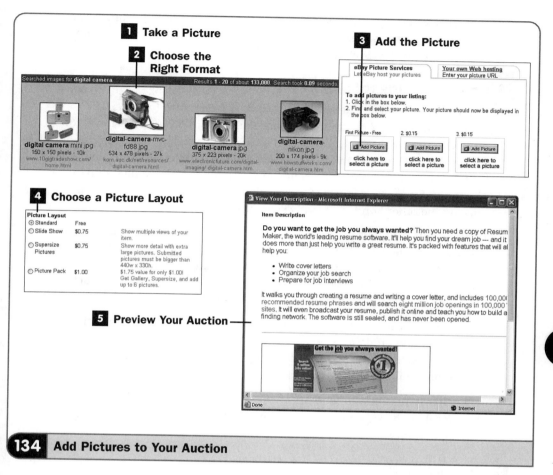

1 Take a Picture

2 Choose the Right Format

3 Add the Picture

4 Choose a Picture Layout

5 Preview Your Auction

134 Add Pictures to Your Auction

134

- Take a photograph with a regular camera and put it into your computer with a scanner—You can buy a good-quality scanner for $100 or less. Scanners do a good job of converting a normal photograph into an image of a high-enough quality that you can put it on your website.

▶ **TIP**

For images intended for use on the Web (as are eBay picture files), you don't need super-high resolution. A resolution of 72dpi is sufficient for most web purposes and ensures a picture file size that's small enough to be downloaded quickly by most viewers' browsers.

- Take a photograph with a regular camera and ask that the photos be made available online or on a CD—When you fill out a form to have your photos developed, the photo developer gives you the option of creating a photo CD or making the images available online. Select one of these options as an easy way to get auction pictures without having to spend any money for hardware.

2 Choose the Right Format

Pictures posted on eBay generally should be in one of two formats: GIF (which stands for Graphical Interchange Format) or JPEG (which stands for Joint Picture Experts Group). Files in the GIF format end in a **.gif** extension; files in the JPEG format end in a **.jpg** extension. Graphics programs and other software give you a choice of formats in which to save image files, and just about all of them let you save files in either of these formats. Digital cameras, on the other hand, frequently save files only as JPEGs.

Both formats compress the graphics files so they aren't too large to be easily displayed on the Web. If graphics are large, they take a long time to download and web surfing slows to a crawl. Either format works fine for your graphics, but if you want your graphics to provide the maximum impact, you should know the following about each format:

134

- JPEG—Does a better job of compressing photographs and art with fine detail and gradations, so choose it if you'll be putting a photograph or detailed image on your auction page. JPEG doesn't do as well with high-contrast images, such as line art.

- GIF—Works best for line art, cartoons, and similar graphics, so choose it for these types of pictures. GIF is not as good as JPEG for displaying photographs.

3 Add the Picture

After you have the picture you want to use, you're ready to add it to your auction. On the **Picture & Details** page of the **Sell Your Item** form, scroll to the bottom of the page to the **EBay Picture Services** section. Click the **Add Picture** button and select the picture you want to add to your auction. The photo continues to live on your hard disk, but a copy of it is uploaded to eBay.

▶ NOTE

If you haven't started the **Sell Your Item** form yet, back up to **129 Start the Sell Form and Choose a Category** to learn how to begin the process of creating an auction listing.

You'll see a thumbnail of your picture on the page when you're done. You can crop the photo by dragging its corner or sides, and you can rotate it 90° by clicking the photo's upper-right corner.

eBay hosts your photo when you add a photo this way. The first photo you use is free, but additional photos cost $0.15 each. If you don't want to use the eBay picture service, you can instead link to a photo you have stored somewhere on the Web—for example, if your Internet service provider gives you storage space, you could upload all your eBay pictures to this space. To use photos stored on some other online web server, click the **Your Own Web Hosting** link and type the URL to your picture.

4 Choose a Picture Layout

Choose the layout for your picture. **Standard** layout is free and is good for most auctions. However, you can instead select a **Slide Show** layout, which shows multiple views of your item and costs $0.75. You can also have **Supersize Pictures** layout, which lets you display large pictures over 440×330 pixels and also costs $0.75 extra, or you can select a **Picture Pack**, which includes up to six pictures, lets you supersize them, and gives you a gallery feature to provide your picture with wider exposure.

134

▶ TIP

For more information about the gallery, see **135** Choose Auction Extras.

5 Preview Your Auction

When you're done making your picture selections, click **Preview Your Listing**. You have to wait a short while as your picture is uploaded to eBay; then you see a preview of your entire auction page, including your picture. Click **Close Window** to return to the **Sell Your Item** form pages.

▶ TIP

Click the **Back** button at the bottom of the **Sell Your Item** form page (not your browser's **Back** button) to back up through the pages of the **Sell Your Item** form if you decide to make changes to earlier selections you've made. Click the **Continue** button to advance through the pages of the form. If you instead use your browser's **Back** and **Forward** buttons, you can lose all the information you entered into your auction page.

135 | Choose Auction Extras

✔ BEFORE YOU BEGIN	→ SEE ALSO
134 Add Pictures to Your Auction	**136** Set Payment and Shipping Options
	137 Review and Post Your Auction

Often, it's the little things in life that matter, and that's certainly true with eBay auctions. You're competing against many thousands of other people for the attention of would-be bidders, so you have to do whatever you can to draw them in.

When you put together your auction, there are a lot of little extras you can add to draw people in. Here's how to add them. Note that all the choices in this module can be found on the **Pictures & Details** page of the **Sell Your Item** form.

1 Use the Listing Designer

135

The **Listing Designer** applies a theme to your picture, such as **Christmas Tree** or **Consumer Electronics**, and lets you control its placement on the auction page. (The cost for a **Listing Designer** theme is $0.10 extra.)

When you choose this option, the **Listing Designer** outlines your auction in a thematic frame to draw extra attention to it. Note that it draws that frame only around the auction itself. When people are browsing on eBay, they won't be able to see the theme—only when they click your auction to view your auction listing page.

To use it, go to the **Listing Designer** section of the **Pictures & Details** page of the **Sell Your Item** form. From the **Select a Theme** drop-down list, select the general category of theme you want, such as **Events**, **Seasonal/Holiday**, or **New** (selecting **New** lists the newest themes). When you select a theme category, the drop-down list just below it lists all the themes available in that category—for example, **Blue Holiday**, **Christmas Tree**, **Father's Day**, **Fourth of July**, and so on for the **Seasonal/Holiday** category. Select the theme you want from the second drop-down list, and you see a preview of it on the right.

When you've chosen the specific theme, select a layout for the theme from the **Select a Layout** drop-down list. When you select a layout, you see a preview to the right.

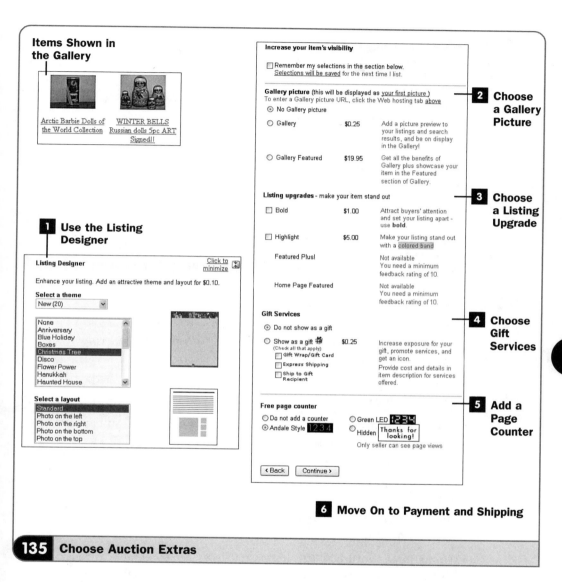

Items Shown in the Gallery

Arctic Barbie Dolls of the World Collection

WINTER BELLS Russian dolls 5pc ART Signed!!

1 Use the Listing Designer

Listing Designer   Click to minimize

Enhance your listing. Add an attractive theme and layout for $0.10.

Select a theme
New (20)

None
Anniversary
Blue Holiday
Boxes
Christmas Tree
Disco
Flower Power
Hanukkah
Haunted House

Select a layout
Standard
Photo on the left
Photo on the right
Photo on the bottom
Photo on the top

Increase your item's visibility

☐ Remember my selections in the section below.
  Selections will be saved for the next time I list.

Gallery picture (this will be displayed as your first picture)
To enter a Gallery picture URL, click the Web hosting tab above
  ⊙ No Gallery picture
  ○ Gallery $0.25   Add a picture preview to your listings and search results, and be on display in the Gallery!
  ○ Gallery Featured $19.95   Get all the benefits of Gallery plus showcase your item in the Featured section of Gallery.

Listing upgrades - make your item stand out

  ☐ Bold $1.00   Attract buyers' attention and set your listing apart - use **bold**.
  ☐ Highlight $5.00   Make your listing stand out with a colored band
  Featured Plus!   Not available You need a minimum feedback rating of 10.
  Home Page Featured   Not available You need a minimum feedback rating of 10.

Gift Services

  ⊙ Do not show as a gift
  ○ Show as a gift 🎁 $0.25   Increase exposure for your gift, promote services, and get an icon.
    (Check all that apply)
    ☐ Gift Wrap/Gift Card
    ☐ Express Shipping   Provide cost and details in item description for services offered.
    ☐ Ship to Gift Recipient

Free page counter

  ○ Do not add a counter   ○ Green LED
  ⊙ Andale Style 1234   ○ Hidden Thanks for looking!
                                Only seller can see page views

  [< Back]   [Continue >]

2 Choose a Gallery Picture

3 Choose a Listing Upgrade

4 Choose Gift Services

5 Add a Page Counter

6 Move On to Payment and Shipping

135 Choose Auction Extras

2 Choose a Gallery Picture

Scroll to the **Gallery Picture** section of the **Sell Your Item** form and select the **Gallery** option if you want your item to be in what eBay calls the *Gallery*. When an item is in the Gallery and someone browses or searches through eBay and comes across your auction, he can see a picture preview of your auction item. Additionally, if someone does a search and asks to see only Gallery items, your item shows up in that search.

▶ KEY TERM

Gallery—An area of eBay that highlights auctions by publishing photographs of their items. You have to pay extra if you want your auction featured in the Gallery.

The cost for listing your item in the Gallery is $0.25. You can also select the **Gallery Featured** option, which gives your auction additional visibility. When you select it, your item periodically appears in the **Featured** section above the normal Gallery. Additionally, your item's picture is nearly twice the size of non-featured Gallery pictures. The cost for this option is substantial—$19.95—so choose it only for high-priced items.

▶ NOTE

eBay does not guarantee the number of times a **Gallery Featured** item will appear in the **Featured** section of the Gallery. The precise number of times is determined by when you list your item and how many other **Gallery Featured** items are in your category.

3 Choose a Listing Upgrade

To draw more attention to your item, you can choose a listing upgrade. To choose one, scroll down to the **Listing Upgrades** section of the **Sell Your Item** form. You have the following options:

- **Bold**—This option boldfaces your listing when people are browsing or searching. It costs $1 extra.

- **Highlight**—This option puts a colored band around your listing when people are browsing or searching. It costs $5 extra.

- **Featured Plus!**—This option gives your auction a more prominent placement in the category list and the search results. Your auction is featured prominently in the **Featured Items** section of the category list and also appears in the regular, non-featured item list. It costs $19.95 per listing extra.

- **Home Page Featured**—This option makes your item eligible to be featured on eBay's home page. The option costs $99.95 if you're selling a single item or $199.95 if you're selling two or more items.

▶ NOTE

You are not allowed to use the **Featured Plus!** or **Home Page Featured** option unless you have a feedback rating of 10 or more.

135

4 Choose Gift Services

If you provide gift services for buyers, you can let them know for a 25-cent additional fee. Scroll to the **Gift Services** section of the **Sell Your Item** page and enable the **Show As a Gift** radio button. You can choose to provide the following services: **Gift Wrap/Gift Card**, **Express Shipping**, and **Ship to Gift Recipient**. You have to provide details about the cost of each of these options and exactly what these services entail in your auction description.

5 Add a Page Counter

Scroll down to the **Free Page Counter** portion of the **Sell Your Item** page and choose a *page counter* if you're interested. If you expect many people to visit, you should add a page counter because it makes people think your item is one many people might want to buy, so it appears to be more desirable. If, however, you don't expect many visitors, don't display a counter because it makes it appear that it's an unwanted item. You can, however, use a **Hidden** counter—visitors won't see the counter, but you will so you have a sense of how many people are visiting your page.

▶ KEY TERM

135

Page counter—A continuously updating digital counter that tells visitors how many people have visited an auction page. If the counter shows many visitors, people are apt to consider your auction item highly valued and might bid more for the item.

▶ NOTE

If you plan to create more auctions in the future, using the same options as you do for this auction, click the **Remember My Selections in the Section Below** check box just below **Increase Your Item's Visibility**. That way, the next auction you create will automatically have all these auction extras preselected. You can still change them, but at least you'll have a head start.

6 Move On to Payment and Shipping

When you've chosen all your auction extras, click **Continue**. You move on to the **Payment & Shipping** page of the **Sell Your Item** form, as explained in **136 Set Payment and Shipping Options**. To back up through the pages of the **Sell Your Item** form, click the **Back** button (not your browser's **Back** button).

136 **Set Payment and Shipping Options**

✔ BEFORE YOU BEGIN	→ SEE ALSO
135 Choose Auction Extras	**137** Review and Post Your Auction

The whole purpose of your auction, of course, is to make money, so you must let potential buyers know how you'll accept payment, how you'll ship the goods, and who will pay for shipping. Here's how to do it:

136

1 Choose Payment Methods

If you haven't started to fill out the **Sell Your Item** form yet, back up to **129** **Start the Sell Form and Choose a Category** to learn how to begin the process of creating an auction listing.

How will you accept payment? At the top of the **Payment & Shipping** page of the **Sell Your Item** form, select all the ways you will accept payment. One of the best ways is to use the **PayPal** online payment method because money is automatically sent from the buyer to your PayPal account.

You can also choose to accept money orders, cashier's checks, personal checks, cash on delivery (COD), and credit cards (if you have a merchant account). You can also specify other payment methods in your item's description.

▶ **TIP**

Money orders and cashier's checks are good choices for payment because they're essentially as good as cash. Personal checks can be a bit more problematic because you must ensure that they clear the bank before you ship your goods. If you choose to accept personal checks, make sure that they clear with your bank before you send the goods. Also, keep in mind that cashier's checks can be forged, so you shouldn't ship the goods until the check clears your bank and is deposited in your account. Only ship goods after you actually see the money deposited to your account.

2 Say Who Will Pay for Shipping Costs

As a general rule, buyers pay shipping costs. It's a well-established practice, and unless you have a specific reason for wanting to pay shipping costs, you should have the buyer pay for them. Make your choice in the **Shipping Costs** section of the **Sell Your Item** form.

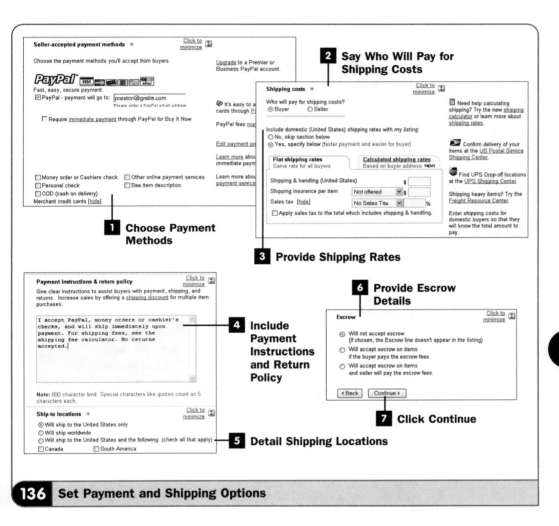

136 Set Payment and Shipping Options

3 Provide Shipping Rates

The buyer will want to know how much he must pay for shipping, so you should provide that information in your auction listing by selecting the appropriate options in the **Shipping Costs** section of the **Sell Your Item** form. If you know the shipping costs for the item and want to provide a flat rate for shipping to anywhere in the United States, enter that information, along with any shipping insurance fees you'll add (if you want to include shipping insurance). If you're going to add sales tax, add it by selecting your state from the drop-down list box next to **Sales Tax** and typing the percent amount of sales tax in the text box next to it.

If you're not sure how much shipping will cost, use the eBay shipping calculator by clicking the **Shipping Calculator** link on the right side of the **Shipping Costs** section. You enter information such as the size and weight of your package and the city to which you are going to ship. The calculator then displays for you the U.S. Postal Service and UPS costs for various shipping options.

▶ **TIP**

When you use the shipping calculator, you don't know from which city the high bidder will be. To be safe, choose the city farthest from your location and use that rate as a flat fee.

You also have the option of including a shipping calculator in your auction that buyers can use to find out how much shipping they'll be expected to pay. To choose that option, click the **Calculated Shipping Rates** tab in the **Shipping Costs** section.

4 Include Payment Instructions and Return Policy

In the **Payment Instructions & Return Policy** section of the **Sell Your Item** form, spell out your payment instructions, even though you've already detailed them in step 1. You should spell out payment instructions in as many places as possible, so there is no misunderstanding about how you'll accept payment. Also, if you have any special instructions, here's the place to include them.

136

▶ **TIP**

When you list your payment options, be sure you don't contradict yourself in different sections of the auction page. Payment information can be listed in two places: in the item description itself and at the bottom, outside the item description. Double-check that you're including the same payment information in both places. If you don't, you might confuse buyers so much they won't bid.

Also be clear whether you will accept returns of your goods, and if so, under what circumstances. And make clear whose responsibility it is for paying shipping for returned goods. Unless there's a good reason otherwise, buyers should always pay for return shipping.

5 Detail Shipping Locations

Will you ship only to the United States, worldwide, or only to specific regions of the world? Enter that information in the **Ship-to Locations** section.

6 Provide Escrow Details

Will you accept **escrow** payments? An escrow payment is when an escrow service such as escrow.com holds the buyer's payment until the goods are shipped to him and he approves the item. The escrow service also handles disputes between buyer and seller. You don't need to use escrow services for low-cost items; an escrow service should be used only if you're selling expensive items such as jewelry, vehicles, or boats.

7 Click Continue

When you're done with the **Payment & Shipping** page of the **Sell Your Item** form, click **Continue** to move on to review your auction and post it. To back up through the pages of the **Sell Your Item** form, click the **Back** button (not your browser's **Back** button).

---

137 Review and Post Your Auction

✔ BEFORE YOU BEGIN	→ SEE ALSO
136 Set Payment and Shipping Options	**145** Track Your Auction

137

The hard work is done; you're almost there. It's time to finally post your auction. Here's how to do it:

1 Review Your Auction's Appearance

If you haven't started to fill out the **Sell Your Item** form yet, back up to **129** **Start the Sell Form and Choose a Category** to learn how to begin the process of creating an auction listing; finish up with **136** **Set Payment and Shipping Options**.

When you click the **Continue** button from the **Payment & Shipping** page, you see a preview of what your auction will look like on the **Review & Submit** page. Look it over carefully to ensure your auction listing looks how you want it to look. If you want to edit the picture, click the **Edit Pictures** link next to the picture. To edit the auction title, click the **Edit Title & Subtitle** link at the top of the page. To edit the auction description, click the **Edit Description** link near the top of the page.

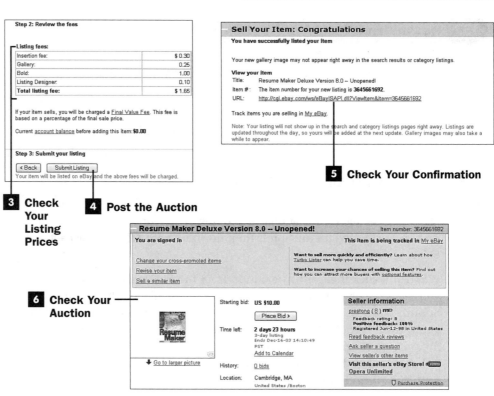

2 Review Your Auction Options

The preview page shows you a **Listing Summary Table** with every aspect of your auction, from the category to title and description, picture and details, and payment and shipping. To change any of your options, click the **Edit** link next to that option; when you're done editing, click the **Save Changes** button at the bottom of the page to return to the **Review & Submit** page.

3 Check Your Listing Prices

At the bottom of the **Review & Submit** page are your individual listing fees along with the total listing fee you have to pay. Keep in mind that this total doesn't include your final value fee. For information about calculating your final value fee, go to **127 Determine Your Selling Price and Estimate Your Selling Fees**.

4 Post the Auction

When you've edited everything to your satisfaction, click the **Submit Listing** button.

▶ NOTE

Make absolutely sure that everything is the way you want it before posting your auction. After it's posted, you might not be able to retrieve it to edit it.

5 Check Your Confirmation

After you click the **Submit Listing** button, you receive a confirmation that your auction has been created. Included in this notice is an item number. Copy that number down for future reference (and so you can get back to the auction). The confirmation notice also contains a link you can click to go to your auction.

6 Check Your Auction

After you receive confirmation, immediately click the link to view your auction. You want to verify that the auction is exactly the way you want it. When you click the URL link, you go to your auction page and see it as the rest of the world will.

Check every aspect of your completed auction. Overlooking things on forms is easy, and this is the first time you'll see your auction listing the way the world sees it. If you find any errors, you might have time to fix them. If no bids have come in—and they shouldn't have because you created the auction only moments ago and it probably isn't visible yet—you can still correct

137

them. To fix any errors, click the **Revise Your Item** link in the upper-right portion of the page.

▶ **NOTE**

It can take up to several hours for the auction to show up on eBay, although it also can be posted immediately. If your link doesn't work at first, click it again after an hour or so. Remember that if you specified a date and time for your auction to appear, it won't appear until then, so don't bother to check ahead of time.

Shortly after creating an auction, you get an email notice from eBay telling you that your auction has been made live and giving you all the vital information about the auction. Keep or print that email for future reference.

20

Power Tips for Handling Digital Auction Pictures

IN THIS CHAPTER:

Here's one of the simplest rules about auctions you'll ever come across: Pictures sell. When you include a picture in your auction, the item has a greater chance of selling—and for more money—than if no picture is included. In short, when it comes to auctions, pictures are worth more than a thousand words—they're worth money as well.

In this chapter, you learn how to get pictures, how to prepare them for posting, how to store them before they can be posted, and how to include them in your auction listing.

138 **About Digital Pictures and eBay**

✔ BEFORE YOU BEGIN	→ SEE ALSO
134 Add Pictures to Your Auction	**124** About Selling on eBay

138

Go to almost any auction page on eBay and you'll find a picture of the item for sale. From jewelry to cards to cars, shoes, toys, and more, almost every auction is accompanied by a picture. There's good reason for that—in an online world, people want to be able to see what they're buying before they bid.

That means you'll be much better off including a picture rather than not including one. But where to get one? There are many ways to get pictures for your auction. The following are the best ways to do it:

- **Take a photograph using a digital camera**—Digital cameras are an excellent way to get pictures into your computer. The cameras store pictures on memory cards. After you take the pictures, you transfer them to your computer. You can save them in a web-friendly graphics format such as *GIF* or *JPEG*.

▶ **KEY TERMS**

GIF and *JPEG*—GIF stands for Graphics Interchange Format and JPEG for Joint Photographic Experts Group. Both are graphics standards that use compression to keep image sizes small but still retain enough detail so the image is of a high quality. JPEG does a better job on photographs and is the format you should generally use when posting pictures to eBay. GIF is better for line art and logos.

- **Take a photograph with a regular camera and put it into your computer with a scanner**—You can buy a good-quality scanner for less than $100. Perhaps you already have one. Scanners do a good job of converting a normal photograph into a digital image of a high-enough quality that you can put it on your website.

▶ **TIP**

If you have a webcam connected to your PC so you can video chat with others, you can use the webcam like a digital camera to take pictures of items you want to sell. Check the documentation for how to do it. The quality won't be as good as a digital camera, but you'll at least get your picture into your auction.

- **Take a photograph with a regular camera and ask that the photo lab convert the picture to a computer format and give it to you on a disk, on CD-ROM, or over the Web**—Pretty much any self-respecting photo service will do this for you these days. It's an easy way to get auction pictures without having to spend any money for hardware.

- **Use America Online's You've Got Pictures feature**—If you're an America Online user, it's exceptionally easy to get pictures into your computer from a regular camera. Take your pictures as you normally would and then take the film into a photo developer that participates in the You've Got Pictures plan. (There shouldn't be a problem finding one because tens of thousands of developers participate.)

  When you fill out your envelope for developing the film, check the America Online box and enter your screen name. Pick up your photos as you normally would—they'll be normal photos. Within 48 hours, the photos will be delivered to your America Online account. When you log in, you'll hear the familiar America Online voice telling you, "You've got pictures!" Use the keyword **Pictures** to go to an area that has an album of all your pictures. Follow the directions for saving them to your computer. When saving the pictures, be sure to save them in the **.jpg** format because that's the format you'll use when posting them on your auction listing.

- **Take a photograph with a regular camera and take the print to a printing or scanning service**—Many printing services, such as Kinko's, will scan photographs and give the digital files to you in any format you want. It's a cheap and easy way to get pictures into your computer without having to buy hardware. Unlike with photo services, you can have single photos scanned this way—you won't have to pay for putting the whole roll of film onto disc.

Getting Pictures from the Web

Another excellent place to get pictures to put in your auction is from the Web itself. The Web is full of pictures of all kinds—and what makes these pictures especially useful for you is that they're already in the proper format you need for posting online. Another bonus is that not only are they in the proper format, often the pictures have been tweaked and manipulated so they'll look best online.

138

▶ **NOTE**

Be aware that pictures you find on the Web might be copyrighted, and you might violate those copyrights if you use the picture without first asking the site for permission. So check before using the picture for your eBay auction.

There are many sources for pictures on the Web, but the best is the Google search engine. To use its picture search feature, go to **www.google.com** and click the **Images** tab. In **140** **Use the Web to Get a Digital Picture** you learn how to download and use pictures from there.

Another way to find pictures of an item you're selling is to go to the manufacturer's website. Many manufacturers include pictures of their products right on the web page. Many online shopping sites, such as **www.buy.com**, also include pictures of products. If you find a picture on a web page, downloading and saving it to your computer is easy, as outlined in **140** **Use the Web to Get a Digital Picture**.

---

139 **Set Up and Take a Picture**	
✔ **BEFORE YOU BEGIN**	→ **SEE ALSO**
151 About Digital Pictures and eBay	**134** Add Pictures to Your Auction

139

You don't have to be a professional photographer to take a good picture. All you need to know are a few basics, and you'll be able to take a picture that shows off your goods.

1 **Choose the Right Place to Take a Picture**

Find a well-lit, uncluttered spot and place a table there for photographing your item. Make sure that the table is large enough to hold the item and that the item isn't near an edge so that it can be easily knocked off.

▶ **NOTE**

Sometimes people steal pictures from other people on eBay—they simply take the photo used on another member's auction page and use it in their auction as if it were their own. This is a no-no. Not only does the picture not belong to those who steal, but it isn't a true representation of the item being sold because it was of someone else's item.

To make it easier for potential bidders to see a smaller item, place a solid-colored sheet underneath the item and put it against a solid backdrop. That way, the photo won't be cluttered, there will be nothing to distract the viewer from the item itself, and the item will stand out in contrast against the backdrop.

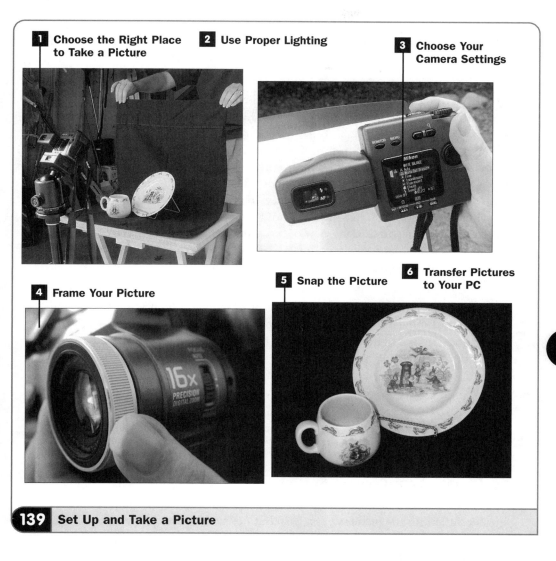

1 Choose the Right Place to Take a Picture

2 Use Proper Lighting

3 Choose Your Camera Settings

4 Frame Your Picture

5 Snap the Picture

6 Transfer Pictures to Your PC

139

139 Set Up and Take a Picture

If you're shooting a large item (such as a car or a boat) outdoors, choose a location without a distracting background. Plan your photo shoot for early morning or late afternoon when the sun won't cast harsh shadows.

2 Use Proper Lighting

Perhaps the biggest problem with digital photos is that they can look dim because they've been under lit, so make sure that you light the item properly. If your camera has a built-in light meter or flash indicator, point your camera at the item to see whether a flash is required. If you need a flash, the item isn't lit properly. (Use the flash as a last resort to light the item; the flash can cause odd shadows and might wash out the item on film. Although the flash is the easiest way to light the item you want to photograph, it's not the best way.)

If you're shooting an item indoors, you have a choice of indirect or direct lighting. With direct lighting, the lights shine directly on the item; with indirect lighting, the light first shines against an object such as a white board, and that reflected light in turn illuminates the item. It's much easier to use direct lighting—and direct lighting works better for most items—so as a general rule, plan to directly light the item. To best light your item, light the item from two or more directions, and place your lights above and to the sides of the item. Move the lights around until the light is best—watch that shadows don't interfere with a clear view of the item. The best lights to use are 100-watt halogen bulbs in clip-on lamps; that way you can easily position the lamps properly and you'll get bright, clean light.

For some items with glossy surfaces such as porcelain or polished metal, you should use indirect lighting. Use sheets of white poster board to surround the item and shine direct light onto the poster board; the poster board will bounce the light onto the item. You'll have to fiddle around with placement until you get the lighting right.

139

▶ **TIP**

If you're taking outdoor photos, the item shouldn't be in direct sunlight. Frequently, slightly overcast days are better than bright, sunny days for picture-taking because you'll have fewer harsh shadows to distract the viewer.

3 Choose Your Camera Settings

For your digital camera, make sure that you take photos at a high enough resolution for the pictures to be crisp but not so high a resolution that the picture files are too large. Anywhere between 640×480 pixels and 1024×768 pixels is a good setting.

Unless you're an experienced photographer, use auto-focus and auto-exposure settings. Getting a picture in focus with the right exposure settings can be frustratingly difficult, and cameras with auto settings do a good job for you.

Also make sure that you've chosen the right distance settings, if your camera can adjust them. Some cameras let you choose a macro setting (useful when the camera lens is only several inches away from an object), a medium setting (for objects a few feet away), or a long-distance setting (when the object is more than 10 feet away).

▶ **TIP**

Be careful when using your camera's flash. Some people tell you never to use flash because it can wash out details from pictures. However, if you don't use a flash, you risk getting dimly lit photos. Experiment with your camera's flash and see whether it harms or helps your photo.

4 Frame Your Picture

All your hard work up until now will amount to nothing if you don't frame your picture properly. Make sure that the item is large enough to be easily seen and takes up most of the frame. Center it for best results. Try framing it from different angles—dead-on, from the right, from the left, from above, and so on—until you find the angle that shows off your item best.

Keep in mind that you can use more than one picture on your eBay auction, so you don't have to have a single best shot—you can shoot the item from multiple angles and post several of the photos.

5 Snap the Picture

If you have a tripod, use that; it will give you the best pictures because it's stable and won't move. If your item has a particular noteworthy detail you want to point out, such as a signature on a baseball card, shoot the entire card; then also shoot a close-up of the signature. In fact, take many pictures from different angles because you'll be able to pick and choose the ones you like best later.

Digital cameras let you preview the pictures before shooting, so preview them first. Additionally, you can review the pictures after you've shot them and delete any you don't like. You can then take more pictures until you have a batch you're satisfied with.

6 Transfer Pictures to Your PC

After you've taken all the pictures of the item, transfer them to your PC using the software that came with your camera or with other graphics software, such as Paint Shop Pro or Photoshop Elements. Create a separate folder for each item you're selling so you can easily find the pictures you want.

139

---

140   **Use the Web to Get a Digital Picture**

✔ BEFORE YOU BEGIN	→ SEE ALSO
138 About Digital Pictures and eBay	**139** Set Up and Take a Picture
	134 Add Pictures to Your Auction

If you don't have a digital camera, the Web is a great place to get photos for use in your auctions. Not only can you find thousands of photos, but the ones you find will already be web friendly, so you'll have less work to do before you post them on your auction. The Web is the ideal place to find photos of manufacturers' goods, such as computers, digital cameras, and so on. If you're selling a vintage item, a one-of-a-kind item, or something you can't find on a manufacturer's website, you'll have to photograph the item yourself (see **139 Set Up and Take a Picture**).

140

▶ **TIP**

If you're grabbing a photo from the Web, make sure that the item you're selling is in as good shape as the photo you're using. If the item is worn or damaged in any way, using a photo of a perfect item is misleading. The buyer would have the right to return the item because you misrepresented it. If your item is in good shape, you can use the picture and add a disclaimer such as "manufacturer's photo of new item," and then describe how your item differs from the picture.

1   **Do a Basic Google Image Search**

The single best place on the Internet for finding photos is the **Images** section of the Google search site. Go to **www.google.com** and click the **Images** tab.

In the search box, type the name of the item you're looking for. Be as descriptive as possible; if you have a model number for the item, include it. Then press **Enter** or click the **Google Search** button.

2   **Use the Advanced Google Image Search**

If you want to fine-tune your search and get a better, more focused selection of images, click the **Advanced Image Search** link. The **Find Results** section of the page lets you determine how Google searches for your search terms. You can choose to have it find pictures related to the exact phrase you type (select **related to the exact phrase**), find pictures related to any term (select **related to any of the words**), search for pictures related to all the terms (select **related to all of the words**), and even exclude pictures that contain certain words (select **not related to the words** and type the words you *don't* want the pictures related to).

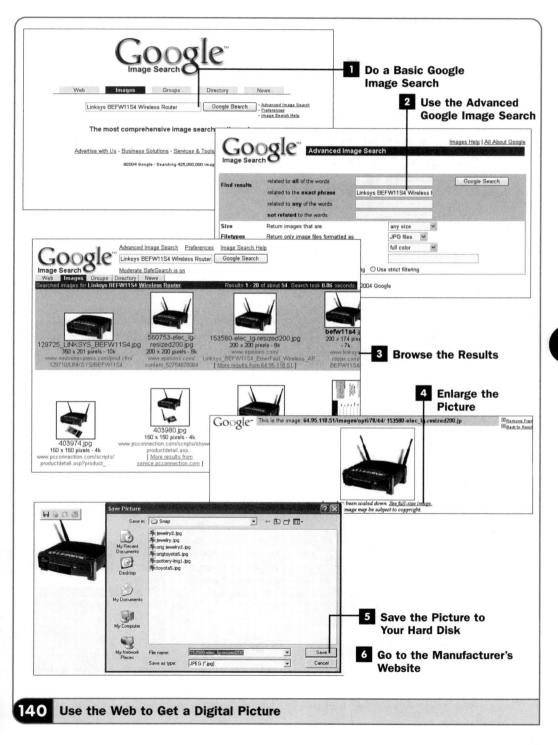

1 Do a Basic Google Image Search

2 Use the Advanced Google Image Search

3 Browse the Results

4 Enlarge the Picture

5 Save the Picture to Your Hard Disk

6 Go to the Manufacturer's Website

140

140 Use the Web to Get a Digital Picture

At the bottom of the screen, you can fine-tune the search by filtering by the size of the images; the file types; whether the images should be in color, black and white, or both; and even from a specific domain.

▶ **TIP**

The Web contains many pornographic images; no matter how innocuous your search terms, you might come across pornographic images when doing a Google search for images. If you want to ensure that no such images appear, select **Use strict filtering** or **Use moderate filtering** in the **Safe Search** section of the screen. **Strict filtering** filters out more pictures but might also filter out some non-pornographic pictures you'll want to see. With **moderate filtering**, a pornographic picture is slightly more likely to slip through, but you'll more likely get a wide range of legitimate pictures as well.

3 Browse the Results

Google searches for images based on your criteria and shows you the results. Each picture it finds has a small thumbnail as well as the URL where the image is located. Google also tells you the size of the picture, in pixels and in bytes (such as 8K, or 8 kilobytes). As a general rule, you don't want pictures to be large, more than about 50K, and preferably much smaller, especially if you're going to use several on your auction page. The larger the picture is in kilobytes, the longer the auction page will take to load and the more likely people are to leave your auction before the images load—which means fewer bidders.

140

Browse through the pictures until you find one you want, and click to select it.

4 Enlarge the Picture

Click the See **full-size image** link directly under the picture to enlarge it. When you do, the image, full-size, appears alone in your browser window.

▶ **TIP**

You should not use a copyrighted image from the Web without first asking permission to use the picture. It can be very difficult to determine whether a picture is copyrighted, however. At a minimum, send a note to the person in charge of the website, telling him that you plan to use the image in an eBay auction and asking whether the image is copyrighted. The best way to find contact information is through the **Contact Us** link or section found on most websites.

5 Save the Picture to Your Hard Disk

When you find a picture you are considering using in your auction, save it to your hard disk. Do this by first enlarging the picture, as detailed in step 4. Then right-click the picture and select **Save Picture As** from the context menu. The **Save Picture** dialog box appears. Browse to the folder where you want the picture saved and click **Save**. Consider creating separate picture folders for each of your auctions as a way to keep them organized.

When saving your picture, give it a descriptive name by typing the name into the **File Name** box in the **Save Picture** dialog box. Typically, the names of files on websites are incomprehensible—filenames such as `153580-elec_lg-resized200.jpg`—and you'll want a more descriptive filename than that.

6 Go to the Manufacturer's Website

If you know the manufacturer of the goods you're selling, consider going straight to its website instead of using Google to find pictures. Many manufacturers post marketing photographs and photos from online manuals. When you find a picture you want to use, save it as outlined in step 5.

---

141 Edit the Picture

✔ BEFORE YOU BEGIN	→ SEE ALSO
139 Set Up and Take a Picture	**134** Add Pictures to Your Auction
140 Use the Web to Get a Digital Picture	

141

No matter how good a photographer you are, you'll most likely have to edit your picture before you post it on your auction page. Perhaps you didn't frame it perfectly, or the lighting is off, or you have to reduce or enlarge it—there are many reasons you might have to edit the photo you've taken.

Many software products can help you edit your images, but for the balance between ease of use and power, you can't do better than Paint Shop Pro. This graphics editor offers a powerful set of editing tools, yet it is surprisingly easy to use. And it even includes one-click picture clean-ups to make editing photos even easier.

You can try the program for free before deciding whether you want to buy it. Go to **www.jasc.com** and download the trial version. If you decide to keep it, you have to pay $80–$100, depending on how you buy it. You can buy it straight from the Web or from retail outlets, and the price of the application varies from place to place.

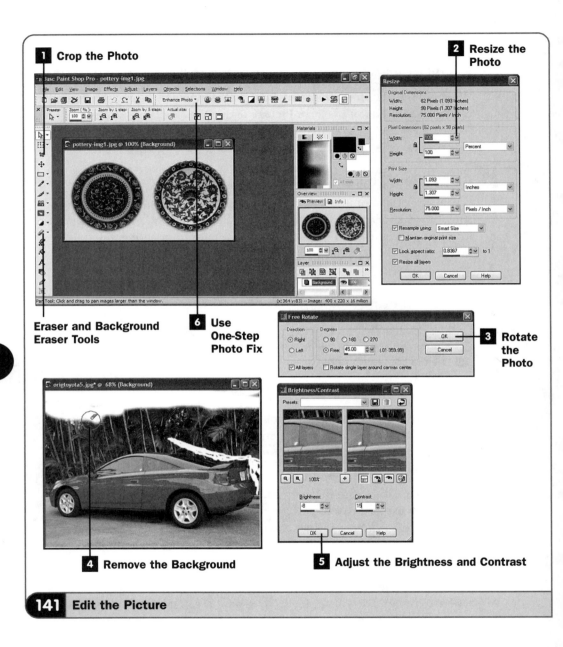

1 Crop the Photo

2 Resize the Photo

Eraser and Background Eraser Tools

6 Use One-Step Photo Fix

3 Rotate the Photo

141

4 Remove the Background

5 Adjust the Brightness and Contrast

141 Edit the Picture

Another excellent choice is Adobe Photoshop Elements. You can try the program for free before deciding whether you want to buy it. Go to http://www.adobe.com/products/photoshopelwin/main.html and download the trial version. If you decide to keep it, you have to pay $99.99. You can buy it straight from the Web or from retail outlets; the price of the application varies from place to place.

If you want a less-powerful but lower-priced piece of software, try LView Pro, which costs $39 without a manual or $70 with a manual. You can also try it for free before deciding to buy it (visit **www.lview.com**). You can buy LView Pro directly from the website.

Editing photos can be very complicated, but here I cover the most basic tasks you'll use for preparing a photo for posting on eBay.

▶ TIP

Paint Shop Pro has an incredible number of tools for editing graphics and photos. To learn about all of them, get *Paint Shop Pro in a Snap* (published by Sams Publishing).

1 Crop the Photo

Probably the most common problem when taking digital photos or using digital photos is that the picture hasn't been framed properly. Perhaps it takes up only part of the screen or isn't centered. Or maybe you've gotten a photo that has several items in it and you're selling only one of them, so you want to get rid of the rest of the images. In all these cases, you have to *crop* the photo.

▶ KEY TERM

Crop—To take out sections of a photograph, leaving behind only the part of the photo you want to remain.

To crop the photo, first launch Paint Shop Pro. Open the image file by clicking the **Open** icon and choosing the photo from the folder where you've stored it. Then click the **Crop** tool in the toolbar on the left side of the screen. In the image area, click and drag the **Crop** tool to draw a rectangle around the area you want to remain. When you release the mouse button, a box appears around the area you're defining. You can move the box by dragging any of the small square handles on the box.

▶ TIP

When you crop a photo, you permanently remove the parts of the photo outside the crop area. Before cropping a photo, you should make a copy of the image file so you have the original if you're not pleased with the crop.

When you're satisfied with the crop area you've defined, double-click the image. Click **Save** to save the newly edited image.

141

❷ Resize the Photo

Another common problem is that the photo is too large or too small to fit on the auction page. In that case, you have to resize the image. To resize an image, open it in Paint Shop Pro and then select **Image**, **Resize** from the menu or press **Shift+S**.

The **Resize** dialog box appears. In the **Pixel Dimensions** area, click the up arrow next to the **Width** or **Height** label. When you click the up arrow, you enlarge your photo size; when you click the down arrow, you reduce the photo size. Note that the width and height measurements are locked—if you change one dimension, the other changes automatically so that you don't distort the image.

Finding the exact size of a photo in inches is easy to do in Paint Shop Pro. With the image open, select **Image**, **Image Information** from the menu bar; you are shown the image size in pixels as well as in inches.

▶ **NOTE**

When you click **Width** or **Height**, you reduce the photo size by a percent—for example, if you select **105**, you're making the photo 105% of its original size. If you want to instead change by pixels, click the drop-down **Percent** box and select **Pixels**.

141

When your photo is of the size you want, click **OK** to close the dialog box and resize the photo.

❸ Rotate the Photo

Sometimes you need to turn your camera sideways to fit in the entire item, or for some other reasons, the photo is rotated improperly. You can easily fix that in Paint Shop Pro. Open the image file and select **Image**, **Rotate**. If you want to rotate the image clockwise 90°, select **Rotate Clockwise 90**; if you want to rotate the image counterclockwise 90°, select **Rotate Counter-clockwise 90**; if you want to rotate the image in any other direction, select **Free Rotate**. In the **Free Rotate** dialog box that opens, select the direction in which you want to rotate the picture, specify the number of degrees you want to rotate it, and click **OK**.

❹ Remove the Background

You might have taken a photograph of the item that includes a distracting background. With Paint Shop Pro, you can easily remove the background to create a photograph that includes only the item itself. Open the photo file in Paint Shop Pro and select the **Background Eraser** tool from the **Tool** palette on the left side of the screen. (The **Background Eraser** tool might be hidden under the **Eraser** tool, so click the arrow next to the **Eraser** tool to see the **Background Eraser** tool.)

A menu appears across the top of the screen, allowing you to change a variety of options for how to use the **Background Eraser** tool, including how large to make the tool itself, the shape of the tool, and similar options. Until you're more familiar with the tool, leave those options as is. However, to make erasing easy, you might want to use a large eraser when erasing large areas and a small eraser when you need to erase the areas directly surrounding the item. To change the size of the eraser, click the up and down arrows next to the **Size** box.

After you're done erasing the background, save the file.

5 Adjust the Brightness and Contrast

Brightness and contrast are major problems for many photos. The photo you took might be too bright or too dark; it might not have enough contrast or too much contrast. To adjust the brightness and contrast, open the photo file in Paint Shop Pro and press **Shift+B**. The **Brightness/Contrast** dialog box appears. The left side of the dialog box shows a portion of the original image; the right side shows the same image, but this version changes as you change the brightness and contrast settings in the dialog box. (With the side-by-side comparison, you can see the results as you work.) To change the brightness and contrast, click the up and down arrows next to **Brightness** and **Contrast**. When you're done, click **OK**.

141

If you want to have Paint Shop Pro automatically adjust the brightness and contrast for you, select **Adjust**, **Brightness and Contrast**, **Automatic Contrast Enhancement**. The **Automatic Contrast Enhancement** dialog box appears. Click **OK** to use Paint Shop Pro's recommended settings. (You can also adjust the settings in this dialog box; when you're done, click **OK**.)

6 Use One-Step Photo Fix

Photos can have a wide variety of problems beyond brightness and contrast, such as ragged edges and images and more. It can be difficult and time-consuming to fix them all yourself. Paint Shop Pro offers a one-step photo fix that fixes them all for you automatically. Open the photograph file in Paint Shop Pro, click the **Enhance Photo** button, and select **One Step Photo Fix**. The fixes are all automatically made to your photo. Save the photo after the changes have been made.

142 Make the Picture Web Friendly

✔ BEFORE YOU BEGIN	→ SEE ALSO
141 Edit the Picture	**143** About Posting Pictures with the eBay Picture Service
	144 About Using External Hosting for Your eBay Auction Pictures

Editing your photo is only the first step in preparing your photo for eBay. You must also make the picture web friendly. The photo must be in a specific web-friendly format and must not be so large that it takes too long for people to download. Paint Shop Pro offers a great set of tools for making your photo ready for the Web.

1 Use a Web-Friendly Palette

When people browse the Web, their monitors do not necessarily display colors and pictures accurately, because of variations in monitors and computer graphics systems. But you can use a web-friendly *palette* made up of colors designed to display properly on the Web, no matter what computer is viewing those photos.

142

▶ KEY TERM

Palette—A group of colors used in a picture. Not all the colors in the palette are necessarily used in the picture, but the picture can use only the colors in the palette and no colors outside the palette.

Paint Shop Pro can change any picture so it uses only colors from a web-friendly palette. Open the picture file in Paint Shop Pro; then select **Image, Decrease Color Depth** from the menu. From the submenu, select **256 Colors (8 bit)**. When the **Decrease Color Depth** dialog box appears, select **Standard/Web Safe** and click **OK**.

2 Resize the Image

Be careful that your picture isn't so large that it takes up too much of your auction page. As a general rule, it shouldn't be more than 400 pixels wide. See **141** **Edit the Picture** for information on how to resize your image in Paint Shop Pro.

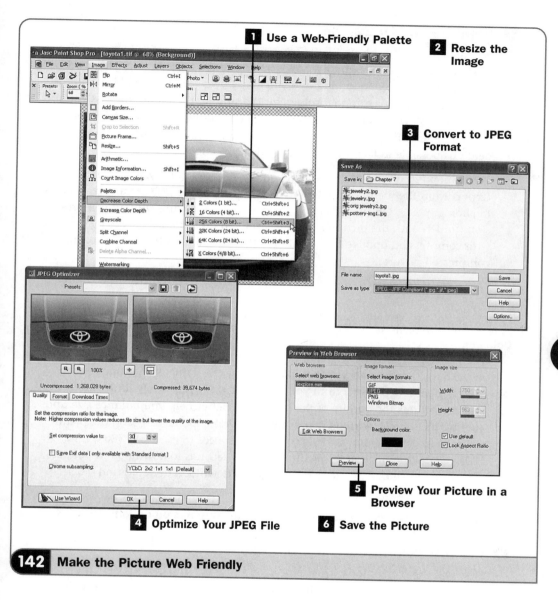

1 Use a Web-Friendly Palette

2 Resize the Image

3 Convert to JPEG Format

4 Optimize Your JPEG File

5 Preview Your Picture in a Browser

6 Save the Picture

142

142 Make the Picture Web Friendly

3 Convert to JPEG Format

The JPEG format is best for posting photos on the Web. If your picture is in another format, convert it to JPEG by selecting **File, Save As**. In the **Save As** dialog box that appears, select **JPEG – JFIF Compliant (*.jpg, *.jif, *.jpeg)** from the **Save as type** drop-down list, and name the file. The original file remains in its original format, but you'll save a new image file in the JPEG format.

4 Optimize Your JPEG File

When creating your photo file for use on the Web, you must balance file size in kilobytes and picture quality. Make the photo too large in kilobytes, and the page takes too long to load and you chase away potential bidders who won't wait for the picture to display. But the smaller the photo, the less detail, and you don't want a photograph of such poor quality that bidders are put off by it. Paint Shop Pro can compress the photo while retaining as much detail as possible to let you balance the two conditions.

Paint Shop Pro offers tools for balancing file size and quality. Select **File, Export** from the menu and select **JPEG Optimizer**. The **JPEG Optimizer** dialog box appears. On the left side is a portion of the picture without compression (underneath the picture is the file size). On the right side is the picture with compression applied to it (underneath that image is the file size of the compressed picture).

▶ **TIP**

Paint Shop Pro can also optimize other web-friendly graphics formats, including GIF and PNG. To optimize them, select **File, Export** and then select **JPEG Optimizer** or **GIF Optimizer**.

142

In the **Set Compression Value to** box, change the value of the compression (the number is a percent) until you find a file size—preferably under 50KB—that still retains the quality of the picture. To better help you balance size and quality, click the **Download Times** tab. That tab reports how long the picture will take to download at various connection speeds (56K, 128K, 380K, and 720K). For example, a 46KB picture takes 8.3 seconds to download at 56K; 3.6 seconds to download at 128K; 1.2 seconds to download at 380K; and 0.6 seconds to download at 720K.

When you're satisfied with the results of your compression options, click **OK**.

5 Preview Your Picture in a Browser

How will the picture look when posted on the Web? You can preview the image you've been manipulating in your web browser. Select **View, Preview in Web Browser** from the menu. The **Preview in Web Browser** dialog box appears. In the **Web Browsers** section, select the browser you want to use to preview the picture. In the **Image Formats** section, select the format of the file you're previewing. Then click **Preview** to see the picture in a web browser the way auction visitors will see it. Close the browser window when you're done viewing.

6 Save the Picture

If you're not satisfied with the picture as it will appear on the Web, continue to work on the file as described in steps 1–4, and then preview the file again. When you're satisfied with the picture, select **File**, **Save** and save the file.

---

143 About Posting Pictures with the eBay Picture Service

✔ BEFORE YOU BEGIN	→ SEE ALSO
142 Make the Picture Web Friendly	**134** Add Pictures to Your Auction
	144 About Using External Hosting for Your eBay Auction Pictures

---

After you've created your photos, you need somewhere to post them. The image files must be on the Web somewhere so you can link to them from your auction page.

The simplest method is to use the eBay Picture Service. The service is built into eBay, accessible directly when you create an auction and is inexpensive—free for the first photo of an auction with marginal fees for every additional photo.

The price you pay is based on the number of pictures you use and the layout you choose in your auction listing. The first picture for each auction listing is free. Each additional picture costs $0.15.

143

▶ NOTE

You can include a maximum of six pictures per auction listing when using the eBay Picture Service.

In addition to the cost per picture, you can also choose special layouts that cost extra (the basic layout has no cost):

- A slideshow that rotates your pictures one after another costs $0.75.

- You can supersize your pictures for an extra $0.75. Supersized pictures display as normal-sized photos, but when someone clicks the **Supersize** link, the photos are displayed in large size, up to 880×600 pixels.

- You can add up to six pictures, supersize your pictures, and get **Gallery** exposure for $1.00 if you select the **Picture Pack** option when creating your auction. (The **Gallery** option gives your auction extra exposure, along with a picture, on eBay pages.)

▶ **NOTE**

If you want to supersize an image, the original image file must be at least 440×330 pixels. eBay can't supersize images that aren't at least that size.

Another bonus of using the eBay Picture Service is that you don't have to know HTML or use any special coding to include your pictures in your auction listing. You post the pictures straight from the create-auction page. For details, see **134** **Add Pictures to Your Auction**.

Your pictures are hosted for as long as your auction lasts. When the auction ends, the pictures are no longer available. Also note that if you upload a picture larger than 400×300 pixels, eBay automatically resizes the picture to 400×300 pixels. The exception is for supersized pictures, which can be displayed up to 880×600 pixels when they're clicked.

---

144 | **About Using External Hosting for Your eBay Auction Pictures**

144

✔ **BEFORE YOU BEGIN**	→ **SEE ALSO**
142 Make the Picture Web Friendly	**134** Add Pictures to Your Auction
	143 About Posting Pictures with the eBay Picture Service

You can still use pictures in your auction listings if you don't use the eBay Picture Service. If you don't use the eBay service, you must find an external picture-hosting service. That means you upload your picture to the hosting service and then include a link to that picture's web location from your auction listing using HTML codes. For details on how to do it, see **134** **Add Pictures to Your Auction**.

Before deciding whether to use an external hosting service, consider these pros and cons:

- You can't use the features of the eBay Picture Service if you host your own pictures. That means you won't be able to use the slideshow or supersize features on your auction page, as described in **143** **About Posting Pictures with the eBay Picture Service**.

- You'll have to pay extra for the eBay Picture Service if you use more than one picture; hosting your own pictures is frequently free. As you'll see later in this section, finding a site that gives you free hosting is easy.

- You can continually reuse pictures with your own hosting service; the eBay Picture Service requires you to upload the pictures for each new auction. When you use your own hosting service, you upload your photos and they stay on that server until you delete them. On the eBay Picture Service, the image files are automatically deleted when the auction ends.

- It's easier to use the eBay Picture Service than your own hosting service. You don't have to figure out how to upload your pictures because the upload process is built in to the auction-creation process.

- If you know HTML, you can control the placement of your photos better if you use your own hosting service. The eBay Picture Service has several set treatments of pictures; you can't deviate from these arrangements. If you know HTML and host your own image, on the other hand, you can customize your picture treatment.

Let's say you've decided to use your own hosting service. How to find one? It's easier than you might think. Try these resources:

- Check with your Internet service provider (ISP). You might not realize it, but many ISPs include storage space as part of your monthly fee. Not uncommonly, you'll have up to 10MB of free server space, which is more than you'll ever need for pictures of auction items.

- Use America Online's **My FTP Space**. America Online includes free storage space as part of its basic service, so if you're a member, you have a place where you can place your picture files. Each screen name can have up to 4MB of storage space. Because you can have up to seven screen names on America Online, you can have up to 28MB of free storage space. For details, use the keywords **My FTP Space**.

- Use a free image-hosting service. There are several of these, including **www.villagephotos.com** and **www.picturetrail.com**. Visit these sites for details about how to sign up.

- Use a for-pay image-hosting service. A number of image-hosting services charge fees for membership and offer extra features not found with the free services, such as editing your photos for you. Among the for-pay services are **www.pongo.com** and **www.pixhost.com**.

▶ **TIP**

Generally, I find that the for-pay services don't offer enough extra features over the free services, such as your own ISP, to be worth paying the extra money.

How you upload your pictures to your hosting service varies from service to service, so see the specific service for details. However, as a general rule, most services allow you to directly upload the pictures yourself using FTP software. A good bet is to use the WS_FTP LE program from **www.ipswitch.com**, which is free for individuals.

143

21

Completing the Sale

IN THIS CHAPTER

You've created a successful auction: Someone has bought the goods. Now it's time to complete the sale, which isn't quite as simple as you might think. You must contact the buyer, arrange for payment, get paid, ship the goods, and pay eBay your seller fees—all the while ensuring that nothing goes wrong and that you don't get burned. The tasks in this chapter explain how to do it all.

145 Track Your Auction

✔ BEFORE YOU BEGIN	→ SEE ALSO
124 About Selling on eBay	**166** Manage Your Auctions with Auction Sentry
137 Review and Post Your Auction	

After you create your auction, you don't really have to do anything except wait until it closes. But what fun would that be? Part of the auction experience is the chase as well as collecting money, so if you're selling at least partially for fun, you'll want to track your auction as people bid.

Even if you're not tracking it for fun, you should know who your high bidder is. Here's how to track your auction and get details on the high bidder.

1 Go to My eBay

Your **My eBay** account includes automated tracking of all your auctions. This feature is particularly useful if you are selling items in more than one auction. To get to your **My eBay** page, click **My eBay** at the top of any eBay page. If you haven't already signed in to eBay, you are asked to provide your member ID and password before you can see your **My eBay** page.

2 Go to the Selling Section

My eBay tracks all your eBay activities, not just what you're selling. To see the live auctions you're currently hosting, click the **Selling** tab in **My eBay**. You see a list of all your current live auctions, including the starting price, current price, number of bids, start date, end date, and time left—in essence, all the relevant information about each auction.

▶ **TIP**

Under the list of your current auctions is a line of information totaling the starting price, current price, reserve price, quantity, and number of bids for all your auctions.

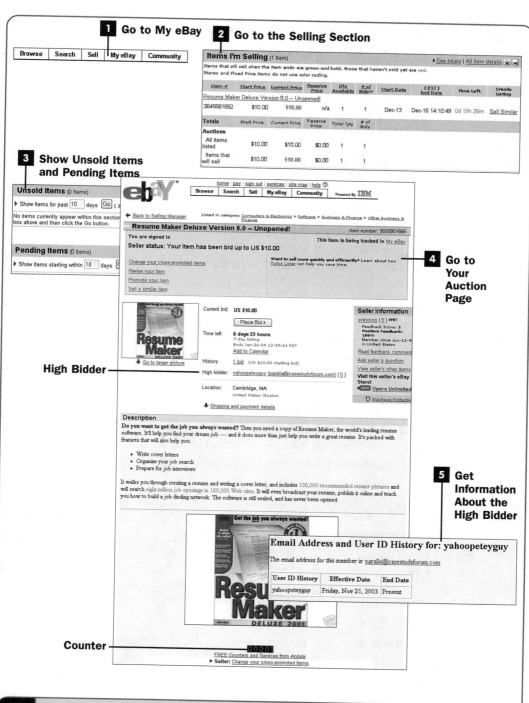

1 Go to My eBay   **2** Go to the Selling Section

| Browse | Search | Sell | My eBay | Community |

Items I'm Selling (1 Item)   ► See totals | All item details

Items that will sell when the item ends are green and bold, those that haven't sold yet are red. Stores and Fixed Price Items do not use color coding.

Item #	Start Price	Current Price	Reserve Price	Qty Available	# of Bids	Start Date	(PST) End Date	Time Left	Create Listing
Resume Maker Deluxe Version 8.0 -- Unopened!									
3645661692	$10.00	$10.00	n/a	1	1	Dec-13	Dec-16 14:10:49	0d 19h 29m	Sell Similar

Totals	Start Price	Current Price	Reserve Price	Total Qty	# of Bids
Auctions					
All items listed	$10.00	$10.00	$0.00	1	1
Items that will sell	$10.00	$10.00	$0.00	1	1

3 Show Unsold Items and Pending Items

Unsold Items (0 Items)

► Show items for past 10 days Go (

No items currently appear within this section box above and then click the Go button.

Pending Items (0 Items)

► Show items starting within 10 days (

home | pay | sign out | services | site map | help ⑦

ebaY | Browse | Search | Sell | My eBay | Community | Powered By IBM

◄ Back to Selling Manager   Listed in category: Computers & Electronics > Software > Business & Finance > Other Business & Finance

Resume Maker Deluxe Version 8.0 -- Unopened!   Item number: 3655801666

You are signed in
Seller status: Your item has been bid up to US $10.00   This item is being tracked in My eBay

Change your cross-promoted items
Revise your item   Want to sell more quickly and efficiently? Learn about how
Promote your item   Turbo Lister can help you save time.
Sell a similar item

4 Go to Your Auction Page

Current bid: US $10.00

   Place Bid ►

Time left: 6 days 23 hours
              7-day listing
              Ends Jan-26-04 13:45:14 PST
              Add to Calendar

High Bidder ──── History: 1 bid (US $10.00 starting bid)

High bidder: yahoopeteyguy (pgralla@casestudyforum.com) (0)

Location: Cambridge, MA
              United States /Boston

► Shipping and payment details

Seller information
prestong (8) me
Feedback Score: 8
Positive Feedback: 100%
Member since Jun-12-9
in United States
Read feedback comment
Ask seller a question
View seller's other items
Visit this seller's eBay Store!
Opera Unlimited
Purchase Protection

↓ Go to larger picture

Description

Do you want to get the job you always wanted? Then you need a copy of Resume Maker, the world's leading resume software. It'll help you find your dream job --- and it does more than just help you write a great resume. It's packed with features that will also help you:

• Write cover letters
• Organize your job search
• Prepare for job interviews

It walks you through creating a resume and writing a cover letter, and includes 100,000 recommended resume phrases and will search eight million job openings in 100,000 Web sites. It will even broadcast your resume, publish it online and teach you how to build a job-finding network. The software is still sealed, and has never been opened.

5 Get Information About the High Bidder

Email Address and User ID History for: yahoopeteyguy

The email address for this member is: pgralla@casestudyforum.com

User ID History	Effective Date	End Date
yahoopeteyguy	Friday, Nov 21, 2003	Present

Counter ──── 00001
FREE Counters and Services from Andale
► Seller: Change your cross-promoted items

145

145 Track Your Auction

3 Show Unsold Items and Pending Items

You can see a list of any unsold items (items you tried to sell at an auction but didn't sell) and your pending items (items you've scheduled to sell at a later date—in other words, items for which you completed the auction form but said that the auction should not start yet).

Scroll down to the **Unsold Items** and **Pending Items** sections of the **Selling** tab; in the text box, enter the number of past days for which you want to display unsold items (or the number of days in the future for which you want to see pending items) and click **Go**.

4 Go to Your Auction Page

The **Selling** tab of your **My eBay** page doesn't include who the current high bidder is for your auction. To find that information, go to your auction page. To get there, click the link to the auction in the **Items I'm Selling** section of the **Selling** tab.

Your auction page opens, and you see a message telling you the status of your auction—for example, that a new high bid has been entered. Scroll down the page until you see the name of the high bidder. You can also see how many people have visited your page if you've put a counter on the page. (For information about including counters, see **135 Choose Auction Extras**.)

5 Get Information About the High Bidder

For information about the high bidder, click the bidder's name where it appears on the auction page. You see the email address and user ID history, which tells you whether this bidder has previously changed her ID.

146

146 Contact the Buyer	
✔ **BEFORE YOU BEGIN**	→ **SEE ALSO**
145 Track Your Auction	**147** About Accepting Payments

Your auction's over and you have a high bidder. Now comes the good part: It's time to collect the money.

The first step in doing that is contacting the buyer. You should get in touch with the buyer immediately and make clear how you'll accept payment. This friendly exchange ensures that you get paid on time so you can ship the goods.

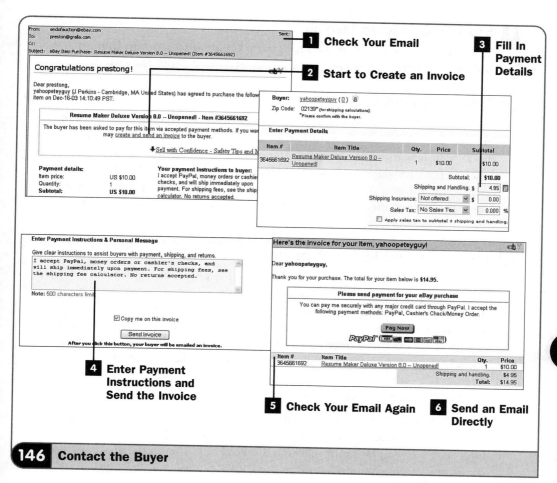

146 Contact the Buyer

1 Check Your Email

When the auction ends, you get an email from eBay informing you who the high bidder is. The email includes the auction title and identifying number; the user ID, real name, and email address of the high bidder; a link to the auction page; details about shipping that you filled in for the auction listing; and details about your payment instructions to the buyer.

▶ NOTE

When a buyer wins an auction, he gets a notification from eBay that he has won the auction, so it won't come as a surprise when you send him an email.

2 Start to Create an Invoice

The email you receive from eBay includes a **Create and Send an Invoice** link. If you want to create an invoice using eBay tools, click the link.

3 Fill In Payment Details

When you click the **Create and Send an Invoice** link, you are sent to a page that creates the invoice for you. The top part of the page includes information about how much is owed you. The eBay invoice tool fills in the final auction price as well as any flat-rate shipping price you entered when you created the auction. You can change the shipping price if you want, although you can't change the final auction price. You can also add shipping insurance and sales tax.

4 Enter Payment Instructions and Send the Invoice

The bottom part of the invoice form includes the payment instructions and space for a personal note you can include in the invoice. The payment instructions have been filled in already, taken directly from your auction page. You can reword them if you want; however, you can't change the actual way you'll accept payment. (If you said on your auction page that you accept personal checks, you can't now say that you don't accept personal checks.) Also, make it clear to the buyer that you won't ship the goods until you've received payment and the payment clears.

If you indicated that you accept *PayPal* payments when you created the auction, the eBay invoice you send to the buyer includes a **PayPal** button. The buyer can pay you by simply clicking the **PayPal** button in the email invoice she receives from you and following the PayPal payment instructions.

▶ **KEY TERM**

PayPal—A person-to-person service that lets people pay each other directly, using email and the Internet. You open a PayPal account and link that account to your credit card or bank. If you use PayPal to receive payments (if you're a seller), you can have PayPal send you a check for the payment you've received.

▶ **TIP**

At the bottom of the invoice page is a **Copy Me on This Invoice** check box. Enable the check box to receive a copy of the invoice you send to the buyer. Always enable this check box so that you have verification of when you sent the invoice to the buyer.

When you're done filling out the invoice form, click **Send Invoice**. The invoice is sent to the buyer—and a copy is sent to you if you enabled the **Copy Me on This Invoice** check box.

5 Check Your Email Again

Because you enabled the **Copy Me on This Invoice** check box (you *did* check that box, didn't you?), you get a copy of the email invoice that is sent to the buyer. Check your email immediately to ensure that the invoice is correct. If it contains any errors, immediately send an email to the buyer to let him know about the errors—and the corrections.

▶ **NOTE**

eBay asks that you send an invoice to the buyer within three days of the end of the auction.

6 Send an Email Directly

If you have your own personal invoice, or prefer to write your own email instead of sending an automated eBay invoice, you can send an email directly to the buyer and include payment information in that message. Use the email address for the buyer that appears when you click the high bidder's member ID on your auction page.

▶ **NOTE**

147

If you've given the buyer a choice of shipping methods, be sure to ask the buyer which shipping method she prefers when you send your email to her.

---

147 About Accepting Payments

✔ **BEFORE YOU BEGIN**

146 Contact the Buyer

Accepting payment sounds like the easiest part of the selling practice, but in fact there's a good deal you need to keep in mind. First, you should follow basic seller's etiquette when accepting payments, so you're more likely to get good feedback and word spreads through eBay that you're a good seller—and also so you don't get burned as a seller.

Money is a touchy issue with many people, and you want to be sure you get payment for your item. However, you also want to ensure that the buyer is satisfied with the process of paying you because you'll get bad feedback on eBay otherwise. Do the following, and you'll ensure that you get paid and that the buyer is happy with the transaction:

- **Be sure you get paid in advance, including for shipping charges**—As you learned in **136 Set Payment and Shipping Options**, you should have made clear on your auction that the buyer will pay for shipping. When you sent your email invoice to the buyer, you should also have explained that you require payment before you'll ship the item purchased. Wait until you get paid before shipping the goods—and you should get full payment, including shipping charges.

- **Ask that a description of the item accompany payment**—When someone pays you, you should get a description of the item along with the payment, including the auction number. Without this information, it is difficult to keep track of what the payment is for, especially if you sell items on several auctions. Make sure that the buyer also sends his mailing address.

▶ **NOTE**

Ideally, the buyer should forward or print the email invoice you sent to him because that invoice includes all the information you need to match a payment with a particular auction.

147

- **When the buyer contacts you to tell you payment is on the way, respond quickly**—Buyers are justifiably worried about who they're buying items from and will judge you according to how responsive you are to them. As soon as you get an email telling you that payment is on the way, send back a note thanking the buyer for the message and explaining that you'll be prompt in sending the item after the payment arrives (or, in the case of a personal check, as soon as the check has cleared the bank).

- **When the payment arrives, send a note to the buyer**—As we all know, things get lost in the mail, and the buyer will want to ensure that his check or money order arrived in good order. When you receive payment, promptly send a note to the buyer stating that. Also tell him when you'll be shipping the item so he'll know when to expect it. If the payment is by PayPal, send the note as soon as you receive payment.

▶ **TIP**

If you're going into business selling at auctions, you can set up a merchant account allowing you to directly accept credit card payments. That way, people who do not use PayPal can pay you using a credit card. Keep in mind that setting up a merchant account is not cheap and can eat into your profits. Some sites charge hundreds of dollars for a setup fee in addition to normal ongoing fees and per-transaction fees. So, it's only worthwhile if you're a heavy eBay seller.

▶ WEB RESOURCE

www.merchantaccount.com

www.interlinkmerchant.com

www.1stamericancardservice.com

You can set up a merchant account to accept credit card payments directly from any of these websites.

Money Orders and Cashier's Checks

For sellers, the ideal way of accepting payments is with PayPal. Payment is immediate and goes straight into your PayPal account. For details on how to sign up, go to **www.paypal.com**.

But if your buyer doesn't pay using PayPal, perhaps the second easiest way to accept payment is with money orders and cashier's checks. For sellers, these options are the gold standard because they're as good as cash and don't have any of the drawbacks of sending cash through the mail.

Keep in mind that cashier's checks can be forged; you shouldn't ship the goods until the check clears your bank and is deposited in your account. So, ship goods only after you actually see the money deposited in your account.

When you get a money order, it has an identification number. The buyer has a receipt that includes the identification number as well, so the check can be traced if there's a problem with it (and the seller can get a replacement for the money order if it's lost in the mail).

A money order is, in essence, cash. The seller has paid cash for it, and you can cash it at your bank or other financial institution. You don't have to wait for it to clear, as you do with a personal check. Instead, the money is yours immediately. Because of this, you should encourage buyers to pay using a money order. A good incentive is to promise to ship the goods within 24 hours of receiving the money order.

Cashier's checks are similar to money orders—they can be issued only when the person obtaining the cashier's check has enough money in the bank to cover the check. As a result, they're as good as cash—or almost. To ensure that the checks are not counterfeit, wait until you've deposited them and the money is actually credited to your account before shipping anything.

▶ TIP

Accepting money from international buyers is easy. If the buyer is in a different country, she can pay with an international money order. The buyer pays for the money order in her own currency. But when you get it, you can take it to your bank and have it converted into American dollars.

147

What You Need to Know About Accepting Personal Checks

Most buyers on auction sites prefer paying by personal check. They're the least trouble for most people because they don't have to go to a bank or post office to get a money order or cashier's check.

Because of the convenience factor for your buyers, you might have to accept personal checks instead of money orders or cashier's checks at your auction. If you say on your auction listing that you won't accept personal checks, you're conceivably cutting down on your potential audience, so you might decide to accept personal checks.

In general, the only issue you have accepting personal checks is that they can bounce. Because checks can bounce, never ship an item until a check clears. When you talk to the buyer about payment, make it clear that you won't ship an item until the check clears.

▶ **TIP**

A bank might report to you that a check has cleared even though the money is not yet in your account. So, before shipping an item, make sure that the money is actually in your account in two ways: Check your account online (if you have online access) and call the bank directly.

148

How to Deal with COD Payment

Another payment method preferred by some buyers is collect on delivery (COD). If you have a buyer who insists on COD, you should insist that he pay the extra COD. charge. When a buyer pays using COD, you ship the item as COD via the U.S. mail; when the buyer gets the item, he pays the postal service the price of your item plus the extra COD charges. The postal service in turn sends you the money (or a check) for the price of the item. Again, if a buyer insists on this form of payment, the buyer should pay the extra charges.

148	**About Accepting Escrow Service Payments**
✔ **BEFORE YOU BEGIN**	→ **SEE ALSO**
147 About Accepting Payments	**149** About Problem Buyers

If you're selling a big-ticket item such as a vehicle or a piece of jewelry, the buyer might want to use an *escrow service*. An escrow service serves as a go-between between you and the buyer. It assures the buyer that he won't get burned because the seller is paid only after the goods are received and accepted by the buyer. The buyer pays the escrow service, and the escrow service in turn pays the seller after the item has been received and inspected by the buyer.

▶ KEY TERM

Escrow services—A service that acts as a go-between in an auction, holding the buyer's money until he receives the items in good order.

It's clear why an escrow service is good for a buyer. But an escrow service is also good for sellers when selling a big-ticket item. It offers the following benefits for sellers:

- **It allows buyers to pay using a credit card**—Unless you've set up a special merchant account with a credit card company, buyers won't be able to pay you directly with a credit card. With escrow services, though, the buyer can pay the escrow service using a credit card, and the service in turn pays you. This convenience and assurance is important when big-ticket items are sold.

▶ NOTE

You need to pay special attention to how you ship items when you're dealing with an escrow service. The services often have strict shipping guidelines, including how you have to package the goods and which shipping companies you're allowed to use. So, when packing your item and arranging for shipping, be sure you are following the rules of the particular escrow service being used.

- **It ensures that you won't have to deal with bad checks or other payment headaches**—Bad checks are a particular problem. If you're paid with a bad check, not only do you not get the money for the item you sold, but banks also often charge a fee for depositing a bad check. Because the escrow service tells you to send the goods only after it receives valid payment, you won't ever have to deal with bad checks.

- **It insures your goods when you ship**—You won't have to arrange for shipping insurance because the escrow service does that for you.

148

Several escrow services are available that you can use, but eBay has a relationship with **www.escrow.com** that makes using that escrow service easy. Payment for using the service is steep, so use it only for big-ticket items. The minimum fee for a single-payment transaction is $22, and the fee varies according to the cost of the item and how the item is being paid for (see the following table).

Costs for Using www.escrow.com

Purchase Price	Check/Money Order	Credit Card	Wire Transfer
$0.01–$1,500	$22 + 0.5%	$22 + 3%	$37 + 0.5%
$1,500.01–$7,500	2.0%	4.5%*	$15 + 2%
$7,500.01–$20,000	1.75%	n/a*	$15 + 1.75%
$20,000.01+	1.5%	n/a*	$15 + 1.5%

Credit card payments are not accepted for over $7,500.

If a buyer wants to use an escrow service, make sure that it's clear who's paying the extra amount for the escrow service. In general, buyers pay for extra services on auction sites, so try to get the buyer to pay the whole amount. However, if you want to get a buyer to use the service, you might have to pay for part or all of the fee.

Paying for an item through an escrow service is a simple process. The following is a step-by-step look at how an escrow service works:

1. The buyer and seller agree that payment will be made using an escrow service and agree who will bear the extra costs of the service.

2. The buyer pays the escrow service the final bidding price of the item, plus the escrow fee (if that was what was agreed to in step 1).

3. The escrow service tells the seller that it has received payment.

4. The seller ships the goods to the buyer.

5. The buyer receives the goods and tells the escrow service that the goods arrived and are what was promised.

6. The escrow service pays the seller. If the buyer and seller agreed that the seller would bear some or all of the extra escrow costs, the seller pays that money to the escrow service.

148

When You Should Use an Escrow Service

An escrow service helps make buying and selling at auctions more secure. But it does add costs to every transaction for which it's used. You shouldn't use escrow services for every transaction—and, in fact, you shouldn't use escrow services for most transactions. When should you use an escrow service, and when shouldn't you? The following is a list of things you need to know:

- **Don't use escrow services for low-cost items, especially if the buyer has positive feedback**—Because of high escrow costs, using an escrow service for low-cost items doesn't make sense, especially if the bidder and seller both have positive track records.

- **If you and the buyer have dealt with each other in the past, you might not need to use an escrow service**—If you've done business with someone else on an auction site frequently, you probably won't need an escrow service when dealing with that person again. However, if it's a big-ticket item, you're still taking a chance if you don't use an escrow service.

▶ **TIP**

An escrow service works well when an overseas buyer wants to pay you in his own currency. The buyer pays the escrow service, and the escrow service pays you in U.S. currency.

You sign up for an escrow service like you do for any other web service—by providing basic information about yourself such as your name, address, and email address. Both buyers and sellers sign up the same way. After you establish an account, you fill out a form every time you want to have a new escrow transaction. The form includes information such as who will pay the escrow fee, who will pay for shipping, the item being sold, and other basic information. All communications are done through email with the escrow service.

149	About Problem Buyers

✔ BEFORE YOU BEGIN	→ SEE ALSO
Just jump right in.	147 About Accepting Payments
	148 About Accepting Escrow Service Payments

149

In the vast majority of cases, you won't run into trouble when accepting payment for an item. But there's a chance that you will. You might have to deal with bounced checks or high bidders who simply won't pay up or respond to your email after they've won the auction. In this section, you learn how to handle these kinds of problems.

How to Handle Bad Checks

When someone sends you a personal check for payment, it might be a bad one and bounce. That's bad on two counts. First, you haven't gotten your money for the auction. Secondly, banks often charge a fee for depositing the bad check.

If you receive a bad check, don't assume the worst—that the buyer was trying to scam you. Instead, send a polite note to the buyer, telling him that his check didn't clear the bank and informing him that you'd like him to send another check and to reimburse you for the bad-check fee your bank charged you. In most instances, this should clear up the problem—the buyer will be more embarrassed than anything else and will send along payment.

▶ **NOTE**

If you get a bad check and ask for repayment, make sure that the buyer doesn't send another personal check—it may well bounce a second time. Instead, have the buyer send a guaranteed form of payment, such as PayPal or a cashier's check.

You might get a buyer who tries to convince you to send the item anyway, saying that he'll send the check immediately. Don't do it. Send the item only after you've received a good check and received reimbursement for the bad one.

► **TIP**

Make clear to the buyer that you don't want cash. Cash is bad because it can be stolen or lost when it's sent through the postal service, and there's no paper trail to follow should a dispute arise between buyer and seller. So, make it clear that you don't accept cash.

If, after some back-and-forth, the buyer doesn't send a good check and reimburse you for the bad one, it's time to cut your losses. Send a polite but firm note saying you want full payment and reimbursement and that, if you don't get it, you'll cancel the high bid, leave negative feedback about the buyer on eBay, and perhaps even take other action. Give the buyer a specific time period in which to send the money. If you don't get it, leave negative feedback. You can then either inform the second-highest bidder (click the **X Bids** link next to **History** on the closed auction listing) that the item is available to her for sale or ask eBay to reimburse the fee you paid for listing the item. Some auction sites, including eBay, reimburse you for a variety of reasons, including receiving a bad check. You won't get back the full amount of what you paid, but you'll get back a portion of it. I show you how to do so in "How to Get Reimbursed If There Are Payment Problems," later in this task.

149

What to Do If the Buyer Never Responds to You

In some instances, the buyer might not respond to your emails so there's no way for you to get payment. If the buyer doesn't respond to your first note, follow up with a second one several days later. Then try a third message a week after that.

► **NOTE**

Some buyers might be more casual about checking and replying to their email than sellers are. Some people (like me) check their email frequently throughout the day, whereas other people check their email only once every few days. If you don't hear back from a buyer within a few days of your sending an email message, it could simply mean that he hasn't checked his email recently and not that he's avoiding contact with you.

Warn the buyer that if you don't hear back within a certain amount of time, you're canceling his bid and leaving negative feedback about him on eBay. If you don't hear back, do what you do when dealing with someone who won't make good on a bad check: Inform the second-highest bidder (click the **X Bids** link next to **History** on the closed auction listing to find the ID of the second-highest bidder) that the item is available for sale at the price at which that bidder dropped out, or get eBay to reimburse you for the fee you paid for listing the item.

How to Get Reimbursed If There Are Payment Problems

If you have payment problems, don't despair: eBay will reimburse your *final value fee* if you have a non-paying bidder. (You still have to pay for all the other costs in the auction listing, though.) To get the credit, follow these steps:

▶ **KEY TERM**

Final value fee—The fee you'll pay only if your item sells on eBay. If the item doesn't sell, you're not charged this fee.

1. Wait between 7 and 45 days after the auction ends and file a **Non-Paying Buyer Alert** form with eBay.

2. Continue trying to get payment from the buyer for 10 days after you file the **Non-Paying Buyer Alert** form.

3. If the buyer still doesn't send money, file a **Final Value Fee Credit Request** form with eBay, and your final value fee will be reimbursed.

For more information about these forms—along with links to the forms—go to http://pages.ebay.com/help/basics/f-npb.html.

150

150 Ship the Goods

✔ BEFORE YOU BEGIN	→ SEE ALSO
136 Set Payment and Shipping Options	**167** Handle Shipping with Shippertools.com

New sellers at auctions think a lot about how to create auctions that sell, and they certainly enjoy accepting payment. But the odds are that they spend little time, if any at all, preparing to ship the items they've sold.

Don't let yourself fall into that trap. For sellers, shipping can be the most important part of the deal in many ways. If the goods are damaged or lost en route to the buyer, or if they're late getting there, you can end up with an unhappy buyer, be in a situation where you are forced to reimburse the buyer, and end up with bad ratings on eBay. If this happens, you'll have a very short life, indeed, as a successful auctioneer. So follow these steps for shipping:

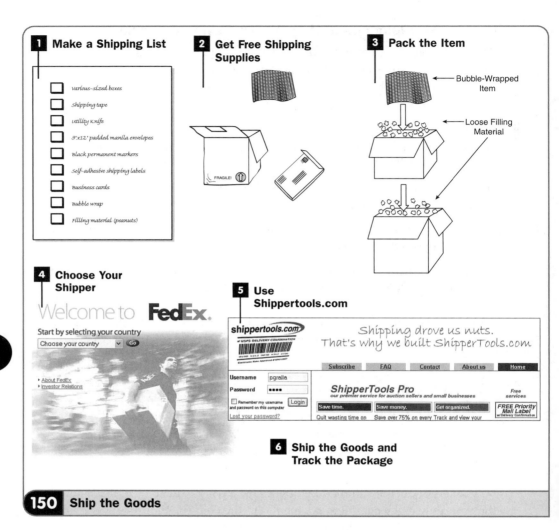

1 **Make a Shipping List**

- various-sized boxes
- shipping tape
- utility knife
- 9"x12" padded manila envelopes
- Black permanent markers
- self-adhesive shipping labels
- Business cards
- Bubble wrap
- Filling material (peanuts)

2 **Get Free Shipping Supplies**

FRAGILE!

3 **Pack the Item**

Bubble-Wrapped Item

Loose Filling Material

4 **Choose Your Shipper**

Welcome to **FedEx.**

Start by selecting your country

Choose your country   Go

▸ About FedEx
▸ Investor Relations

5 **Use Shippertools.com**

shippertools.com

Shipping drove us nuts.
That's why we built ShipperTools.com

Subscribe   FAQ   Contact   About us   Home

Username pgralla
Password ••••

☐ Remember my username and password on this computer   Login
Lost your password?

ShipperTools Pro
our premier service for auction sellers and small businesses

Free services

Save time.   Save money.   Get organized.   FREE Priority Mail Label w/Delivery Confirmation on

Quit wasting time on   Save over 75% on every   Track and view your

6 **Ship the Goods and Track the Package**

150

150 **Ship the Goods**

1 Make a Shipping List

Although the types of supplies you need to keep on hand vary according to what you're shipping, here's a good starting point. Keep these items on hand and you'll be well prepared for most kinds of shipping:

- Various-sized boxes
- Clear shipping tape
- Utility knife
- 9"×12" manila envelopes

- Black permanent markers

- Self-adhesive shipping labels

- Business cards, if you have any

- Bubble wrap

- Filling material, such as Styrofoam peanuts

2 Get Free Shipping Supplies

One of the hidden costs of selling items is the cost of shipping supplies. All those boxes, packing tape, and other things you need can add up pretty quickly. But there are ways to get them for free—or at least inexpensively.

Before buying supplies, see what you have around the house that can be recycled. Almost anything you buy new will be packed in a box, so save those boxes. If space is a problem where you live, and you can't store all the boxes, take off the tape holding the boxes together and fold the boxes flat. You can store many boxes when they're flat.

One of the best places to get no-cost supplies is your place of work. Don't take new supplies home and use them. But at most offices, an enormous amount of material, such as boxes, is thrown away. Office supplies, computers, software, printers, and other office equipment come in boxes that are usually discarded. Much of this material makes great shipping containers. Check for boxes that are being thrown away, Styrofoam-packing peanuts, bubble wrap, oversized heavy-duty envelopes, and anything else that looks like it will do the trick.

150

▶ TIP

Before taking anything home from the office, of course, check to ensure that you're allowed to do so. In fact, if you check with your office manager and tell her what you plan to do, you can make an arrangement to take as much of the discards home as you can on a regular basis.

If you buy goods through mail-order suppliers or over the Web—or if you buy at auctions—you have a ready-made supply of materials. Don't throw away the boxes, bubble wrap, peanuts, and similar items you receive when things are delivered to you through the mail.

Ask friends to save the supplies for you as well. Yes, you might have to swallow your pride a little when asking, but they'll be happy to comply. After all, what are friends for?

▶ **TIP**

Retail stores in your town or neighborhood are good sources of supplies as well. In particular, they have many boxes they throw away on a regular basis.

When recycling shipping supplies like this, be sure that the boxes or supplies are in good shape. Carefully examine the boxes to ensure that they're not torn or worn and that they're still sturdy enough to protect the goods you're shipping. The U.S. Postal Service requires that any markings on boxes you reuse for shipping must be completely obliterated with permanent markers. When looking for boxes to recycle, keep in mind that boxes with fewer markings are better.

Also, check with your shipper to see what they supply. Many shippers supply a wide range of free items. The U.S. Postal Service, for example, provides some kinds of free supplies when you ship using Priority Mail and Express Mail. Services such as Airborne Express and Federal Express also offer free packaging. Check at your local post office or call your shipping company.

You won't always be able to get free supplies from your office, home, or shippers. In that case, you must pay for them. Your local office supply store is well stocked and is a good place to turn. Also, look for stores such as Mailboxes Etc. (which are being converted to UPS Stores) that specialize in shipping goods—they always have a big selection of shipping supplies. You can reach the company on the Internet at **www.mbe.com**.

150

▶ **WEB RESOURCE**

www.staples.com

www.officedepot.com

You can order shipping supplies online at office supply sites such as these.

3 **Pack the Item**

All your great work in creating an auction that sells can be destroyed by improperly packing the item you're shipping—if you're not careful, the item can arrive damaged. Follow this advice for how to pack items for shipping:

- **Always assume that packages will be dropped, thrown, and man-handled**—For everything you ship, use more packaging material rather than less to keep the item safe.

- **Ship fragile items in a box inside a box**—If you're shipping glass, pottery, or similarly fragile items, use the two-box method. First, wrap the fragile item in bubble wrap or a similar material. Then put it in a box filled with peanuts or a similar protective material and seal the box. Put that box, in turn, inside a larger box filled with peanuts or protective material. Finally, seal and address the larger box.

▶ TIP

Selling isn't just about making a single sale; it's about developing relationships. So, include a note with the item you ship, thanking the buyer for payment and including your contact information and a business card. It will go a long way toward making future sales.

- **Put goods such as Beanie Babies inside a sealed, protective plastic bag, and buy a tag protector to protect the tag**—Beanie collectors prize tags that are as new looking as possible. Then protect the bagged item with peanuts or similar filling material inside a box. Seal and address the box.

- **Put collectible cards such as baseball cards and Pokémon cards inside special hard, protective sleeves before shipping them**—These specially designed sleeves ensure that the cards aren't damaged when they're shipped. Still, pack protective material around the sleeves or ship them in a shipping envelope that contains protective material to ensure that no damage occurs.

- **Protect flat items such as photographs and small posters by placing them between two pieces of sturdy cardboard**—You don't want the items to be bent when they're shipped.

- **Ship posters in cardboard tubes**—Cardboard tubes do a good job of protecting posters. The posters might be curled when they arrive, but they'll soon flatten out.

4 Choose Your Shipper

You can choose from many shippers, including the U.S. Postal Service (**www.usps.gov**), Federal Express (**www.fedex.com**), Airborne Express (**www.airborne.com**), and United Parcel Service (**www.ups.com**), among others. Although there are differences among them, those differences aren't dramatic enough to make one much better than another—here's an instance where your personal preference should take precedence. Take into account how convenient the shipper is to you, whether it'll pick up from your house, and similar things. Depending on where and what you're shipping, the rates of all the carriers vary.

150

▶ **TIP**

If the buyer has a P.O. box, you have to ship using the U.S. Postal Service because most shipping companies, including United Parcel Service and Federal Express, don't ship to post office boxes.

Whichever shipper you choose, be sure that the shipper lets you track the status of your package and has a return-receipt service, so you'll know when the goods are delivered. Also, be aware that the method you choose to ship should take into account the buyer's preferences as well. If the buyer lives in an area that a particular delivery service doesn't go to or that causes difficulty in some other way for the buyer, you need to use a different method of shipment. And keep in mind that if, on your auction page, you let potential bidders know you're flexible in how you'll ship items, you're more likely to attract bidders and thus get higher prices on your items.

▶ **TIP**

Make sure that the shipping costs you list on your auction page are accurate. To ensure they're accurate, buy a low-cost shipping scale from an office supply store. Then weigh the item along with the packaging in which you'll ship it. After you know the weight of the item and packing material, get the shipping price using eBay's shipping tools as detailed in **136** Set Payment and Shipping Options.

151

5 Use Shippertools.com

The most efficient way to handle the entire shipping end of the transaction is by using an online site such as **www.shippertools.com**. For details on how to use it, see **167** Handle Shipping with Shippertools.com.

6 Ship the Goods and Track the Package

Now comes the easy part—ship the goods. Bring the packaged item to the post office or shipping company, or have a company pick it up at your residence or place of business. Get a receipt so you can track your package; most shippers let you track your packages online.

---

151 **Pay the eBay Fees**

✔ BEFORE YOU BEGIN	→ SEE ALSO
127 Determine Your Selling Price and Estimate Your Selling Fees	**137** Review and Post Your Auction

The auction is over—well, not quite. You still have to pay your auction fees. Don't be tempted to skip payment; if you do, you'll be kicked off eBay. For information about the various fees, see **127** **Determine Your Selling Price and Estimate Your Selling Fees**.

1 Go to Your Seller Account Page

Go to your **Seller Account** page by clicking **My eBay** and then clicking the **Accounts** tab. You are shown the amount of money you owe to eBay for all your auctions combined (if you haven't paid your fees for them all).

2 View Account Status

Before paying eBay, make sure it hasn't made a mistake in figuring your selling fees. Click the **View Account Status** link, and fill out the form asking for the time period you want to view your seller account. Include the dates of your most recent auctions so you can check on them. Click the **Submit** button. You come to a page that summarizes your account activity and provides details on any outstanding fees you owe. Scroll to the bottom of the page to see your auction fees.

3 Pay Your Selling Fees

You have four options by which to pay your eBay fees: PayPal, your checking account, your credit card, or a money order. Click the appropriate link in the **Pay Your eBay Seller Fees** area on the **Accounts** tab and follow the directions for paying.

▶ NOTE

When you pay using your checking account, you don't actually write a check. Instead, you fill in information about your checking account and money is automatically withdrawn from it. You pay by credit card by filling in information about the card. When you click the link to mail a check or money order, you are sent to a page with information about your auction, including how much is due. Print that page, detach the bottom portion, and send it in with your check or money order.

4 Make Sure That Your Payment Went Through

If you paid your fees using an instant payment method such as PayPal or your credit card, the payment should go through immediately and no outstanding balance should be owed to eBay. Go back to your **My eBay Accounts** page and make sure that the **Pay Your eBay Seller Fees** box is empty.

151

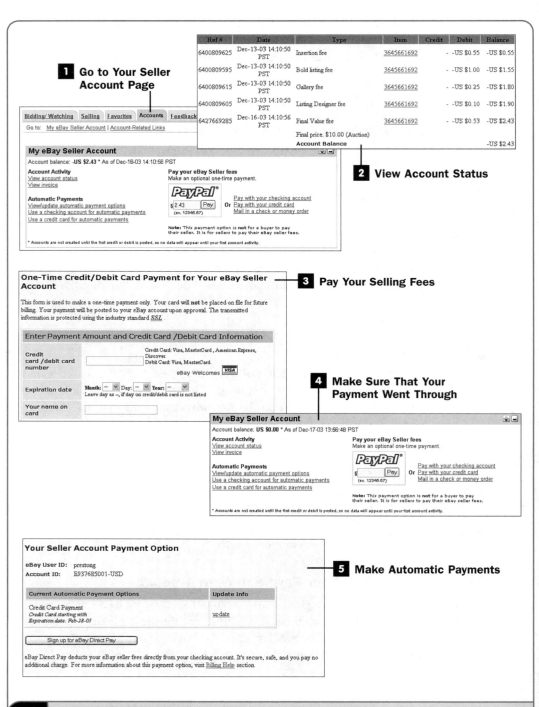

1 Go to Your Seller Account Page

2 View Account Status

3 Pay Your Selling Fees

4 Make Sure That Your Payment Went Through

5 Make Automatic Payments

151

5 Make Automatic Payments

Forgetting to make your eBay payments is easy, so you can set up your seller account so you pay eBay automatically every month by arranging for the site to take money from either your checking account or your credit card account. To sign up, click the **Use a Checking Account for Automatic Payments** or **Use a Credit Card for Automatic Payments** link on your **My eBay Accounts** page and fill in the forms. After you're done, if you want to check that automatic payment has been enabled or change the way you pay automatically, click the **View/Update Automatic Payment Options** link on your **My eBay Accounts** page.

151

22

Advanced Tools for Sellers

IN THIS CHAPTER:

Anyone can find an item to sell and then create an auction—the basics are fairly straightforward. But not everyone can create an auction that sells. Or two auctions that sell. Or more. If you get serious about selling on eBay, you need to get serious about the tools you use.

In this chapter, you learn about a variety of tools that can help you create better auctions, ranging from tools provided by eBay to HTML tags you can use to dress up your auction pages.

152 About Advanced Seller's Tools

✔ BEFORE YOU BEGIN	→ SEE ALSO
124 About Selling on eBay	**145** Track Your Auction
137 Review and Post Your Auction	

152

You'll find a variety of tools to help you sell better on eBay. Some, such as Turbo Lister and Selling Manager, are available directly from eBay, either on the site itself or as a download. But other types of tools are available as well, such as using a knowledge of HTML to add colors and fonts to your auction or knowing the basics of how to write ad copy that sells.

▶ TIP

If you have items you want to sell but don't want to have to sell them yourself on eBay, there's now a way to do it. In fact, you don't even need an Internet connection. Instead, you can pay one of a variety of services that take your goods, create an eBay auction, and complete the sale for you, all in return for a fee. Among the services that do this are **www.auctiondrop.com** and **www.quikdrop.com**.

When using these selling tools, keep in mind that the best tools won't help you if you don't have something good to sell and aren't smart about setting the right price. For more information on finding goods to sell, turn to **125** **About Finding Items to Sell**. And for help determining how much to charge for your goods, see **127** **Determine Your Selling Price and Estimate Your Selling Fees**.

eBay offers three particularly useful tools for medium- to high-volume sellers. eBay **Turbo Lister** lets you create professional-looking listings and upload literally thousands of items in bulk uploads. **Seller's Assistant** helps you create auctions as well (see **154** **Manage Multiple Listings with Seller's Assistant**). Use it to create multiple auctions quickly. **Selling Manager**, **Seller's Assistant**, and **Selling Manager Pro** primarily help you after you've created the auctions; they're for the most part sales management tools that can track all your auctions, ensure that you get paid and ship the goods on time, and help with paperwork and finances.

153 Create Multiple Listings with Turbo Lister

✔ BEFORE YOU BEGIN	→ SEE ALSO
137 Review and Post Your Auction	145 Track Your Auction
	154 Manage Multiple Listings with Seller's Assistant
	155 Manage Bulk Listings with Selling Manager

If you frequently create auctions and are looking for a way to create them more quickly and in bulk, you owe it to yourself to give **Turbo Lister** a try. It's free, it's simple to use and, after only a few minutes, you'll have created your first auction. Here's how to use it:

1 Download and Install Turbo Lister

Go to **http://pages.ebay.com/turbo_lister** and click the **Download Now** button. You are sent to a page that has two download links: one that installs the program from the Web and one that lets you download a full installation program. You should install the program from the Web because that version checks whether you already have some components that don't need to be reinstalled. Click **Turbo Lister Web Setup** to install from the Web; click **Turbo Lister Full Setup** to download a file and install it from your computer. In both cases, you should close all open programs before installation.

153

If you install from the Web, you get a security warning asking whether you want to install eBay **Turbo Lister**. Click **Yes** and follow the installation directions. If you instead choose to download the installation file, remember where you save the file on your hard disk; then double-click the file and follow the installation instructions.

After you install the program, run it by either telling it to run at the end of the installation process or double-clicking its icon on the desktop.

2 Create a New Turbo Lister File

When the program starts, you are asked whether you want to create a new **Turbo Lister** file. *Creating a file* is not the same thing as *creating an auction*. When you create a file, you tell **Turbo Lister** to use your eBay username, and then only later on do you actually create an auction.

To create a file, click **Next** and enter your eBay user ID and password. Click **Connect Now** when the next screen comes up, enter your contact information, and click **Finish**.

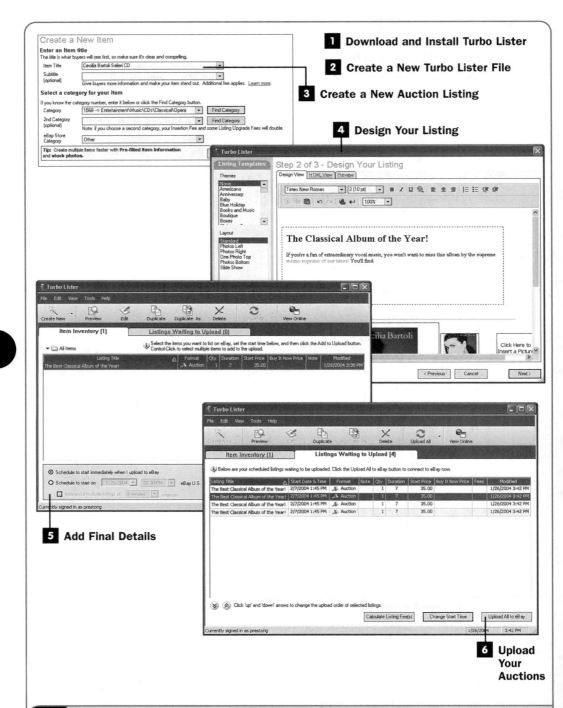

1 Download and Install Turbo Lister

2 Create a New Turbo Lister File

3 Create a New Auction Listing

4 Design Your Listing

5 Add Final Details

6 Upload Your Auctions

153 Create Multiple Listings with Turbo Lister

3 Create a New Auction Listing

After you enter your contact information, you come to a screen that lets you create a new auction listing. Select the kind of auction you want to create—a normal **Auction**, a **Fixed Price** listing, an item for your **Store** (if you have an eBay store), or a real estate listing in an **Ad Format**. Then click **Next**.

The next page asks your item's title and category. Fill in the information as you would if you were creating the auction directly on eBay. (For more information, turn to ⑫⑨ **Start the Sell Form and Choose a Category**.)

▶ TIP

For certain items, such as music CDs, you can use the **Turbo Lister** software to automatically get photos and prefilled information about what you're selling, such as the description of the item. Click the **Try Now** button near the bottom of the screen to do so.

When you're done filling in the information about the title and category, click **Next**.

4 Design Your Listing

The next screen lets you choose a template, write your description, and include art. (For more information about writing a good description and formatting it using HTML, turn to ⑬⓪ **Write the Title and Description** and ⑬① **Format Your Description with eBay's HTML Editor**.) From the left side of the **Turbo Lister** screen, select the template you want to use. Use the built-in HTML Editor to format your description with HTML commands, and select a picture by clicking **Click Here to Insert a Picture** and then browsing through your hard disk to find the picture you want to use. To add a counter to your auction, click the **Select a Counter** button at the bottom of the page.

Before you move on to the next step, click the **Preview** tab to see what your auction will look like. When you're done, click **Next**.

5 Add Final Details

On the next page, fill in the final details about the auction, such as its duration, the price you're charging for the item, payment details, shipping information, and similar data. When you're done, click the **Save** button.

At this point, your auction is saved in the program but has not yet been posted to eBay. After you click **Save**, you come to a screen that has all the auctions you've already created but that have yet to be posted to eBay. From this screen, you can specify the actual starting date of the auction by filling in the information at the bottom of the screen next to **Schedule to Start On**.

153

To create another auction, click the **Create New** button and follow the instructions outlined in steps 3–5.

6 Upload Your Auctions

When you've created several auctions you want to post to eBay, highlight each and click **Add to Upload**. Note that this action doesn't yet upload your auctions. Instead, it adds them to a waiting queue.

▶ TIP

To find out which eBay fees you have to pay for all the auctions you've selected to upload, go to the **Listings Waiting to Upload** tab and click **Calculate Listing Fee(s)**.

To actually upload your items, click the **Listings Waiting to Upload** tab. Then click **Upload All to eBay**; all your auctions, including your graphics, are uploaded and your auctions begin.

---

154   Manage Multiple Listings with Seller's Assistant

154

✔ BEFORE YOU BEGIN	→ SEE ALSO
124 About Selling on eBay	145 Track Your Auction

The **Turbo Lister** software described in 153 **Create Multiple Listings with Turbo Lister** does a good job if you're interested in creating auctions in bulk. But it doesn't offer tools for managing customer emails and tracking sales information. For that, you can use eBay's **Seller's Assistant**. It costs $9.99 per month—and $15.99 per month for the professional version—so you should subscribe only if you're making a reasonable amount of money by selling on eBay.

The **Seller's Assistant Pro** version is the same as the basic version but offers a variety of tools for handling high-volume sales and bulk listings. In these steps, you learn how to use the basic version because that's what most people will use. The **Pro** version works the same except for additional features.

For both versions, you download software to your PC and manage your auctions using that desktop software. In that way, it's similar to **Turbo Lister**. You use the **Selling Manager** software, described in 155 **Manage Bulk Listings with Selling Manager**, over the Web rather than from software downloaded to your computer's hard disk.

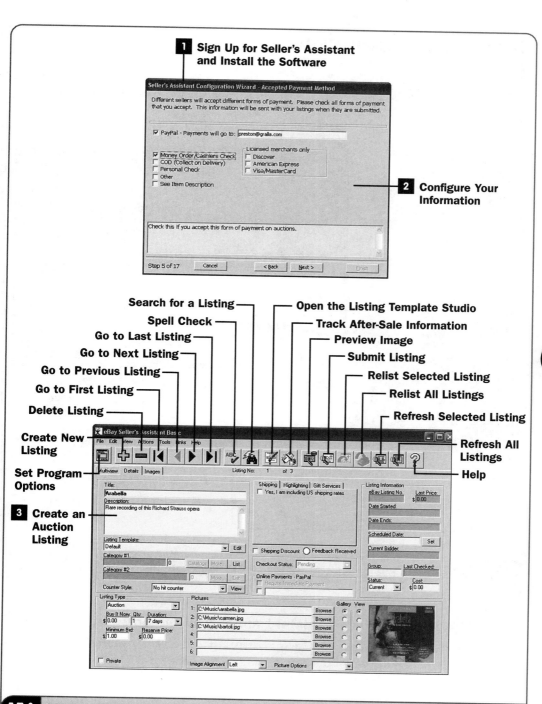

1 **Sign Up for Seller's Assistant and Install the Software**

Seller's Assistant Configuration Wizard - Accepted Payment Method

Different sellers will accept different forms of payment. Please check all forms of payment that you accept. This information will be sent with your listings when they are submitted.

☑ PayPal - Payments will go to: preston@gralla.com

☑ Money Order/Cashiers Check
☐ COD (Collect on Delivery)
☐ Personal Check
☐ Other
☐ See Item Description

Licensed merchants only
☐ Discover
☐ American Express
☐ Visa/MasterCard

2 **Configure Your Information**

Check this if you accept this form of payment on auctions.

Step 5 of 17   Cancel   < Back   Next >   Finish

Search for a Listing
Spell Check
Go to Last Listing
Go to Next Listing
Go to Previous Listing
Go to First Listing
Delete Listing
Create New Listing
Set Program Options
3 Create an Auction Listing

Open the Listing Template Studio
Track After-Sale Information
Preview Image
Submit Listing
Relist Selected Listing
Relist All Listings
Refresh Selected Listing
Refresh All Listings
Help

eBay Seller's Assistant Basic
File Edit View Actions Tools Links Help

Listing No: 1   of 3

Multiview Details Images

Title:
Arabella
Description:
Rare recording of this Richard Strauss opera

Listing Template:
Default   Edit
Category #1:
0   Catalogs More List
Category #2:
0   More   List
Counter Style: No hit counter   View
Listing Type
Auction
Buy It Now: Qty: Duration:
$0.00   1   7 days
Minimum Bid: Reserve Price:
$1.00 $0.00
☐ Private

Shipping | Highlighting | Gift Services |
☐ Yes, I am including US shipping rates

☐ Shipping Discount ○ Feedback Received
Checkout Status: Pending
Online Payments - PayPal
☐ Require Immediate Payment

Pictures
1: C:\Music\arabella.jpg   Browse
2: C:\Music\carmen.jpg   Browse
3: C:\Music\bartoli.jpg   Browse
4:                   Browse
5:                   Browse
6:                   Browse
Image Alignment Left   Picture Options

Listing Information
eBay Listing No: Last Price:
$0.00
Date Started:
Date Ends:
Scheduled Date:
Set
Current Bidder:
Group: Last Checked:
Status: Cost:
Current $0.00

Gallery View

154

154   **Manage Multiple Listings with Seller's Assistant**

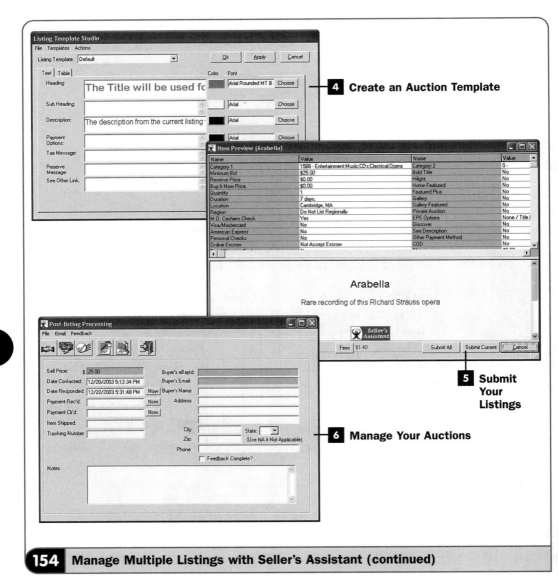

4 Create an Auction Template

5 Submit Your Listings

6 Manage Your Auctions

154 Manage Multiple Listings with Seller's Assistant (continued)

1 Sign Up for Seller's Assistant and Install the Software

Go to **http://pages.ebay.com/sellers_assistant** and click the **Subscribe Now!** link. Two links appear at the bottom of the page—one for the basic version and one for the **Pro** version—so be sure you click the right one.

▶ **TIP**

You can try either version of **Seller's Assistant** for free for 30 days, so if you give it a try and decide not to use it, you won't be out any money. Just be sure to let eBay know you don't want to use it before the end of the trial period. You get an email at the end of the free trial period reminding you that you're about to have to pay for the service, so that's a good time to unsubscribe.

After you accept the eBay agreement, you are brought to a page where you can download the software. Download it by clicking the download link. Remember where you save the file on your hard disk, find the file, double-click it, and follow the installation instructions.

After you install **Seller's Assistant**, run it by double-clicking its **Desktop** icon. The first time you use the software, you have to type your eBay user ID and password and click the **Subscribe** button to start using the program. After you subscribe, it takes some time for the program to download all the latest categories from eBay. Even if you have a high-speed connection such as a cable modem, it can take more than 10 or 15 minutes to download all the various components. On a dial-up connection, it takes even longer.

154

2 **Configure Your Information**

You are asked a series of questions, including your location, how you'll accept payment, who pays for shipping costs, and similar questions required to create auctions. After you're finished, click **Finish** and then click **Done**.

3 **Create an Auction Listing**

Create a new auction listing by clicking the large + button in the upper-right portion of the screen. Fill in all the information about the auction, including title, description, type of auction, cost, shipping price, and similar information. Add pictures by clicking the **browse** buttons in the **Pictures** area at the bottom of the page.

4 **Create an Auction Template**

One of the more powerful features of **Seller's Assistant** is its capability to create templates you can automatically apply to all your auctions. A template includes fonts and colors that are applied to your text, as well as the payment options you want included on all your auctions. Click the **Listing Template Studio** button and create your template. When you're done, click **OK**.

▶ **TIP**

To use the template you've created with any auction listing, select a template for that auction from the **Listing Template** drop-down list.

5 Submit Your Listings

Click the **Submit** button and you see a preview of your listing, including all its information such as price, duration, and location. When you're satisfied with the listing, click on **Submit Current** to submit only the current auction. If you want to see all your listings that have yet to be submitted, click the **Multiview** tab, which shows you all your listings. Click **Submit All** to submit all your auction listings.

▶ **TIP**

Seller's Assistant includes many more tools, such as a spell checker and a way to search through all your auctions. Use the toolbar at the top of the screen to access many of the program's selling tools. You can also use the **Tools** menu to access other tools, such as a calculator and calendar.

154

6 Manage Your Auctions

The power of **Seller's Assistant** comes into play after your auctions are complete and uploaded. You are able to automatically notify buyers that they've won, follow up with payment reminders, track all your payments, send shipping notifications and thank-you notes, and leave feedback. To use these tools, click the **Post-listing Processing** button.

When you click the button, the **Post-listing Processing** screen appears; this screen includes a series of buttons, each of which helps with a different post-auction activity. Clicking one button sends a notice to the high bidder that she is the winner; clicking another button notifies the buyer that you've received her payment; another button notifies the buyer that you've shipped the item; another button lets you leave feedback about the buyer; and another button lets you view feedback about a buyer. Additionally, the main part of the screen shows you details about the auction, such as its selling price, when you contacted the buyer, when you received payment, when you shipped the item, and so on. There is no direct link to PayPal, so **Seller's Assistant** does not automatically gather information about PayPal payments.

155 Manage Bulk Listings with Selling Manager

✔ BEFORE YOU BEGIN	→ SEE ALSO
124 About Selling on eBay	**145** Track Your Auction

The **Seller's Assistant** program, detailed in **154** **Manage Multiple Listings with Seller's Assistant**, runs as a desktop application—that is, it runs as a piece of software on your computer. But not everyone wants to download and run software because it can lead to system conflicts and be time-consuming.

If you'd prefer to manage multiple listings directly on the Web, you should use **Selling Manager**. Like **Seller's Assistant**, you must subscribe to the **Selling Manager**. A **Selling Manager** subscription costs $4.99 per month, but if you already have a **Seller's Assistant** account, you won't need to pay extra for it; it will be included in the price for **Seller's Assistant**. You can try **Selling Manager** for free for 30 days. To get started, go to **http://pages.ebay.com/selling_ manager/** and click the **Subscribe Now** button. Then follow the subscription instructions. Here's how to use the program after you've subscribed:

1 Go to Selling Manager

155

Click the **My eBay** tab at the top of any eBay page and sign in. Then click the **Selling Manager** tab. (The tab shows up only after you've subscribed to **Selling Manager**.) You see a quick summary of all your eBay selling activity, including current listings, listings slated to begin in the next day, and listings in which items have already sold. The summary shows the totals for each area, including the gross amount of money you've made.

▶ TIP

Your listings don't show up immediately under the **Selling Manager** tab after you sign up for **Selling Manager**. It can take several hours for them to be imported from eBay.

2 Check Your Active Listings

In the **Selling Manager Summary** list, click the **Active Listings** link to see a list of all your currently active auctions. Each active auction includes vital details such as the number of bids, the current price, the item number, the time the auction ends, and a link to the auction.

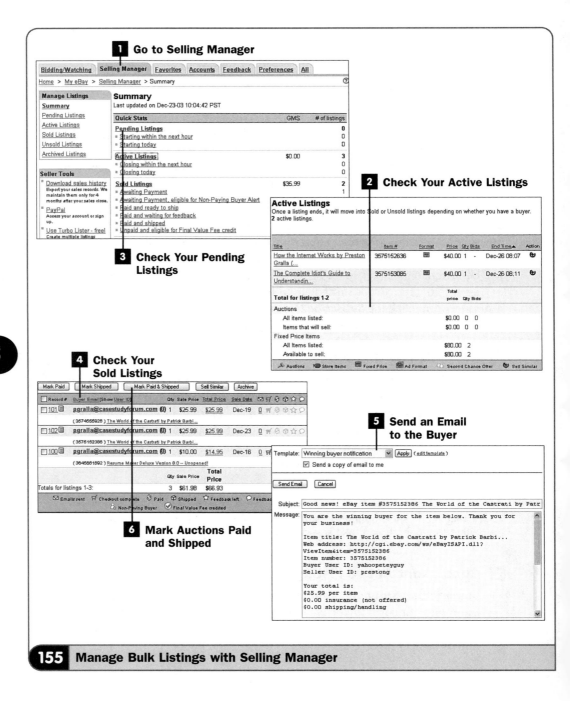

1 Go to Selling Manager

2 Check Your Active Listings

3 Check Your Pending Listings

4 Check Your Sold Listings

5 Send an Email to the Buyer

6 Mark Auctions Paid and Shipped

155

155 Manage Bulk Listings with Selling Manager

From the **Active Listings** page, you can also easily create new auctions based on any existing current auction. Click the small symbol at the far right of the listing, underneath the **Action** column, to start a new auction using the same information from the existing auction as a starting point. Edit the information to complete the auction.

▶ **NOTE**

The **Active Listings** page also shows, at a glance, the format of each auction, such as a fixed-price auction, a traditional auction, and so on. Look at the icon in the **Format** column and check the bottom of the page for a guide to the icons.

3 Check Your Pending Listings

Click the **Pending Listings** link on the **Summary** page to see all your current listings. The display is similar to that for the **Active Listings**. Click any listing to edit it. You should check your pending listings from the **Pending Listings** page to ensure that they contain the proper information and edit them before they go live.

4 Check Your Sold Listings

Click the **Sold Listings** link to see all the items you've successfully sold. This is the most useful portion of the **Selling Manager** software because, when you sell many items, you can easily lose track of which have been sold, which have been paid for, which have been shipped, and so on.

155

The **Sold Listings** page shows you, at a glance, the statuses of all the items you've sold and includes the buyer, the sales price, the sale date, and other relevant information. On the far right side of each item is a series of icons that tell you whether the items have been paid for or shipped, whether you've sent an email to the buyer, and similar information.

5 Send an Email to the Buyer

From the **Sold Listings** page, you can easily send an email to the buyer, notifying her that she's the high bidder or reminding her to pay you. Click the buyer's name to open a prewritten email you can customize. After you've finished customizing the message, click the **Send Email** button to send it to the buyer. On the **Sold Listings** page, an icon appears in the auction entry showing that an email has been sent.

6 Mark Auctions Paid and Shipped

As you are paid by buyers and as you ship items to them, make notes of these landmarks in **Selling Manager** so you can easily track all your selling activity. Put a check in the box next to the auction for which you've been paid or for which you've been paid and shipped the goods, and click the

Mark Paid, Mark Shipped, or **Mark Paid & Shipped** buttons at the top of the auction list. You come to a page asking for confirmation. Click **Confirm Status** and the proper icon shows up next to that auction on the **Sold Listings** page in **Selling Manager**. As your auctions proceed, keep marking them in this way so you have a complete record of the statuses of all your auctions.

▶ **TIP**

Selling Manager does not actually link to your emails or to any payments that have been made to you. That means you have to track those transactions yourself, either on paper or using another program, and then input them into **Selling Manager**.

156 About Writing Effective Ad Copy

✔ BEFORE YOU BEGIN	→ SEE ALSO
130 Write the Title and Description	131 Format Your Description with eBay's HTML Editor
	157 Jazz Up Text and Headlines with HTML
	158 Colorize and Change Fonts and Add Effects with HTML
	159 About Including HTML on eBay Auction Pages

156

Countless auctions compete with your auction. So how do you ensure that bidders and buyers come to *your* auctions? Write effective auction copy—titles and listings that catch buyers' attentions and get them competing with each other to buy what you have for sale. Here's how to write the most effective auction copy to create auction listings that give you the best chance to sell your goods.

Use Eye-Catching Titles

Perhaps the single most important thing you can do to ensure that you sell your items for the most money is to write an eye-catching title. As people browse through auction listings, that's all they're going to see—your auction's title. If your title doesn't catch their eye, and if it doesn't include specific, accurate information about what you're selling, you won't hook the buyers.

Follow these tips to write a title that draws in buyers:

- **Don't use unnecessary words**—Pare down the title until it's as brief as possible. Every word should matter and convey important information.

- **Use words that draw attention to your auction**—Words in titles such as *rare* or *beautiful* draw immediate attention. Use them—but only if they're true.

▶ **TIP**

The words in titles are used when people search an auction site. So, the title should include as many descriptive keywords as possible. Don't use so many descriptive adjectives that you forget to include the basic facts about the object! That way, your auction will be found by the most people.

- **Use abbreviations commonly found on auction sites**—eBay has a limit of 45 characters for auction titles. Study the titles of auctions in your categories to see which abbreviations are commonly used. For example, you can use N/R or No Res to mean *no reserved price*, 14K instead of *14 carat gold*, and 17C to mean *seventeenth century*.

- **Use the proper acronyms when selling collectibles**—There's a whole language of acronyms you can use when selling collectibles, such as NRFB (never removed from box). Study the category of item you're selling to learn which abbreviations to use. Be careful, though, not to use abbreviations for the most important words in your auction title, such as BK for *book*. If you did that, people searching on the word *book* wouldn't find your auction.

- **Avoid using special keyboard characters**—Every auction site is filled with titles and words that have special keyboard characters in them, such as L@@K!!!!. Avoid them. They're so overused that people pass right over them.

- **Point out what's unique or special about what you're selling**—Do you have a one-of-a-kind item or one in mint condition? Is it a particular brand or model number that is in great demand? Think of what sets your item apart from the mass of other auction items out there, and make sure that comes across in the title.

- **Pay extra for a boldfaced listing**—Boldface draws attention to your listing. It only costs $1, so it can be money well spent.

- **Don't stretch the truth**—In your attempt to draw in buyers, you might feel compelled to stretch the truth to make your item sound more appealing or more unique than it really is. Avoid doing that. If you promise more than your auction delivers, you'll only annoy potential buyers who will avoid your auctions in the future. And if you get a bad reputation on an auction site, it's hard to live it down.

156

How to Write Descriptions That Sell

If you've done your job right, the title will be enough of a draw for potential bidders to get to your auction page. But that's only the beginning. Now you need people to actually bid and buy. The title is like a pleasing storefront display that brings people into the store. After buyers come into the store, they expect to see displays and goods so they're enticed to buy what you have to sell.

▶ **TIP**

In the same way a store should be appealing and its goods put nicely on display, your description should be laid out nicely and clearly and be enticing enough so people want to buy what you're selling.

Follow this advice and you'll write the best descriptions to help sell your items at auctions:

- **Be comprehensive in your description**—The more detail you provide, the more likely someone is to bid on what you have up for sale. Be sure to list all the item's features, especially anything that makes it unique. You're not limited in how much space you use for your description, so feel free to use the space.

- **Be enthusiastic in your description**—If you're not excited about the item you have for sale, how do you think the bidder will feel? You want to impart a sense of enthusiasm and energy in the description you write.

- **Accurately portray the condition of the item you're selling**—Don't try to hide the fact that your item has flaws or defects or that it has been used. The buyer will find out the truth and, if you've been inaccurate in your portrayal of the item, the buyer might ask for his money back. In any event, you're more likely than not to get negative feedback. On the other hand, don't dwell solely on the item's defects—you mainly want to point out what's good about it.

- **Stress the benefits of the item you're selling, not just its features**—Let's say you're selling a digital organizer. If you were going to stress only its features, you might write, **Comes with 128MB RAM.** That's not much of a sell. If, instead, you write, **It will store your entire yearly schedule, address book, all your to-do lists, your expense accounts, your favorite MP3 files, and more in its 128MB of RAM,** you're stressing its specific benefits. You're more likely to get bidders when you can sell them on the benefits of the item you have for sale.

▶ **TIP**

If you don't grab potential bidders in your first sentence, you're going to lose them. That's the time to stress the benefits of what you have for sale, its uniqueness, its special features, and anything else you can think of that will make people want to buy it.

- **End your description with a summarizing sales pitch**—The last words of a listing can be the primary thing people remember after reading your listing, and those words are probably the last thing they'll read before making a bid. Be sure that the end of your description sums up the item and stresses all its benefits with enthusiasm.

- **Anticipate questions that potential buyers might have about the item**—Stand back for a moment and imagine yourself as the buyer of what you have for sale. What questions do you think buyers would ask about the item, and what more might they want to know? Include the answers to these questions in your description.

- **Include brand name, manufacturer, years of manufacture, and other similar information**—There are collectors of everything imaginable. You might not realize it, but collectors might specialize in the precise brand or manufacturer of what you have for sale. It's important to include these details in your descriptions.

Three Things to Include in Every Auction Listing

If you write eye-catching titles and descriptions that sell, you'll help ensure that your item is bid on and bought. But there's more advice you should follow, as well. You should include the following three things in every auction listing, without fail:

156

- **Tell people to email you with questions or for more information**—If people feel you're open to answering questions, they'll be more likely to trust you and be more likely to bid. If someone takes the time to email a question to you, it means you've piqued her interest and are more likely to make a sale.

▶ **TIP**

If you're going to encourage bidders to email you with questions, you should check your email several times a day and respond promptly to questions. Otherwise, you'll lose bidders—and the sale.

- **Include details about shipping, insurance, and payment**—You want to leave no questions in the bidder's mind about how the transaction will work. Giving precise details about important post-auction items such as shipping and insurance will put bidders at ease because they know exactly what to expect.

- **Describe your expertise, if any, in the category of the thing you're selling**—Are you an expert in Depression glass? A collector of Nancy Ann dolls? If you have special expertise or are a collector of what you're selling, let people know that and then tell them why you value the item you're selling. Not only will it lend an authoritative voice to your auction, but other collectors will feel a kind of kinship with you and will be more likely to bid. You might also gain new friends with common interests in this way.

► **TIP**

Some sellers like to use the ignoramus approach to selling—they say they have little expertise about the item they have for sale, they got it from their divorced sister's aunt's grandmother, and so on. If bidders have specific questions, the seller tells them to email the questions and the seller will find the answer. This approach reassures buyers that the seller is not trying to misrepresent the item; additionally, the seller might feel that there's a way to get a bargain from someone who doesn't really know the high quality of the goods he's selling.

157 **Jazz Up Text and Headlines with HTML**

✔ BEFORE YOU BEGIN	→ SEE ALSO
2 Use HTML Tags	**156** About Writing Effective Ad Copy
6 About Proper HTML Coding	**159** About Including HTML on eBay Auction Pages
130 Write the Title and Description	
131 Format Your Description with eBay's HTML Editor	

157

Use *HTML* as the best way to make your headlines and text stand out and help draw attention to your auction. It's true that you can use eBay's built-in HTML Editor to do this, as outlined in **131** **Format Your Description with eBay's HTML Editor**, but using the eBay Editor limits what you can do. HTML offers a world beyond what's offered with the eBay Editor.

► **KEY TERM**

HTML—Short for Hypertext Markup Language, HTML is the language of the Web. In short, it instructs browsers how to display web pages.

HTML is the language that tells web browsers how to display web pages. Fancy fonts, big headlines, graphics—all of that and more is possible with HTML. When you go to a web page, your browser looks at the HTML code "behind" the text you actually see and then displays the text following the HTML instructions embedded in the web page.

In this section, you learn the basics of HTML and find out how to jazz up your text and headlines with HTML commands.

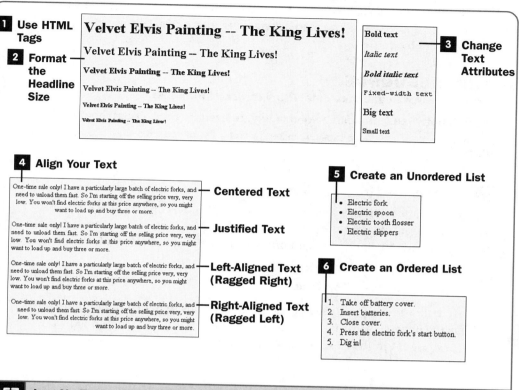

157 | **Jazz Up Text and Headlines with HTML**

1 Use HTML Tags

HTML works by using *tags* that tell a browser how to display a page. Each tag has an instruction to do a particular thing, such as displaying text at a certain size, displaying it as bold or italic, or displaying a graphic.

▶ KEY TERM

Tags—HTML instructions that tell a browser how to display text, graphics, or other items. Tags usually come in pairs: a starting tag to tell the browser how to display the item and an ending tag that tells the browser to no longer use the tag information. For example, to make an item boldface, you surround it with the tags <b> and </b>.

HTML tags are enclosed within angle brackets (the less-than and greater-than signs). Usually, tags contain a pair of instructions—the first one turns on the action, and the second one turns it off. For example, if you wanted to make text on a page boldfaced, you'd put the tag <B> in front of the text you wanted to make bold and the tag </B> after the text you wanted to make bold, like this: <B>This is boldfaced text</B>. Note that it doesn't matter whether you use uppercase or lowercase letters in your tags. You can use <B> and </B> or <b> and </b>.

▶ **WEB RESOURCE**

http://www.willcam.com/cmat/html/crossref.html#list

http://hotwired.lycos.com/webmonkey/reference/html_cheatsheet/

HTML uses many tags; visit these websites to find a list of common tags and how to use them.

2 Format the Headline Size

To format headings, you use the <H> and </H> tags and include a number that determines how large the heading should be. You can use numbers from 1 to 6, with 1 being the largest and 6 being the smallest. Here's how you use the tag:

<H1>Velvet Elvis -- The King Lives!</H1>

Note that the number used by the closing tag has to match the number used by the opening tag—in other words, if you use H1 in the opening tag, you must use H1 in the closing tag. All headings are automatically put in bold-face.

157

▶ **NOTE**

Heading sizes work differently from the rest of HTML. In headings, smaller numbers produce large headings and vice versa. In other words, using **1** produces a large heading and using **6** produces a small heading. In the rest of HTML, though, the reverse holds true. When using the font tag, for example, the smaller the number, the smaller the text.

The following list details the various sizes of headings. As a practical matter, you'll probably use only headings 1 and 2 for your auctions because smaller sizes don't function as headings at all—they're simply too small.

HTML Heading Tag	Approximate Point Size of Text
H1	24 points
H2	18 points
H3	14 points
H4	12 points
H5	10 points
H6	8 points (9 points on the Macintosh)

3 Change Text Attributes

Many times you'll need to format text in your description for emphasis or special display—for example, to italicize or boldface text. Several tags affect the attributes of the text, and they all work the same way. Let's take the tag for making text bold. As explained earlier, to make text boldfaced, use the <B> and </B> tags, like this:

<B>I'm bold text.</B>

To make text italic, use the <I> and </I> tags. Note that you can nest text-formatting tags, like this:

<B><I>I'm bold italic text.</I></B>

▶ NOTE

You should always turn off tags in the reverse order that you turned them on. (Use <B><I> and </I></B> rather than <B><I> and </B></I>, for example.) In many cases, how you turn them off won't matter, but occasionally it can make a difference, so get into the habit of turning them off in this way.

HTML has quite a few text-formatting tags like these. The following table lists the major tags and describes what they each do. Each of these tags requires a closing tag, which is the tag preceded by a forward slash (/). The <STRONG> tag is closed with the </STRONG> tag.

157

HTML Text Formatting Tags and What They Do

Tag	Description
<B>	Makes text bold
<I>	Italicizes text
<U>	Underlines text
<STRIKE>	Puts a line through text, like ~~this~~
<SUB>	Makes text appear as a subscript, like $_{this}$
<SUP>	Makes text appear as a superscript, like ^{this}
<TT>	Makes text appear in a fixed-width font, usually `Courier`
<STRONG>	Makes text stronger, generally by making it bold
<EM>	Gives text more emphasis, generally by making it italic
<BIG>	Makes text larger than the surrounding text
<SMALL>	Makes text smaller than the surrounding text

Keep in mind that browsers sometimes display HTML pages differently from one another—the fonts might display at slightly different sizes, for example. If you want, you can preview your page in several browsers. However, the vast majority of people use Internet Explorer, so if you use that browser to view your HTML, you can ensure that you are reaching the largest potential audience.

▶ **NOTE**

Be very careful when using underlined text on your auction page—as a general rule, you should avoid that formatting option. Normally, when text appears underlined, it means that it is a link. Therefore, people can be confused by underlined text and think it's a link, and they'll click it to no avail.

You can use text formatting in concert with headings and paragraphs, not just individual words and sentences. If you wanted part of a heading to be italicized, for example, you would code it like this:

<H1>The <I>Best</I> Electric Gadgets</H1>

Remember that the **<H>** tag automatically makes text bold, so don't use the **<B>** tag along with it.

4 Align Your Text

157

You can use HTML to align your headlines and text on the page. There's good news and bad news about aligning text using HTML. Here's the good news: It's very easy to do.

Here's the bad news: It's very easy to do because you have so little control over how text aligns. In fact, you really have only these choices:

- You can align the text to the left.

- You can align the text to the right.

  When you align text to the right or the left, the text runs *ragged* on the other margin, which means all the text doesn't line up precisely on that margin. Typically, when you use a word processor, you have ragged-right text, which means the text is aligned on the left side and is ragged on the right. This book, for example, uses left-aligned, ragged-right text.

- You can center the text.

- You can justify the text, which means the text lines up precisely on both the right and left margins.

▶ **NOTE**

When you don't use any HTML alignment commands in your text, it automatically is displayed as left aligned, ragged right in a browser.

The most basic way to align text is to use alignment commands along with the paragraph (<P>) tag, like this:

<P ALIGN="center">

<P ALIGN="justify">

<P ALIGN="left">

<P ALIGN="right">

Doing that aligns all subsequent paragraphs in the manner you've chosen. To stop the alignment, use the closing </P> tag.

5 Create an Unordered List

Lists are a great way to present information in auctions. You can use them to draw attention to highlights of the goods you're selling. With an unordered list, each item on the list is preceded by a bullet.

To create an unordered list, use the <UL> and </UL> tags around the entire list of items. Then precede each item in the list with the <LI> (list item) tag. The <LI> tag doesn't use a closing tag. Here's how to create an unordered list:

157

<UL>

<LI>Electric fork

<LI>Electric spoon

<LI>Electric tooth flosser

<LI>Electric slippers

</UL>

The default bullet is a filled-in circle. If you want, you can change the bullets to either hollow circles or hollow squares. To change the bullet character to a hollow circle, type this:

<UL TYPE="circle">

To change the bullet to a hollow square, type this:

<UL TYPE="square">

Use the **UL TYPE=** tag at the beginning of the list, in place of the plain <UL> tag. When you end the list with the </UL> tag, you reset the bullet type to the default filled-in circle.

▶ **TIP**

Remember that you can combine tags. For example, you can boldface each entry in your list or make bold just a few words in each entry in your list.

6 **Create an Ordered List**

You can create another type of list—an ordered list. An ordered list is one in which each item is numbered or lettered sequentially. HTML does all the work for you—you don't actually have to insert the numbers or letters. Space is automatically inserted between the number or letter and each item on the list to make the list more legible. If you reorder the list or add or take away items from it, HTML automatically adjusts the letters or numbers for you.

To create an ordered list, use the <OL> and </OL> tags around the list, along with the list item tag (<LI>), like this:

<OL>

<LI>Take off battery cover.

157

<LI>Insert batteries.

<LI>Close cover.

<LI>Press the electric fork's start button.

<LI>Dig in!

</OL>

The preceding instructions create a numbered list. But you can also create lists using letters and have even more control—you can use uppercase or lowercase letters or uppercase or lowercase Roman numerals instead. To do it, use the <OL> tag with the **TYPE** attribute, which tells the browser how to display the list. For example, if you wanted to display the list alphabetically in uppercase letters, you'd use this tag:

<OL TYPE=A>

To display the list alphabetically in lowercase letters, use this tag:

<OL TYPE=a>

To display the list in uppercase Roman numerals, use this tag:

<OL TYPE=I>

To display the list in lowercase Roman numerals, use this tag:

<OL TYPE=i>

158 Colorize and Change Fonts and Add Effects with HTML

✔ BEFORE YOU BEGIN

2 Use HTML Tags
6 About Proper HTML Coding
130 Write the Title and Description
157 Jazz Up Text and Headlines with HTML

→ SEE ALSO

156 About Writing Effective Ad Copy
159 About Including HTML on eBay Auction Pages

You can use HTML in more ways to jazz up your auctions. You can use different fonts, add color, and add special effects such as lines across the page. Follow the same basic HTML rules about tags defined in **157** **Jazz Up Text and Headlines with HTML** and follow these instructions:

1 Change the Typeface

The text that appears on eBay is standard Times Roman font. You can make your auction listing more unique by changing the font. To change the font, use the following command:

<FONT FACE="*fontname*">text goes here</FONT>

In this command, ***fontname*** is the name of the font you want to use. If you wanted to use the Helvetica font, the command would look like this:

<FONT FACE="Helvetica">text goes here</FONT>

You should use only common fonts that are found on most people's computers. In other words, try to use the normal fonts that came on your computer, and stay away from extra fonts you've bought or that came with other programs. Arial and Helvetica, in addition to Times Roman, are always good bets. The following table lists fonts typically found on Windows computers; the next table lists fonts typically found on Macintoshes.

158

▶ NOTE

If you've used a font not on the recommended list, a visitor to your auction page can still see the text in her browser. If her computer has the font you specified, it displays it. If it doesn't have that font, it uses the closest approximation of the font on her computer to display the text.

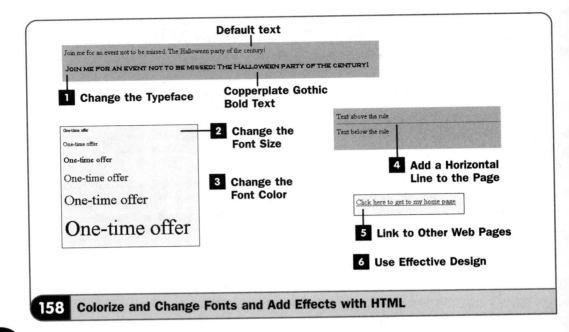

Default text

1 Change the Typeface

Copperplate Gothic Bold Text

2 Change the Font Size

3 Change the Font Color

4 Add a Horizontal Line to the Page

5 Link to Other Web Pages

6 Use Effective Design

158   Colorize and Change Fonts and Add Effects with HTML

158

Fonts Typically Found on Windows Computers

Arial

Arial Black

Arial Narrow

Arial Rounded MT Bold

Book Antiqua

Bookman Old Style

Century Gothic

Century Schoolbook

Courier

Courier New

Garamond

Helvetica

Times New Roman

Verdana

Fonts Typically Found on Macintosh Computers

Chicago

Courier

Geneva

Helvetica

Monaco

New York

Palatino

Times

2 Change the Font Size

You can change the size of the font in much the same way as you can change the size of the title of the headline (see **157 Jazz Up Text and Headlines with HTML**). As with a headline, you don't specify an exact size for the text. Instead, you specify a relative size, with the most practical being from –0 (the smallest) to 6 (the biggest). To change the size of the text, use the following command:

<FONT SIZE="2">text goes here</FONT>

The sample figure shows the range of sizes available to you in the Times New Roman font.

You can combine changing the font with changing the font size to display a variety of fonts in different sizes. If you want to display the largest text available (size 6) in the Helvetica font, use the following command:

<FONT FACE="Helvetica" size=6>text goes here</FONT>

158

▶ TIP

There's no real reason to use small font sizes when creating your auction. You want everything clear and readable, and using small fonts will only frustrate potential bidders.

3 Change the Font Color

To really jazz up your auction page, you can use colored text. You can add color to headlines or body text. In fact, you can add color to any text on the page. Here's the command for changing the color of text:

<FONT COLOR="blue">This is blue text.</FONT>

You can name up to 140 colors in this way. The list is too long to include here, but you can specify many common colors including blue, green, red, yellow, gold, orange, pink, purple, and violet. Many uncommon colors are available as well, such as tomato, PaleGoldenRod, and MidnightBlue.

▶ WEB RESOURCE
www.w3schools.com/html/html_colornames.asp
This site offers a complete list of HTML font color names and hex color codes you can use.

▶ NOTE
You can also specify a color by issuing the command **<FONT COLOR="#*colorcode*">text goes here</FONTfont>**, where *colorcode* is a hex code (a combination of six letters and numbers) that specifies a specific color. The code for blue is **0000FF**, so the following command would make text blue:

<FONT COLOR="#0000FF">text goes here</FONT>.

4 Add a Horizontal Line to the Page

If you want to separate sections of your text, you can draw a horizontal line, called a *rule*, across the page. To do so, insert the <HR> tag. The <HR> tag doesn't use a closing tag. It places a line break above and below the rule and inserts the proper amount of white space. The rule itself is an embossed, shaded line that goes across the entire width of the browser.

158

5 Link to Other Web Pages

HTML allows you to link to other pages so someone can click a link in your auction page and immediately go to another web page. You can use this HTML link feature to link to all your other auctions, increasing visibility for them all. If you have a business on the Web where you sell items similar to the one you're selling at the auction, you can link to your business web page as well. You also can link to pages that offer more information about the item you have for sale. In fact, the ways you can use this feature are endless.

Here's the code you use for linking to other pages:

<A HREF= "*URL*">Here's a link</Aa>

In this code, **URL** is the location of the web page to which you're linking, such as **http://www.myhomepage.com/moreauctions.html**.

Say you're linking from the auction page to your own home page and the URL (web location) of your page is **http://www.myisp.net/users/mypage.html**. Here's the command you'd issue to create the link to your home page:

<A HREF= "http://www.myisp.net/users/mypage.html">Click here to get to my home page</A>

When you use this command, only the **Click here to get to my home page** text actually shows up on your auction page on the Web. The text shows up as an underlined link, the same as any other link you're used to seeing.

▶ **TIP**

When you use the **A REF=** HTML tag, you must include the **http://** portion of the URL in the address.

6 Use Effective Design

After you learn how to use HTML, you'll probably want to go crazy using different fonts, text sizes, and text colors. You might be tempted to start changing them willy-nilly on your auction page so your auction looks like a patched-together ransom note. Be advised: Use different fonts, colors, and sizes sparingly. When you mix too many elements on a single page, the text becomes confusing and difficult to read and might chase potential bidders away. Use all your HTML options judiciously to draw attention to your auction's important points.

159 About Including HTML on eBay Auction Pages	
✔ **BEFORE YOU BEGIN**	→ **SEE ALSO**
2 Use HTML Tags	**131** Format Your Description with eBay's HTML Editor
6 About Proper HTML Coding	
157 Jazz Up Text and Headlines with HTML	
158 Colorize and Change Fonts and Add Effects with HTML	

Now you know the basics of HTML, but how do you go about using HTML tags on eBay? Keep in mind that on eBay you fill out a form to create an auction listing. After that form is filled out, the auction site automatically creates your listing, which is, in fact, an HTML page. The best way to include HTML on your eBay auction page is to create your HTML-enhanced text in Notepad or some other text-editing program, copy all the HTML to the Windows or Mac Clipboard, and then paste the encoded text from the Clipboard into the **Sell Your Item** form on eBay.

▶ **NOTE**

Different browsers might display HTML differently. HTML can't completely control how each browser displays pages. So, the headline sizes, font sizes, and other features of the page can look different on different browsers. All browsers can display standard HTML commands, but a lot of HTML is *nonstandard*—that is, it might work fine on some browsers but not on others. You should therefore use simple HTML commands; if you want your pages to look good on every browser, test the pages with different browsers.

Here are a few important things to keep in mind when using HTML on eBay:

- **You can't use HTML in your auction title**—HTML codes interfere with eBay's search function so people won't find your item when searching. Furthermore, eBay doesn't recognize HTML codes in auction titles and won't display the effects even if you choose to use them.

- **Review your HTML before and after posting it**—Nothing can make you look worse than presenting a sloppy-looking auction listing with odd commands, characters, and spaces showing. Review your HTML-enhanced text before pasting it into the **Sell Your Item** form, and then review the final listing carefully before posting it. You can easily make tiny errors in HTML that have big consequences when your page is posted.

159

To review your HTML, make sure that you've coded it in Notepad. Then save the code as a file with an **.html** extension (for example, **testauction.html**). After you've saved it, open the file: Select **File**, **Open**; browse to the folder where you've put the file; and open the file. You can now preview the HTML. If there's a problem, fix it in Notepad, open the file in your browser again, and check whether the problem is fixed. Keep previewing and editing the code until you've got it right.

23

Starting an eBay Business

IN THIS CHAPTER:

It's easy to catch the eBay selling bug after you find out how easy selling online is. If you're successful at selling online, at some point you'll have to make a decision whether eBay is more than a side hobby for you and whether you should get serious about your selling.

If you ever get serious about selling, consider setting up an eBay store. It's a great way for volume sellers to get high visibility, low listing fees, and credibility with buyers. eBay stores also help you with your promotion and merchandising efforts.

This chapter shows you how to set up your eBay store, list items for sale, and market your store and rake in the money.

160	**About eBay Businesses**

✔ **BEFORE YOU BEGIN**	→ **SEE ALSO**
124 About Selling on eBay	**152** About Advanced Seller's Tools
	161 Set Up an eBay Store

160

If you're serious about selling and frequently sell many different items, you'd do well to set up your own online storefront on eBay, called an *eBay store*. An eBay store is your own private area on eBay, where you can sell your goods and customize the way your store looks. eBay stores offer a variety of benefits for serious sellers:

▶ **KEY TERM**

eBay store—An online storefront on eBay where you can sell your goods and customize the way the store looks and how the items are displayed and organized.

- **Lower listing fees**—When you set up your own store, you pay less for each auction listing.

- **Less time building auction listings**—You don't have a time limit for each item you auction—you can list them for 30, 60, 90, or 120 days or permanently until you take the listing down from your store.

- **More promotional opportunities**—eBay will help you promote your store in a variety of ways, and you can use a cross-promotional tool for even more promotion.

- **Potentially more profits**—eBay claims that those who sell using eBay stores have a 25% average increase in sales the first three months after opening an eBay store.

- **Free monthly reports**—You'll get reports on vital information such as monthly gross sales, conversion rates, and number of buyers.

- **More professional-looking auctions**—When you have a storefront, you're trusted more by buyers. In fact, some buyers specifically look for eBay stores from which to buy.

You have to pay a monthly fee to open a store. A basic store costs $9.95 per month. If you build it into a thriving business, you can spend $49.95 to be a featured store and $499.95 per month to be an anchor store. These higher-priced options come primarily with a great deal more promotion efforts on the part of eBay.

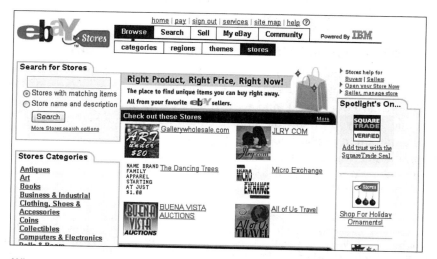

When you open an eBay store, eBay helps promote your business with special listings and links.

To open your eBay store, you must be a registered eBay seller and have your credit card on file with eBay. You also must have a minimum feedback rating of 20 or pay a $5 fee to get an ID Verified listing. And you must be able to accept credit card payments from an Internet payment service such as PayPal or through a credit card merchant account.

▶ TIP

To accept PayPal payments, you must have an email address and register at **www.paypal.com**.

161	Set Up an eBay Store
✔ **BEFORE YOU BEGIN**	→ **SEE ALSO**
160 About eBay Businesses	**162** About Listing Items for Sale at Your Store
	163 Market Your Store
	164 Make the Sale

Setting up an eBay store is surprisingly easy—it requires only a few minutes of your time and some thought. Remember, though, that you have to be able to accept credit card payments from an Internet payment service such as PayPal or through a credit card merchant account. After that payment option is set up, here's how to start your own eBay store:

1 Click eBay Stores; Then Click Open Your Store Now

From the eBay home page, click the **eBay Stores** link in the **Specialty Sites** area near the top of the page. Then click the **Open Your Store Now** link. If you're not currently logged in to eBay, you'll have to log in before you can continue. After you log in, you come to a page that informs you that you need a minimum feedback rating of 20 or to be ID Verified. If you don't have a minimum feedback rating of 20, click the **ID Verified** link and fill out the form to be ID Verified. It costs $5 to be verified.

▶ NOTE

The eBay verification service requires that you enter your credit card number and driver's license number, so have those handy when you fill out the **ID Verified** form. If you're not comfortable giving out that information, you won't be able to be verified. Also, the service asks questions about your mortgage payments and credit card limits. If you don't know them, put in any number and you'll get an error message along with a phone number to call. When you call that phone number, you'll be able to be verified.

2 Choose Your Store Name

When you're presented with a form asking for information about the store you're creating, the first bit of information you're asked to provide is the name of your store. Don't just type the first name that comes to mind—in many ways, this step is the most important one of all for setting up an eBay store. You should choose a name that describes what your store specializes in selling; the store name should be unique, recognizable, and easy to remember. Having the store name reflect exactly what you sell will also make it more likely to show up in Internet search engines when someone is looking to buy particular kinds of goods.

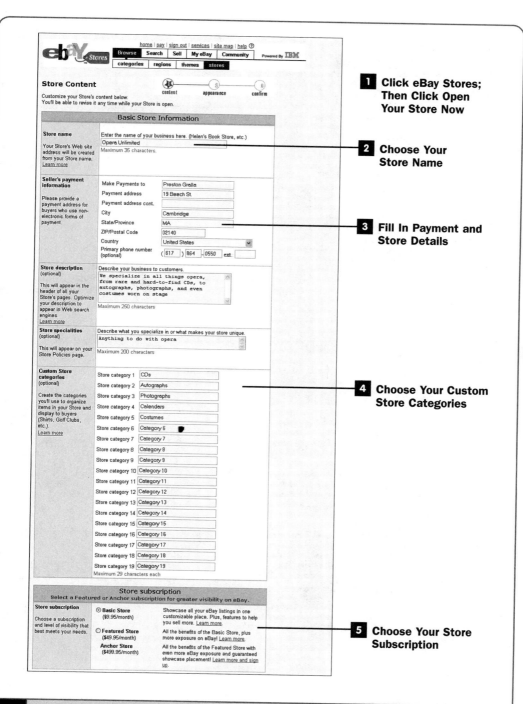

Store Content

Customize your Store's content below.
You'll be able to revise it any time while your Store is open.

content — appearance — confirm

Basic Store Information

Store name

Your Store's Web site address will be created from your Store name. Learn more

Enter the name of your business here. (Helen's Book Store, etc.)

Opera Unlimited

Maximum 35 characters.

Seller's payment information

Please provide a payment address for buyers who use non-electronic forms of payment.

Make Payments to — Preston Gralla
Payment address — 19 Beech St.
Payment address cont.
City — Cambridge
State/Province — MA
ZIP/Postal Code — 02140
Country — United States
Primary phone number (optional) — (617) 864 - 0550 ext.

Store description (optional)

This will appear in the header of all your Store's pages. Optimize your description to appear in Web search engines. Learn more

Describe your business to customers.

We specialize in all things opera, from rare and hard-to-find CDs, to autographs, photographs, and even costumes worn on stage

Maximum 250 characters

Store specialties (optional)

This will appear on your Store Policies page.

Describe what you specialize in or what makes your store unique.

Anything to do with opera

Maximum 200 characters

Custom Store categories (optional)

Create the categories you'll use to organize items in your Store and display to buyers (Shirts, Golf Clubs, etc.). Learn more

Store category 1 — CDs
Store category 2 — Autographs
Store category 3 — Photographs
Store category 4 — Calendars
Store category 5 — Costumes
Store category 6 — Category 6
Store category 7 — Category 7
Store category 8 — Category 8
Store category 9 — Category 9
Store category 10 — Category 10
Store category 11 — Category 11
Store category 12 — Category 12
Store category 13 — Category 13
Store category 14 — Category 14
Store category 15 — Category 15
Store category 16 — Category 16
Store category 17 — Category 17
Store category 18 — Category 18
Store category 19 — Category 19

Maximum 29 characters each

Store subscription

Select a Featured or Anchor subscription for greater visibility on eBay.

Store subscription

Choose a subscription and level of visibility that best meets your needs.

⊙ **Basic Store** ($9.95/month) — Showcase all your eBay listings in one customizable place. Plus, features to help you sell more. Learn more.

○ **Featured Store** ($49.95/month) — All the benefits of the Basic Store, plus more exposure on eBay! Learn more.

Anchor Store ($499.95/month) — All the benefits of the Featured Store with even more eBay exposure and guaranteed showcase placement! Learn more and sign up.

1 Click eBay Stores; Then Click Open Your Store Now

2 Choose Your Store Name

3 Fill In Payment and Store Details

4 Choose Your Custom Store Categories

5 Choose Your Store Subscription

161

161 Set Up an eBay Store

About Your Store

Store payment methods	☑ PayPal ☐ COD (cash on delivery)
	☑ Money Order or Cashiers Check ☐ Other online payment services
Choose all methods you'll accept, and enter any additional explanation if needed.	☐ Personal Check ☐ See Item Description
	Only for sellers accepting credit card purchases through their own merchant account.
	☑ Visa/MasterCard ☐ Discover ☐ American Express

Additional payment explanation (optional)

Maximum 200 characters

6 Provide About Your Store Information

Store ship-to locations	⊙ Will ship to United States only
	○ Will ship internationally (worldwide)
	○ Will ship to the United States and the following regions only:
	☐ Canada ☐ Africa
	☐ Europe ☐ Mexico and Central America
	☐ Australasia ☐ Middle East
	☐ Asia ☐ Caribbean
	☐ South America
	○ Will arrange for local pickup only (no shipping)

Additional shipping explanation (optional):
Describe international shipping details, pickups for large items, etc.

Maximum 200 characters

Shipping Costs	Who will pay for shipping costs? ⊙ Buyer ○ Seller
Store sales tax	0 % charged in No Sales Tax ▾
If you don't collect sales tax, you can leave this blank.	Additional sales tax explanation (optional):
	Maximum 200 characters
Store customer service & return policy	Describe any policies such as "satisfaction guaranteed" or "… Buy as is
	Maximum 90 characters
Additional store information (optional)	
Describe any additional policies or information about your Store here. This will appear on your Store Policies page.	Maximum 200 characters
About Me Page	Note: Your About Me Page will be automatically included in … Don't have one? Create one now.
Export of Store Listings (optional)	Drive more traffic to your listings by exposing them to third-p… engines and product comparison sites. eBay can provide a f… partners to pick up. Learn more
Let third parties download a file of your listings. Learn more	○ Don't make a file available
	○ Make a file of my Store Inventory listings available
	Note: Use of the information you permit eBay to make available to any third party will be in accordance with such third party's terms and conditions. eBay is not responsible fo… such third party.

[Clear Form]   [Continue ➤]

Announcements | Register | Safe Trading Tips

Copyright © 1995-2003 eBay Inc. All Rights Reserved.
Designated trademarks and brands are the property of their respec…
Use of this Web site constitutes acceptance of the eBay User Agree…

7 Customize Your Store's Appearance

Store Appearance

Store Color Scheme	⊙ Pre-selected color scheme
Choose a color scheme for your Store or enter your own custom colors. Learn more.	Coral ▾ Preview colors below
	○ Custom colors
	Background # [ ] ▣
	Foreground # [ ] ▣
	Text # [ ] ▣
	Example: FFFFFF
Store Graphic	⊙ Predesigned graphic
Choose a graphic from the options below or insert the URL to your custom graphic. Learn more.	Music ▾ Preview graphics below
	○ Custom graphic
	http://www.mysite|com/images/opera.gif
	Graphic size is 310 x 90 pixels. Larger and smaller logos will be automatically resized to fit these dimensions.

Opera Unlimited   Seller, manage Store
Maintained by prestong (8) me 〈store〉

We specialize in all things opera, from rare and hard-to-find CDs, to autographs, photographs, and even costumes worn on stage

Opera Unlimited Search	**0** items found in **All Categories** View: **All Items**	Buy It Now only	Auction only
	There are no items in this category.
	Try these search alternatives
☑ in titles & descriptions	• Sorry, all items have been purchased. Try viewing here.
[Search]	

eBay official time 09:29:18 PST

8 Visit Your Store

161

Keep in mind that the name of your store determines your store's website address. So, if your store name is Opera Unlimited, for example, its address will be http://stores.ebay.com/operaunlimited. (When determining your address, eBay takes out special characters—apostrophes, spaces, &, !, $, and so on—and makes all letters lowercase.)

Also, keep these rules in mind when choosing a store name:

- It must start and end with a letter or a number.

- It cannot start with four or more consecutive letter *As* (either lowercase or uppercase).

- It cannot start with a lowercase or uppercase *e* followed by a number.

- It cannot contain the characters <, >, or @.

- It cannot contain three consecutive letter *Ws* (**www** or **WWW**) any-where in the name.

- It cannot contain two or more consecutive spaces or non-alphanumeric characters.

- It cannot end with a top-level Internet domain abbreviation such as **.com**, **.net**, **.org**, **.mil**, and so on.

- It cannot be identical or very similar to another company's name that is protected by a trademark. It cannot contain the word *eBay*, *Half.com*, *Butterfields*, or *Billpoint*, or be very similar to any of those names.

③ Fill In Payment and Store Details

The payment information eBay asks you to provide is straightforward: Include the name and address that payments should be made out to.

The store description, like the store name, is of primary importance. It appears in the header of all your store pages and is therefore highly promi-nent. The store description (although optional) is the primary means of telling people about what makes your store unique and trustworthy. If you've been in business for several years, let people know that—and certainly tell them what goods you specialize in. Because people often use search engines to find products they're shopping for, you also want your store description to be picked up by search engines. So use words that people would typically use when searching—for example, *sneakers* rather than *running accoutrements*. Include products and brand names you often have in stock, but don't include products and brand names you don't stock.

161

▶ **NOTE**

Don't include links to websites outside of eBay in your store description—doing so violates eBay policies.

Filling out your store specialties is optional. The specialties appear only on your Store Policies page and are not prominently displayed. However, if you do specialize in certain products, list them in this text box.

4 Choose Your Custom Store Categories

You can organize your store by choosing up to 19 different categories. Think of *categories* as your store's aisles—categories are how people browse through your store. These categories can be unique to your store; they do not have to match eBay's categorization scheme.

Choose a set of categories that best reflects the variety of goods you have for sale and that helps potential buyers find what they're looking for. You can categorize by type of item, by price levels, by brand names, and so on. You might also want to have special categories, such as Today's Specials or Half-Off.

To choose a category, type the name of each category you want in your store using the **Store Category** text boxes. You can have up to 19 categories, and each category name can have a maximum of 29 characters.

161

5 Choose Your Store Subscription

You can choose to make your store a basic store ($9.95/month), a featured store ($49.95/month), or an anchor store ($499.95/month). Featured stores and anchor stores get more exposure than do basic stores, but apart from that, there is not an enormous amount of difference among these options.

▶ **NOTE**

A featured store gives you extra exposure compared to a basic store by giving you priority placement in the **Shop eBay Stores** section that appears on search results pages on eBay, featured placement on the **eBay Stores** home page, and extra positioning in the **eBay Stores Directory** for categories where you have items listed. An anchor store gives you all that plus one million impressions per month for your store throughout eBay.com, priority placement in the **Shop eBay Stores** section that appears on search results pages on eBay, and showcase placement of your logo on the **eBay Stores Directory** pages.

6 Provide About Your Store Information

The bottom of the form contains information such as the payment methods you accept, where you will ship to, who pays for shipping costs, customer service and return policies, and any additional information you might want to appear on your **Store Policies** page. Your store will include an automatic link to your **About Me** page, so if you don't have one, now is a good time to create one (click the **Create One Now** link in the **About Me** section).

Pay particular attention to the **Store Sales Tax** section of the page. Some states require that you collect sales tax, and others don't; some states require that you collect sales tax only if you sell to others in your own state. For more information, contact your state government.

When you're done filling out the store-creation form, click the **Continue** button.

7 Customize Your Store's Appearance

The next page that appears lets you choose your store's color scheme, pick a graphic (you can select one of eBay's graphics or use one of your own), and use HTML to design your store. (For more information about using HTML on eBay, see **157 Jazz Up Text and Headlines with HTML**, **158 Colorize and Change Fonts and Add Effects with HTML**, and **159 About Including HTML on eBay Auction Pages**. For information about graphics on eBay, see **138 About Digital Pictures and eBay**.

When you're done designing your store's appearance, click the **Save Changes and Publish** button.

8 Visit Your Store

Your store now exists on eBay. You'll get an email message confirming your store's URL and containing information about how to make changes to your store. Because you haven't yet listed any items for sale, your store will be empty of goods, but you should still visit it before listing items for sale so you can make sure the store looks the way you want it to before you open for business.

162 About Listing Items for Sale at Your Store

✔ BEFORE YOU BEGIN	→ SEE ALSO
161 Set Up an eBay Store	160 About eBay Businesses
124 About Selling on eBay	163 Market Your Store
147 About Accepting Payments	164 Make the Sale

Selling items through your store differs somewhat from selling them at regular auctions. In essence, you're selling at a traditional online site rather than at an auction. Here are the main differences between selling items on an eBay auction and selling items from your eBay store:

- **When you sell through your store, you use the Buy It Now feature**—Your items are not presented in an auction format but rather a traditional store format. Because you list the items for sale, you put a purchase price on them; when someone wants to buy, he buys the item without having to bid.

- **The items you list for sale at your store do not show up in eBay's normal browsing and searching**—However, eBay promotes the stores, so it sends traffic to them using other methods. And your store and items show up when people search through eBay stores.

- **In your eBay store, you can list items for longer times than you can in normal auctions**—You can list for 30, 60, or 90 days or select **Good 'Til Canceled**, which lets you renew the listing every 30 days.

- **You pay only $0.05 for each listing**—This is compared to a minimum of $0.30 in normal eBay auctions.

- **Items you list in your store use the categories you set up when you created your storefront**—For more information, see **161 Set Up an eBay Store**.

162

Even after you set up an eBay store, you can continue to sell items using normal eBay auctions in addition to selling on your eBay store. If you have some items you want to sell in the traditional auction way, you can continue to do so. You'll be charged the normal eBay auction fees, and your items will appear in the normal eBay auction listings. Those normal auctions also show up in your store so your store can be a mix of items you auction in the normal way and items available through your store and the **Buy It Now** approach.

▶ **NOTE**

Auctions you created before you opened your store do not appear in your store. Only auctions you create after your store opens appear in the store's listings, and they appear in eBay's browse and searches as well.

You list items for sale in your store in the same way you list items for sale in normal auctions. List an item by clicking the **Sell** button at the top of any eBay page. After verifying your seller and credit card information, select **Sell in Store Inventory**, click **Continue**, and then list the item as described in **128 About the eBay Sell Your Item Page**.

163 Market Your Store

✔ BEFORE YOU BEGIN	→ SEE ALSO
161 Set Up an eBay Store **162** About Listing Items for Sale at Your Store	**164** Make the Sale

If you build it, they won't necessarily come. After you open your store, don't expect the world to beat a path to it. You'll have to work to get visitors and then work on promoting your items to them. Using your own ingenuity and eBay's built-in promotional tools, you can pack your new storefront with potential customers.

1 Pay Extra Listing Fees

When you list a new item to be sold, you have the option of paying extra fees to highlight the listing. A wide variety of promotional opportunities are available, including a front-page highlight, a highlight on category pages, bold-faced titles, and many other options. Costs range from a $1 fee for a bold listing to $99.95 for a single featured item on eBay's home page, which is listed under the **Featured Items** area near the bottom of the home page.

163

▶ NOTE

Be careful not to overspend when buying promotional spots on eBay. If you're going to choose a $99.95 listing, it only makes sense to do so if you're selling multiple items and fully expect to sell most of them.

2 Use Your About Me Page

Your **About Me** page is a great promotional tool for your store. The page lets you list any information about yourself and your interests and automatically includes information about your store as well. But a surprising number of people—including sellers—don't create an **About Me** page. To do it, click the **My eBay** button at the top of any eBay page, click the **Preferences** tab, and click **Create a Personal 'About Me' Page**. Follow the simple directions for creating one.

3 Build Your Own Website

Millions of people use eBay, but many more millions of people *don't* use eBay. Your potential customers are not only existing eBay customers but also those who don't use the auction site. You can draw people to your eBay business from outside of eBay by building your own website and linking to your eBay business from the website.

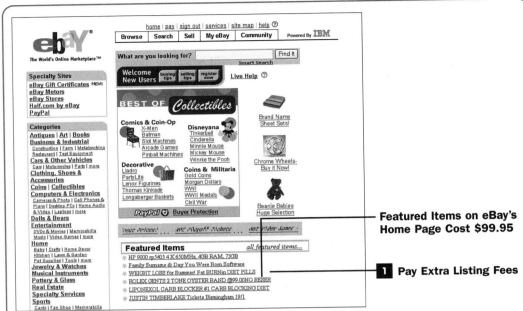

Featured Items on eBay's Home Page Cost $99.95

1 Pay Extra Listing Fees

2 Use Your About Me Page

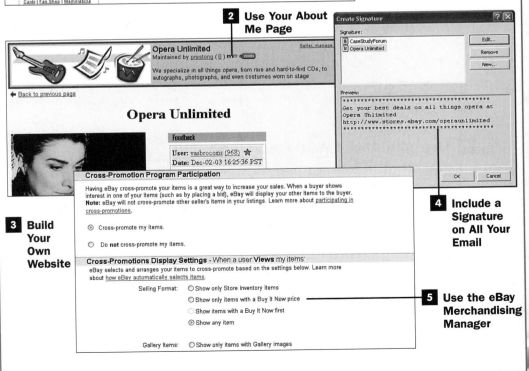

3 Build Your Own Website

4 Include a Signature on All Your Email

5 Use the eBay Merchandising Manager

163

4 Include a Signature on All Your Email

Email software lets you automatically include a signature at the bottom of every email you send. That signature can be any text you want. Create a signature that tells people about your eBay store. If you're like most people, you send email to dozens of people a day, and signatures are a great, free way to get the word out about your eBay store. Check your email software to see how to create a signature.

▶ **TIP**

In Microsoft Outlook, you can create a signature for your email messages by selecting **Tools, Options.** Then select the **Mail Format** tab and click **Signatures.** From there, follow the easy directions for creating one.

5 Use the eBay Merchandising Manager

The eBay Merchandising Manager is a great way to cross-promote the items you have for sale in your store. When someone is on a bid confirmation page for one of your items, for example, you can cross-promote other items in your store she might want to buy. For example, if you're selling a CD of the opera *La Traviata*, you can sell posters of the opera, or photographs of the composer Verdi, or other Verdi operas.

164

If you're an eBay member, you can use the eBay Merchandising Manager for free. From your **My eBay** page, click the **Preferences** tab and then click **Participate in eBay Merchandising.**

164 Make the Sale

✔ BEFORE YOU BEGIN	→ SEE ALSO
161 Set Up an eBay Store	163 Market Your Store
162 About Listing Items for Sale at Your Store	

When people buy items from your eBay store, it's a different experience from when they buy at a normal auction. Instead of bidding, they buy immediately. From your point of view, you don't do anything different—you collect the money and ship the goods.

But you should understand your customer's buying experience, so here's how they'll buy from your store:

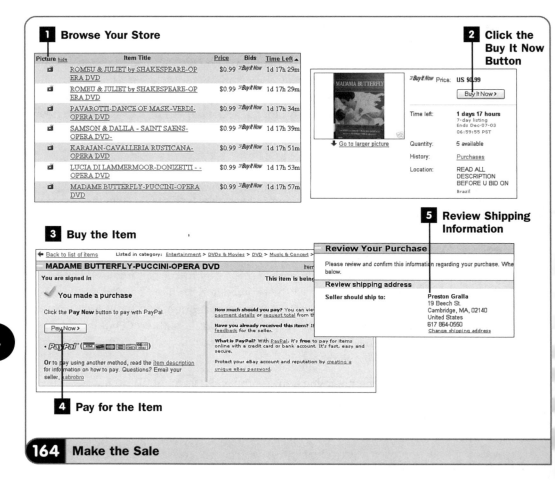

1 Browse Your Store

Potential buyers come into the main page of your store, where they can browse for items. They'll be able to search through only your store and browse by the categories you've set up.

2 Click the Buy It Now Button

Rather than bid, as in a traditional auction, visitors to your store buy the item immediately by clicking the **Buy It Now** button.

▶ NOTE

All auctions include **Time Left** information, but in the instance of a **Buy It Now** item, you don't wait until the auction is over until the seller ships the goods to the buyer.

3 Buy the Item

Before actually buying the item, visitors to your eBay store get a chance to stop the sale or to go through with it. When they've decided to go through with the purchase, they buy it—no bidding is required.

4 Pay for the Item

When you set up your store, you determined the method of payment and your buyers have to pay using one of your acceptable options. PayPal or credit cards are the best methods of payment because they do not require any handling on your part. If you've set up a store, you expect to do a high volume of business and so you can't afford to have to handle every payment.

5 Review Shipping Information

After the buyer has paid, he reviews his shipping information and submits it. The information is submitted to you in the same way it is in a regular auction. For details, see **150 Ship the Goods**.

164

24

Use eBay Power Tools

IN THIS CHAPTER:

As you've seen throughout this book, eBay is a sprawling, massive service with an enormous number of features, many of which are hidden or untapped. Millions of people use eBay every month, and because people can make significant amounts of money on it, eBay has become a highly competitive marketplace.

To help you get the most out of eBay, I've assembled these eBay power tools—software, add-ons, and websites that will help you sell and buy better and have an overall more enjoyable eBay experience.

165   About eBay Power Tools

✔ BEFORE YOU BEGIN	→ SEE ALSO
152 About Advanced Seller's Tools	**150** Ship the Goods

To help you more easily use eBay, build the best auctions that make the most money possible, and let you receive payments and ship goods more easily, entire subindustries and software and services have sprung up around eBay.

Some of these services are centered on websites that sell you services, such as the **www.shippertools.com** site that lets you easily ship and track your goods. Some services are software you download and use on your computer, as you do any other kind of software. Typically, this type of software is *shareware*. In some instances, the shareware software won't work after the specified time elapses, and in other instances, the software continues to work but in a limited fashion or it constantly throws up nag screens reminding you to pay for the software.

▶ KEY TERM

Shareware—Software you can try for free for a certain amount of time, such as 30 days, and that you're expected to pay for after that time period ends.

▶ NOTE

eBay includes many built-in tools to help sellers. For details, see **152** **About Advanced Seller's Tools.**

When using these outside tools and services, keep in mind that most are not associated with eBay. If an affiliation exists, eBay lets you know on its site or the service's site itself lets you know. If no affiliation exists between the site/service and eBay and you have trouble with the site or service, turn to the site itself, not to eBay.

Most of the outside services available for eBay help sellers, and that makes sense because the services can help you make more money from eBay than if you didn't use them. But keep in mind that the costs of all these services can quickly add up. As a seller, be careful that you're actually coming out ahead financially by using these services. It will do you no good if you spend more money on these services than you're getting in return.

166 Manage Your Auctions with Auction Sentry

✔ **BEFORE YOU BEGIN**

124 About Selling on eBay

If you do a good deal of selling and buying on eBay, keeping track of all your auctions can be tough. The **My eBay** page offers some help, but there's a lot it can't do, such as automatically place bids for you or keep track of how much money you've made on your auctions.

If you're serious about selling and buying, your best bet is to use software to help. A great deal of software is available to do this for you, but an excellent package is Auction Sentry, which offers features for both sellers and buyers. Auction Sentry is shareware, which means you can try it for free but you'll have to pay for it if you want to continue to use it for more than 10 days (it costs $14.95). To pay for it, after you install the program, click **Help** and then click **Register Auction Sentry**.

166

Auction Sentry offers many features for buyers and sellers, and I can't cover them all here. Instead, you'll just see how to get started and use the basics.

1 Download, Install, and Launch Auction Sentry

Go to **www.auctionsentry.com** and click **Download Your Free Trial Now**. Note where on your computer's hard disk the file downloads. After it downloads, double-click the file and follow the installation instructions. After it's installed, double-click the program's desktop icon to run it.

To track your auctions and to bid for you, Auction Sentry needs to know your eBay user ID and password. Select **Tools**, **Options** to open the **Options** dialog box; then click the **Identification** tab and fill in your ID and password. Enable the **Remember This Information** check box so you don't have to type your ID and password every time you use the program.

▶ TIP

To get the most out of Auction Sentry, you should synchronize your PC's clock with eBay's. To do so, select **Tools**, **Options** and click the **Time Synchronization** tab in the **Options** dialog box. Enable the **Synchronize PC's Clock with eBay's** check box and click **OK**.

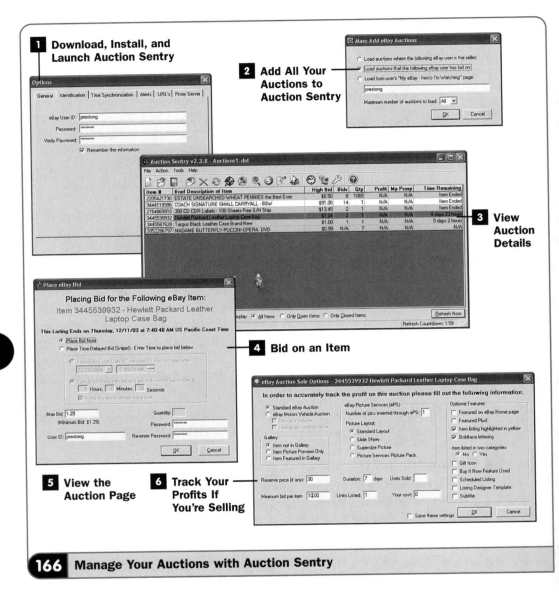

1 Download, Install, and Launch Auction Sentry

2 Add All Your Auctions to Auction Sentry

3 View Auction Details

4 Bid on an Item

5 View the Auction Page

6 Track Your Profits If You're Selling

166   Manage Your Auctions with Auction Sentry

166

2 Add All Your Auctions to Auction Sentry

You need to tell Auction Sentry to start tracking your auctions for you. You can add your auctions one at a time to the program by typing the auction number at the lower left of the **Auction Sentry** screen and clicking **Add eBay Auction**, but this can be exceedingly time-consuming and tedious, and you might forget to add auctions.

A better option is to have the program track all your auctions automatically. Select **Mass Add eBay Auctions** from the **Action** menu, type your eBay user ID into the text box, select **Load Auctions That the Following eBay User Has Bid On**, and click **OK**. If you want to track only those auctions in which you're the *seller*, select **Load Auctions Where the Following eBay User Is the Seller**.

After several minutes, the program loads all the auctions in which you're participating, or in which you have participated—including those in which you've been outbid.

3 View Auction Details

Auction Sentry shows you the most important details about each auction in which you're participating, including the item's description, the number of items for sale, the high bid, your bid, whether you've made a profit (if you're the seller), and how much time is left in the auction (or whether it has already ended).

4 Bid on an Item

You can use the program not for auctions you create, but ones you bid on. To bid on any item, right-click it in the main list and select **Bid on This Auction!** from the context menu. A **Place eBay Bid** dialog box appears. Fill in your bid. You can either place the bid immediately or use the software to snipe at the last minute.

166

5 View the Auction Page

To go to any eBay auction in which you're participating, double-click the auction in the main list. Your web browser launches, and you are sent to the auction page. You should go to the auction page at some point after you've asked Auction Sentry to place your bid, just to ensure that it's done what you've asked it to do.

6 Track Your Profits If You're Selling

If you're a seller, you can use Auction Sentry to track your profits. Right-click an auction in the main list and select **Update Profit Tracking on Selected Row** from the context menu. Then fill out information about the auction, including what type of auction it is, whether you've paid extra for features such as giving it boldfaced lettering, what your minimum bid is, and so on. Then, when the auction closes and you get paid, the software automatically tracks your profits for each auction as well as your total profits.

▶ **TIP**

When you use Auction Sentry to track your profits, you have to enter the selling price information in the screen when you select **Update Profit Tracking on Selected Row** from the context menu. Based on that information, and the fees you pay for eBay, the software calculates your profits. The profit calculation is shown on the same screen on which you enter your pricing and other information when you select **Update Profit Tracking on Selected Row** from the context menu.

---

167   **Handle Shipping with Shippertools.com**

✔ **BEFORE YOU BEGIN**

150 Ship the Goods

167

For most people, the worst part of selling on eBay is shipping the items. Finding goods to sell, creating the auction, watching the bidding, and collecting the money is fun; filling out shipping labels, taking your items to the post office, and then trying to track down shipping problems is drudgery.

The **www.shippertools.com** site neatly solves the problem. With this software package, you can print shipping labels, get discounts on shipping services such as delivery confirmation, and easily track all the items you're shipping. Shippertools.com uses the U.S. Postal Service for delivery. Here's how to use it:

1 Register at the Site

The Shippertools.com service isn't free—you pay $6.95 per month, so it's worthwhile only if you sell a great deal of items every month and need some way to manage it all. You can cancel at any time, but every month you'll be billed $6.95 until you cancel.

To register, go to **www.shippertools.com**, click **Subscribe**, and follow the instructions. The site accepts payment only through PayPal, so you need a PayPal account if you want to use the service. For details, go to **www. paypal.com**.

After you're done registering and paying, log in to the site by entering your username and password on the left side of the screen. (Use your Shippertools.com ID and password, not your eBay ID and password.)

2 Create a Shipping Label

The site's most useful feature is its capability to create customized shipping labels you can affix to your packages. You create the form online and then print the labels on your printer.

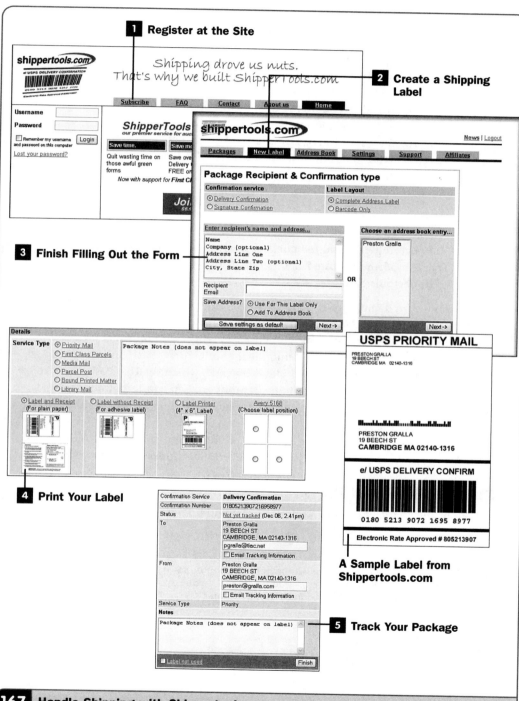

1 Register at the Site

2 Create a Shipping Label

3 Finish Filling Out the Form

4 Print Your Label

A Sample Label from Shippertools.com

5 Track Your Package

167

167 Handle Shipping with Shippertools.com

To start creating a shipping label, click the **New Label** tab and fill out the **Confirmation Service** area at the top of the form. You can choose to have delivery confirmation or signature confirmation. Here's how each differs:

- **Delivery confirmation**—You receive a confirmation from the U.S. Postal Service that the package has been delivered. It confirms that the package was delivered to the address but does not require that the recipient sign for it. Normally, the service costs $0.45 for Priority Mail and $0.55 for First Class, Media Mail, Parcel Post, and other package services. With labels from **www.shippertools.com**, Priority Mail delivery confirmation is free and you get all other delivery confirmation for $0.13.

- **Signature confirmation**—The recipient must sign for the package when it is delivered, so you receive a confirmation that the recipient actually received the package and signed for it. Signature confirmation normally costs $1.80 per delivery, but when you use **www. shippertools.com**, it costs $1.30 per delivery.

167

You also have a choice of two label types: complete address label or barcode only. The **Complete Address Label** option prints a complete address label including the delivery confirmation barcode, sender and recipient addresses, and type of shipment (Priority Mail, Media Mail, Parcel Post, and so on). When you print the label, it includes a barcode, which the U.S. Postal Service scans while the package moves to its destination. You can then track the package. As the name implies, the **Barcode Only** option prints only the barcode and not the full address. The U.S. Postal Service can deliver the package using only the barcode. Unless there's a specific reason you don't want the shipping address on the label, select the **Complete Address Label** option.

3 Finish Filling Out the Form

Fill in the recipient's name, address, and email address, and then click **Next**.

▶ TIP

When filling out the shipping form, you have the option of saving the person's address information to your Shippingtools.com address book. If you expect to ship to the same person again, enable the **Add to Address Book** option.

4 Print Your Label

The next page that appears shows the name and address of the person to whom you're shipping the item, lets you select the type of mailing service (Priority Mail, First Class, and so on), and lets you select your printing format. For example, if you have adhesive labels, select that format; if you have Avery 5168 labels, select that format; and if you're going to print to plain paper and then cut out and tape the labels, use that format.

After you select the print format, click **Next**; from the next page that appears, click **Display Label.** You can then preview your label before printing using the Adobe Acrobat reader. After you preview the label, click the print icon to print the label.

▶ WEB RESOURCE
www.adobe.com
If you don't have a copy of Adobe Acrobat, you can get it for free from this site.

5 Track Your Package

To track the status of all your packages, click the **Packages** tab. You'll see a list of all your packages, including the recipient, the status of the package, the date it was shipped, and a confirmation number. When the package is confirmed as delivered, the Status line shows that the package has been delivered. For more detailed tracking information about any package, click the confirmation number.

168

---

168 | **Calculate eBay Selling Fees with FeeFinder**

✔ BEFORE YOU BEGIN	→ SEE ALSO
127 Determine Your Selling Price and Estimate Your Selling Fees	**136** Set Payment and Shipping Options

---

If you're looking to make money on eBay, knowing your selling fees is key—how much you'll have to pay eBay for each auction. These fees can add up quickly and can be hard to calculate ahead of time. For example, you can pay extra for features such as getting your auction highlighted, putting it into a gallery, getting it boldfaced, and so on. Then there are the normal fees for each auction, and the PayPal fees, and the shipping fees....

▶ NOTE
Making it all more complicated is that those fees can change at a moment's notice. And because eBay and PayPal don't necessarily send emails when they change their fee structures, you won't necessarily know when those fees change.

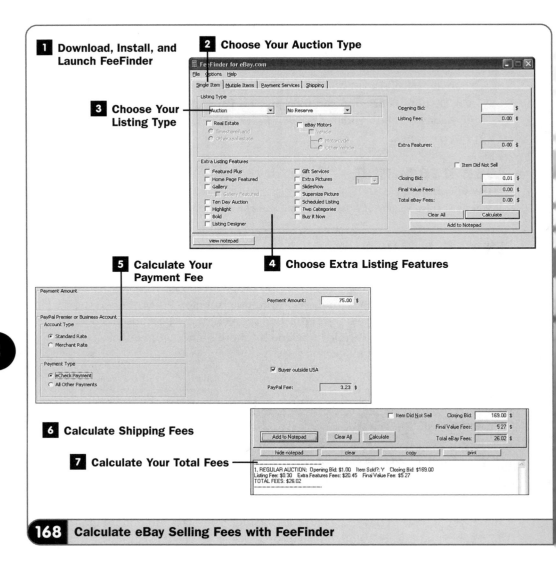

1 Download, Install, and Launch FeeFinder

2 Choose Your Auction Type

3 Choose Your Listing Type

5 Calculate Your Payment Fee

4 Choose Extra Listing Features

6 Calculate Shipping Fees

7 Calculate Your Total Fees

168

168 Calculate eBay Selling Fees with FeeFinder

That's where FeeFinder comes in. This software makes calculating your selling fees easy. Just fill in a series of screens, and the software calculates the fees for you. FeeFinder is shareware, which means you can try it for free but you have to pay for it if you want to continue to use it for more than 30 days (it costs $12.99). To pay for it, after you install the software, select **Purchase Registration Code** from the **Help** menu.

1 Download, Install, and Launch FeeFinder

Go to www.hammertap.com and look for the button labeled **FeeFinder**. Click the button and then click **Download FeeFinder Today!**. Note where on your computer's hard disk the file downloads. After it downloads, double-click the file and follow the installation instructions. After it is installed, double-click the program's desktop icon to launch it.

2 Choose Your Auction Type

Your basic choice is to track fees for single-item auctions or multiple-item auctions. Dutch auctions are always multiple-item auctions, and traditional auctions are single-item auctions. However, fixed-price auctions can be either single-item or multiple-item. Click the appropriate **Single Item** or **Multiple Items** tab for the type of auction you want to track.

3 Choose Your Listing Type

Will the auction you're tracking be a traditional auction, a fixed-priced auction, or a Dutch auction? Select the proper type from the first drop-down list in the **Listing Type** area. If you are selling real estate or running the auction through eBay Motors, be sure to enable the appropriate check box because pricing is different for these types of auctions compared to other auctions (for more information about eBay Motors, see **171 About Selling Cars and Vehicles**).

168

4 Choose Extra Listing Features

Will you be paying for extra features for the listing, such as a highlight, Featured Plus, extra pictures, and so on? If so, enable the appropriate check boxes for all the options that apply to your auction. Note that FeeFinder recalculates your fees with each new option you add or take away. When you're done, click **Calculate** and then click **Add to Notepad**. The Notepad appears at the bottom of the FeeFinder screen and shows a running list of all your payments. The FeeFinder Notepad is not the Windows Notepad, but instead is part of the FeeFinder program.

▶ TIP

To view the contents of the FeeFinder Notepad, click **View Notepad** in the bottom-left corner of the FeeFinder screen. The Notepad shows you information about all the auctions on which you're working, not just the current one.

5 Calculate Your Payment Fee

When you accept payment from PayPal, you have to pay a fee based on the amount of payment you're accepting. To find this amount, click the **Payment Services** tab, enter the payment amount, and select the account type (Standard Rate—a regular account—or Merchant Rate—a merchant credit card account). When you're done, click **Calculate** and then click **Add to Notepad**. Information is added to the FeeFinder Notepad. The Notepad adds these extra fees to your normal eBay listing fees.

▶ **TIP**

You should keep complete records of all your auctions and their associated costs. Use FeeFinder to print your fees for each auction. Make sure that you always add the auction fees to the Notepad, and when you're done, click Print.

6 Calculate Shipping Fees

To calculate your shipping fees, click the **Shipping** tab. You won't actually calculate your shipping fees from within FeeFinder. Instead, the program includes links to shipping calculators on websites of the U.S. Postal Service, United Parcel Service, and similar services. Click the link to the service you plan to use; then use the calculator at that site. When you're done, write down the shipping costs on a slip of paper, and then enter them into FeeFinder.

Keep in mind that the shipping fees charged by shipping services are typically less than the shipping fees you charge to buyers. Your actual shipping charges should include the shipping fees you pay plus expenses such as boxes, padding, and so on. You might also want to charge a minimal fee for handling to cover the amount of time you'll spend shipping the item.

7 Calculate Your Total Fees

Add together each of the fees you've calculated, and you'll come up with the total fee you'll pay for the auction. You'll also find the information in the Notepad section of the program.

---

169 Build Better Auctions with the Omni Auction Builder

✔ BEFORE YOU BEGIN	→ SEE ALSO
124 About Selling on eBay	152 About Advanced Seller's Tools

One of the best ways to ensure that your items sell is to create great-looking auctions with customized colors and layouts. But few of us are artistic enough to do that, and if you have to create many different auctions, designing an eye-catching auction page for each item can be time-consuming.

Omni Auction Builder solves that problem neatly. It lets you fill out a series of simple forms and choose from prebuilt layouts and returns beautiful auction pages.

Omni Auction Builder is shareware, which means you can try it for free but you have to pay for it if you want to continue to use it for more than 30 days (it costs $20). To pay for it, go to **www.omniauctionbuilder.com**.

1 Download, Install, and Launch Omni Auction Builder

Go to **www.omniauctionbuilder.com** and click the **Download the Free 30-Day Trial Now!** link. Note where on your computer's hard disk the file downloads. After it downloads, double-click the file and follow the installation instructions. After it is installed, double-click the program's desktop icon to launch it.

2 Choose Your Auction Title and Layout

Click the **Auction Layout** button on the left side of the screen; in the **Title and Layout** tab that appears, type a title for your auction and select from the preformatted layouts.

To customize the layout, click the **Layout Properties** tab and select the auction's properties—in essence, you'll be choosing the color of each element of the layout.

3 Write the Description of Your Auction

The description is the text that people see when they come to your auction. Click the **Auction Properties** button on the left side of the screen, click the **Description** tab, and type the auction description.

▶ NOTE

Omni Auction Builder can create auctions not just for eBay, but also for other auction sites. You don't need a separate version of the program for each auction site—just tell the program where to post your auction when it's time for posting.

169

169

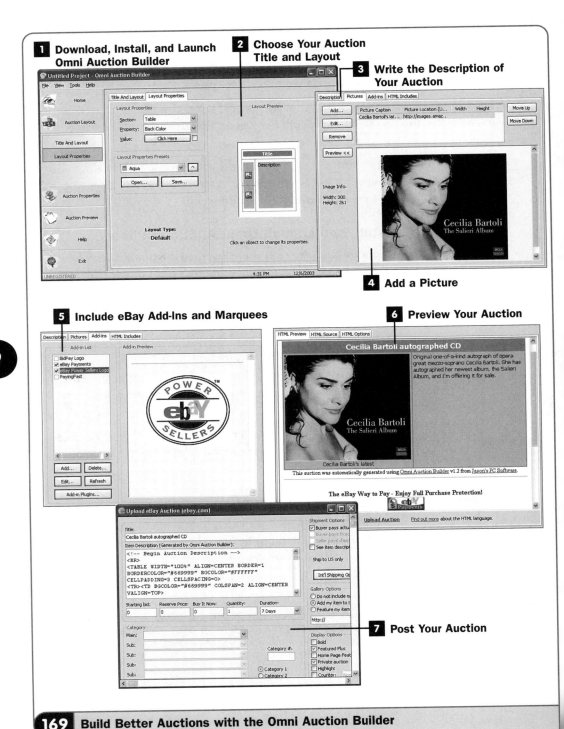

169   Build Better Auctions with the Omni Auction Builder

4 Add a Picture

You can add one or more pictures to your auction. Click the **Auction Properties** button on the left side of the screen, click the **Pictures** tab, and click the **Add** button. Then type the location of your picture (the URL for the website where the image file exists) in the **Picture Location** box and click **OK**. Note that the picture must be on a website, not on your hard disk, to show up on eBay. (For information about posting pictures on eBay, see **134 Add Pictures to Your Auction** and **138 About Digital Pictures and eBay**.)

To preview your picture, click the **Preview** button. To turn off the preview, click the **Preview** button again.

5 Include eBay Add-Ins and Marquees

The Omni Auction Builder program can automatically include logos such as the eBay Power Sellers logo. To add such icons to your auction, click the **Auction Properties** button on the left side of the screen, click the **Add-Ins** tab, and enable the check boxes for the logos you want to be part of your auction. Note that the software is slightly outdated—**eBay Payments** is no longer an eBay service and has been replaced by PayPal. For details about PayPal, go to **www.paypal.com**. The **BidPay** service has been replaced by Western Union Auction payments. For details, go to **http://www. auctionpayments.com**.

169

▶ TIP

You can use the **eBay Power Sellers** logo only if you qualify for it. To become a power seller, you must consistently sell a significant volume of items, have a 98% or higher positive feedback rating, and offer a high level of service to buyers. For details, go to **http://pages.ebay.com/services/buyandsell/welcome.html**.

You can also add scrolling marquees that contain text that scrolls across the screen. To do that, click the **Auction Properties** button on the left side of the screen, click the **HTML Includes** tab, and select the marquee you want to use.

6 Preview Your Auction

Click the **Auction Preview** button on the left side of the screen; after a few moments, you'll see a preview of what your auction will look like when it's posted on eBay. If you're not happy with it, change the layout, picture, and other properties as outlined in the previous steps.

7 Post Your Auction

When your auction is ready for public viewing, click the **Upload Auction** button on the left side of the screen and select either **eBay Uploader** or **eBay Submission Helper**. Whichever option you select lets you choose the details of your auction, including your asking price, shipping and handling information, payment methods, and so on. When you're done, follow the instructions for uploading your auction to finish and make your auction live.

▶ **NOTE**

Both **eBay Uploader** and **eBay Submission Helper** let you choose the details of your auction and upload them to eBay. But **Submission Helper** offers more help and advice, whereas **Uploader** is faster to use.

---

170 Get the Most Out of eBay with the eBay Toolbar

✔ BEFORE YOU BEGIN	→ SEE ALSO
Just jump right in.	**166** Manage Your Auctions with Auction Sentry

170

If you do a lot of buying on eBay, you might like access to all your auctions to be only a click or two away. As you've seen in this chapter, you can use add-in software such as Auction Sentry to track your auctions. But eBay offers a simple, free toolbar that latches onto Internet Explorer to let you track your auctions, search for auctions, and bid on auctions from within your browser. It also lets you track the auctions that you've created. The *eBay Toolbar* is simple to use and install and doesn't cost a penny. It won't help you do any selling, but for buyers and sellers it's a great, easy tool.

▶ **KEY TERM**

eBay Toolbar—An add-in to Internet Explorer that lets you track your auctions, search for auctions, and bid on auctions from right within Internet Explorer.

1 Download and Install the Toolbar

Go to **http://pages.ebay.com/ebay_toolbar/** and click the **Download Now** button. You come to a page that explains the terms of the toolbar's use. Read the terms, and if you agree with them, click **Download Now** again.

After several minutes, a security warning dialog box might appear. You will be asked whether you want to install the eBay Toolbar. Click **Yes**.

After a little longer, the toolbar installs. You'll notice that a small eBay logo appears in your system tray, telling you that the toolbar is running.

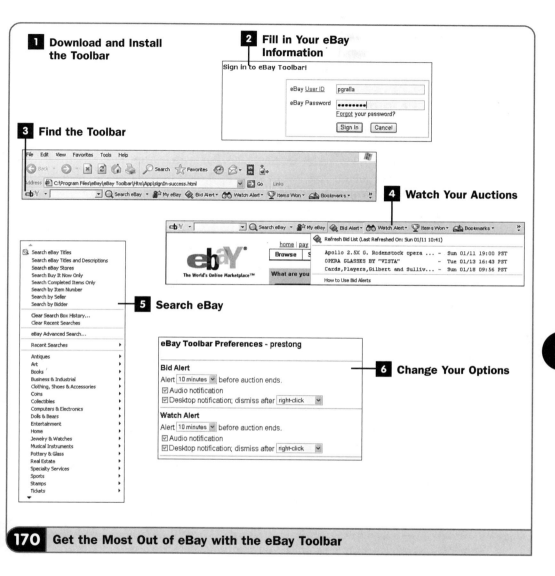

170

170   Get the Most Out of eBay with the eBay Toolbar

2 Fill in Your eBay Information

You now have two browser windows open. Close the one that reads **Please Close This Window**. In the other one, enter your eBay user ID and password to sign in to eBay.

▶ NOTE

If you don't sign in to eBay when you run the eBay Toolbar, you won't be able to track your auctions or bid on them.

3 Find the Toolbar

Your eBay Toolbar runs directly within your browser, as a toolbar underneath your address bar or underneath any other toolbars you might have added.

4 Watch Your Auctions

Perhaps the eBay Toolbar's most useful function is its capability to watch auctions on which you're bidding and report to you on what it finds. To watch auctions on which you're bidding, click the **Watch Alert** button. This Toolbar feature works with your own eBay watch alert that you set up from **My eBay**. With the **Watch Alert** button, you can create your eBay watch alerts without having to visit eBay to set them. It watches the auctions for you and sends you notifications when necessary.

The eBay Toolbar can also alert you when an auction on which you are bidding is about to end. Click the **Bid Alert** button to see a list of all auctions on which you've bid. The Bid Alert feature can alert you 10, 15, 30, 60, or 75 minutes before the auction ends, depending on your preference.

170   ▶ **NOTE**
You must be connected to the Internet if you want to use the eBay Toolbar because the Toolbar connects to the eBay site to do its work.

5 Search eBay

No matter where you are on the Web, you can search eBay without actually having to manually visit the site. In the eBay Toolbar's search box, type the item you want to search for and press **Enter**. You are sent to the eBay site, and the search is performed. You can also customize your search in many ways—for example, searching a particular category or subcategories and searching by seller, item number, and so on. To do that, type your search term and click the small arrow next to the **Search eBay** button. A menu appears, allowing you to customize your search. Select the option you want and then press **Enter**.

6 Change Your Options

You can change how the eBay Toolbar works—for example, by determining how long in advance of the end of an auction you should be sent an alert. To change your options, click the arrow next to the **eBay** logo in the Toolbar, select **eBay Toolbar Preferences**, and fill out the form.

25

Sell Cars and Vehicles

IN THIS CHAPTER:

When most people think of eBay, they think of collectibles or relatively low-priced goods. But eBay is also a great place to sell automobiles, motorcycles, boats, and parts for them—in fact, almost anything that moves and uses a motor can be sold on eBay.

eBay Motors uses the same eBay auction techniques as the rest of eBay for selling, with some differences. In this chapter, you learn how to take advantage of eBay Motors to sell your vehicle at the best price.

---

171 About Selling Cars and Vehicles

✔ **BEFORE YOU BEGIN**

124 About Selling on eBay

171

Why sell your car on eBay? After all, you have local newspapers where you can place classified ads, so why bother to go to the trouble of listing your car online?

The answer is simple: reach and money. When you list your car on eBay, you reach far more people than your local newspaper can. And when you reach more people, you're more likely to get more money for your car.

Additionally, you can get people to bid against one another, with the possibility of getting a higher price than if you list a single price on a classified ad.

Finally, eBay lets you provide much more detail in a listing than you can in a classified ad, including an entire gallery of photographs of your car or vehicle.

When selling your vehicle on eBay, you must also do more preparation than when listing it in a newspaper classified ad. Because you'll be in direct competition with many others selling their cars, you must do your homework about pricing and be smart about how you describe your car.

▶ **NOTE**

If you choose to sell your car on eBay, you're not alone. According to eBay, some 300,000 vehicles were sold on the site in 2003.

When selling a car, you follow the same basic steps as selling any other item on eBay, although with a few important differences. We cover how to prepare for selling and how to sell your car in **172** **Use the "Sell Your Vehicle" Checklist** and **173** **List Your Vehicle**.

172 Use the "Sell Your Vehicle" Checklist

✔ BEFORE YOU BEGIN	→ SEE ALSO
171 About Selling Cars and Vehicles	**127** Determine Your Selling Price and Estimate Your Selling Fees

There's a lot you need to do before you list your car on eBay, including determining its best selling price, copying down important information such as its mileage and VIN, and more.

To help you do all that, eBay has created an eBay Motors seller's checklist. In this task, you learn how to use the checklist to prepare for selling your vehicle.

1 Download and Print the Checklist

Go to **http://pages.ebay.com/motors/sell/Sell_Your_Vehicle_Checklist.pdf** and print the checklist. Note that to view the checklist, you must have a copy of Adobe Acrobat Reader, which you can download and use for free from **www.adobe.com**. As you go through the rest of the steps in this task, you'll copy information onto your printed checklist.

2 List Vehicle Information

Part 1 of the checklist covers basic vehicle information. First write down your car's *vehicle identification number (VIN)*. You can usually find it on the driver's side of the front windshield of your car, on the driver's side doorjamb, or on your car's registration. Then write down the vehicle's year, make, model, mileage, type of transmission, warranty, and similar information, as required by the checklist. Make notes of the vehicle's equipment, such as whether it has leather seats, air conditioning, and so on.

▶ KEY TERM

Vehicle identification number (VIN)—A unique identification number assigned to every vehicle that can be used to track information about the vehicle, such as whether it has been stolen or involved in an accident.

3 Take Pictures of Your Vehicle

Your auction page should include a variety of photos of your vehicle—the **Photo Checklist** in the **Vehicle Information** section advises which views to use. Take photos of your car with a digital camera. (For help taking and handling digital photos, turn to **74** Import Photos from a Digital Camera and **138** About Digital Pictures and eBay.)

172

1 Download and Print the Checklist

eBay **Motors**   **Sell Your Vehicle Checklist** ☑

Part 1: Vehicle Information

VIN: ☐☐☐☐☐☐☐☐☐☐☐☐☐☐☐☐☐ *(17-digit if 1981 or later)* Mileage: _____
Year: _____ Make: _____ Model: _____ Sub-Model: *(if applicable)* _____
Engine Cylinders: *(circle one)* 3 | 4 | 5 | 6 | 8 | 10 | 12 Title Type: *(circle one)* Clear | Salvage | Other
Transmission: *(circle one)* Manual | Automatic   Warranty: *(circle one)* Existing | None

Major Vehicle Equipment

☐ Anti Lock Brakes (ABS) ☐ Air Conditioning ☐ Cruise Control ☐ Dual Front Air Bags ☐ Dual Power Seats
☐ Leather Seats ☐ Moon Roof ☐ Multi Compact Disc ☐ Navigation System ☐ Power Door Locks
☐ Power Windows ☐ Premium Sound ☐ Tilt Wheel ☐ Traction Control

Photo Checklist

Exterior
☐ Left side ☐ Right side ☐ Front
Interior
☐ Front seats ☐ Back seats ☐ Trunk
Special
☐ Engine bay ☐ Odometer close-up ☐ Customization

2 List Vehicle Information

3 Take Pictures of Your Vehicle

4 Write Down the Vehicle Description

Part 2: Vehicle Description

Vehicle description and history: Helps answer common questions about the vehicle.
☐ Are you the original owner or know the ownership history?
☐ Have you made any modifications to the car: accessories, wheels, etc.?
☐ Do you have maintenance records on the vehicle?
☐ Do you have a warranty? (If so, provide details about remaining coverage and transferability.)

Vehicle condition: Helps buyers know what to expect when purchasing and bidding.
☐ Is there any condition not shown in your vehicle photos: mechanical, interior, exterior, cigarette odor?
☐ Does your vehicle feature any unique customization or added accessories that you'd like to showcase?
☐ Have you performed any recent maintenance on the vehicle, such as tire replacement or major service?
☐ Are there any current mechanical or cosmetic issues or near-future needed maintenance (like tires)?

Terms of sale: Helps make the sale easier and quicker if the buyer is prepared.
☐ Do you have the title available? If not, specify timing and availability.
☐ Any specific time frame for sale or payment conditions?
☐ Will you accept escrow payments?
☐ Any other paperwork required for a legal sale of a vehicle in your area (such as smog inspection)?

5 Determine a Selling Price

172

Part 3: Vehicle Pricing

Starting Price
Setting it low will encourage the most bidding activity.

Reserve Price
The Reserve Price should be set at the minimum price you will accept. Don't have a Reserve Price in mind? Consider researching similar vehicle values at eBay Motors, or try other vehicle pricing resources such as Kelley Blue Book.

Buy It Now.
You can stimulate immediate sales with Buy It Now. If a buyer wants your vehicle at your Buy It Now price, they can click to buy it directly instead of bidding on the vehicle. It can be a fast way to sell your vehicle since anyone can accept your Buy It Now price at any time. Avoid setting the Buy It Now too high such that no bidders would ever consider Buy It Now.

STEP 5 Review Edmunds.com Pricing Report

2002 Volkswagen Jetta   **TMV** True Market Value®
4 Dr GL Sedan   Pricing

	Trade-In	Private Party	Dealer Retail
National Base Price	$10,647	$11,481	$12,871
Optional Equipment	$431	$465	$581
Automatic 4-Speed Transmission	$431	$465	$581
Color Adjustment Black	$22	$23	$26
Regional Adjustment for Zip Code 02140	$-43	$-46	$-52
Mileage Adjustment 50,000 miles	$-1,457	$-1,457	$-1,457
Condition Adjustment Clean	$0	$0	$0
Total	$9,600	$10,466	$11,969
Certified Used Vehicle			$13,069

Price Another Vehicle

An Edmund's Pricing Report Can Help You Set a Selling Price

172 Use the "Sell Your Vehicle" Checklist

4 Write Down the Vehicle Description

Part 2 of the checklist covers common questions you might be asked about the vehicle, such as whether you are the original owner or know the ownership history, whether you've made modifications to the vehicle, whether you have maintenance records, whether you have a warranty, and whether it is transferable. You'll also be prompted to cover any cosmetic or other problems with the vehicle; any specializations you've made to it; and information about the terms of the sale, such as whether you have a specific time frame, whether you'll accept escrow payments, and whether the title is available. Keep in mind that Part 2 of the checklist only includes check boxes; it assumes that you are collecting the paperwork or evidence to support the answers to the questions. So be sure to keep the paperwork near at hand.

▶ NOTE

You must have your vehicle's title if you want to sell it. If you don't have the title, get it from your state's Department of Motor Vehicles. If you're making car payments, your bank or other lender might have the title. You'll have to pay off the loan before you get the title. And for a list of every state's Department of Motor Vehicles, go to **http://pages.ebay.com/ebaymotors/help/basics/dmv.html**.

Also note whether you need to gather any extra paperwork to sell the car, such as getting a smog inspection.

5 Determine a Selling Price

Part 3 of the checklist covers the vehicle pricing. When you sell your vehicle, you can set a *reserve price*, so that if that price isn't met in the bidding, you won't have to sell your car at a cost less than you think it is worth. You can also sell your car using eBay's **Buy It Now** feature. For both approaches, though, you must determine a selling price. The best way to do that is to check the estimated value of your car at two car sites: Edmund's at **www.edmunds.com** and Kelley Blue Book at **www.kbb.com**.

▶ KEY TERM

Reserve price—A secret price you set for the item you're selling; if the bids don't reach that price, you don't sell the item.

---

173 Li**st Your Vehicle**		
✔ **BEFORE YOU BEGIN**		→ **SEE ALSO**
128 About the eBay Sell Your Item Page		**137** Review and Post Your Auction
172 Use the "Sell Your Vehicle" Checklist		

After you've completed the seller's checklist, you're ready to list your vehicle on eBay Motors. Give yourself plenty of time for this task because how you handle it will determine whether your car sells and what its eventual selling price will be. When you sell a vehicle, you use the same general page you do to create listings for other items, although some differences exist. For more information about selling items on eBay and filling out an auction page, go to **124 About Selling on eBay.**

1 Open the Auction Form

Click the **Sell** link at the top of any eBay Motors page and then click **Sell Your Item on eBay Motors Now!**. If you're not logged in to eBay, you must log in before you can continue. After you log in, click **Sell Item at Online Auction**.

▶ **NOTE**

If you want to sell your vehicle at a fixed price, select **Sell at a Fixed Price**.

2 Choose Categories and Enter a VIN

First, select whether the vehicle you want to list is a passenger vehicle, motorcycle, and so on. Then select the vehicle's manufacturer and model. When you're done, click **Continue**. On the next page, enter your vehicle's VIN and click **Continue**. When you do this, your auction page is automatically populated with specific information about your vehicle, based on its VIN.

▶ **NOTE**

If you're selling a car older than a 1991 model, it won't have a VIN that can be used to automatically fill in auction information. In that case, or in an instance in which you can't locate the VIN, in the **Listing a 1991 or Older Vehicle?** section of the page, click **Continue** and fill out information about the car.

3 Write the Auction Title and Description

You come to a page on which you write the auction title and a description of the vehicle. If you entered a VIN for a 1992 or newer vehicle, some information will already be filled in.

For basic information about how to write a title and description, turn to **130 Write the Title and Description**; to learn how to use HTML to format the description, turn to **131 Format Your Description with eBay's HTML Editor**. And for more advice on how to create titles and descriptions that sell, see **156 About Writing Effective Ad Copy**, **157 Jazz Up Text and Headlines with HTML**, and **158 Colorize and Change Fonts and Add Effects with HTML**.

Use the information from your seller's checklist, as detailed in **172 Use the "Sell Your Vehicle" Checklist** to fill out the page, including equipment, mileage, whether there is a warranty and title, and so on.

173

1 Open the Auction Form

3 Write the Auction Title and Description

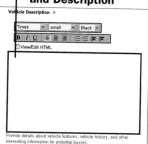

2 Choose Categories and Enter a VIN

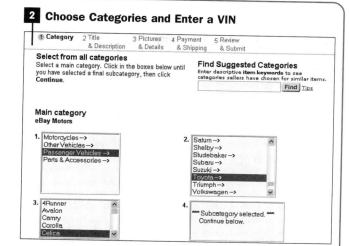

5 Choose Payment and Shipping Information

6 Review and Submit Your Auction

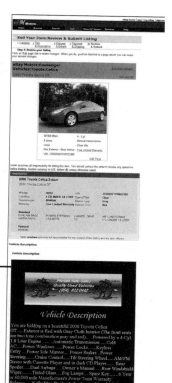

4 Include Pictures and Details

173

When writing a description and history of a vehicle, there are some special things you should include or be aware of. Put yourself in the shoes of the buyer and imagine what you would want to know about a used car. In particular, consider these tips:

- Include the car's ownership and maintenance history, as far as you know it.

- Highlight any special features, options, or equipment such as a sunroof or special sound system.

- If you have a warranty that can be transferred, mention that and include details.

- Note any damage, wear and tear, and mechanical or cosmetic problems with the vehicle.

- If your car has been in an accident, mention that.

▶ **TIP**

It's important to be as accurate and honest as possible in your description so you don't later run into problems after the sale has been made—you don't want the buyer claiming you misrepresented the condition of the car.

173

In the **Terms of Sale** section of the auction page, you should include the terms of the sale. Again, be as explicit as possible here. Do you have any requirements that a deposit (or partial payment) be made? If so, how long does the buyer have to make the deposit? Sellers frequently ask that a partial payment be made within 24–72 hours. How will you accept payment? PayPal is an excellent way to accept payment and has become the standard on eBay. (For more information, go to **www.paypal.com**.) Will you accept escrow payments? Will you ship the car, and if so, who will pay for shipping costs? How will the title be transferred—in person or some other way?

▶ **NOTE**

Consider having your vehicle inspected before selling it and making the inspection available online to potential buyers. A posted inspection makes people more likely to bid on the vehicle. For details, go to **http://pages.ebay.com/ebaymotors/services/ inspection/inspection.html**. If you do have an inspection done, enable the **Vehicle Has Been Inspected** check box on the auction creation page and provide information about the inspection in your description.

When you're done filling in the **Describe Your Item** page of the auction-creation form, click the **Continue** button located at the bottom of the page.

4 Include Pictures and Details

Next, you select the details of your auction, including its length, starting price, whether you want a reserve price, and similar information. You fill out this page just as you do a normal eBay auction. For details, see **132 Choose Pricing, Duration, and Location**. Make sure that you include pictures; without them, it's unlikely that anyone will buy your vehicle. It's best to include several photos, with a variety of views, as outlined in the seller's checklist. For information on how to post pictures to your auction page, see **134 Add Pictures to Your Auction**.

When you're done with the **Provide Pictures & Item Details** page of the auction-creation form, click **Continue**. There might be a slight delay as your pictures upload.

5 Choose Payment and Shipping Information

On the **Enter Payment & Shipping** page, you detail the terms of the sale. Be as explicit as possible here. Do you have any requirements that a deposit (or a partial payment) be made? If so, how long does the buyer have to make the deposit? Sellers frequently ask that a partial payment be made within 24–72 hours after the auction ends. How will you accept payment? PayPal is an excellent way to accept payment and has become the standard on eBay. (For more information, go to **www.paypal.com**.) Will you accept escrow payments using an escrow service such as **www.escrows.com**? Will you ship the car, and if so, who will pay for shipping costs? How will the title be transferred—in person or some other way?

After you fill out the **Enter Payment & Shipping** page, click the **Continue** button at the bottom of the page.

173

▶ NOTE

There are two places on the selling form where you enter payment and shipping information. Double-check that the information is consistent in both places and that you don't contradict yourself.

6 Review and Submit Your Auction

The next page you see asks whether the vehicle has been modified in any special way or whether it's what eBay considers a "special vehicle type." (The special vehicle types are listed on the page.) If the vehicle has not been modified and is not a special vehicle, it qualifies for the eBay warranty. (For details, go to **http://pages.motors.ebay.com/services/assurance.html**.) When you're done with the page, click **Continue**.

You come to a page that shows the completed auction, including your eBay fees. Review the page and click the **Back** button if you want to change any details. When you're done, click the **Submit Listing** button at the bottom of the page. Make absolutely sure that everything is the way you want it before submitting the listing. For details, see **137** **Review and Post Your Auction**.

---

174 Use the CarAd Listing Tool

✔ BEFORE YOU BEGIN	→ SEE ALSO
172 Use the "Sell Your Vehicle" Checklist	**173** List Your Vehicle

---

A lot of money is at stake when you're selling a vehicle—many thousands of dollars. Because of that, you should use every tool you can to sell it and sell it at the best price. As you learned from **173** **List Your Vehicle**, creating a listing to sell a vehicle can be a tedious, time-consuming process.

To help make your listing go more smoothly, and to create the best-looking auction possible, consider using CarAd, a for-pay service owned by eBay that makes listing your vehicle as easy as filling in a series of forms. The service includes templates and layouts to make your auction as enticing as possible. It costs $9.95 per listing.

174

1 Have Your Seller's Checklist Ready

You're going to need all the information you normally would gather when selling a vehicle, so prepare your seller's checklist as detailed in **172** **Use the "Sell Your Vehicle" Checklist**.

2 Register at CarAd

Go to **www.carad.com** and click the **Register Now** button. You'll be asked information such as your name, address, and so on. You must also include your eBay ID and password, so if you haven't registered on eBay yet, you must do so before using CarAd.

The registration screen also includes some basic information that will be included in your listing, such as the terms of the sale, how you'll accept payment, whether you'll accept escrow payments, shipping information, and so on. You can always change this later, but you'll save time if you enter the information correctly when you register. When you're done, click the **Register** button and then click **Click Here to Continue**. The **Profile** page appears.

1 Have Your Seller's Checklist Ready

2 Register at CarAd

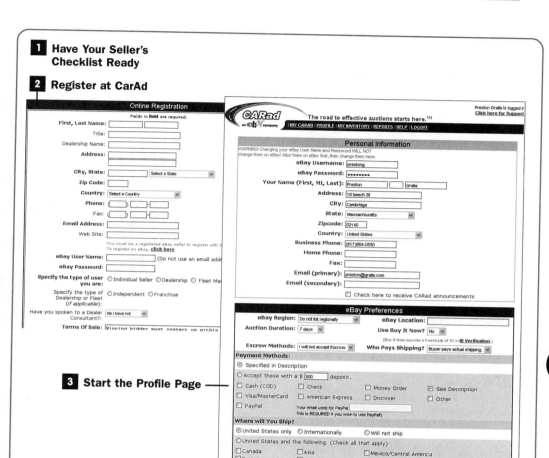

3 Start the Profile Page

4 Choose Templates and Complete the Profile

174

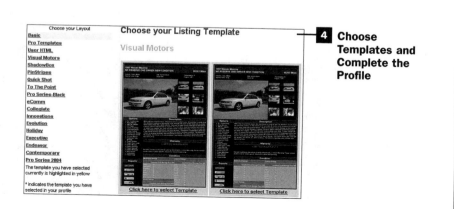

174 Use the CarAd Listing Tool

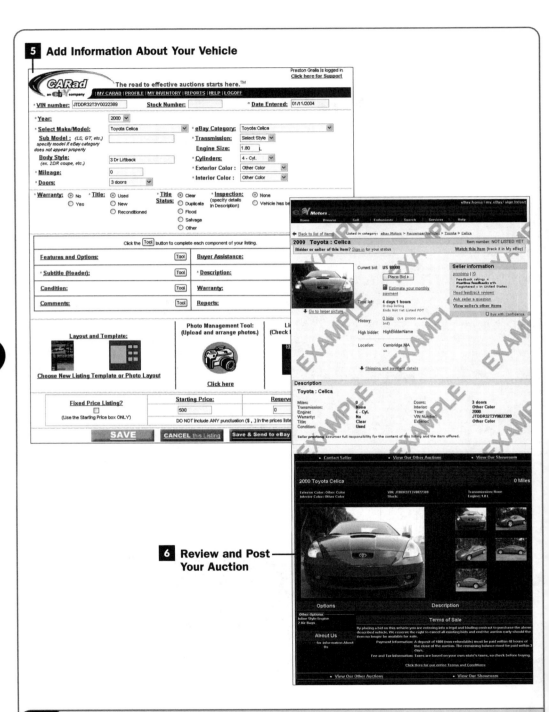

5 Add Information About Your Vehicle

174

6 Review and Post Your Auction

174 Use the CarAd Listing Tool (continued)

3 Start the Profile Page

CarAd has been designed not only for people selling one vehicle, but for dealers and those who sell multiple vehicles. Because of that, it bases everything on a *profile* you create. The profile is, in essence, the layout for your auction page, so when you create a profile, you're creating a template for your auctions. The profile includes information such as which layout to use and the terms of the sale, but not individual details about the vehicle you're selling— that you complete later.

Start filling out the **Profile** page, including information such as shipping, payment methods, and so on. Much of this data is picked up from the registration page, but you have a chance to change it now, so review your information.

4 Choose Templates and Complete the Profile

One of the best features of CarAd is the multiple templates you can use for laying out your auction. To select your favorite template, click the **Choose Listing and Photo Layouts** link on the **Profile** page. On the left side of the **Choose Your Listing Template** page, review the layouts. Click a layout name to see a preview on the right. When you find a layout you want to use, click the **Click Here to Select Template** link beneath it.

174

▶ TIP

If you have your own template or HTML code you want to use in your auction listing, you can do that in CarAd as well. From the list of templates, select **User HTML** to use your own HTML code in a listing.

You then have a choice of several photo templates to use. Each template includes a different number of photos and arrangement of photos on the page. When you find the one you want to use, click the **Click Here to Select Template** link beneath the template preview.

When you're done choosing your templates, complete the rest of the **Profile** page, including information about any fees and taxes, terms and conditions, and other basic information about your auction. There is also an **About Us** section you can use to provide more information about you—especially useful if you are a dealer.

When you're done, click the **Update Profile** button at the bottom of the **Profile** page.

▶ **NOTE**

The **Showroom Layout** section of the profile applies only to dealers, so you don't need to fill it out unless you're a dealer. It lets you include not only the vehicle you're selling on eBay, but also other inventory you have that's available for sale at your showroom but not online.

5 Add Information About Your Vehicle

After you've updated your profile, a mostly blank page appears with a series of icons along the bottom. Click an icon to add information about your vehicle to your auction page. There are icons for adding a car, a motorcycle, or another kind of vehicle (planes, boats, trucks, and so on). Keep in mind that the form is used by dealers as well as individuals, so there are icons that might not be useful to you (such as the **Add to Inventory** icon). Just ignore the icons you don't need to use.

A page appears asking for the vehicle's VIN. Type the VIN to populate the auction with information about your vehicle. Then click **Decode VIN**. If you don't have a VIN, click **Skip Decode** instead. (If you don't have a VIN, no data will populate the form for you. You can still create your auction, but you have to enter information manually.)

A page appears with the information about the specific car you're planning to sell, including the make and model, the category, what equipment it has, and so on—the same information you would include in a normal auction as detailed in **173** **List Your Vehicle**. Fill in the required information. (If you entered the VIN, some of this data is already entered.)

▶ **TIP**

It's important to include pictures of the vehicle you want to sell. To upload them, use the **Photo Management Tool**. It lets you choose your pictures and arrange them based on the photo template you chose in step 4.

6 Review and Post Your Auction

Don't post your auction yet; you should first preview it to ensure that it's what you want to appear. In the **Listing Preview** section of the information page, click the **Click Here** button to preview your auction page. After you preview it, edit it until you're pleased with it. To post the auction, click **Save & Send to eBay**. To save the auction for later editing or posting, click **Save**. To work on the auction at a later date, log back in to CarAd and, from the page that appears, select the auction.

175 About Accepting Payment for Your Vehicle

✔ **BEFORE YOU BEGIN**	→ **SEE ALSO**
147 About Accepting Payments	**148** About Accepting Escrow Service Payments
	149 About Problem Buyers

The hard work is over. You created your auction, you watched the bids come in, and you have a high bidder. Now all you need to do is collect the money.

Well, not quite. It's a little more complicated than that because selling an $8,000 car is a bit different from selling a $4.75 Yu-Gi-Oh card.

Many of the basics are the same, however, so for information about completing an eBay sale, go to **145** **Track Your Auction**.

However, some differences exist between completing a regular sale and collecting the money on eBay Motors, and completing a regular sale and collecting the money on eBay:

- **You should collect the down payment as detailed in your terms**—When you created your listing, you most likely asked that a down payment (or a partial payment) be made within a certain amount of time—for example, 48 hours after the close of the auction. As soon as the auction ends, send an email to the high bidder, reminding him when the down payment is due and of how he can pay you. The quickest and easiest way is using PayPal. For details, go to **www.paypal.com**.

  In instances where the buyer is financing the car, he gets the loan money from a financial institution and then makes a payment to you. In instances where the buyer is using an escrow service, the escrow service serves as a go-between. See **148** **About Accepting Escrow Service Payments** for more details.

- **You should have the title and other papers ready**—The buyer will require the title to the vehicle; depending on your state and the terms of the sale, the buyer might ask for other paperwork as well, such as a contract showing the selling price of the car (this information might be required so he can pay the proper amount of taxes on the car). Make sure that all your papers are in order and that the sales price was also printed on the title.

- **Arrange for final payment**—After you have received the down payment, make arrangements for final payment. Again, this depends on the terms you've asked for. In some cases, the buyer might not want to make final payment until he has seen the condition of the vehicle. If the buyer is financing

175

the sale, he might first get the money from his financial institution and then pay you; in some instances, the buyer might want the financial institution to pay you directly.

- **Arrange for the vehicle to be picked up**—After payment, make arrangements for the vehicle to be picked up by the buyer. If you've agreed to ship the car, make it clear who is responsible for getting the shipping done, you or the buyer.

175

26

Sell Tickets

IN THIS CHAPTER:

Got a ticket to an event of any kind that you need to sell? No need to skulk to the ballpark and risk being an illegal scalper, or try to sell concert tickets at a loss to friends. With eBay, you get a worldwide audience for your tickets.

Selling tickets differs somewhat from selling other items on eBay, and this chapter tells you what you need to know.

176   About Selling Tickets

✔ BEFORE YOU BEGIN

124 About Selling on eBay

The basics of selling tickets on eBay are no different from selling any other item, although you obviously have to include ticket-specific information such as the location of the seats you're selling.

The big question for sellers is whether it's legal to sell tickets on eBay. The answer is *yes*, although with certain limitations on the price you're allowed to charge. Some states have antiscalping laws that regulate the price you're allowed to charge for tickets when you resell them—you might not be allowed to sell them for more than the face value, or you might be able to sell them for only a few dollars over the face value. Other states have no such regulations. And the regulations might apply only if you live in the same state in which the event will take place.

The following table, taken from eBay, outlines what you need to know before selling:

Location of Event	Location of Seller	Location of Bidder	eBay Policy
Regulated location	Same as event	Any location	Seller cannot accept bids above state-established pricing limitations.
Regulated location	Different from event	Same as event	Seller can accept bids without limit, but bidder cannot exceed state-established pricing limitations.

Location of Event	Location of Seller	Location of Bidder	eBay Policy
Regulated location	Different from event	Different from event	Seller can accept bids without limit.
Nonregulated location	Any location	Any location	Seller can accept bids without limit, and bidders can bid without limit.

States that regulate ticket sales have different rules. For example, Connecticut and North Carolina have pricing limitations of face value plus $3, but Missouri limits the price to face value for sporting events but has no limit on other events.

▶ WEB RESOURCE

http://pages.ebay.com/help/policies/event-tickets.html
For details about which states regulate ticket prices, visit this page of the eBay website.

eBay tries to follow each of the state's regulations. It determines where you live by your eBay registration information and determines where the event is taking place by the information you put in the auction page. eBay requires that you disclose the actual face value of the tickets. If you falsely represent the face value of tickets, you can be permanently suspended from eBay and could also be subject to criminal prosecution in the state in which you live. And obviously, you won't have any eBay consumer protections if you violate the law. So, if you're selling tickets, keep your nose clean and follow the letter of the law.

176

▶ TIP

When creating your auction, make sure that your auction doesn't end after the ticket date. This might sound obvious, but it's easy to forget these kinds of last-minute details.

If you haven't bought the tickets yet but you know that you're going to buy them in order to turn around and sell them on eBay, you might be able to use the Ticketfast delivery service that can deliver tickets through email. Ticketfast delivery is available only if you buy your ticket from **www.ticketmaster.com**, and only for certain events. So, if you're buying from Ticketmaster, check to see whether you can use the Ticketfast option.

177   Create a Ticket Auction

✔ BEFORE YOU BEGIN	→ SEE ALSO
124 About Selling on eBay **176** About Selling Tickets	**145** Track Your Auction

It's easy to sell tickets on eBay—just create an auction for them as you do for any other item. However, as you'll see in this task, you should take into account some special things when selling tickets.

1 Prepare Your Ticket Information

Selling a ticket requires that you have very specific information about it, not just the date and time but also the seat, row number, and similar information. So have your ticket at hand when you're filling out your auction listing.

Additionally, as explained later in this task, in some circumstances you might have to make available to eBay a scanned image of the ticket, so scan your ticket and have the electronic file accessible on your computer. Finally, check **http://pages.ebay.com/help/policies/event-tickets.html** for information about whether you have any limitations on how much you are allowed to accept for your tickets.

2 Start the Auction Page

Click the **Sell** button at the top of any eBay page; then select **Sell Item at Online Auction** and click **Continue**. (For details about starting an auction page, see **129** **Start the Sell Form and Choose a Category**.) When the **Sell Your Item: Select Category** page appears, select **Tickets** as your category and **Event Tickets** as the subcategory. Click **Continue**.

▶ NOTE

You can also select the **Experiences** or **Other** subcategory when you select **Tickets** as your main category. The **Experiences** subcategory is primarily for package tours and theme park tickets. The **Other** category is for anything that can't otherwise be categorized but belongs in the ticket area, for example, VIP passes to clubs and raffle tickets.

3 Fill In the Auction Title

For the title of your auction, make sure that you include the word *tickets*, the name of the artist or team, and the venue. Buyers frequently find tickets based on keyword searches, so if you put all the right words into your title, buyers are more likely to find your auction. Specifically, when writing a title, be sure to include the following:

- The word *tickets*
- The number of tickets
- The artist/team name(s)
- The event date and location
- The seat vicinity or any unique features about the tickets

You can add a subtitle for an additional fee of $0.50. If you think the title doesn't convey enough information about the tickets, it might be worthwhile to pay for a subtitle.

4 Fill In the Item Specifics and Description

In the **Item Specifics: Tickets** section, provide the event type, the number of tickets, the venue location, the section and row of the tickets, and so on. It's vital that you do this correctly because this information is used when someone does a **Tickets Finder** search. If you don't enter the information in this section, your tickets won't show up in the **Tickets Finder** search results.

▶ NOTE

In the **Item Specifics: Tickets** section, when you select from the pull-down menus, your browser might refresh itself whenever you make a choice. Don't be disconcerted; this is normal behavior and nothing is wrong with what you're doing.

177

The free-form **Item Description** you type should be concise but should include all the pertinent details about the tickets and event. In particular, be sure to include the following:

- The title of the event (artist, team, game, and so on).
- The event date and time.
- The event venue location and venue name.
- The number of tickets.
- The seat location (section and row).
- Any unique information about the seats, such as whether they're together, if they're obstructed views, if they're front-row seats, whether parking is included, and so on.
- A venue seating map or a sight-line picture that shows the view from the seats. You can get free venue maps from eBay at **http://enterprise.channeladvisor.com/tickets/?ssPageName= CatTixchanneladvisor**. You can also get maps of many venues from **www.seatdata.com**.

177

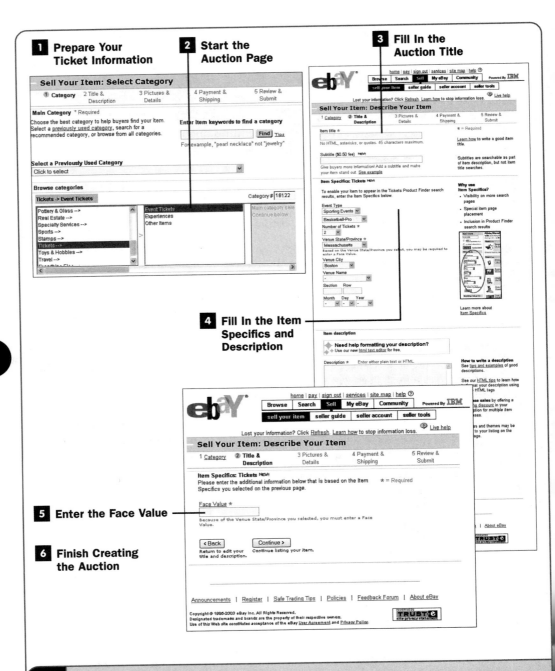

▶ **TIP**

Make sure that you have the electronic file containing scanned tickets. eBay might ask you to upload the scanned ticket (although in the many auctions I've created, I've never been asked for a scanned ticket). Still, be prepared!

When you finish with the description, click **Continue**.

5 Enter the Face Value

Depending on the state in which you live, you might have to enter the face value of the tickets, and you might not be able to charge much more than the face value. If you are required by eBay to list the face value, a page appears asking that you list the face value of the ticket. When you're done, click **Continue**.

6 Finish Creating the Auction

You'll be asked to fill in details of the auction, such as its duration, a minimum price for the tickets, and so on, as well as shipping information. For information about how to fill in the auction details and shipping information and how to review and post your auction, turn to **132** **Choose Pricing, Duration, and Location**, **135** **Choose Auction Extras**, **136** **Set Payment and Shipping Options**, and **137** **Review and Post Your Auction**.

When choosing shipping information, be sure to give people a pricing option for an overnight mail service, such as Federal Express, to ensure that the tickets will get to them on time. If you have tickets that can be delivered using Ticketfast, mention that as well.

▶ **TIP**

It's not a bad idea to require an overnight service as a shipping method because that way there will be no disagreements over whether the tickets arrived in time. With a service such as Federal Express, you can also track your shipment and get confirmation that it was received by the buyer.

178 **About Accepting Money and Shipping the Tickets**

✔ BEFORE YOU BEGIN	→ SEE ALSO
147 About Accepting Payments	**150** Ship the Goods
	151 Pay the eBay Fees

You accept payments for tickets on eBay the same way you do for other items, so for more details on how to get your money from the buyer, turn to **147** **About Accepting Payments**. The same general rules hold true for shipping tickets as for shipping other items, so for details about shipping, see **150** **Ship the Goods**.

However, you should take into account a number of things when accepting payments for and shipping tickets:

- Accept only immediate payment methods, such as PayPal. Tickets are time sensitive, and after their date passes, you can't sell them anymore. If you accept payment methods that require mailing (such as checks or money orders), the payment could get held up or lost, you could be sent a bad check, or similar problems might occur. As you're waiting for the payment to arrive or the check to clear after you've deposited it, the ticket event date might creep up and pass you by. In that case, you'd be out of luck because the buyer could back out. (For details about setting up a PayPal account and receiving PayPal payments, go to **www.paypal.com**.)

- Immediately follow up your auction closing with an email to the high bidder. Because tickets are time sensitive, you want to have enough time to relist them if something goes wrong with the first buyer.

178

- Require that payment be made within one or two days of your auction closing. Again, tickets are time sensitive; if you don't receive payment within the time you've allotted, relist the tickets in another auction.

- If you're buying a ticket from Ticketmaster that you later plan to sell on eBay, consider asking that you get it through Ticketfast. With Ticketfast, you get a file in Adobe Acrobat (`.pdf`) format, which you can print and use as a ticket. If you get a Ticketfast ticket, you can email the Ticketfast file to the buyer, and delivery will be immediate and done.

- When shipping tickets, use a next-day delivery service such as Federal Express or UPS that enables you to track your shipment. That way, you will have a record that your ticket was received and the buyer cannot claim she never received it. You can also use the U.S. Postal Service for next-day delivery.

179 Make Sure You Don't Get Burned Selling Tickets

✔ BEFORE YOU BEGIN	→ SEE ALSO
149 About Problem Buyers	

Because tickets are time sensitive, if you run into problems with a buyer, you could end up not being able to sell your tickets. When selling tickets, you must be more careful dealing with buyers than when selling most other items.

Most of eBay's fraud protections are designed to cover the buyer, not the seller. To ensure that you don't get burned by buyers of your tickets, you must take matters into your own hands. Follow these tips, and you'll help make sure that you don't get burned:

- **Accept only PayPal payments**—PayPal payments are instantaneous. You're either paid or you're not—no bounced checks, "the money is in the mail" excuses, or similar problems. In short, you're guaranteed payment. For details about setting up a PayPal account and accepting payments, go to **www.paypal.com**.

- **Know your buyer**—Check the buyer's feedback information so you know ahead of time whether you might have a problem buyer on your hands. To check out another eBay member's feedback, click his name on an auction page, and you'll see all the feedback that he has received.

- **Set a minimum positive rating for buyers**—When you create your auction, in your description tell potential buyers that you'll only sell to those who have a certain minimum feedback rating. You can tell a member's feedback rating by looking at the number in parentheses after the member's ID. What minimum rating you'll accept is based on personal preferences, but be careful if someone doesn't have a rating above 5 or 10.

▶ **TIP**

If you set a minimum positive feedback rating for your bidders, you won't have to deal with people who have bad track records or who are so new to eBay that you can't tell what kind of track records they have. You can also specify that you won't sell to anyone with any negative feedback whatsoever.

- **Ship using a tracking number and insurance**—If you ship the tickets with some type of tracking or delivery confirmation and the buyer claims she never received the ticket, you have confirmation that she did.

179

- **Ship tickets only after you've received payment and the payment has gone through**—This one sounds obvious, but you'd be surprised at how persuasive some scammers can be and the excuses they can dream up. So never violate this rule.

- **Create a blocked bidder/buyer list**—If you've had a bad experience with a bidder or have heard of other sellers who have, you can block specific people from bidding on your auction. Go to **http://offer.ebay.com/ws2/eBayISAPI.dll?bidderblocklogin** and follow the instructions on this eBay page to block specific members from bidding on your auctions.

179

PART VI

Build a Blog

IN THIS CHAPTER

27

Blogging Basics

IN THIS CHAPTER:

Not long ago, Merriam-Webster, Inc. announced that *blog* had been selected as the number one word for the year. It defined a blog as "a website that contains an online personal journal with reflections, comments, and often hyperlinks."

There are articles on how the blogging community has pointed out inconsistencies in national news stories. During the election process in 2004, blogs were used for organizing and getting news out to innumerable political groups. Blogs are praised and belittled in equal amounts in the press, but people are reading them more and more and thus they are here to stay.

It's pretty cool that the blog has become as prominent as fast as it has, but the blog is not limited to personal musings about life, politics, or music by any means. A well-designed and maintained blog can be used by a company to interact with its customers. It can deliver news with comments directly attached to the story. It can be a source for users of a product to interact with each other. It can become a way to ask questions of your readers and have them help you define the direction of your site. A blog can also be a great tool for a large group of people who are addressing the same problem. It enables them to communicate with one another in a place where the conversation is maintained and kept public, unlike email. I can think of no site that is active and vibrant that does not have a blog associated with it in some way or another.

180

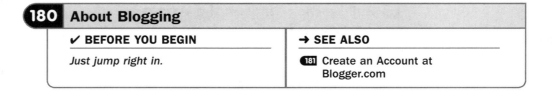

180 About Blogging

✔ BEFORE YOU BEGIN	→ SEE ALSO
Just jump right in.	**181** Create an Account at Blogger.com

The key to blogging is not the setup or anything that you can learn here—the key is making it a part of your day and adding content as regularly as you can. If you want your blog to be successful, you need to be prepared to work on it on a schedule and to look at the comments as they come back so you can use the input in your work.

To get an idea of what a good blog can do, you are going to look at a couple before you create one of your own.

Review the Cooking with Amy Blog

Let's review **http://cookingwithamy.blogspot.com**.Cooking with Amy is a blog that is operated by **Amy Sherman** of San Francisco. Her blog on various cooking, eating, and living topics was rated by **Forbes.com** as one of the best blogs on the Net. If you take a look, it is a perfect example of a blog. There are **postings** on a regular basis that detail recipes, vacation spots, and restaurants. On the left side, there are **links** to other sites that Amy thinks are worth visiting along with an **About blurb** that gives you an idea of what the site is about. Farther down the page are **archives** so that you can go to all the postings since the inception of the site in 2003.

There is a **Search** function so that you can find subjects you want in the archives easily.

At the bottom of every entry is a link to **comments**. There aren't comments on every posting, but look through some. As I write this, Amy is somewhere in Mexico enjoying the sun and food and, as she posts from Mexico, her readers are giving her feedback and telling her where to go and what to try.

Amy's blog is more than a simple static website.

Review the Electablog Blog

Electablog is a very different sort of blog than **Cooking with Amy**. **Electablog** is a political blog and showcases the views of the author **Dave Pell**. If you explore this blog, you'll find that there is not a way to add comments to the posts (which sort of makes sense on a political site, where most posts would degenerate into name calling). The owner of the site is not interested in becoming a forum to express other viewpoints in an unregulated sort of way.

180

The links on **Electablog** are interesting. Each is an email link you can use to notify friends who you think might be interested in a particular posting. The **Link** button also provides a page with each article on its own page so that you can link to it directly. This is very handy because linking to a blog directly gets you to the latest posting and not necessarily the posting you wanted.

Review a Macromedia Blog

Last, open and review **http://www.markme.com/mesh/**.

This is a **Flash** developer's blog by **Mike Chambers** from **Macromedia**, the software company that makes **Flash** (and a lot of other professional web development software). This blog tends to be very technical and deals almost exclusively with **Flash**, but it shows the blog as a way for a company to get information out and get comments back.

On the day I am writing this, Mike has mentioned that several people have emailed him for new features they would like to see added to **Macromedia's Flash** product. Mike notes that these things are already possible to do by changing some of the preferences in the product, so he is using the blog as a tech support tool. This allows him to answer a question for one or two people, but in such a way that will help many people who might read the post on his blog today—or anytime in the future because the answer is archived.

Businesses can very effectively use blogs to get information to and from their users in an easily searchable format without having to wait for the mail or conferences or the next release of a product.

Plan Your Blog

Planning out your blog on paper and setting goals will help you create a blog that will bring people back. With planning, you are going to be able to keep up to date and have the best features to help you and your viewers get the most out of it. Here are some questions to ask yourself to get you started:

- **What is the subject of your blog?** Any reason is fine, but knowing what that is before you start is a good way to make sure you don't get off track.

- **Do you want to have your viewers comment back?** Are you expecting to respond to your viewers, and do you want their feedback?

- **Do you want people to link to your individual pages or just your overall blog?** If you want people to use pieces of your blog and be able to access them from other sites without going to your current page, you should think about that early on.

- **Are you going to be able to keep your blog up to date?** As someone who kept up a blog daily for some time, I can tell you this is not trivial. If you can't do it daily, set the expectation of your viewers so that they aren't coming back more often than you are posting. If you disappoint people, they will find other places on the Web in which to go.

181

---

181 Create an Account at Blogger.com

✔ BEFORE YOU BEGIN	→ SEE ALSO
180 About Blogging	**182** Build a Blog Through the Wizard

After you have an idea of the things that can be done in blogs in general, you need to pick a service. There are a lot of different ones: Microsoft (**spaces.msn.com**), TypePad (**www.typepad.com**), Salon.com (**www.salon.com/blogs/**), and many others offer yearly or monthly subscriptions or are free. When you are ready to do your blog, you should look at the different services. For this task and the others in this book, you are going to use **Blogger**, which can be found at **http://www.blogger.com**.

1 Go to http://www.blogger.com

2 Take the Blogger Quick Tour

3 Click on the Create a Blog Now button

4 Accept the Terms of Service

181

Create an Account at Blogger.com

1 Go to http://www.blogger.com

Blogger is one of the original blogging tools and is used today by many of the most popular blogs. It is easy to use and powerful enough to do most anything you want with your blog.

2 Take the Blogger Quick Tour

The **Quick Tour** gives you a really good idea of what blogging is all about and lets you see the features available to you in the program. Some of these features include being able to post from an email through instant blogging with the **BlogThis!** button, and using **AudioBlogger**, which lets you blog over the phone to your site and makes your call available as an MP3 audio file from your site.

3 Click on the Create a Blog Now Button

Click on the **Create a Blog Now** button. The first thing you need to do with **Blogger** is to create an account for yourself. This is a lot like creating an account anywhere. You'll need a username, a password, a regular name that people can call you, and your email address.

4 Accept the Terms of Service

To create the account, you have to accept the terms of service. When you click on the **Continue** button, you will have created your account. After you have your account set up, the wizard will continue on to create your first blog, which you are going to do in the next task.

182

182 Build a Blog Through the Wizard	
✔ **BEFORE YOU BEGIN**	→ **SEE ALSO**
181 Create an Account at Blogger.com	**189** Edit Your Blog from the Dashboard
	190 Add a Post

When you get your **Blogger** account, you can keep going to create your blog. Lets review a few points mentioned previously. After all, blogs take commitment. Are you committed to your subject and to checking your blog for responses? Have you outlined your writing before sitting in front of that lonely, blank, and very spacious text entry box? If so, proceed.

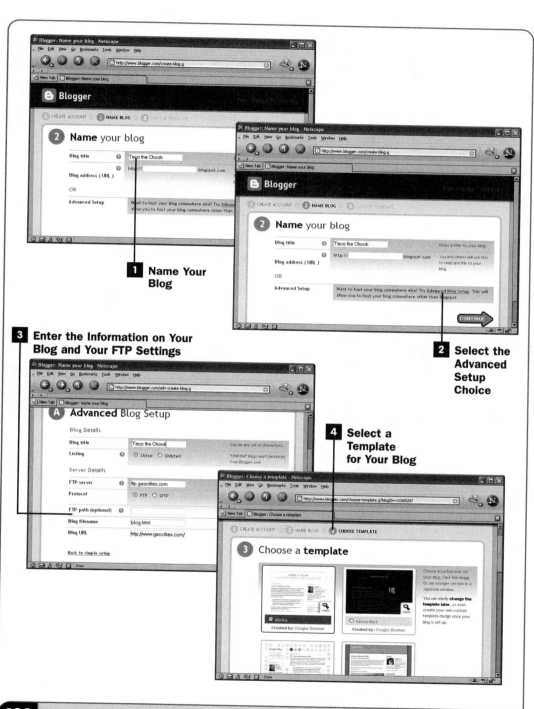

1 Name Your Blog

2 Select the Advanced Setup Choice

3 Enter the Information on Your Blog and Your FTP Settings

4 Select a Template for Your Blog

182

182 Build a Blog Through the Wizard

Also, in this section I will illustrate an advanced setup. I will use the **Blogger** website to prepare my blog. I will then have my blog sent to my website, for display there. Some people choose to do it this way. If you're comfortable with displaying your blogs on the **Blogger** site only, the **FTP** information is something you should skip.

1 Name Your Blog

In the **Blog title** space, name your blog. This is going to be the name that appears on the page and what people are going to remember. I am going to call my blog "Taco the Chook."

2 Select the Advanced Setup Choice

If you have a premium service such as **GeoCities Pro** and have an **FTP** address you can use for your site, you can host your blog yourself at your site. Because this choice allows you more options than if you host the site at **Blogger.com**, we are going to write the tasks to work with **FTP** hosting on your own site so that you can see all the options and learn how to use them.

If you want to have **Blogger** host your page, simply enter a name for your page at **Blogger.com** and then click the **Continue** button. Remember that if you host your site at **Blogger.com**, some of the options we show in these tasks will not be available.

3 Enter the Information on Your Blog and Your FTP Settings

For the blog title, name your blog as you did in step 1. Unfortunately, when you switch to the **Advanced Blog Setup**, the name is not carried with you.

Select whether you want your blog listed or not. Listing your blog will allow it to show up in the lists of blogs from **Blogger.com**. You might or might not want this link. You can always change your mind later, so for now choose to have your blog listed.

In the **Server Details** section, you will need to add the **FTP** information for your site. Add the address for the **FTP** server and pick the protocol for the files to be sent—select **FTP** (not **SFTP** [Secure **FTP**], unless you have your server set to use **SFTP**). The **FTP** path is used on some servers, but you shouldn't have to worry about that unless your service provider has given you that information.

The wizard is going to create an actual blog page, so you need to specify the name for the page. I am calling mine **blog.html**.

In the Blog URL field, you need to tell Blogger what you want the address to be. I am going to set mine to **http://www.geocities.com/tacothechook/ blog/** so that it has its own directory on my site. Click on **Continue** to move on to the template selection.

4 Select a Template for Your Blog

There are several templates for you to use but none of them match the templates you used in **GeoCities**. However, there are several that would work for me. I am going to select the **Son of Moto** template, which I think might match my chicken site better than most of the others.

Pick the template that will work best for your site. It is possible to change templates after your blog is set up, so the choice is not critical. Click on **Continue** to finish. You are now able to start posting to your blog.

183 Make Your First Post

✔ BEFORE YOU BEGIN	→ SEE ALSO
181 Create an Account at Blogger.com	**189** Edit Your Blog from the Dashboard
182 Build a Blog Through the Wizard	**190** Add a Post

183

You are ready to start posting to your site, which you need to do to view your site. You can't really have a blog without having some content there.

1 Click on the Arrow to Start Posting

You are now in the **Blogger Dashboard** in the Posting section where you can create new postings. This is an **HTML Editor**.

2 Create Your First Post

Enter a title for your first posting and some text in the **Edit** area.

Give your first post a name and enter what you want to have on your site. This is where you are going to be able to edit and create new posts in your blog.

For your first post, add some text as a greeting and whatever content you want to start your blog.

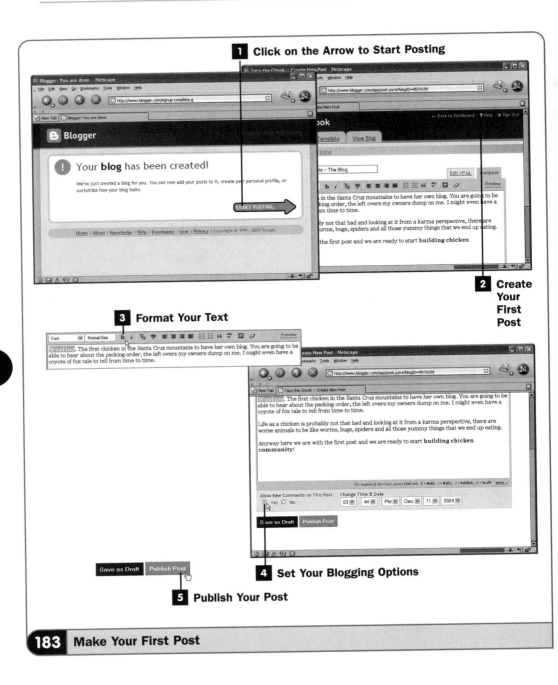

1 Click on the Arrow to Start Posting

2 Create Your First Post

3 Format Your Text

4 Set Your Blogging Options

5 Publish Your Post

183 Make Your First Post

3 Format Your Text

You can select portions of your text to highlight in one way or another using many of the same tools you might have available in many word processors.

You can add text decoration such as color, boldface, and alignment, or you can create links here and add pictures using the tools above the **Text Edit** area.

4 Set Your Blogging Options

You can set the blogging options for the post below the **Text Edit** area. Set the **Allow New Comments on This Post** radio button to **Yes**. This will enable users to add comments to the post. There will probably be some postings where you don't want to allow users to post their comments. You can set that here. You can also set the time and date for the posting if you would like.

5 Publish Your Post

After you are done with your post and your settings, click on the **Publish Post** button to publish your post.

---

184 View Your Blog

✔ BEFORE YOU BEGIN	→ SEE ALSO
182 Build a Blog Through the Wizard	186 Browse Blogs
183 Make Your First Post	

184

You have a post done on your blog, so you should be able to see the blog on your site. You might have chosen to host your site with **Blogger** or on your own site if you have access to a site with **FTP** access.

1 View Your Blog

In your browser, go to your blog. In my case, that is **http://www.geocities.com/tacothechook/blog/blog.html**.

When I created the site, it asked for the name of the path for the blog and the name of the file—so you need to go to the address you entered to view the blog.

However you get to your blog, it comes up and you can see where the text you entered in the wizard displays on the page.

2 Click on the View My Complete Profile Link

The link to your profile—which you can edit on the **Blogger Dashboard**—doesn't show anything because you need to go there still and enter the information you want to show up here. For your viewers, this is a place where they can get to know you in more general terms than your opinions.

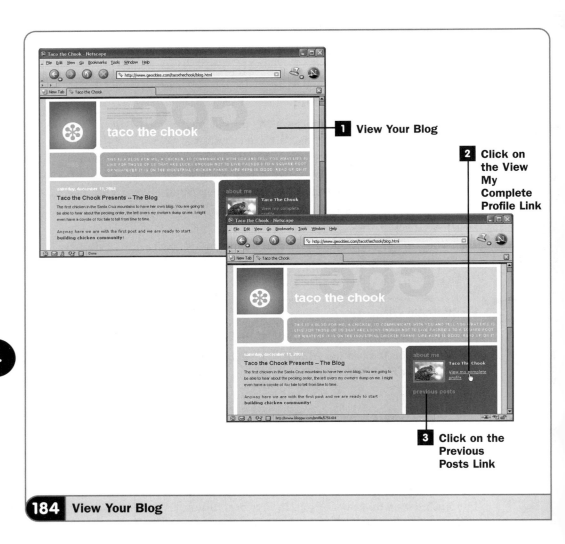

1 View Your Blog

2 Click on the View My Complete Profile Link

3 Click on the Previous Posts Link

184 View Your Blog

184

3 **Click on the Previous Posts Link**

The **Previous Posts** link won't go anywhere because you only have the one post. When you add more postings, both the **Previous Posts** and **Archives** links will work so your viewers will be able to go back through your postings.

185 Read Blogger News

✔ BEFORE YOU BEGIN	→ SEE ALSO
184 View Your Blog	**188** Set Your Blogger Profile

After you have an idea of how to build a blog, you have a whole "blogosphere" to explore with ideas and techniques. One of the best places to find information on blogging and specifically on **Blogger** is, of course, the **Blogger** site. You are going to look at the **Blogger Dashboard** in depth in the next chapter, but we'll take a quick look now so that you can explore the news before you go on with more techniques.

1 Log In to Your Blog

You are now on the **Dashboard**. You will go through this more in upcoming tasks.

Scroll down to the **Blogger News** section.

This is the area of the **Dashboard** where **Blogger** posts its news articles. The articles change—some are more interesting than others and some are aimed at different levels of users. When I wrote this chapter, there was a link to the news about the word *blog* being the number one word of the year; a link to **Lynda.com**, where you can buy a **Learning Blogger** CD-ROM; and a link to a book on blogging by a luminary of the blogging community.

2 Click on the Blogger Knowledge Link

The **Blogger Knowledge** page has some duplication with the **Blogger** news on the **Dashboard**, but there is a list of the latest knowledge items that you can browse.

Across the middle of the page, there are also links to **Blogger Basics** and **Working with Blogger**, which is a tutorial and help site, and a link to advanced use and support.

3 Go Back to the Dashboard

All your reference information is accessible from the **Dashboard**.

4 Click on the Link to Blogger Help

On the **Blogger Help** page, you'll find answers to the top questions about using **Blogger**. There is an article search, and topics are broken out by section in the main area of the page.

185

1 Log In to Your Blog

3 Go Back to the Dashboard

2 Click on the Blogger Knowledge Link

4 Click on the Link to Blogger Help

185

185 Read Blogger News

186 Browse Blogs

✔ BEFORE YOU BEGIN	→ SEE ALSO
184 View Your Blog	187 Comment on Other People's Blogs

From the **Dashboard**, you can also browse through what the **Blogger** staff thinks are currently the most interesting blogs. This will give you the same sorts of ideas that you got when you browsed through the blogs in 182 **Build a Blog Through the Wizard**.

The sites linked there change all the time, so what you see won't be what I see here today, but you should glance through some of them and look for the techniques that you think make them stand out.

1 Click on One of the Blogs of Note

I went to the scifidaily site (**http://scifidaily.blogspot.com/**) because it was near the top of the list today. You will have a different set of blogs to choose from because they are added every few days.

On the site, there are a few things I see that are worth noting and probably are on the blog you selected to look at.

186

2 Look for a Mission Statement

Look for a **mission statement** on the blog you clicked on. At the top of the scifidaily blog, there is a mission statement of what the blog is there for: "The latest news, reviews, diatribes, and banter on science-fiction/fantasy films, TV shows, etc...."

Having a mission statement will let your viewers know what to expect on your blog and can set the tone for their involvement by asking them to participate in the discussions. To do that, the people at scifidaily have even posted instructions to teach viewers about the different ways to comment on the articles.

3 Check Whether the Site Is Hosted at Blogspot.com

Blogs can be hosted on either your site or at **Blogspot.com**. Check in the address bar of your browser to see whether the site is hosted at the Blogspot server instead of at one of the sites belonging to the hosts. You have set your site to be hosted via **FTP**, but you are going to be able to change it to publish at **Blogspot.com** in a later task.

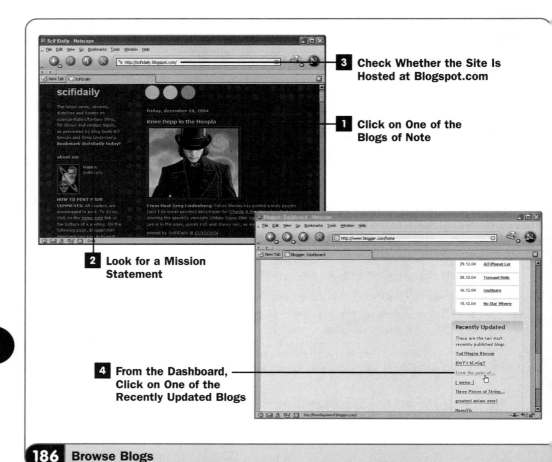

186 Browse Blogs

---

4 **From the Dashboard, Click on One of the Recently Updated Blogs**

Unlike the **Blogs of Note**, which are recommended by the Blogger community, the **Recently Updated** blogs are the ones that have just received an update or a new post. You can click through these, but remember that the subject matter and the content are as varied as there are people on the Web.

187 **Comment on Other People's Blogs**

✔ **BEFORE YOU BEGIN**	→ **SEE ALSO**
184 View Your Blog	**186** Browse Blogs

One of the points of blogging is that you can comment on people's postings. You can interact with the postings and the owner of the site can have a directed discussion with you and with others. To interact, though, you need to post comments on sites.

1 Go to http://tacoposting.blogspot.com

This is the site I have set up for you to post comments to. You will note that the site is set up on Blogspot.com. Using this site will enable you to mess around and not bother anyone with a full-scale blog with a community already posting and commenting to it.

2 Click on the Comments Link

The example comments for the posting are shown.

3 Click on the Post a Comment Link

This looks like the second time that you have to click on the **Comment** link. Let me explain. The first time you clicked the link, you came to the page to review current comments for this blog. The second time you click on the **Comment** link, you are taken to the form at **Blogger**, where you can enter your comment on the post.

4 Fill Out Your Comment and Publish It

You can add what you like to a posting, including **HTML** source code. When you're finished, click the **Publish Your Comment** button to post your comment.

5 Go Back to the Blog and Look at the Comment You Added

It might take a moment for the comment to appear. If it doesn't, you can click on the **Refresh** button in the browser and it should show.

187

1 Go to http://
tacoposting.blogspot.com

2 Click on the Comments Link

3 Click on the Post a
Comment Link

4 Fill Out Your Comment
and Publish It

5 Go Back to the Blog and Look
at the Comment You Added

187

187   Comment on Other People's Blogs

28

Use Your Blogger Dashboard

IN THIS CHAPTER:

With your blog up and running and an idea of where to find tutorials and support for **Blogger**, you are ready to learn how to administer your blog through the **Blogger Dashboard**.

---

188 **Set Your Blogger Profile**

✔ BEFORE YOU BEGIN	→ SEE ALSO
182 Build a Blog Through the Wizard	**181** Create an Account at Blogger.com
	185 Read Blogger News

Many bloggers don't understand their own importance. There are many self-proclaimed experts out in blogging land. If you want to get serious consideration for your blogs, you must show that you, the author, are worthy of the consideration. In this section, we will work on the **Blogger profile**, a way to let readers know more about you—as well as your ideas.

188

1 Log In to Your Blog and Go to the Dashboard

If you checked the **Remember Me** button in the past, the browser will remember your login information so that when you log in from this computer, you will be logged in to your page automatically. If you use this one computer all the time and no one else has access to the page, this saves you time.

▶ NOTE

If you are on a computer that is set up to use a single account for more than one user, clicking the **Remember Me** button allows the next person who happens to go to the **Blogger** website total access to your page. This person could cause mischief by rewriting your blog to ruin your reputation. So, don't check this box on a shared computer. Typing an **ID** and **password** isn't too much work, right?

2 Click on the Edit Profile Link on the Dashboard

This is where you can edit your user profile. Your profile provides information that can appear on your blog separate from your daily postings. You can place information about yourself or your company that will act as your mission statement for the site.

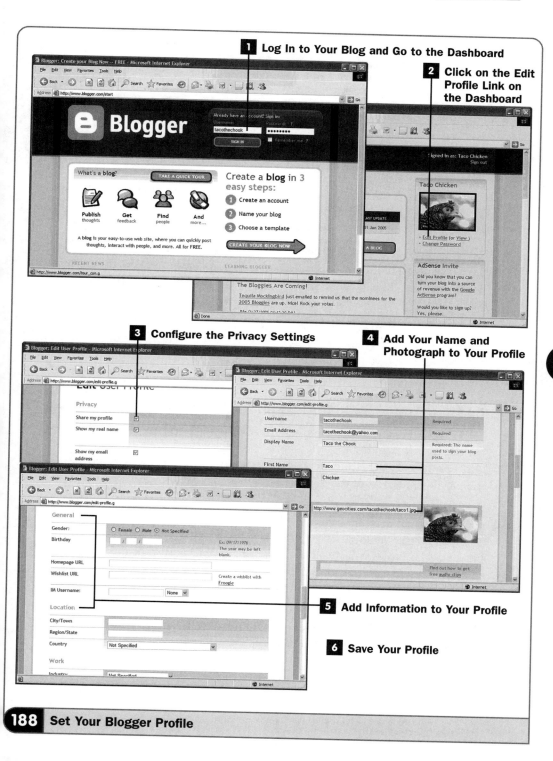

1 Log In to Your Blog and Go to the Dashboard

2 Click on the Edit Profile Link on the Dashboard

3 Configure the Privacy Settings

4 Add Your Name and Photograph to Your Profile

5 Add Information to Your Profile

6 Save Your Profile

188

188 Set Your Blogger Profile

▶ **TIP**

What do I mean by *your company*? I mean a company or business you own. If you work for another company and consider it your own true love, you should check your company for any policies on employee blogs. You must follow your company's confidentiality policies whether you have a conversation in a bar or write a blog. Some employees have been fired over material they posted in a public blog.

3 Configure the Privacy Settings

In the **Privacy** section of the profile, you can choose to have your profile available from your site. You can choose to show your real name by selecting the check box. This replaces your username with your real first and last names, which you can enter in the **Identity** section below.

You can also set the profile to show all your blogs if you have more than one. If you are doing a blog for business, you might not want to select that option. However, if you have a cooking blog, a political blog, and a hobby blog, you might want people to be able to visit your different blogs.

The **Show My Email Address** box is important if you want users to be able to reach you outside of the blog. Generally, you'll want to have the address there unless you are concerned you will be overwhelmed with email from the site.

188

4 Add Your Name and Photograph to Your Profile

Your first and last names will only appear if you check the **Show My Real Name** check box in the Privacy section. If this is not checked, readers will only see the **Display Name** you have configured. Your picture will show in the profile regardless of the settings in the **Privacy** section.

5 Add Information to Your Profile

The items in the remaining sections are more useful for personal sites than business sites, but if your business has a bricks-and-mortar location, you might enter your address in the **Location** area.

6 Save Your Profile

Scroll to the bottom of the **Profile** screen and click the **Save Profile** button. You can now view your new profile or click to go to your blog.

189 Edit Your Blog from the Dashboard

✔ BEFORE YOU BEGIN	→ SEE ALSO
182 Build a Blog Through the Wizard	**185** Read Blogger News
	186 Browse Blogs

The central location at **Blogger.com** where you can edit your posts and the various settings of your site is the **Dashboard**. From here, you can access each of your blogs, get help from experts, link to blogging news, and create and update your profile. Have you already logged on to the **Dashboard** to look at other blogs or maybe your profile? This time you will be using the **Dashboard** to access and change the settings for your site.

1 Log In to Your Account and Go to the Dashboard

You are back at the **Dashboard** for your account. If you have more than one blog, they will show up in the list of blogs in the left column.

If you are still logged in from the last task, you can click on the **Back to the Dashboard** button at the top of the page.

2 View the Settings for the Blog

Viewing your blog from the **Dashboard** allows you to manage postings—the default view on the page. You can also manage your settings and your templates, and you can view your blog from several links throughout the different screens.

In the **Edit Posts** screen you can create a new post, and you can specify how many posts to show in the window as you edit.

If you click on the title of any post you have there, the text for the blog appears. You can read the post from here or click on the **Edit** button to edit the post. You might find this very useful if you are like me and have a spontaneous nature but not always the best judgment. It can be very nice to add or remove parts of your posting.

You can delete your individual posts from here as well.

At the top of the page you also have a **Search** field so you can find your postings through keywords if they appeared too long ago to show up in the list.

189

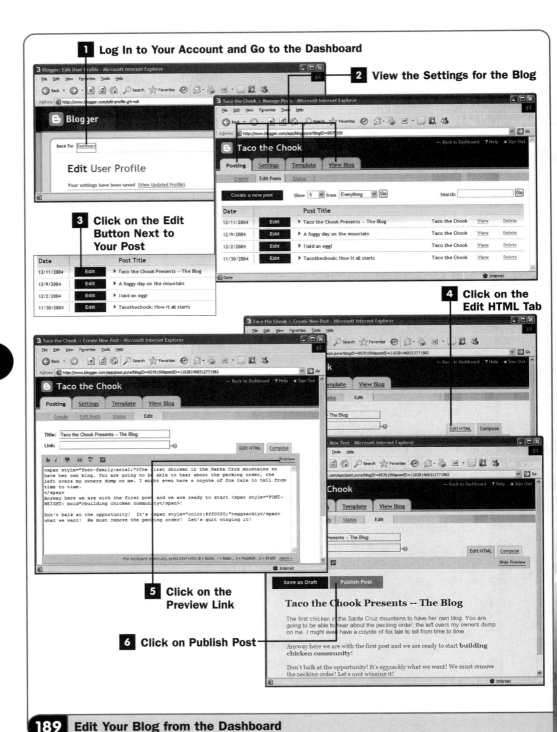

3 Click on the Edit Button Next to Your Post

Your post is now visible in an edit area, where you can make changes to the text you posted.

Add some text to your post, or select some of the text and change the font or color. These are just some of the things you can do. Need to issue a correction? You can even do that. Don't ask me how I know....

4 Click on the Edit HTML Tab

When you look at the HTML code of the page, you can see that wherever you made changes to the format of the text, there are now HTML tags wrapped around the text with the style that you have specified.

I alluded to **CSS styles** in Chapter 8, "Work with Text," and noted that they were the preferred way to set the visual styles for your text. The templates in **Blogger** use **CSS styles** by default. If you want to use regular **HTML**, though, you can enter that code here by hand and it will be rendered by **Blogger**.

5 Click on the Preview Link

Your blog entry will be updated and the one page you changed will be published back to the site.

190

6 Click on Publish Post

After publishing the page, you should see a screen that tells you that your blog has been published. If you want to look at your site now, click on the **View Blog (In a New Window)** link.

---

190 Add a Post

✔ BEFORE YOU BEGIN	→ SEE ALSO
182 Build a Blog Through the Wizard	**189** Edit Your Blog from the Dashboard
183 Make Your First Post	

Adding a post is very much like editing a post. (You added your first post when you created your **Blogger** account.)

1 Click on the Blog Name in the Dashboard

Of course logging on is a must; and after you have, you are at the **Dashboard**. Let's do some edits to any existing blog you might have written. Click on the title of any existing blog.

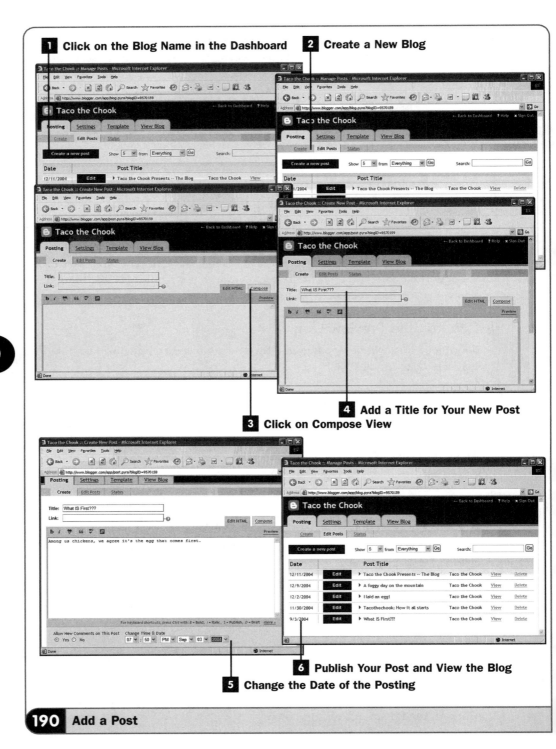

1 Click on the Blog Name in the Dashboard   **2** Create a New Blog

4 Add a Title for Your New Post

3 Click on Compose View

6 Publish Your Post and View the Blog

5 Change the Date of the Posting

190 Add a Post

2 Create a New Blog

Clicking on the **Create** tab link, the one in the tab bar, summons the same **Edit** text box you might have used to create your first post **184** **View Your Blog** and to edit that post. **191** **Change Settings**. Begin writing some text. You can view it as HTML in the **Edit HTML** view on the top right of the **Text Edit** area or in the **Compose** view where you have more tools available to edit the text and add formatting.

3 Click on Compose View

In the **Compose** view, you can create your next post. As you write, switch between the **Edit HTML** and **Compose** tabs. Use different fonts and paragraph styles. Light up your life with a few bulleted comments. You'll soon find this tool provides many of the most important word processing functions. This enables you to focus on your message. There's even a spelling checker you should use to avoid embarrassing mistakes.

4 Add a Title for Your New Post

For your second post, give some additional information for the blog so that you can experiment with it later and add or delete parts of it. If you don't like it, you can always delete it.

190

5 Change the Date of the Posting

Change the date of the posting to a date a day or so ago. At the bottom of the Text Edit area, you can change the date on the post so that if you have an idea that you want to post and don't do it when you think of it, you can go back later and fill in the hole in the list of postings.

You can edit the post later and change the date back, but for now, setting it to a day or so ago will help you see how posts are organized in the blog.

6 Publish Your Post and View the Blog

The post you made would normally go to the top of the blog so that people could read the latest post first, but in this case, because you changed the date, the new post appears below the first post.

---

191 **Change Settings**

✔ BEFORE YOU BEGIN	→ SEE ALSO
182 Build a Blog Through the Wizard	188 Set Your Blogger Profile

---

Changing your settings is easy and you can do it as often as you like. When you change your settings, you will be prompted to save the settings and then to republish the site. Republishing your site is covered in 194 **Republish Your Blog**.

1 **Add a Description and Save Your Settings**

Click on the **Settings** tab in the **Dashboard**. You should be in the **Basic Setting** view of the **Settings** tab, which opens by default when you click on the **Settings** tab.

Type in a description for your site and set the **Show Email Post links** to **Yes**. When you are done, scroll down to the bottom and click on the **Save Settings** button. It's best to save your work from time to time. Doing this now ensures we're okay if the power goes out right now!

191

The description you enter here tells the viewer your reason for having the blog. If you are working on a site for business, you should put your mission statement here.

When you set the **Show Email Post links** to **Yes**, it creates a link at the bottom of your post, which enables people to email the posting to their friends. This is particularly cool if you want to get a message out. Instead of having to copy and paste things to another email program, you can just have them sent directly with **Blogger**.

2 **Configure the Publishing Destination**

This is where you would change the path of your files on your **FTP server** if you configured the website to publish your blog to your personal website via FTP. For now, you do not want to make any changes here.

You also can change your site to be hosted from the **Blogspot.com** free hosting server.

1 Add a Description and Save Your Settings

2 Configure the Publishing Destination

3 Configure Your Blog's Formatting

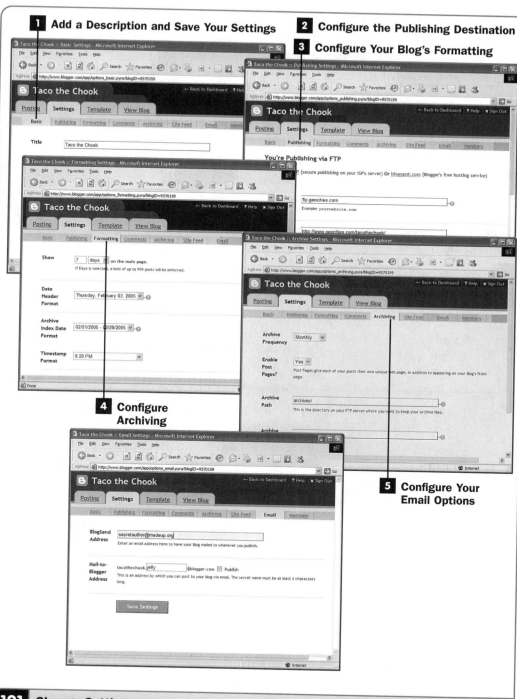

4 Configure Archiving

5 Configure Your Email Options

191

191 Change Settings

3 Configure Your Blog's Formatting

The **Formatting** view is where you can change the date and time formats. You can also set your time zone. This helps the reader understand the context of your blog. Blogs are created and edited and read across the world 7×24. If a reader in Russia posts a comment and knows it is 03:00 your time, she won't expect an answer for some time. Treat your readers nicely, and they will treat your blogs with respect.

There are also settings here to convert your returns to breaks when the post is displayed as you type in the editor. You *do* want this to happen. If it doesn't happen, the returns you type in the editor will not appear in your posts. The default is for this to be on—so keep it on.

4 Configure Archiving

Your blog is backed up regularly by **Blogger.com** and sent to a file on your server. You probably want to do this so that if there is some data loss somewhere, you can get into your posts. It is set to back up monthly by default. If you want the files archived, you will have to give a path to the archive file folder. You should consider a daily archive and selecting to **Enable Post Pages** to give each post its own URL. This allows others to quote your blog or reference the whole document by **URL**.

191

5 Configure Your Email Options

The **Email** view enables you to set a couple of great features in **Blogger** that you definitely want to have turned on.

BlogSend Address is an address archive that shows where every one of your posts is mailed. This provides you a handy backup of your blog—sent to your email address. This is really handy when you use it in tandem with the next feature, **Mail-to-Blogger Address**.

Mail-to-Blogger Address enables you to enter a "secret name" in the **Text Entry** box and create a unique email address that only you know, such as **tacothechook.jelly@blogger.com**. After the email address is created, you can use your email program to post to your blog. This means you can email from your phone, someone else's computer, or any other way you can send email without having to actually use the **Blogger** interface. When you choose this option, you'll want to click on the **Publish** box, which enables your email postings to go straight to the blog rather than being held as a draft for your approval later.

Enter your email address in the **BlogSend Address** and create a secret name for the **Mail-to-Blogger Address**. This has to be at least four characters long.

▶ **TIP**

If you do email your posts, be sure to add **#end** at the end of the part of your email that you want to be the post. If you don't, some email programs will add some text, often advertising to your email and thus to your posts. Also, if your blogs are used to help sell your company, sell your image, and so forth, don't use this feature. Secret email addresses don't stay secret long.

192 Change Templates	
✔ **BEFORE YOU BEGIN**	→ **SEE ALSO**
182 Build a Blog Through the Wizard	**188** Set Your Blogger Profile

After you have a handle on how the mechanics of the **Dashboard** work, you might want to change your template to change the look of the site dramatically.

1 Configure a New Template

In the **Template** tab, you have only a few choices, but they are very powerful. At the top, you can select to pick an entirely new template. (You will do that in a moment.) You can add the **Blogger NavBar**, which gives you a way to search your blog and to link to other recently updated blogs. The main area of the page, though, enables you to see the HTML code that actually runs your **Blogger** page.

192

If you want to make changes to the **HTML** of the template, you can—but remember that if you do, it might stop working the way you expect.

2 Select Your New Link

Look through the selection of templates; and, when you find one you would like to change to, click on the **Use This Template** button.

As you are looking through the selection of templates, you can click on the View icon on the corner of each thumbnail if you want to see one in more detail.

3 Click on a New Template

When you select a new template and click on the **Use This Template** button, you will get a warning that any customizations will be lost. You haven't made any customizations to the template, so click **OK** on the warning.

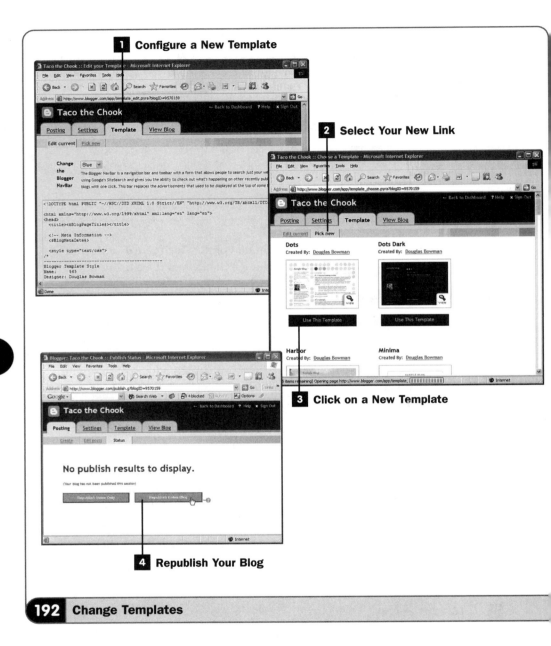

1 Configure a New Template

2 Select Your New Link

3 Click on a New Template

4 Republish Your Blog

192 Change Templates

4 Republish Your Blog

You can now view the site in a new window to see the new template you have applied.

193 Limit Who Can Comment on Your Blog

✔ BEFORE YOU BEGIN	→ SEE ALSO
182 Build a Blog Through the Wizard	**188** Set Your Blogger Profile
	194 Republish Your Blog

There are several options for allowing people to comment on your postings. You can permit anyone to comment, which allows a wide audience, but you are likely to get comments from people who are only posting to cause problems because there is no accountability for anonymous posters. You can limit postings to people who are registered with **Blogger.com**, which is still a large group of people, or you can limit postings to members of your team. To set up a team, see **199 Enable Your Blog for Team Blogging**.

1 Navigate to Your Comments Options

Select the Settings tab and, after this is done, select the **Comments** tab.

2 Configure Your Comments Options

By default, comments are set to show. If this option is turned off, your posts will appear with no comments below them. Consider what's best for your blogs and choose the best option for you. If you are just starting out, seeing zero comments can be more insulting than helpful.

3 Set the Who Can Comment Drop-Down

If the **Who Can Comment** drop-down is set to **Anyone**, anyone can comment on a post with total anonymity, which gives you the best reach for your blog and encourages the highest level of participation.

If you limit the comments to members only, you will have comments from the **Blogger.com** community (which is large). However, your customers or friends might not be members, so this option is not as attractive as letting Anyone comment.

The third option is to only allow team members to post to your blog. This option enables you to limit the people who can post to a minimum. The advantage is that you can allow this same group to post as well, so you create a team blogging application that you can use for a work group to brainstorm and work together without having outside users comment back.

Decide what is best for you and make the correct setting.

193

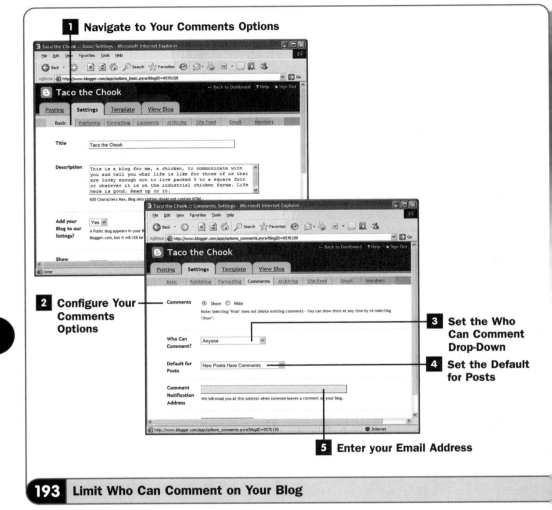

1 Navigate to Your Comments Options

2 Configure Your Comments Options

3 Set the Who Can Comment Drop-Down

4 Set the Default for Posts

5 Enter your Email Address

193   **Limit Who Can Comment on Your Blog**

4 Set the Default for Posts

When you set the **Default for Posts** to not have comments, new posts won't have comments in them until you edit the specific post and allow comments, which you can do from the **Posting** tab and the **Edit Posts** view. This enables you to edit comments before they're read by others.

This is a good compromise if you want comments, but not on every post. It also allows you to deal with hecklers effectively.

If you leave the default to **New Posts Have Comments**, you can turn them off on a case-by-case basis for each post on the **Posting** tab, **Edit Posts** view.

5   Enter Your Email Address

Enter your email address in the **Comment Notification Address** field. Press **Save Settings** and then republish your blog.

When you add a **Comment Notification Address**, you can specify where **Blogger** will send copies of each comment that is posted to your server. For a while, it is useful to have on so that you know when you get a comment. Later, as you get more and more comments, you might want to turn off this option so you don't drown in email.

---

194   Republish Your Blog

✔ **BEFORE YOU BEGIN**	→ **SEE ALSO**
182 Build a Blog Through the Wizard	**189** Edit Your Blog from the Dashboard
	190 Add a Post
	191 Change Settings
	192 Change Templates

194

You need to republish your blog to make the options you change stick in some cases. You can either republish one page or your whole site. If you publish just the page you are working on, you might have some pages that don't reflect the changes. Specifically, if you change your template and have several posts online already, you'll want to republish your whole site so that you can apply the new templates to each post's page on your site.

1   Click on Any of the Views in the Settings Tab

At the bottom of each view is a button to save the changes to the site.

2   Click on Save Changes.

Your page redraws, and at the top there are now two buttons. The **Republish** button will republish your entire site and apply whatever changes you made to the settings and templates to all the pages on the site.

If you click on the second button, **Republish Index**, only the main page of the site will be updated.

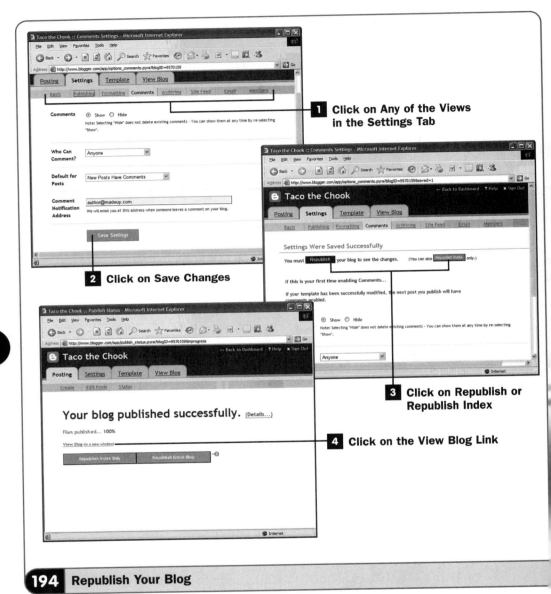

1 Click on Any of the Views in the Settings Tab

2 Click on Save Changes

3 Click on Republish or Republish Index

4 Click on the View Blog Link

194 Republish Your Blog

3 Click on Republish or Republish Index

Use the **Republish Index** option when you have modified a single post or
changed an option that is going to appear in your profile or in only one page
of the site. If you are doing anything you think might involve more than one

page, use the Republish button. The only reason not to use the **Republish** button would be to avoid the delay waiting for the republishing to finish. As your blog grows the number of pages, republishing takes longer and longer.

4 Click on the View Blog Link

When you change your settings, you should take the time to go to the page and view it in the browser to be sure the changes you made work the way you want.

194

29

Use Advanced Blogging Tools

IN THIS CHAPTER:

Your blog is looking good. You can have people comment on your postings. Your viewers can mail your postings to their friends and colleagues. You can change the templates for your blog easily to change the look of your site. You have really built a simple way to interact with many people at one time.

From here, you can add advanced tools from Blogger.

---

195 **Add Links to Your Blog**

✔ BEFORE YOU BEGIN	→ SEE ALSO
182 Build a Blog Through the Wizard	**26** Create Links to Other Pages

---

Adding links to your blog is very much the same as adding a link to a page that isn't a blog. Remember that the point of adding a link is to provide more information for your user. However, if you do provide a link out of your blog, your user is not going to read the rest of your post. One practical solution is to put your links at the end of the post so that the viewer is likely to read the post and then click on the choices at the end of the post.

195

Regardless of how you arrange your links, the process for creating them is the same.

1 Click on Your Blog in the Dashboard

If you have more than one blog in your account, you will have several names from which to choose. Click on the name of the blog you want to edit.

2 Select a Post to Edit

You can select any post to edit. You can do many common editing functions you might be familiar with now. For example, you can make links during blog creation or during later edits. You can add and move lines of text. This is a full-featured tool, similar to other full-featured tools you might have used elsewhere.

3 Select a Piece of Text

Select a piece of text you want to become your link. Avoid selecting multiple lines. Each link should provide a good summary of what other content will be accessed through the link. Multiple lines with multiple messages won't do. By the same token, going for one word won't be descriptive enough. Some believe it's bad web form to use the word *here* to designate a link, such as, "View more about foobar industries here," with *here* being the link text. Instead, make foobar industries the link and be more direct.

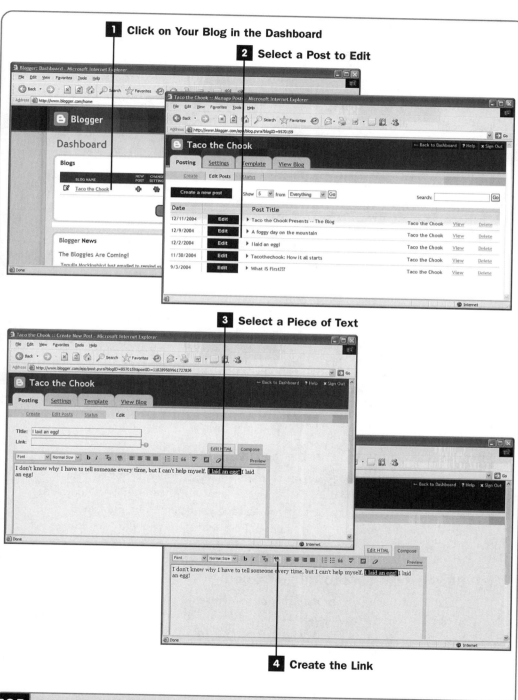

1 Click on Your Blog in the Dashboard

2 Select a Post to Edit

3 Select a Piece of Text

4 Create the Link

195

4 Create the Link

Click the **Link** icon. In the **Link** dialog box, enter the address of the page to which you want to link. Click on **Publish Post** to save your change to your blog.

In my page, I am going to link to a site where you can buy eggs for hatching. Be sure to add the **http://** portion of the address if you are going to link to a page away from your site. If your blog is hosted on your site and you are linking to a page locally, you don't need to use the **http://** in the address.

196   Change the Location of Your Blog

✔ BEFORE YOU BEGIN	→ SEE ALSO
182 Build a Blog Through the Wizard	**71** Configure the Settings to Publish Your Site
	72 Publish Your Page

196

When you set up your blog, you might have set it up to be hosted on your own site. You probably entered your FTP information and passwords so that your blog would have the same address as your regular site. For example, my blog is at **http://www.geocities.com/tacothechook/blog.html**, which makes it feel like part of my site. If you decide to separate your blogs from your regular website, you can have your blog hosted at **Blogspot.com**, which is a free domain set up by **Blogger** for your blog to reside.

1 Click on Publishing in the Settings Tab

On the **Publishing** tab, you can change where your blog is hosted. You might have it set to be published on your website. You should write down the settings in this screen because if you change your blog to be published from **Blogspot.com**, you are going to need these settings if you want to change back to publishing on your own site via **FTP**.

2 Click on the Link to Blogspot.com

Clicking on the link to **Blogspot.com** will erase all the information you set up for any other blog location. You might want to write down other blogging location information before you click on the link. This enables you to replace it later if you want.

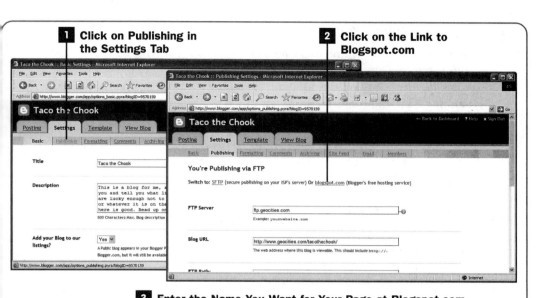

1 Click on Publishing in the Settings Tab

2 Click on the Link to Blogspot.com

3 Enter the Name You Want for Your Page at Blogspot.com

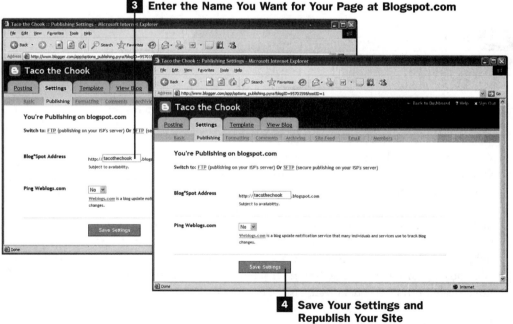

4 Save Your Settings and Republish Your Site

196

196 Change the Location of Your Blog

3 Enter the Name You Want for Your Page at Blogspot.com

When you click on the link to publish on **Blogspot.com**, you'll need to enter a name for your site on **Blogspot**. In my case, I am going to make the address **tacothechook.blogspot.com**. If you have a rather common name for your blog, you might need to try a few different names to find one that is available.

You can leave the **Ping Weblogs.com** set to **No**. This is a service that keeps track of which blogs have been changed so that readers can track multiple blogs from one place.

4 Save Your Settings and Republish Your Site

Now you can send people to your blog at the address you entered. Having the option of publishing your site on a shared server such as **Blogspot.com** is great if you are not sure whether you are going to keep the same address for your personal site. You can even have the blog and not have a regular site.

197

197 Archive Your Blog	
✔ **BEFORE YOU BEGIN**	→ **SEE ALSO**
182 Build a Blog Through the Wizard	**71** Configure the Settings to Publish Your Site
	72 Publish Your Page

When you spend the time to set up a blog and maintain it with regular posts, you want to be sure the contents are archived and available for people to read as separate HTML pages. When you blog, all your posts are in the **Blogger** database and available for browsing through the **Blogger** interface. However, when you archive your posts, there is an additional level of pages created—one for each posting and one for the index of the archive. This allows people to link directly to old postings of your blog from their pages. Although the **Blogger** database where your postings are kept is safe, having a separate set of pages with the data you have posted is a good backup in case of emergency.

1 Click on Archiving in the Settings Tab

The **Archiving** tab has all the settings you need to organize the archives of your site.

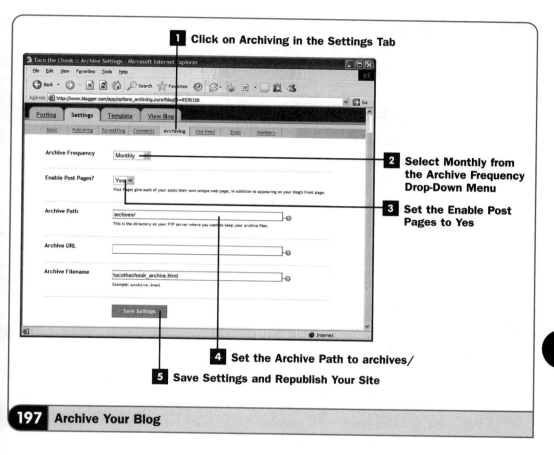

1 Click on Archiving in the Settings Tab

2 Select Monthly from the Archive Frequency Drop-Down Menu

3 Set the Enable Post Pages to Yes

4 Set the Archive Path to archives/

5 Save Settings and Republish Your Site

197 Archive Your Blog

2 Select Monthly from the Archive Frequency Drop-Down Menu

You can choose to set the archiving frequency to **Daily**, **Weekly**, or **Monthly**. The more postings you have, the more you might want to set the frequency to **Daily** so that each page doesn't have too many postings on it. If you have several posts daily and set your archive to **Monthly**, you are going to have too many postings per page for viewers to find things easily.

3 Set the Enable Post Pages to Yes

When you set the **Enable Post Pages** to Yes, you create a unique page for each post, which allows people to link to each post at a unique address.

4 Set the Archive Path to archives/

The **Archive Path** is the location where your archive pages are going to be saved. You need to be sure that you add the slash to the end of the folder name.

5 **Save Settings and Republish Your Site**

Your changes are saved, and the site reflects your changes only after you republish your site.

---

198 **Create a Site Feed**

✔ **BEFORE YOU BEGIN**

182 **Build a Blog Through the Wizard**

198

One of the really interesting features of **Blogger** is that you can syndicate your content so that other bloggers and people with websites can have either just the postings, or the postings *and* the content appear on their sites (with attribution to you, of course). If you are providing content that others want to use on their sites, you will have your ideas available to even more readers.

1 **Click on Site Feed in the Settings Tab**

All the settings for your site feed appear on the **Site Feed** view.

2 **Set the Publish Settings**

Set the **Publish Site Feed** to **Yes**. Set the **Descriptions** to **Full**. Set the **Site Feed Filename** and **Site Feed URL**.

When you create a site feed for your blog, or syndicate your blog, you can set your feed to either include the full content of each post or just the first paragraph. Sometimes you want to have your content be just a tease so that people click to come back to your site. Sometimes you might want to have the full content of your postings be available to the people that use your feed.

Set the **Site Feed Filename** to **atom.xml**. You can select another name, but it is the convention for **Blogger** not to change the name.

The **Site Feed URL** is where you are going to have your **.xml** feed file saved.

3 **Save Your Settings and Then Republish Your Site**

Your changes are saved, and the site reflects your changes only after you republish your site.

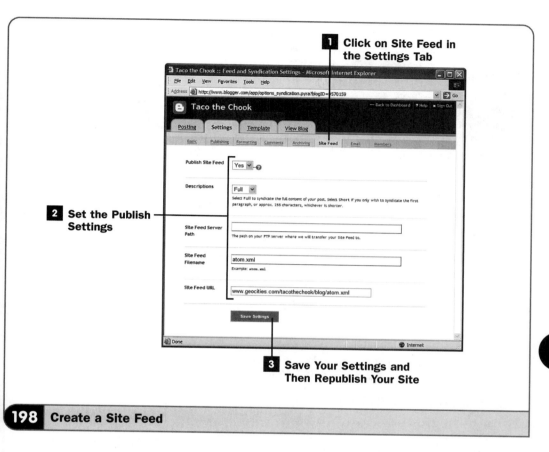

1 Click on Site Feed in the Settings Tab

2 Set the Publish Settings

3 Save Your Settings and Then Republish Your Site

198 Create a Site Feed

199

---

199 Enable Your Blog for Team Blogging

✔ **BEFORE YOU BEGIN**

182 Build a Blog Through the Wizard

One thing you might want to do is have other people add to your blog as a team. One of the sites you looked at earlier was the scifi blog, which is maintained by a set of people, all posting and working together. If you are running a blog for a community, you can set it to have multiple contributors as well. You will add members to your team. Don't worry if things don't work out. The interface that lets you add members lets you delete them if you must.

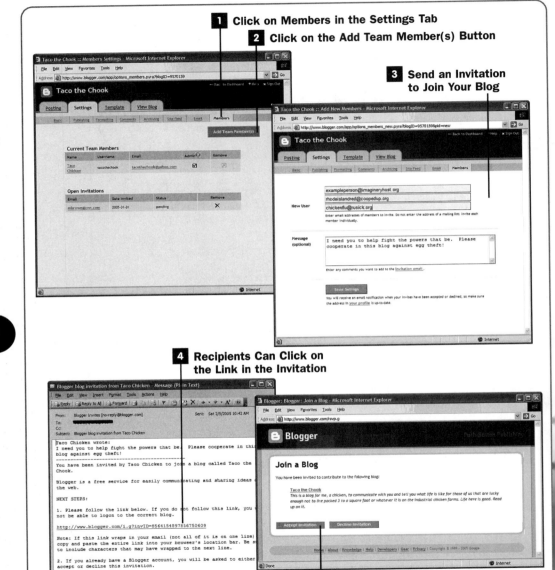

1 Click on Members in the Settings Tab

2 Click on the Add Team Member(s) Button

3 Send an Invitation to Join Your Blog

4 Recipients Can Click on the Link in the Invitation

5 Invitation Recipients Can Click on the Accept Invitation Button

199 Enable Your Blog for Team Blogging

1 Click on Members in the Settings tab

In the **Members** view, you can see who is a member of your blog and you can add new members to your blog.

2 Click on the Add Team Member(s) Button

From the **Add Team Member(s)** screen, you can add multiple people to the email asking them to join your blog.

3 Send an Invitation to Join Your Blog

Each person you add will get an email with a link to click on to join the blog.

4 Recipients Can Click on the Link in the Invitation

Each email will contain in its body the message you entered in the invitation. When your new members click back on the link, they will be able to post to your blog.

5 Invitation Recipients Can Click on the Accept Invitation Button

On the **Join a Blog** page (with your invitation), recipients can click on the **Accept Invitation** button to add themselves to your blog.

199

Index

Symbols

A

B

E

F

G

H

I

J - K

L

M

O

P

Q - R

S

T

X - Y - Z

Key Terms

Don't let unfamiliar terms discourage you from learning all you can about creating Web pages. If you don't completely understand what one of these words means, flip to the indicated page, read the full definition there, and find techniques related to that term.

Alpha channel   *Data saved with an image for reuse when needed, such as selections, masks, and creator information.*   **Page 251**

Attribute   *A modification of an HTML tag that lets you choose options over how that tag should be used—for example, by choosing a font to display on a web page.*   **24**

Blog   *A website that is in diary-like format, in which there are a series of short, dated entries. Many blogs also allow for readers to post comments on the site.*   **53**

Canvas   *The working area of an image, as defined by the image's outer dimensions.*   **331**

Cascading Style Sheets (CSS)   *Cascading Style Sheets (CSS) is a language related to HTML that the browser can read to impart visual styles to HTML pages. In web development, you might hear that best practice is to separate content from visual presentation. This allows your page to be very flexible in how it appears. You can have the same information that is presented for a web browser on a computer, a cellular telephone, a kiosk, an Internet-equipped television, or who knows what. The only thing that would have to change is the style sheet that tells the device how to show the same information differently (suited to each medium).*   **158**

Character entity   *Special characters that are not represented in the HTML code as regular characters, but that can be added to a page with small blocks of code. For example, the & symbol won't show up in the page if you add it from the keyboard as you do in a word processor. Instead, if you type & in your HTML, the browser displays that as a regular ampersand when the page is viewed.*   **162**

Closing tag   *A tag that tells a browser to stop displaying text in a certain way, or to stop displaying an element on a web page.*   **21**

Color depth   *The number of colors a computer is set to display. Older computers only display 256 colors or less—called 8-bit color. If your visitors come to your site and only can view 256 colors but your images use more, they will see images that are grainy or dithered.*   **128**

DNS (Domain Naming Service) server
An Internet server that translates web addresses such as www.samspublishing.com to 63.240.93.138. When you type in a web address, the request is first sent to a DNS server that translates the address into an IP address. Your computer then uses the IP address to contact the website you want to visit.   **5**

Dutch auction   *An auction in which multiple items are up for sale. All the winning bidders on the items in a Dutch auction pay the same price for the items, the lowest successful bid.*   **Page 420**

eBay store   *An online storefront on eBay where you can sell your goods, and customize the way the store looks and how the items are displayed and organized.*   **516**

eBay Toolbar   *An add-in to Internet Explorer that lets you track your auctions, search for auctions, and bid on auctions from right within Internet Explorer.*   **546**

Empty tag   *An HTML tag that does not get a closing tag, and that will not accept a closing tag.*   **22**

Escrow services   *A service that acts as a go-between in an auction, holding the buyer's money until he receives the items in good order.*   **471**

Final value fee   *The fee you pay only if your item sells on eBay. If the item doesn't sell, you're not charged this fee.*   **405**

FTP (File Transfer Protocol)   *A web protocol much like HTTP (Hypertext Transfer Protocol) that moves information around the Web. The difference between the two is that HTTP opens a connection between the server and the browser, downloads the information (like a web page), and then closes the connection so that other browsers can access the server. FTP creates a connection and then leaves that connection open for a time to allow files to move to and from the server. This forces the server to focus on fewer dedicated connections at one time than an HTTP server.*   **222**

GIF and JPEG   *GIF stands for Graphics Interchange Format and JPEG for Joint Photographic Experts Group. Both are graphics standards that use compression to keep image sizes small but still retain enough detail so the image is of a high quality. JPEG does a better job on photographs and is the format you should generally use when posting pictures to eBay. GIF is better for line art and logos.*   **440**

Grayscale picture   *A black-and-white picture that has gradations of gray in it.*   **237**

Hexadecimal   *A numbering system that uses 16 unique symbols: the numbers 0 through 9, and the letters A through F. These symbols are used individually, or combined. So, for example, the number 15 is represented in the decimal system by F.*   **40**

Hosting service   *A service that will let you post your pages to it, and keep all your pages on its server, so that people can visit it.*   **45**